OBJECT-OR
APPLICATION
FRAMEWORKS

TED LEWIS *and*

GLENN ANDERT

PAUL CALDER

ERICH GAMMA

WOLFGANG PREE

LARRY ROSENSTEIN

KURT SCHMUCKER

ANDRÉ WEINAND

JOHN M. VLISSIDES

MANNING

Greenwich
(74° w. long.)

The publisher offers discounts on this book when ordered in quantity.
For more information please contact:

Special Sales Department
Manning Publications Co.
3 Lewis Street
Greenwich, CT 06830
or
73150.1431@compuserve.com
Fax: (203) 661-9018

Design and Typesetting: Stephen Adams
Copy editor: Margaret Marynowski

Recognizing the importance of preserving what has been written, it is the policy of Manning Publications to have the books they publish printed on acid-free paper, and we exert our best efforts to that end.

Library of Congress Cataloging–in–Publication Data

Object-oriented application frameworks / Ted Lewis, editor.
p. cm.
Includes bibliographical references and index.
ISBN 1-884777-06-6
1. Object-oriented programming (Computer Science) I. Lewis, T. G. (Theodore Gyle), 1941– .
QA76.64.0243 1995
005.1'1—dc20 94-48023
CIP

95 96 97 98 BB 10 9 8 7 6 5 4 3 2

Printed in the United States of America

Contents

Preface

One of the next major steps in object-oriented design and programming is framework design and programming. Frameworks are being commercialized by NeXT and Taligent, and to a lesser extent, by IBM, Microsoft, SunSoft, Borland, and Hewlett Packard. I think that the introduction of the Taligent products in 1995 will stimulate widespread interest in frameworks: what they are, how they work, and how they compare with one another.

This paperback tutorial/survey is designed to address the anticipated surge of interest in what has previously been a little-understood technology. I hope to do so in three parts: an introduction to the underlying principles of object-oriented design, a comparative survey of frameworks for personal computers and UNIX workstations, and an illustration of the uses of frameworks. Part I should make the book appealing to the beginner, and Parts II and III should appeal to the software project leader, MIS manager, or advanced programmer. This is a professional book, not a textbook.

What exactly is an object-oriented framework? It is an object-oriented class hierarchy plus a built-in model of interaction which defines how the objects derived from the class hierarchy interact with one another.

This rather simple definition belies the power of frameworks. In practical terms, the framework approach leverages capital-intensive software investment through reuse, and provides a much higher-level application programming interface, so that applications can be developed ten times faster. It is the next giant step in the progression toward more powerful desktop computers. Steve Jobs recognized the significance of object-oriented frameworks when he called his new company *NeXT* and his framework-based operating system *NeXTStep*.

Frameworks are not new-fangled research exotica, but rather the essential core of what is happening in software these days. The two most glaring examples of the framework approach come from Taligent Inc. and NeXT Inc. Both operating systems are based on the MACH kernel (or other multithreading systems, such as OS/2 or Apple's System 8.0), and both are layered with object-oriented software services in the form of object-oriented frameworks. The Taligent operating system makes more extensive use of frameworks than any other system, except perhaps the Apple Newton.

The purpose of the Taligent operating system is to win the battle of the desktop in the next round of operating systems wars. Of course, the players want to shift the balance of power to their own advantage as the PC industry converts from a 16-bit to a 32/64-bit architecture based on RISC processors such as PowerPC, DEC Alpha, and SuperSPARC. These better-performing processors with radically different architecture make existing PC operating systems obsolete. But what will replace them? This is the 100-billion-dollar question.

I believe whatever the outcome of these wars, the object-oriented framework concept will be at the core of the technology of the twenty-first century. I hope this book helps you get started on your journey toward understanding the subtleties of this new technology.

TED G. LEWIS, PHD

PART I

A Guide to Object-Oriented Design

Every book must start somewhere, so we will start at the beginning, with an overview of the history and origins of object-oriented programming and frameworks. What are they, how did they come about, and why are they so important? These, and other mysteries of the Universe, are covered in four adventure-packed episodes.

The advanced reader might want to skip Part I, especially if he or she already knows the ins and outs of objects, polymorphism, inheritance, class libraries, and Norwegian science. The rest of us can use these introductory chapters to brush up on some important ideas. For example, Chapter 1 quickly takes us up to the contemporary software scene, where programmers are making significant advances in productivity, pushing rapid application development to the limit, and making more money than ever. Chapter 1 is also an excellent place to find basic definition of terms that will linger throughout the rest of the book. While technically lightweight, this first foray into the object-oriented jungle will reward the reader with an orthodontically correct view of the subject.

Chapter 2 gets to the heart of the matter by defining what a framework is, and what it can do. This chapter's stark simplicity will be much appreciated by even the most dedicated nontechnical reader. In addition to introducing the very important model of interaction called MVC (Model-View-Controller), its clear writing, advanced thinking, and global perspective will place you on the edge of your sofa.

Things get tougher in Chapters 3 and 4, because here is where we start to get specific. First, Chapter 3 drags you through the design of a small application framework. The Table framework is a reusable component that creates and manages spreadsheet-like data. In addition to displaying data in a two-dimensional format like Excel or Lotus 1-2-3, the Table framework works as part of a larger framework (MacApp). This illustrates the way programmers of the future will work: borrowing instead of reinventing the software wheel.

Chapter 4 pushes these ideas a bit further, by overlaying a visual or diagram-like programming system on top of a framework for the Macintosh called Objex. This clever bit of programming magic encapsulates both design and code for storage, GUI, I/O, graphics, and MVC applications under the glossy cover of a point-and-click diagramming language based on the mathematically elegant Petri Network. This chapter also contains the first evidence to support the wild claims about programmer productivity that we make in the first chapter.

CHAPTER 1

Origins of the Species

Preview

The object-oriented design and programming revolution is based on the fundamental ideas of objects, classes, methods, messages, encapsulation, inheritance, polymorphism, and dynamic binding. Some of these are new words for old ideas, while others are names for new concepts in software design. How did we get here from the old-fashioned procedural programming heritage, and what do all of these new words mean? The following is an illustrated guide to the new way of thinking about, designing, and writing software.

The two great programming paradigms of the past three decades have been procedure-orientation and object-orientation. The procedural paradigm has served us well, but now it is time for something more powerful, because machines and consumer expectations have grown in power and sophistication. So, how do we deliver powerful software while sidestepping the software crisis? The answer goes all the way back to 1967, to Norway—not Japan, not Germany, and certainly not the USA.

In this chapter you will learn that object-orientation is a better way of writing modular programs. The modules of an object-oriented program encapsulate function, in the form of procedures, and state, in the form of storage variables. This, combined with the generality and flexibility of a programming trick called *polymorphism*, defines the object-oriented paradigm. Oh, and then there are *inheritance* and *dynamic binding*. But then, if we tell you what these are in the first page, you won't buy the book!

1.1 After 25 Years, Why Now?

First, a warning to the reader. The word *OOP* is not a faux pas on the part of the author, but rather an abbreviation of *object-oriented programming*. Another frequently-used phrase in this book is *object-oriented design*, abbreviated *OOD*.

Second warning. This chapter introduces OOP and OOD at the most elementary level. If you are beyond the novice level, skip to the next chapter, or if you are an expert OOP programmer and simply want to read about frameworks, skip to the next part.

1.1.1 In the Beginning

OOP and OOD are at least two decades old, and the ideas have been around for perhaps even longer. The fundamental idea of composing software from a collection of modules called *objects* goes way back to the dawning era of software design, even before personal computers. Even before video games! In 1967, a new programming language called *Simula67* was invented for the purpose of writing simulation software. But, rather than raise interest in simulations, it went unnoticed by just about everyone except for a few leading-edge software academics. The academics liked Simula67 because it showed how to cluster data around procedures, thus simplifying software design, coding, and maintenance.

Data and procedure clustering prevented unauthorized access to data in a Simula67 program. Only procedures that belonged to the same cluster were allowed direct access to the cluster data. In a sense, Simula67 substituted function calls for data access everywhere it occurred in the program.

Clusters prevented indiscriminate data access. They set up software fences, and access procedures were software gates for controlling access. Thus was born the idea of *encapsulation*—one of the central ideas of OOP, so important in fact, that we have used an enclosed box to represent it, in Figure 1.1. Encapsulation is defined as any mechanism which separates a program variable from code which changes its state. Furthermore, encapsulation implies some form of access protection, a topic of great interest to programming language designers in the 1970s. But, we are getting ahead of our story.

Maybe because Simula67 was aimed at simulation programmers instead of general application development programmers, or maybe because it was invented in Scandinavia, it remained somewhat obscure until the same ideas were rediscovered by the computer scientists at Xerox Corporation's think tank, Xerox PARC (PARC is an abbreviation of Palo Alto Research Center). In the 1960s, 1970s, and early 1980s, Douglas Englebart and others at PARC had fun inventing things like menus and windows, the mouse, and computer-to-computer networks. One of their

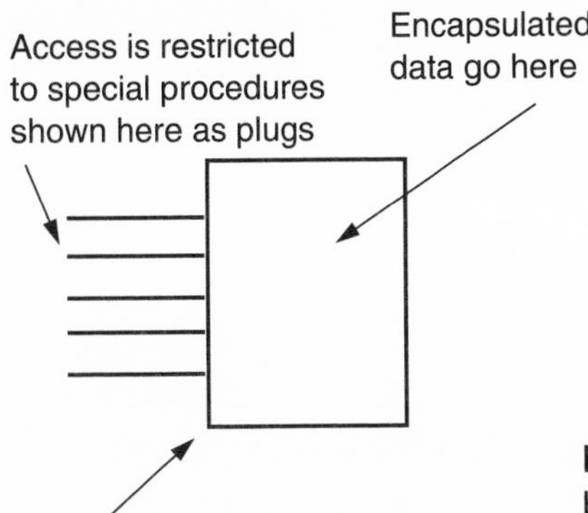
Access is restricted to special procedures shown here as plugs
Encapsulated data go here
The basis of an object is the concept of encapsulation shown as a box with access procedures shown as plugs

Figure 1.1 *Encapsulation* is the basis of OOP: All data are closed off from the outside world, and only special procedures called *methods* or *member functions* are allowed to directly access the encapsulated data

goals was to make computers so simple that even a child could program them. To do this, they had to eliminate much of the complexity of traditional procedural programming, e.g., FORTRAN and Cobol had to go.

So, with the help of Allan Kay, Adele Goldberg, Larry Tesler, and others, the ideas of OOP were collected together to create yet another language, this time called *Smalltalk-80*, which incorporated the fundamentals of OOP. And, once again, the world pretty much ignored it!

1.1.2 The Software Crisis Scare

Two things happened in the 1980s which reversed the poor fortunes of OOP. First, computer hardware got faster and cheaper, and second, software got bigger and much more expensive. In fact, software costs soared to the point of creating a *software crisis*. The combination of these two trends is dramatized in Figure 1.2, which shows that the cost per hardware unit was plunging while the cost per software unit was soaring. (The cost per statement of a large program is higher than the cost per statement of a smaller program. So, Figure 1.2 is truly a comparison of the per-unit costs of software versus hardware. On the other hand, the cost of a single transistor decreases by a factor of about 4 every three years!).

Rapid advances in building faster and cheaper hardware were quickly absorbed by software that made intensive use of graphical user interfaces (GUIs). GUI software made using computers so simple that a new breed of applications was quickly invented. Drawing programs that processed

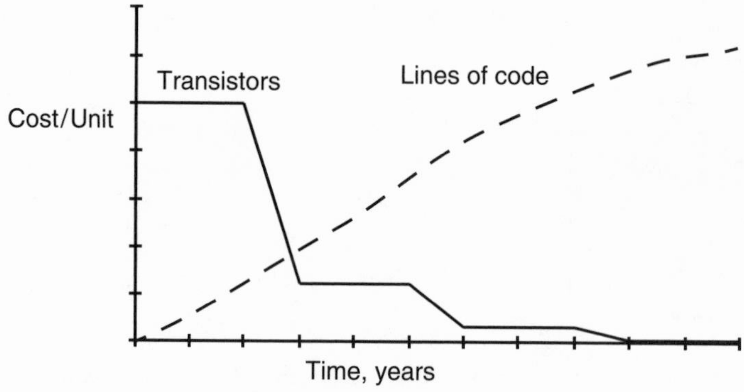

Figure 1.2 Cost trends in the 1970s and 1980s. Unless something is done about software, these trends will continue into the year 2000

pictures instead of text could run on inexpensive personal computers for the first time. Ordinary people could build financial models by merely pointing and clicking. These new toys looked suspiciously like the Xerox PARC computers designed for the children of silicon valley families living next to PARC. And guess what—the drawing programs were object-oriented! (This idea just kept showing up in all the right places).

One person's fool's gold is another person's treasure. The Xerox executives failed to appreciate the profit potential of cute little computers with object-oriented GUIs that everyone could operate. Profit potential was not over the head of Steve Jobs of Apple Computer, who saw clearly that OOP held the long-sought-after answer to the big questions of computer life. Apple bought the idea of OOP, along with most of the people who worked for PARC! (Larry Tesler became head of Advanced Technologies, and Allan Kay became what he always wanted to be—an icon). They made a small computer at a selling price comparable to a car instead of a house, and the Macintosh was born. The Macintosh changed the world in more ways than one, but to the OOP world, it was a godsend.

1.1.3 The Plot Thickens

The plot thickens even more, because the second problem of the 1980s persisted: the soaring cost of software was put into orbit by GUI programming. As it turns out, while Apple was busy making money from Xerox PARC's ideas, Apple was also contributing to the software crisis. GUI programming, networking, multiple-processor systems, and rising customer expectations were all driving programmers to the brink as software became bigger, more complex, and more elaborate. What was a programmer to do?

The software engineers of the 1980s had a solution, but they did not know how to implement it. *Reuse* is the so-called *mega programming* idea, whereby software components are scavenged from old programs then reused to construct new programs. Could the software crisis be held at bay through reuse of software components? It seemed like a good idea, but how? The reuse craze swept the land at about the same time rap music overwhelmed MTV. Oh, and OOP was reborn because the OOP paradigm is perfect for reuse. Not only did OOP properly encapsulate, but it also recycled old code into new.

As they say, the rest is being rewritten as history. OOP solved a major computing problem, making it possible to program faster and cheaper hardware much faster and cheaper than using the old-fashioned procedural style exemplified by FORTRAN, Cobol, Pascal, and C. The faster hardware made programmers stop worrying about the overhead of OOP, so they had time to worry about bigger and costlier application software. But, the side benefits of OOP reuse put a stop to the growth in complexity of the new GUI-intensive applications.

Apple Computer tried to promote OOP with MacApp, which was the first widely used reusable OOP tool. But the idea was still slightly ahead of its time. Then Apple Computer stumbled in its loyalty to founder Jobs, so he took his OOP ideas to NeXT Inc., and NeXTStep was born out of the OOP stew. Later, IBM thought that OOP was such a good idea, it bought the languishing technology from Apple and together they formed Taligent Inc., and another contender in the "OOP is for reuse" contest joined the frenzy.

1.1.4 Back at the (AT&T) Ranch

Meanwhile, the procedural programming gang was not giving up without a fight. Cute little computers were not going to rule the world, at least not while there were UNIX hackers, C language diehards, and AT&T. Smalltalk might be pure and perfect, Object Pascal elegant, and MacApp simply too advanced, but C was the *lingua franca* of real programmers. If it was not an extension of C, how could it be more than a toy?

Bjorne Stroustrup of AT&T Bell Labs offered a solution just in time to rally the UNIX programmers who were as out of date in the new OOP decade as disco. Stroustrup added object-oriented features to C, and gave the concoction a clever name, C++. Actually, C++ source code was originally converted into ordinary C by a program called *CFRONT* which AT&T gave away. The converted program was run through a C compiler to get executable binary code. Therefore, C++ was not really pure and perfect. Even today, C++ is euphemistically called a *hybrid OOP,* because a clever programmer can use it to write either a procedural or object-oriented program.

The invention of C++, Object Pascal, and other hybrids has weakened the foundation of OOP, because encapsulation is not strictly enforced in such upstart languages. Yet, these hybrids have been largely responsible for the slow conversion of procedural programmers to the OOP style of programming. In the 1990s the story is largely one of transition from pure procedural to pure object-oriented programming.

So, by the late 1990s, OOP will have replaced top-down structured programming as the software fad of the decade. Programmers will discard their worn-out ideas based on procedural languages and adopt an OOP language. If it were not so true, we would not have to say it, but OOP is to the 1990s what structured programming was to the 1970s. And, OOP is truly a paradigm shift because most of what you know about procedural programming is harmful to understanding the OOP paradigm.

1.1.5 Giving Life to Meaning: OOP As a Paradigm

What exactly is the OOP paradigm? Table 1.1 summarizes the terminology of both paradigms. In the new paradigm, *procedures* are no longer the fundamental software building blocks, rather, *objects* are. Now embedded in objects, procedures are activated only when a *message* is sent from one object to another. Objects and messages are the stuff of software design.

The procedural paradigm must be discarded to clear the way for an entirely different view of data, data types, and access to data. We will begin to tell that story in the next section. In the remainder of this book, we will illustrate these ideas and discuss how they are used to reverse the software crisis, stave off spiraling development and maintenance costs, and save the computer world. Well, maybe not, but at least you will become an expert

Table 1.1 Procedural paradigm versus OOP paradigm

Procedural	OOP (approximately equivalent)
Functional decomposition	Responsibility-driven design
Information hiding	Encapsulation
Module	Object
Procedure call	Message
Procedure	Method or member function
Runtime call	Dynamic binding
Runtime declaration	Instantiation
Structured design	OOD
Type	Class

on a technology that is sure to change the way you write programs, design systems, and amuse your friends at cocktail parties.

1.2 What Makes an Object an Object?

The OOP idea of a module is different from the procedural idea of a module. In the OOP paradigm, the purpose of a module is to encapsulate data along with processing functions, making the function/data cluster one simple, compact, elegant unit of software. Such modules are called objects, and in their purest form objects contain functions called *methods* or *behaviors* and states called *instance variables.* (In C++ methods are called *member functions* and instance variables are called *member variables.* If you can ignore these differences in terminology, then OOP begins to make sense).

1.2.1 Visualizing Objects

Figure 1.3 shows an object as a box enclosing data with externally accessible ports representing methods. The encapsulated data of the object are called its instance variables or state. Thus, an object is a programming entity which encapsulates both function and state. That's it, folks: an object is an encapsulation of data along with the procedures for manipulating the data. Well, almost.

Think of objects as having *attributes*: function attributes are implemented as access procedures, and state attributes are implemented as instance variables. We will introduce other attributes as needed, but in

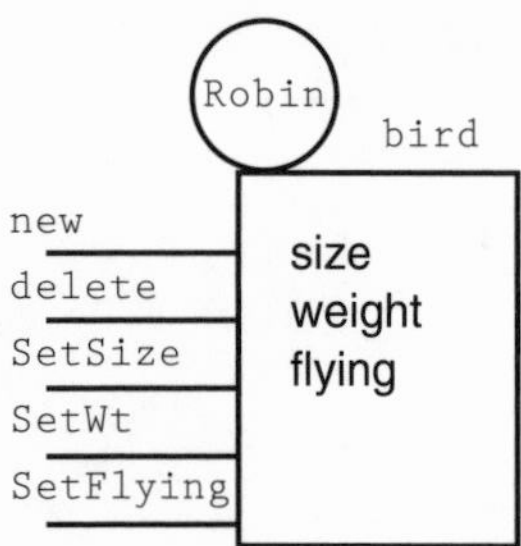

Figure 1.3 An example of an object called `Robin`, of type `bird`, with encapsulated data *size*, *weight*, and *flying*, and access procedures `new`, `delete`, `SetSize`, `SetWt`, and `SetFlying`

their simplest form objects are merely clusters of data and functions. Figure 1.3 illustrates some other attributes of objects. Each object has a name; in this case, `Robin` is the name of the object.

1.2.2 Classes Are Not Objects

All objects belong to a class of objects called the *class attribute*. Thus, `Robin` is an object which belongs to the class of `birds`. Think of a class as a template or blueprint for the creation of objects. When a house is constructed from a blueprint, it is one of many possible instances of the same blueprint. If you live in a California housing development, you will know what I mean. Similarly, an object is an instance of a class. An object is the actual thing, but a class is only a blueprint.

Objects take up storage space inside of a computer's memory just like a house takes up space along the street. A class does not take up space, however, because it is merely a specification. (Well, almost. The code which implements the methods of a class take space in program memory). Thus, a class is an abstract definition of encapsulated function and state.

The difference between a class and objects derived from it is shown in Figure 1.4. Note that an object is drawn with a circle around its name, to distinguish it from a class, which has no circled name. I guess you could say an object just ain't got no class. But, all objects are derived from classes.

Example

Consider the drawing program fragment shown in Figure 1.4, which renders ovals and rectangles on a screen. Ovals and rectangles are geometric shapes; hence they belong to the class called `Shape`. `Shape` can be used as a blueprint for all geometric shapes. It defines both state and function of objects derived from it.

The state of any object created from `Shape` is simple in this case. Coordinates (`top, left`) and (`bot, right`) are corners of a rectangular

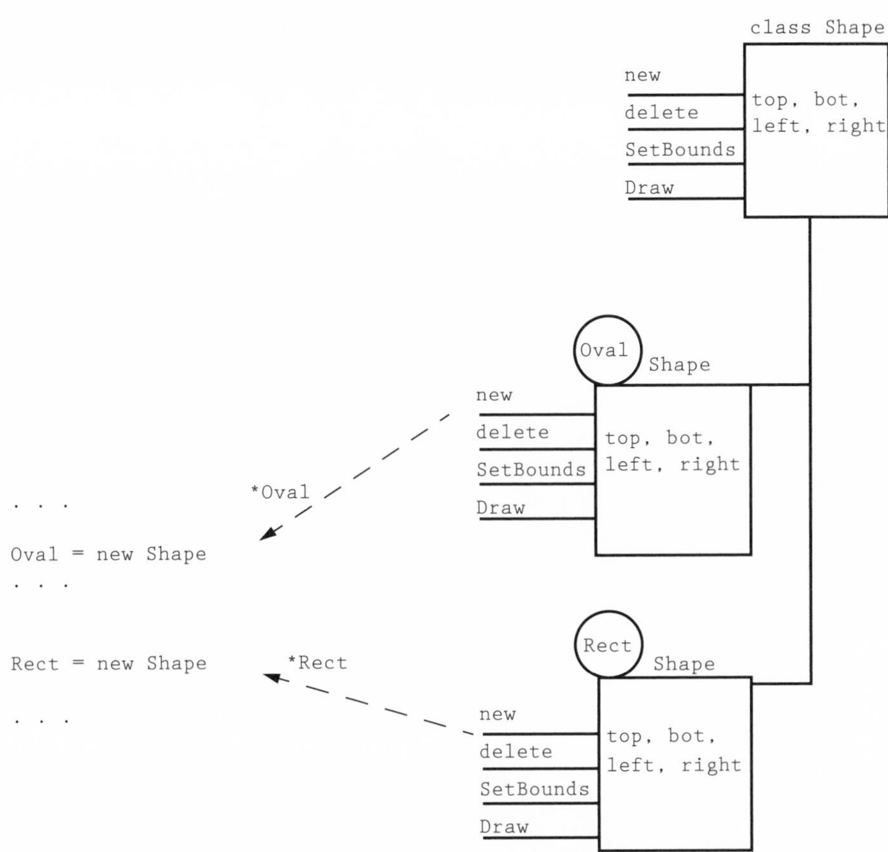

Figure 1.4 Two objects created from one class definition. An instance is a clone of a class. The *star notation* of C is used to designate a pointer, e.g., `*Oval` and `*Rect` point to their respective objects (Caution: This example is purposely oversimplified.)

region on the screen where shapes are to be drawn. All we have to do is send a message to each object that tells it where to draw itself, and then send another message to draw. The details of drawing are delegated to the object itself.

The method `new`, which is part of all class definitions, is said to respond to a message from the running program to create storage space for the Oval object, for example. This is shown as a dotted line between the main program's code, and the method `new` defined on each object. The dotted line is also labeled with the name of a pointer which is returned to the main program so that it can keep track of the location of each object.

1.2.3 Creating Objects

An object is created by a process called *instantiation.* To use a biological analogy, we say the object is cloned from its class. Any number of objects may be instantiated from a single class by the electronic equivalent of cloning. Figure 1.4 shows only two objects, but the number of objects is limited only by the amount of memory.

The operator `new` is used to instantiate an object. Memory is allocated to hold the instance variables for the object, and the memory location is returned through a pointer to the object.

The class procedures are not copied into the object, because this would be too wasteful of memory. (Keep in mind that one class may define many objects; each object references the same procedures). But, the object contains a reference to its access procedures, which are defined by its class. Thus, every object reuses the procedures defined by its parent class. (As promised, we got around to reuse—more later).

All objects also respond to a `new` operation. When an object is deleted, its storage space is returned to main memory, and its location pointer is set to null.

In addition, `new` causes the object's *constructor function* to execute, and `new` causes the object's *destructor function* to execute. So, we can also say that the `new` operation constructs an object, and the `new` operation destroys it. The code for a constructor and destructor is part of the class definition as well. Such *prologue* and *epilog* code is useful for automating housekeeping chores such as initializing a linked list or deleting all lingering storage after an object that references it is gone.

Example

Returning to our drawing program, suppose the main program sends a message to one or both of the objects to draw themselves on the screen. The actual draw operation is encapsulated inside of each object, so the main program need not provide any code. Instead, the main program sends a message to the object to activate its `Draw()` method. The main program might contain something like this in C++:

```
Rect -> Draw(); //Send a message to Draw a Rectangle
Oval -> Draw(); //Draw an Oval
```

Some of the functions in Figure 1.4 are application-dependent operations for manipulating the state of the object. For example, we send a `SetBounds ()` message to an object to tell it where to draw itself. `SetBounds` changes the state of an object (`top, bot, left, right`) in preparation for drawing inside of a rectangle whose upper lefthand corner is at location (`top, left`), and whose lower righthand corner is at location (`bot, right`).

The drawing example of Figure 1.4 will be continued and enhanced as our story unfolds. However, it is only fair to warn the reader that the example just given is an oversimplification of what really goes on in a C++ program. In fact, there are bugs in the drawing program example. But, be patient and the bugs will be fixed in the next chapter.

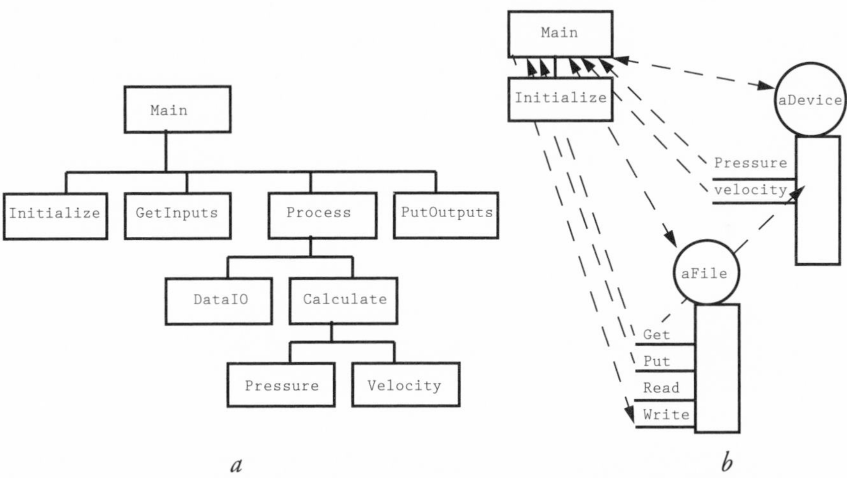

Figure 1.5 Conceptual comparison of Procedural (*a*) versus Object-Oriented (*b*) Program Design. The call graph (*a*) is read from top to bottom and left to right to give the order of procedure execution. On the contrary, the order of method calls in an object-oriented program is not discernible from the OOD wiring diagram

1.3 Polymorphism and All That Jazz

Objects are plugged together much like stereo components are connected by wires to make a complete system. Programming by wiring together communicating objects results in an *object-oriented program*. The wiring diagram is the object-oriented design (OOD), corresponding to the program. Software wiring is done by *message-passing*, shown in Figure 1.4 as dotted lines labeled with one or more message parameters.

But, object-oriented programming is more than wiring together funny modules called objects and then reverting back to the old procedural paradigm. Sure, encapsulation is merely information-hiding in disguise, methods are merely procedures, and messages are just another form of procedure call. Is this all? (I know you are still skeptical).

1.3.1 Those Magnificent Polymorphic Methods

The OOP paradigm extends the ideas of encapsulation and message-passing in a number of other powerful ways. For example, message-passing changes program structure, see Figure 1.5. Instead of a hierarchical *call graph* of procedures, an object-oriented program contains a network of communicating objects. Instead of functional decomposition, which structured programming preached for so many years as the foundation of procedural programming, OOD uses encapsulation to derive the program's design. See the difference?

The diagrams of Figure 1.5 do not show all of the important differences. Still, if you closely examine the OOP version of Figure 1.5(b) you might see subtle but important structural differences. For example, in place of `if-then-else` and `case` select statements, an OOP contains *polymorphic methods*. We will illustrate this important concept by extending our previous drawing example.

Suppose we expand on the drawing program fragments shown in Figure 1.4 to arrive at the program structures shown in Figure 1.6. In Figure 1.6(a) we have constructed a traditional procedural program for drawing either an oval or a rectangle. The boxes represent procedures, and the solid lines represent the flow of control through the program. Read the diagram from top to bottom, and left to right. The main program executes `SetUpWind()` first, followed by `ChooseShape`. The `*` in the `ChooseShape` box means this procedure is repeated. Similarly, an `0` in a box means it is selected from among alternatives. Thus, the procedural program in Figure 1.6(a) can be paraphrased as follows:

```
main;
    SetUpWind();                {Create Drawing Window}
    while....
        ChooseShape(shape);     {Return a shape type from user}
        Get(top, bot,...);      {Return location from user}
        case shape of...
            1: DrawOval();      {Use different procedures...}
            2: DrawRect();      {... one for each type}
        endcase
    endwhile
endmain
```

The dotted lines show the flow of values back and forth between the global variables in the main program and the procedures. First, input values flow to the globals, and then from the globals back out to the procedures. This is necessary because the procedures discard their local values each time they are exited. That is, they do not have state-like objects.

Second, note that the procedural program's control structure must be altered to add another type of drawing. Suppose we wanted to draw a triangle. We would have to modify the internal structure of the program in addition to adding a new procedure to draw triangles. This is because of the `case` selection at the core of the program. Modifying the `case` selection is tantamount to redesigning the program.

1.3.2 Bad-Mouthing the Competition

It's not that we dislike the procedural paradigm, but OOP is a better way. We will summarize some problems with the procedural program for your reading enjoyment:

- The procedural paradigm is based on *functional decomposition.* This leads to `case` selection with corresponding functions to handle "exceptions." It also means that a maintenance programmer must alter the basic program structure even to add a small amount of new functionality.
- Functional decomposition only partially encapsulates data and functionality, so that functions are more difficult to reuse. It is unlikely that another application will use any of the code or design of the application. It is simply too difficult and dangerous to scavenge reusable components from the procedural code.
- Functions and global data are scattered all over the program, making maintenance a nightmare. Additions tend to increase the

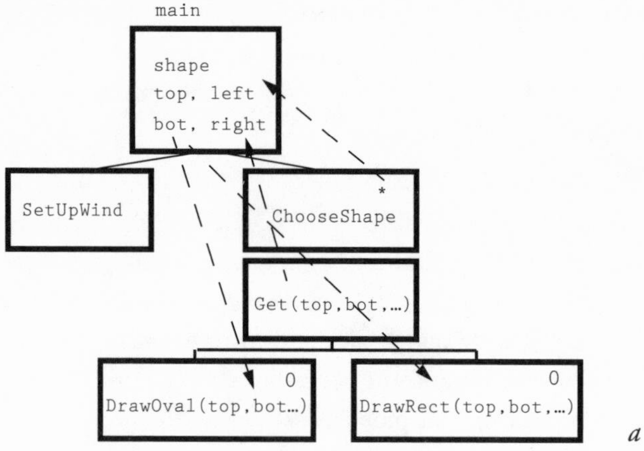

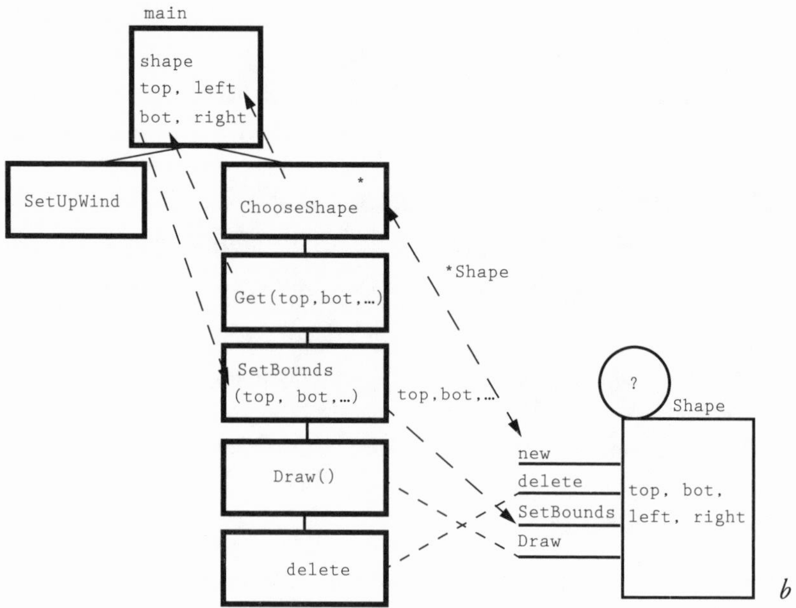

Figure 1.6 Comparison of a procedural versus object-oriented drawing program. (*a*) Procedural drawing program uses case selection. (*b*) Object-oriented drawing program uses dynamic binding and polymorphism

number of globals as well as the number of control statements, both of which are the major source of uncontrolled complexity. Procedural programs become less stable as they age, because they become more complex.

It is doubtful that the simple example of Figure 1.6(b) will convince you that all of these are negative traits of procedural programs. But, we have had three decades of experience with procedural programming that more or less prove these points. What does this have to do with polymorphism?

1.3.3 Dynamic Binding

To work up to polymorphism we have to study the OOP version of the drawing application, see Figure 1.6(b). Here is how it works. First, there are still global variables, but the traffic to and from them is lower. These are really working variables used for input and output and are not part of the state of the program. The state of the program is encapsulated in objects rather than scattered throughout the program. This will be a big plus for the maintenance programmer.

The control structure looks almost the same—the differences are subtle, but important. The most important difference is in the elimination of the `case` selection structure. In its place, we have dynamic creation and binding of an object with its own state and functionality. When the `ChooseShape` routine gets the user's inputs (the kind of shape wanted—oval or rectangle), it also creates the appropriate object by cloning it from the shape class. `ChooseShape` returns a pointer to the shape to be drawn.

Example

Here is a roughly equivalent textual version of the program, written in a C++ like notation:

```
main:
    SetUpWind();                      //Create drawing window
    for(...){
            ChooseShape(shape);       //Creates Object, Returns a
                                          pointer to it
            Get(top,bot,...);         //Returns location from user
            shape->SetBounds(top,bot,...);//Change state of object
            shape->Draw();            //Draw whatever you want
            delete shape;             //Destroy object
    }
}
```

The SetBounds method is applied to whatever shape is created by ChooseShape. But, the shape is not known until the program runs. We call this *dynamic binding* because the message is bound to the object at the latest possible moment, i.e., when the program is running.

To illustrate where the dynamic creation occurs, consider the following pseudocode for ChooseShape. We have taken liberties with C++ in this example, and actually, this code is not yet correct. The fixes will be added in the next section, but for now, simplicity is worth a small amount of indiscretion with C++:

```
ChooseShape(aShape): {
    Get(ShapeKind);                  //Ask user for what kind of shape
    switch(ShapeKind) {              // R=Rect, O=Oval
    case 'R' : aShape = new Shape; //Construct, return value to aShape
                break;
    case 'O' : aShape = new Shape; //aShape is a pointer to an object
                break;
    }}
```

We will return to an explanation of how Rect and Oval are implemented. The point of this example is to illustrate dynamic binding which is defined as the connection that takes place at runtime between communicating objects. Messages are bound to an object when the program runs instead of when the program is written. Therefore, messages are bound either to a Rect or an Oval, but not both. The returned pointer designates which object receives a message to run its SetBounds and Draw methods.

The Draw() message is sent to the appropriate object so that it can draw itself. We say that the Draw method is *polymorphic* because it takes on different implementations at different points in the program. If the object created by ChooseShape is a rectangle, the Draw() message is bound to a Rect object's Draw method. If ChooseShape returns a pointer to an Oval object, the Draw() message is dynamically bound to the Draw method of an oval object.

So why the big name for such a simple idea? *Poly* means many, and *morphic* means shape. Therefore, methods in OOP have many forms, even though a single name designates them.

1.3.4 But Can I Do It With a Callback?

Polymorphism may seem unnatural to a traditional procedural programmer. Think of a program with two or more procedures having exactly the same name and parameters. How would the program distinguish one from the other? But even in a procedural language which allows procedure pointers we can distinguish procedures from one another by where they are stored in memory.

In fact, a *callback* procedure is implemented by passing a procedure pointer to another procedure, which in turn calls back the passed procedure, see Figure 1.7. The main program uses one `Draw()` procedure to handle both cases. The address of the drawing routine is passed to `Draw`, and then `Draw` calls the appropriate routine. This illustrates how to implement object-oriented programming ideas in procedural languages such as C.

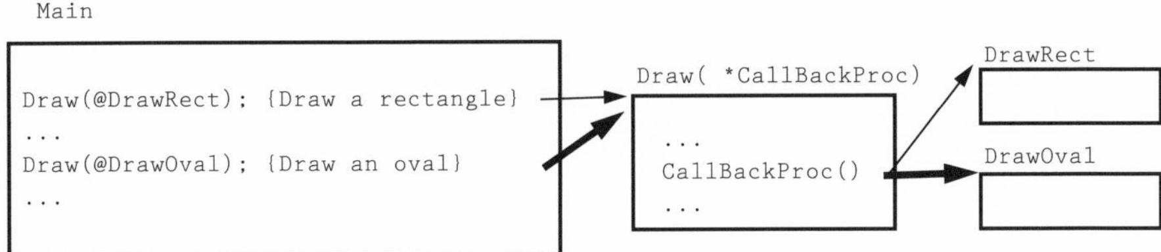

Figure 1.7 Use of callback procedures to simulate polymorphism in procedural programs. Main calls `Draw`, and `Draw` calls the appropriate callback procedure. The address of the callback procedure is passed instead of its name

Getting back to object-oriented programming, note that in Figure 1.6(b) we have labeled the object with a question mark because we do not know until run-time whether it is an `Oval` or a `Rect`. In either case, each time we repeat the loop of the program an object is created, drawn on the screen, and then destroyed. In an actual program, we would have to delay the computer to see the drawing before it is removed by the delete function.

1.3.5 Hurrah for Our Side!

Regardless of the impressive number of syllables in terms like *polymorphism* and *dynamic binding*, these concepts do not by themselves abate the software crisis. Still, we claim that OOP programming is an improvement of major proportions over procedural programming, because:

- The code is made more general and flexible because `case` selection is replaced by dynamic binding, resulting in smaller, simpler code.
- A greater degree of encapsulation means greater opportunity for reuse. Like greed on Wall Street, reuse is good.
- Maintenance is easier because all `Draw` message-passing is centralized and rarely needs to be changed. Polymorphism means we can write different draw methods for different objects, but never change the calling routine's `Draw()` message.
- Complexity is reduced because there is little growth of the global state. The state is contained within each object, rather than scattered through the code in the form of global variables.
- Objects may come and go, but the basic structure of the program remains relatively static. This opens up opportunities for the reuse of design as well as code, a subject we will dwell on repeatedly throughout this book.

Using polymorphic and dynamic objects leads to greater generality and flexibility, but to do battle with the software crisis we need design and code reuse. These are achieved through a concept which has no equivalent in procedural programming: *inheritance* is the key to unlocking the pent-up power of reuse.

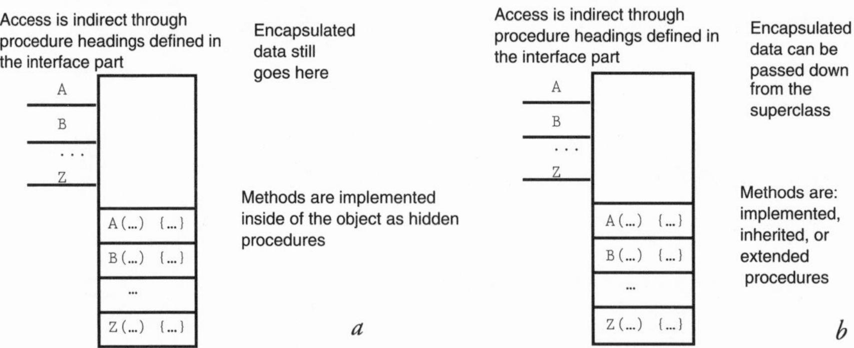

Figure 1.8 Functions are implemented as hidden procedures. (*a*) Direct implementation is simple. (*b*) Inherited and extended implementations are obtained through subclassing

1.4 Inheritance Is the Key to Reuse

The foregoing example still obscures some important details. For example, how are the different `Draw` methods actually implemented? How does the hierarchy in Figure 1.4 distinguish between a rectangle and an oval? Messy details, all right, but they are related to important concepts called *inheritance, subclassing, overriding,* and *extension.* Without these, OOP would not be a key technology for solving the software crisis through reuse.

1.4.1 The Fix

First, suppose we fix the problem of implementing functions in an object. Specifically, how do we implement the drawing methods of the simple example of Figure 1.6(b)? The fix involves correcting an oversimplification in both Figures 1.3 and 1.6(b).

Figure 1.8 introduces a model of an object which includes its implementation part. In Figure 1.8(a), we see the simplest possible implementation part corresponding with the procedures listed in the interface part (Also, hidden functions can be defined in the implementation part, and used only by the object's methods).

The world would be a drab place if everyone looked and acted exactly like their parents. OOP would be just as drab if objects looked and acted exactly like their classes. Genetic variation is introduced in biological populations through sex, but this is a family book, so we have to use something else. OOP uses a hierarchy of classes and overriding of methods to gain variability.

1.4.2 The Act of Inheritance

To introduce variations in OOP, we create a class hierarchy through a series of subclasses, see Figure 1.9. A *subclass* is a class that inherits the properties of a parent class, called the *superclass.* When we say a subclass inherits properties, we mean that the declaration of state and function are the same for the subclass and the superclass. Thus, *inheritance* is the process of obtaining properties through a relation such as parent–child, superior–subordinate, or general–specific.

The methods of a subclassed object may be defined directly as in Figure 1.8(a), but they may also be inherited from a superclass, as shown in

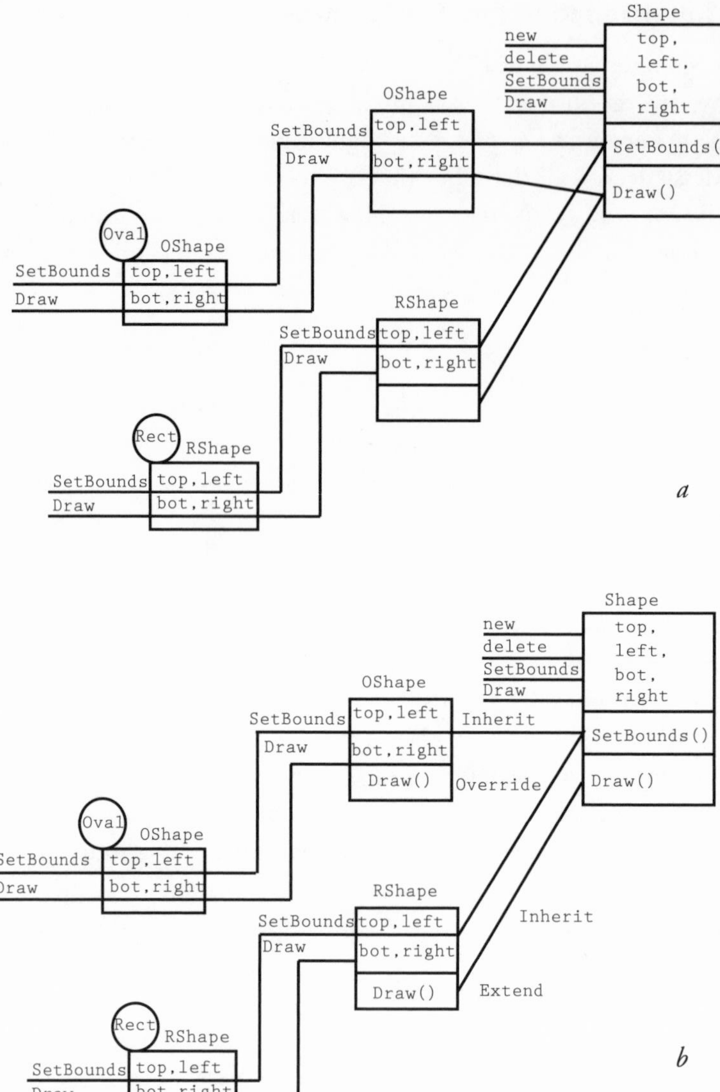

Figure 1.9 Use and reuse through inheritance. In simple inheritance (*a*), the subclasses are identical to the superclass, but in (*b*), the subclasses have been modified by overriding and extending the superclass methods

Figure 1.8(b). Inheritance means that a method's code is copied from the superclass. *Inheritance* is the act of reusing properties of superclasses.

Now, two things can happen when a subclass inherits from its superclass. First, the methods of the superclass can be inherited without any changes. This is the boring case, which hardly any respectable programmer would use.

1.4.3 Override and Extend

Alternatively, inherited methods can be altered in one of two ways. An *override* occurs when the method's name is retained, but its code is completely replaced by code in the subclass. An *extension* occurs when the method's name is retained and the superclass code is retained, but the code is extended to do additional things. We illustrate these two possibilities in Figure 1.9.

Figure 1.9(a) corrects the oversimplified hierarchy given earlier in Figure 1.4. The `Shape` class is subclassed twice; once to obtain `OShape`, and again to obtain `RShape`. Both subclasses are still class declarations, rather than objects, and both subclasses can be cloned to make objects, or subclassed further to make more classes.

Example
In C++, the classes in Figure 1.9(a) would be declared as follows:

```
class Shape : public {
    private :
     int top, left, bot, right;    // Instance variables
    public :                       //Method Prototypes…
    void SetBounds( int top, left, bot, right);//Set Drawing Area
    void Draw( void);              //Polymorphic Draw
}

class OShape : Shape {};//Direct inheritance
class RShape : Shape {};//Direct inheritance
```

Figure 1.9(a) graphically depicts the two-step process. First the `Shape` class is subclassed twice, once for each new type of object we want. Then, each subclass is used as a blueprint for its corresponding object. The `Rect` object is created from the `RShape` subclass, and the `Oval` object is created from the `OShape` subclass. Later in the program, we dynamically create the objects which are labeled `Oval` and `Rect` in Figure 1.8(b). These objects inherit the state of their parent classes:

```
main{
    RShape *Rect;                      //Pointer to rectangle object
    OShape *Oval;                      //Pointer to oval object
...

Rect = new RShape;//Instance of a rectangle
Oval = new OShape;//Instance of an oval
}
```

The two objects are twins. They are also clones of their parents, because they inherit all attributes of the parent `Shape`, in every detail. Specifically, they have inherited the same code for `SetBounds` and `Draw`. Therefore, they will appear exactly the same on the screen. The `Draw` methods of both objects draw exactly the same diagram!

This is not what we wanted. To introduce genetic mutations into the family tree we must resort to an override. This is shown in Figure 1.9(b) for the `OShape` subclass. Note that the `SetBounds` method is copied from the parent class Shape, but that the `Draw` method is replaced in `OShape`. The polymorphic `Draw()` message is handled differently by objects derived from `OShape` than by objects derived from `Shape`.

Example

The C++ code equivalent of the sleight of hand called subclassing with override is:

```
class OShape : Shape {
    void Draw(void) };      //Override inherited Draw, roll your own

void OShape::Draw(void) {  //Implementation is separate and hidden
    DrawOval() };         //Fill in the blank with whatever you want
here
```

The code above does two things. First, the `Draw` declaration in the class `OShape` knocks out the inherited `Draw`. Second, the implemented `Draw` for subclass `OShape` implements anything the programmer wants. Now, when `Oval` objects need to be drawn, they use this version of `Draw` instead of the one in `Shape`.

The approach taken in subclass `RShape` is different, simply to illustrate extension. Instead of replacing the entire `Draw` method of `Shape`, we use it, and add a bit more code. Suppose the `Draw` of `Shape` does setup work, and the `Draw` of `Rect` is delegated to actual drawing. We could use the inherited `Draw` first, followed by the actual drawing code.

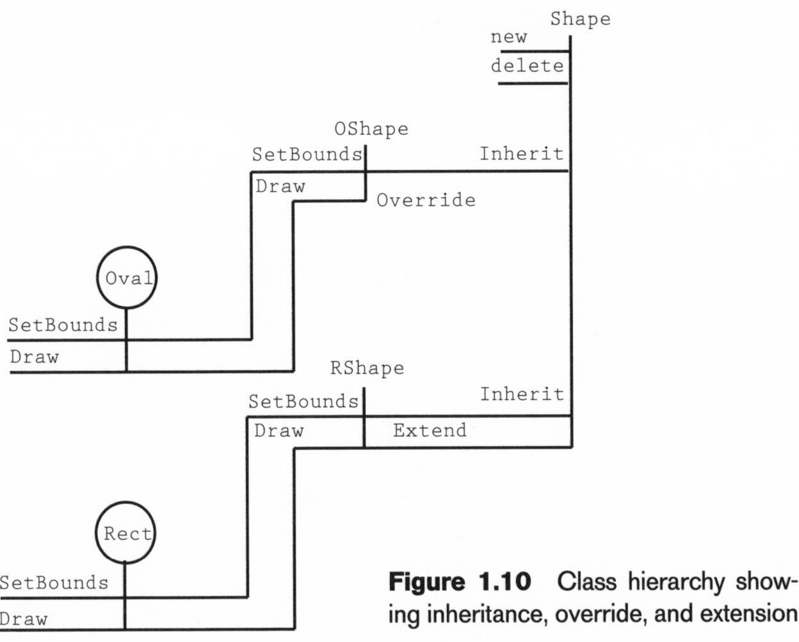

Figure 1.10 Class hierarchy showing inheritance, override, and extension

```
class RShape : Shape {//Subclass Shape
    inherited::Draw();//Perform Shape::Draw()
    PaintRect();//Lay down lines
}

void Shape::Draw(void) {//A possible inherited Draw ...
    SetRect(top, left, bot, right); // ... or a reasonable equivalent
}
```

The extension is clever, for sure, but more importantly, extension reuses code that may be useful in a number of drawing objects. Thus, it is not necessary to repeat the redundant code everywhere it is needed.

Inheritance is the key to reuse. First, we needed subclassing to create the inheritance hierarchy of classes. Figure 1.10 shows an abbreviated class hierarchy and the corresponding simple inheritance, overrides, and extensions. The state information and implementation parts have been removed from Figure 1.10 as a simplification. Named vertical lines correspond to classes and subclasses. Circles represent objects, and lines connecting methods represent inheritance and extension.

Without inheritance, OOP would not be a key technology for solving the software crisis through reuse. Without all of the other features discussed in this chapter, OOP would not have survived its rocky road to fame.

1.5 Summary of the Main Points

We will summarize some important consequences that might have escaped you because of the distracting references to sex:

- Objects are abstractions which separate an interface from the implementation.
- Class hierarchies use subclassing to build even higher level abstractions through composition.
- Interface parts are used to design an object-oriented program as a collection of message-passing objects. We do not need any implementation parts to design an entire program.
- The implementation part is used to construct the functionality of a program. We can economize by reusing as many implementation parts as possible. This is done by inheritance, but inheritance is often too restricted, so we can modify the strict inheritance hierarchy by overriding and extending implementation parts.
- We might conclude from the foregoing points that a program's design is equivalent to its object interfaces and message structure. While this is not entirely correct, it is close to the truth. At any rate, the implementation part is not part of a program's design. This separation of implementation from design is one of the most powerful arguments for replacing the procedural paradigm with the OOP paradigm.

Further Reading

[Budd90] T. Budd, *An Introduction to Object-Oriented Programming*, Addison-Wesley, Reading, MA, 1990.

[Cox86] B. Cox, *Object-Oriented Programming: An Evolutionary Approach*, Addison-Wesley, Reading, MA, 1986.

[Korson90] T. Korson and J. D. McGregor, Understanding object-oriented: A unifying paradigm, *Communications of the ACM*, **33** (9), 40–60, Sep. 1990.

CHAPTER 2

Framework Fundamentals

Preview

A framework is more than a class hierarchy. It is a class hierarchy plus a model of interaction among the objects instantiated from the framework. In addition, a framework reverses the traditional idea of component reuse. Instead of a programmer writing a main program which calls reusable procedures, a programmer instantiates objects from the framework's class hierarchy and then provides methods for the framework to call. Thus, a framework is a generic application program which a programmer tailors by providing highly specialized routines which are called by the framework.

The building blocks of a framework are class hierarchy design, abstract classes, iterators, and the MVC interaction. We will examine two fundamental approaches to hierarchical design and then launch into the gory details of how to make a framework. The diligent reader is rewarded with the virtue of virtual functions, and the uses of polymorphism. The purple-heart reader is treated to seething C++ code, and an illustration of how most GUIs work. Taken in sum, these are the fundamentals of frameworks.

2.1 Inheritance Relation = Class Hierarchy

The previous chapter showed how inheritance leads to a class hierarchy, but it did not explain how to decide what hierarchy makes sense, nor how to design a good class hierarchy. Actually, a lot has been written about how to design class hierarchies, giving the impression that it is an exotic topic. But it is really very simple. Hierarchies are nearly always based on either a *is-a* or *has-a* relation. The stark simplicity of the is-a and has-a relations deserves an equally stark explanation:

- A *has-a* relation defines a container hierarchy.
- A *is-a* relation defines a categorization hierarchy.

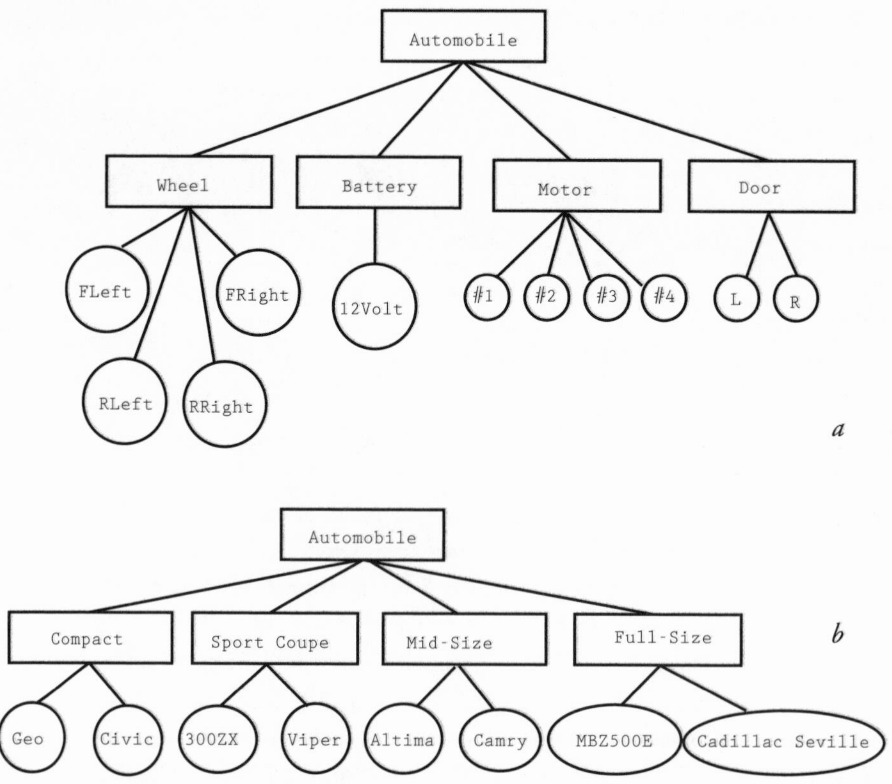

Figure 2.1 Comparison of container and categorization hierarchies. (*a*) Container relations (has-a) for a single automobile. (*b*) Categorization relations (is-a) for a collection of automobiles

2.1.1 Containers

Figure 2.1(*a*) illustrates a partial container hierarchy for modeling a simple automobile as a collection of container objects. Objects instantiated from the hierarchy contain four wheels, one four-cylinder motor, a twelve-volt battery, and two doors. At least the battery is included at no extra cost!

In OOP jargon the `Automobile` class models an object which has-a wheels, batteries, motors, and doors. Thus, the hierarchy of containment obscures detail at the top, and uncovers detail as you move down the hierarchy. Like a politician's campaign promise, each layer uncovers hidden detail.

Another observation is useful when considering the container classes of a has-a relation. The subclasses enumerate the objects contained within the class. Thus, the subclasses of Wheel enumerate the objects contained in `Wheel` as `FLeft`, `FRight`, `RLeft`, and `RRight` wheels; `Battery` has-a 12Volt battery; `Motor` has-a `#1`, `#2`, `#3`, and `#4` cylinder; and `Door` has-a `L` and `R` doors. Enumeration of objects is as important in some programs as counting your children after leaving Disneyland.

2.1.2 Categories

In contrast, Figure 2.1(*b*) illustrates a partial categorization hierarchy for modeling the same simple automobile. In this approach, the class of automobiles is divided into subclasses: `Compact`, `Sport Coupe`, `Mid-Size`, and `Full-Size`. The OOP subclasses correspond with subcategories in the application program. That is, an automobile is-a compact, sport coupe, mid-size, or full-size. In turn, a `Compact` is-a `Geo` or `Civic`. A `Sport Coupe` is-a `300ZX` or `Viper`, and so forth, all the way down to a `Yugo`.

In a categorization hierarchy, the is-a relation defines a specialization rather than an enumeration. Instead of containing other objects, specialized objects override general attributes in favor of more specialized attributes. This is an important distinction:

Container classes model enumerated objects, while categorization classes model specializations.

2.1.3 Politics

At the risk of waxing philosophical for a moment, we might say that the OOP process attempts to model the world as objects which contain other objects, or as objects which are specializations of more general classes. This mouthful says that we have two guiding principles to help determine how to construct a class hierarchy. Which is the best philosophy, containers or specializations? The answer depends on the application, and which high priest of OOP you idolize.

In most cases, categorization is the most general, because it is more likely to render class hierarchies which are reusable across several applications. The container relation usually leads to application-dependent code. For example, in Figure 2.1(a), what happens if we want to model a four-door automobile?

Life is not so simple, however, and there are cases where a container relation is better and more general. The following section illustrates a combination of container and category relations which models most common storage structures. Keep in mind that we seek a simple hierarchy in which both design and code can be reused.

2.2 Your First Class Hierarchy

Consider the following programming problem: you want to design a class hierarchy for data storage in an arbitrary program. The hierarchy should be complete in the sense that it can be used to store almost any kind of data structure, and it should be general enough to be useful in almost any kind of program. If you should take on this difficult assignment, be careful which relation you use.

2.2.1 Factoring

First things first. We will apply the principle of encapsulation to the problem of data storage by making data structure objects encapsulate data, as well as all of the functions we want to perform on the data. For example, methods might be needed in an arbitrary program to:

- `Add()` adds an object to a collection.
- `AddQueue()` adds an object to a FIFO queue.
- `Contains()` returns TRUE if an object is in a collection.
- `DelQueue()` removes an object from a FIFO queue.
- `DiskRead()` reads a data structure from a disk file.
- `DiskWrite()` saves a data structure to a disk file.
- `Find()` finds an object in a collection.
- `Hash()` returns a hashing value.
- `IsEmpty()` returns TRUE if a collection is empty.
- `IsEqual()` returns TRUE if two objects are the same.
- `Pop()` is the stack pop.
- `Push()` is the stack push.
- `Remove()` removes an object from a collection.

- `Size()` returns the size of a collection.
- `SortDown()` rearranges a collection into descending order.
- `SortUp()` rearranges a collection into ascending order.

Next, we will separate these operations into classes (categories), as follows. The operations which are common to all collections of data are placed into the most general class. The operations which are more specialized are placed into specialized subclasses.

The most general category becomes the most general class, which we call a `Collection`. The operations on `Collection` are:

- `Add()` adds an object to a collection.
- `Contains()` returns TRUE if an object is in a collection.
- `DiskRead()` reads a data structure from a disk file.
- `DiskWrite()` saves a data structure to a disk file.
- `Find()` finds an object in a collection.
- `IsEmpty()` returns TRUE if a collection is empty.
- `IsEqual()` returns TRUE if two objects are the same.
- `Remove()` removes an object from a collection.
- `Size()` returns the size of a collection.

The remaining operations are more specialized equivalents of these operations. For example, we equate the following:

```
Add() : AddQueue() : Push()
Contains() : IsEqual()
Remove() : DelQueue() : Pop()
```

These equivalents correspond to specializations of storage. Therefore, we set up a general class having these operations defined on all storage objects derived from the general class, and then we use overrides to specialize each subclass. The `Add()` operation implements `AddQueue()` when the storage discipline is a FIFO queue, `Push()` is used for `Stack` objects, `Insert()` is used for `HashArray` objects, and so forth. The resulting specialization hierarchy is shown in Figure 2.2.

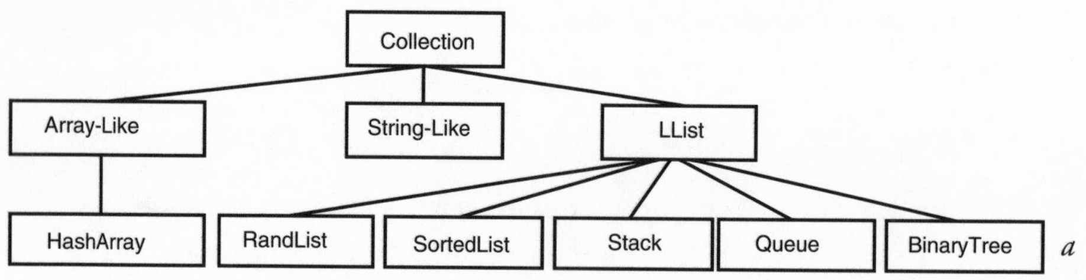

Collection
Add
Contains
DiskRead
DiskWrite
Find
IsEmpty
IsEqual
Remove
Size

String-Like
Add
Contains
DiskRead
DiskWrite
Find
IsEmpty
IsEqual
Remove
Size

Array-Like
Add
Contains
DiskRead
DiskWrite
Find
IsEmpty
IsEqual
Remove
Size

HashArray
Add
Contains
DiskRead
DiskWrite
Find
IsEmpty
IsEqual
Remove
Size
Hash

LList
Add
Contains
DiskRead
DiskWrite
Find
IsEmpty
IsEqual
Remove
Size

RandList
SortedList
SortUp SortDown
Stack
Queue
BinaryTree

b

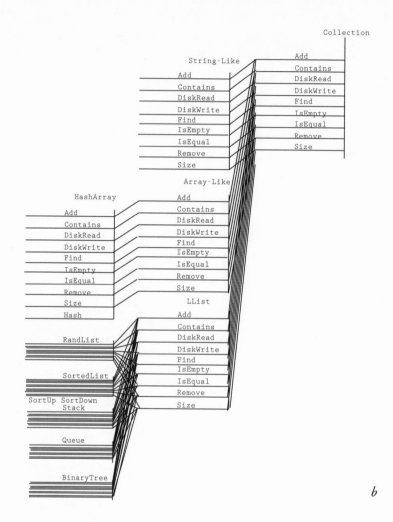

Figure 2.2 Category relation (is-a) class hierarchy for data storage objects. (*a*) The class hierarchy. (*b*) The inheritance hierarchy

The remaining operations have no equivalent. They are further specializations which show up as extensions in further subclassing. For example, in Figure 2.2 we clearly associate the `Hash()` function with the `HashArray` subclass, and the `SortUp()` and `SortDown()` functions with the `SortedList` subclass.

2.2.2 Abstraction

The is-a relation establishes specialization from the top (root) to the bottom (leaves) of the inheritance tree, as shown in Figure 2.2(a). But, the processing action takes place in the descendants of a `Collection` because the descendants define the object's state. The concept of delegating the implementation of tailored functions to a lower class object is called abstraction in OOD. But unlike poverty, *abstraction* is rewarded in the lower classes of an OOP.

Contemplate what it means to be a `Collection` *object.* Such an object is meaningless because the `Collection` class merely defines an interface, never an implementation. We call `Collection` an *abstract class* (aka *metaclass* in some circles) because it has no state, and therefore cannot define an object. An abstract *class* defines an interface, only. We use abstract classes to define *patterns* and interfaces in an object-oriented design. You might say that patterns and interfaces are the building blocks of object-oriented designs.

2.2.3 Virtuality

When we are certain that we are going to override a method in an abstract class we resort to using a *virtual function.* Abstract classes have abstract methods in which the name and parameters of the method are merely interfaces. Their behaviors are defined much later in an override. Thus, a virtual function is an interface or template for the real thing.

Sometimes virtual functions are more than another pretty face. A clever design might define an implementation part for all virtual functions in spite of the inevitable override simply as a guard against a forgetful programmer. If no override occurs, the program can fall back on a default definition in the abstract class. (Okay, so I lied when I said an abstract class contains no implementations. But, this is just a trick.).

In summary, an abstract class may contain virtual functions which are abstractions of their descendants. When we have tied together enough abstractions we end up with a design, and not an implementation. This is why it is safe to say that an OOD incorporates both design and code reuse.

The relation used to establish Figure 2.2(a) is also used to establish an abstract design, see Figure 2.2(b). In this design, we override the methods of the abstract class Collection in each subclass. The overrides specialize subclasses, giving them proper behaviors for each type of object. `Add()` is implemented as a `Push()` for stacks, and as an `Insert()` for hash tables.

In addition, because the design shown in Figure 2.2(b) is based on specialization (as well as the is-a container relation), we can use extension to add more specialized functionality as we descend the hierarchy. Thus, `SortUp()` and `SortDown()` specialize `LList` into `SortedList`, and `Hash()` specializes `HashArray`. The children of five-fingered parents are given six fingers by simply adding an additional finger after birth!

2.2.4 Polymorphism to the Max

So what we have done is to use *polymorphism* to the maximum in the design of a class hierarchy which presents a simple, consistent interface to all users. This interface is defined by an abstract class, `Collection`, which characterizes all subclasses derived from it. Whether the storage structure implements a stack, queue, or hash array depends on the operations specified by the abstract class and implemented by the dynamically created objects. This is another case where polymorphism replaces pages of ugly `if-then-else` code with one set of (abstract) methods for accessing all storage structures.

2.3 Frameworks Defined

The previous example illustrates nearly all of the basic principles of OOP: encapsulation of state and function, polymorphism, inheritance, and specialization through overrides and extensions. We have used everything, and have no unexplained parts left over! Except, which philosophy does the class hierarchy in Figure 2.2 use?

The clean is-a relation established by the `Collection` class hierarchy is deceptively simple. The problem arises when we start to think about what each object derived from a `HashArray`, `RandList`, `SortedList`, `Stack`, `Queue`, or `BinaryTree` collection stores. If these storage objects contain other objects, then is the hierarchy based on a has-a or an is-a relation? For instance, suppose a storage structure from subclass `RandList` contains a randomized list of automobiles instantiated from Figure 2.1(a). These container objects form the state of the `RandList` object. Is the hierarchy based on has-a or is-a?

The source of the confusion stems from how we interpret the class hierarchy. When we construct a class hierarchy prior to running the program, the relations are static. When objects are constructed during program execution, the relations are dynamic. This dynamic interaction is missing in the picture we have painted thus far. We need a model of interaction to go along with a program's static design.

Now it is time to define the key idea of this entire book! An object-oriented *framework* provides both static and dynamic parts of an object-oriented program.

A framework is an object-oriented class hierarchy plus a built-in model which defines how the objects derived from the hierarchy interact with one another.

A framework is more than a class hierarchy. It is a miniature application complete with dynamic as well as static structure. It is a generic application we can reuse as the basis of many other applications. And, before I forget it, frameworks are specialized for a narrow range of applications, because each model of interaction is domain-specific, e.g., designed to solve a narrow set of problems. A framework is the product of many iterations in design. It is not something that you invent in a big bang, and then go about reusing for years. Frameworks evolve over long periods of time, and like good wine, the older they are the better they are. But because this is a short book, we will make it appear as if the frameworks described herein were products of instant invention.

2.4 Iterator Interactions in Frameworks

The example class hierarchy of Figure 2.2 is not a framework because it lacks generic interactions among the various classes of storage. That is, it lacks a dynamic part. We are about to change that with another class hierarchy of dynamic relations called *iterators.*

An iterator is an object whose sole purpose in life is to enumerate the elements of container objects. This is the analog of scanning a data structure with a loop in a procedural program. For example, the elements of an array `A[1..N]` are enumerated by the loop:

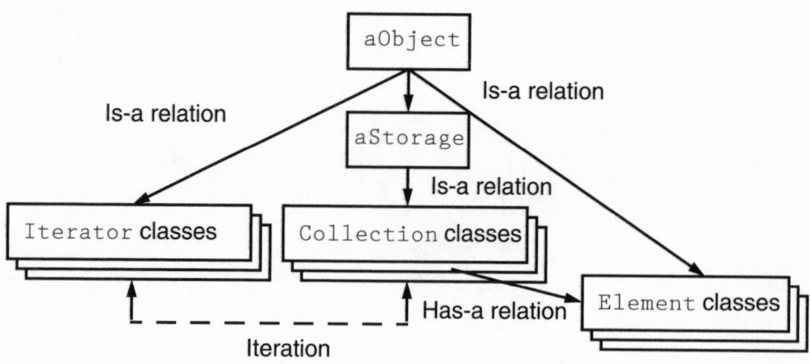

Figure 2.3 Class hierarchies and interactions among classes in the data storage framework. Solid lines denote subclasses, while the dashed line denotes interactions

```
for( i = 1; i ≤ N; i++){… A[i]…}
```

An iteration model of interaction is shown in Figure 2.3 for a simple data storage framework. Note the is-a relation (specialization) between the most general class `aObject` and all subclasses in the framework. In addition, notice the has-a relation (container) between the `Collection` classes and the elements that are stored in the `Collection` objects. Finally, note the model of interaction (dynamic part) which establishes a third kind of relation in the framework, i.e., the interaction.

2.4.1 Iterator Class Hierarchy

Iterator classes inspect each element in a collection one by one. For example, if the storage class is an `Array-Like`, and the method is `Find()`, the corresponding iterator class scans all elements of `Array-Like` objects one-by-one, from beginning to end. The scanning is carried out using the `Next()` function defined for all iterators. Each time a message is sent to `Next()`, it returns the next element of a list; e.g., `Next()` retrieves the elements of a container object one at a time. Such methods are sometimes called *generators.*

The iterator classes mirror the `Collection` classes shown in Figure 2.4. But, why are iterators separated from the classes they iterate? This seems like a violation of encapsulation.

Separation of iterators from collection classes holds two advantages. First, it reduces the size of each collection class. Large class sizes impose

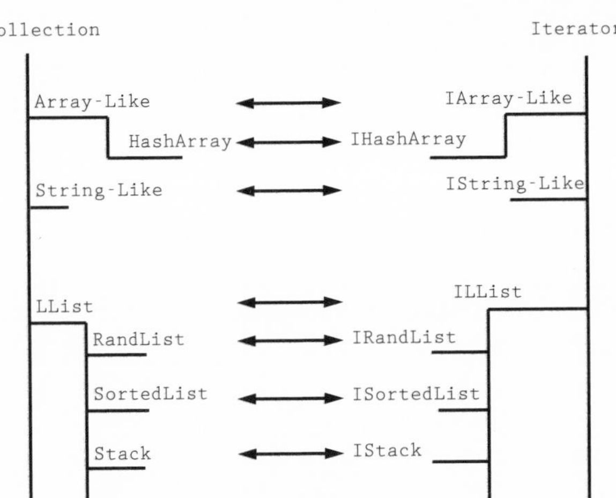

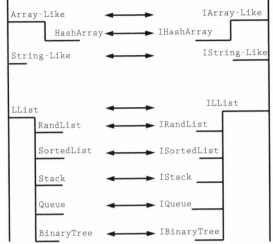

Figure 2.4 Correspondence between `Iterator` class hierarchy and `Collection` class hierarchy

considerable overhead in terms of memory and the time needed to compile, link, and run.

The second and most important advantage is the ability to multiply traverse a single object. If an iterator was included in each class, an object's elements could not be traversed by two or more iterators at the same time because the first iterator would have to be reset for the second traversal, which would destroy the state of the first traversal.

If an iterator is separated from its collection class, then each time an iterator is instantiated, it creates its own state of traversal. This permits multiple instantiations of iterators on the same collection object.

2.4.2 Gory Details

Sure, this is a messy detail, but it is an important concept. If you are satisfied that this illustrates the concept of framework interaction, then there is no penalty for skipping the following example. But, if you need to be convinced, study the code below.

Example

The raw, seething code below says it all. We want to scan a list of objects. The RandList class is instantiated as a container object. To keep things general, after an object is stored its pointer is placed in the linked list called alist. We scan alist by going hand over fist down the nodes of alist, getting pointers at each node. The objects are obtained by following the pointers stored in nodes of alist:

```
main(){
    RandList    *alist;      //List
    AObject     op;          //Object pointers in alist
    alist = new RandList();//Instantiate container object
    IRandList next(alist); //See the constructor of IRandList
    while (op = next()){;} //Return the very next element until it
                           //Reaches the end of the collection
    }
```

In this example, the RandList iterator is created through the function called MakeIterator() which is provided in each collection class so that it can create an iterator during run-time. The constructor function of IRandList illustrates how a class sends a message to MakeIterator() each time an object of the class is instantiated:

```
    IRandList(CLCollection*col)
    {   seq = col ? col->MakeIterator() : 0};
```

The MakeIterator function is defined in class IRandList as follows. The notation :: separates the class name from the method name:

```
    IRandList *RandListPtr :: MakeIterator(){
        return new RandListIter(this); //Create iterator}
    RandListIter :: RandListIter(Collection *s){
    cs = (RandList*)s; // get the first element in the list
    // if first element is not empty, set the state.
        cs = cs ? cs->first : 0;
    }
```

2.5 MVC: The Mother of All Interactions

What the world needs more than a good pizza is a general model of interaction that every good framework can depend on. The Model-View-Controller (MVC) interaction proposed by Reenskaug is the oldest, and is perhaps the most widely used model. It first appeared in the Smalltalk-80 programming environment [Goldberg83], but has made guest appearances in MacApp [Alger90], The Andrew Toolkit, NeWS Development Environment and Stepstone's ICpak 201 [Knolle89], portions of ET++ [Weinand89], and Smalltalk/V. [For the full-length book version of MVC, read Alexander87, Urlocker89, Wirfs-Brock90, Booch91, and Dodani89.] For a discussion of MVC by its original author see the very readable [Reenskaug95].

We can construct an MVC-based GUI framework using three classes, see Figure 2.5. The Model class holds the domain-specific data that is to be represented and manipulated by the GUI application. The View class renders all or some of these data on the screen. The Controller class is responsible for accepting asynchronous input from the mouse and keyboard, and for passing appropriate messages to the Model and View classes to allow editing of the model data.

For example, suppose your application is a word processor. The model stores the text data, the view renders the text in a window, and the controller handles keystrokes. Simple.

An application is created from an MVC framework by subclassing. Specializations in the subclasses further refine the MVC classes to allow display and editing of the model data. Views and controllers may have

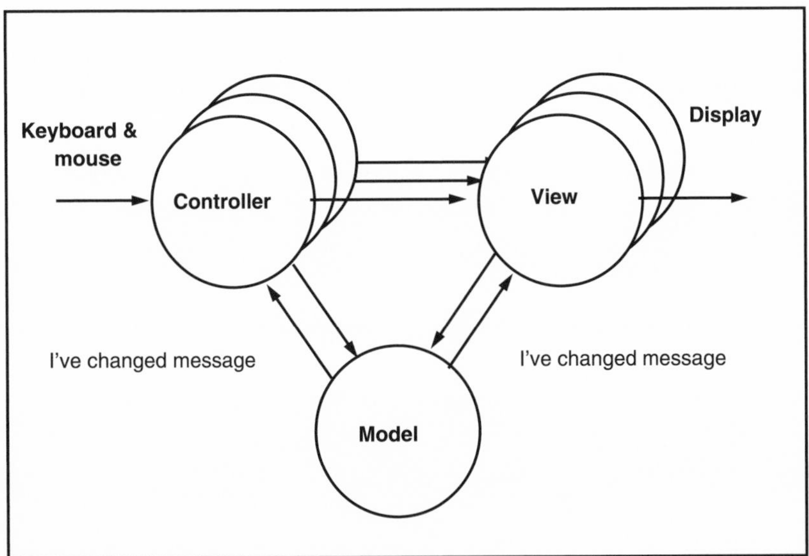

Figure 2.5 MVC interaction: a model with multiple view-controller pairs

only one model, but models may have many views and controllers; see Figure 2.5.

2.5.1 MVC Updates

Views and controllers are generally tied closely together. The reason for this becomes obvious if you consider the difference between editing data in a spreadsheet view versus a chart view. The kinds of interactions involved in the spreadsheet are quite different from the interactions involved in a graphics view.

The possibility of multiple views introduces the problem of keeping all of the views consistent with the state of the data when it is edited through one of the views. This is the so-called *MVC update problem,* which is usually handled by keeping a list of all views, so that an update to one is propagated to all others.

We can see the MVC update in action in Figure 2.5. Each time a view changes, the "I've changed" message is propagated to all other views through the model object. This deceptively simple idea turns out to be enormously useful and powerful. In fact, the MVC interaction is so important that we will waste three more sections belaboring these points.

2.5.2 Model

The model contains domain-specific data that are displayed and manipulated by an application. They can range from integers (representing counters or thermometers) or arrays of characters (simple text editors), all the way to dynamic lists of structures, records, or other complex data structures. A model does not need to know anything about its views or controllers.

2.5.3 View

A view controls the visual representation of all or parts of a specific model. Common functions such as refreshing or scrolling a window may be contained in this class, but application-specific functions such as "display this array as a spreadsheet" will be implemented as subclasses by the application developer.

Views may represent the entire model or only certain aspects. The view must know about the model it is representing, but needs no knowledge of any other views.

2.5.4 Controller

Controllers are associated with both views and models. A controller accepts user input from various input devices such as the keyboard and mouse, and sends appropriate messages to the view and the model.

Controllers must know about the model and view they are associated with, but need no information about other controllers.

Communication between the model and the view–controller pair is captured in abstract classes, so the MVC design can be reused for every new view and application. This can save considerable design effort every time the MVC framework is used.

Views and controllers are registered with their model when they come into existence, and any time the model's data are changed the model broadcasts an "I've changed" message to all of its dependents. Each dependent view and controller can then access the model's data and update itself appropriately. Parameters passed with the "I've changed" message may allow views and controllers to decide if they need to update for a given change.

An example of the MVC update in an actual framework is shown in Figure 2.6. Notice how the interaction flows through overridden methods on its way to the multiple views. This automation of interaction in the dynamic structure of a framework is responsible for the power and flexibility of frameworks. Someone has to be responsible, and unlike a toolbox of reusable subroutines, a framework assumes the responsibility typically off-loaded to the programmer.

2.5.5 MVC Around the World

Suppose we jump ahead a little and preview the coming attractions. The MVC interaction is a well-known collaboration model, with years of use in the Smalltalk-80 environment [Krasner 88]. Alger has demonstrated the feasibility of using it with the Macintosh user interface [Alger90]. Ferrel lists "a general mechanism for multiple views of content" as a desirable objective for Aldus Corporation's Vamp framework, but does not tell how it is to be implemented [Ferrel89]. [Knolle89] implements a version of MVC using DepObject, a general dependency mechanism in ICpak 201 in Objective-C. The Andrew Toolkit [Palay88] uses a similar change propagation mechanism inherited from a superclass in the

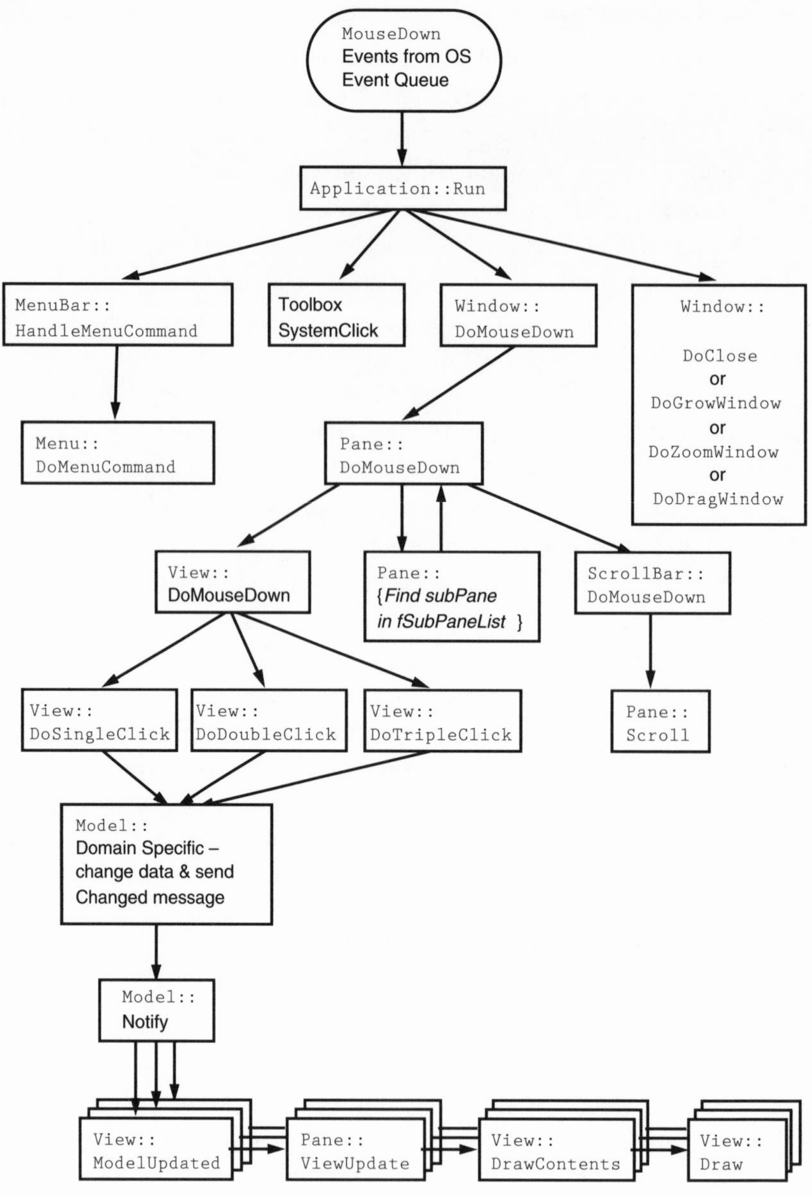

Figure 2.6 Framework communication triggered by user clicking mouse button

custom object-oriented environment called *Class.* Both ICpak 201 and the Andrew Toolkit combine the view and controller into a single object.

I hope this convinces you that the MVC interaction is important. We shall see it again in later chapters. Take notes.

2.6 Summary of the Main Points

Here are some things about frameworks which set OOP and OOD apart from traditional procedural programming:

- Design is the process of constructing a framework. Top-down design is as outdated as patent leather shoes.
- Implementation is the process of instantiating objects from a framework. Code-writing is held to a minimum because we can reuse so much of the code already available as methods on predefined classes.
- Testing is the process of verifying that objects have been instantiated properly. Objects are assumed to be correct, because they have been reused so many times that the bugs have long ago been worked out.
- A framework calls user-supplied routines, instead of the other way around. A framework is not a class library which a programmer dips into whenever a subroutine is needed.
- A framework is reusable within a narrow domain. It is not all things to all programs.
- Frameworks evolve rather than suddenly appear after a "big development bang." Like a high-school sophomore, frameworks often take years to become useful to society.

Further Reading

[Alger90] J. Alger, Using model-view-controller with MacApp, *FrameWorks, The Journal of Macintosh Object Program Development,* **4** (2), 1990.

[Booch91] G. Booch, *Object-Oriented Design with Applications*, Benjamin/Cummings, Redwood City, 1991.

[Dearle90] F. Dearle, Designing portable application frameworks for C++, *Proceedings of the 1990 USENIX C++ Conference*, April 9–11, San Francisco, 51–61, 1990.

[Dodani89] M. Dodani, C. Hughes, and J. M. Moshell, Separation of Powers, *Byte,* **14** (3), 255–262, 1989.

[Ferrel89] P. J. Ferrel and R. F. Meyer, Vamp: The Aldus application framework, *OOPSLA '89 Conference Proceedings,* New Orleans, 185–189, Association of Computing Machinery, Oct. 1989.

[Goldberg83] A. Goldberg, *Smalltalk-80: The Interactive Programming Environment,* Addison-Wesley, Menlo Park, 1983.

[Johnson88] R. E. Johnson and Brian Foote, Designing reusable classes, *Journal of Object-Oriented Programming,* **1** (2), 22–35, 1988.

[Knolle89] N. Knolle, Variations of model-view-controller, *Journal of Object-Oriented Programming,* **2** (3), 42–46, 1989.

[Krasner88] G. Krasner and S. Pope, "A cookbook for using the model-view-controller user interface paradigm in Smalltalk-80, *Journal of Object-Oriented Programming,* **1** (3), 26–49, 1988.

[Palay 88] A.J. Palay, et al., The Andrew Toolkit: An overview, In *USENIX Proceedings Winter Technical Conference,* Dallas, Feb. 1988.

[Reenskaug95] T. Reenskaug, *Working with Objects,* Manning/Prentice Hall, Greenwich, 1995.

[Schmucker86] K. J. Schmucker, MacApp: An application framework, *Byte,* **11** (8), 189–193, Aug. 1986.

[Thompson89] T. Thompson, The NeXT step, *Byte,* **14** (3), 265–269, Mar. 1989.

[Urlocker89] Z. Urlocker, Abstracting the user interface, *Journal of Object-Oriented Programming,* **2** (4), 1989.

[Weinand89] A. Weinand, E. Gamma and R. Marty, Design and implementation of ET++, a seamless object-oriented application framework, *Structured Programming,* **10** (2), 1989.

[Wilson90] D. Wilson, L. Rosenstein, and D. Shafer, *Programming with MacApp,* Addison-Wesley, Reading, 1990.

[Wirfs-Brock90] R. Wirfs-Brock and R. E. Johnson, Surveying current research in object-oriented design, *Communications of the ACM,* **33** (9), 104–124, 1990.

CHAPTER 3

Visit to a Small Framework

Preview

This is a good time to look at a complete framework for a domain-specific task of great interest in many applications: creating tables. Specifically, we will design a framework for handling most of the functionality of tables, spreadsheets, and other row-and-column data. We will call this the `TableView` *framework*, and the tool that it incorporates will be called *Table Builder*. `TableView` is a class for displaying tabular data, and Table Builder is a tool for customizing table views.

Views are reusable software building blocks that render and manipulate data. All views share a common application programming interface and data model architecture. This architecture allows them to communicate with each other, the data they manage, and the rest of the application. The data model architecture employs *data wrappers* and a Data Manager which enable each view to manage and store its data without knowledge of the data's internal format. In addition, the architecture provides a mechanism for propagating changes made to the data rendered in one view to all other interested views.

The architecture of this framework and its relationship to other frameworks is shown in Figure 3.1. This architecture also provides a means of communicating changes in data between one view and another; e.g., it supports the MVC model.

A sample application, DreamGrader, is used to illustrate the `TableView` building block, and the Table Builder customization tool. DreamGrader is a simple but functional classroom grading application that uses the data model architecture to combine two view building blocks, `TableView` and `3DChartView`, into a single application. Developing the DreamGrader application required only a few days of effort and 1,000 lines of code. When one compares the 1 year and 50,000 lines of code required to

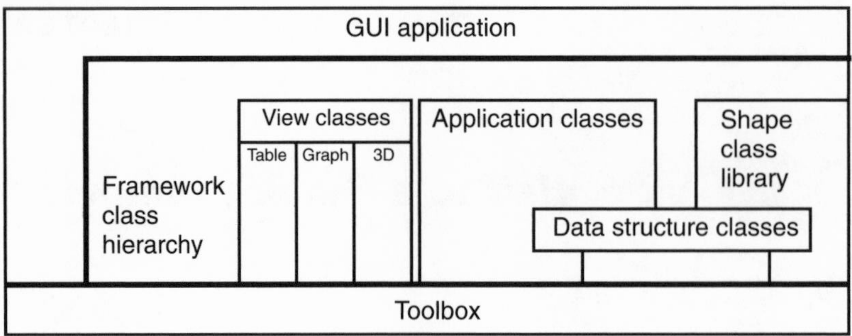

Figure 3.1 Application components using frameworks to do graphics (shapes), data structures, tables, graphs, and 3D charts. `TableView` is a domain-specific application framework

implement the `TableView` and `3DChartView` building blocks, the productivity gains provided by the ViewBuilder approach are clear.

3.1 The Component Architecture

In addition to showing how to design and construct a specific framework, this chapter gives us the opportunity to introduce another idea. Frameworks support the concept of *component* software. The idea is simple: frameworks are building blocks, and blocks of frameworks are the components we use to build even larger structures. Think of it this way: classes are framework building blocks, and frameworks are application building blocks. The component concept overcomes the limitations of frameworks, because a single framework is too domain-specific to support all of the things an application wants to do.

Before we can discuss the composition of large applications as a collection of components, we need a unifying data model to integrate the different components. This is where a data model architecture comes in. A *data model architecture* serves as a format-independent link between the application's data and all components that access that data. Since we are interested in views, the components described in this chapter are going to be called *view components* or *view building blocks*. Each view component comes with a view customization tool which allows developers to specialize the view according to their particular needs. These tools provide options to the designer, giving him or her control over the visual aspects of the resulting view and the behavior of the data it renders.

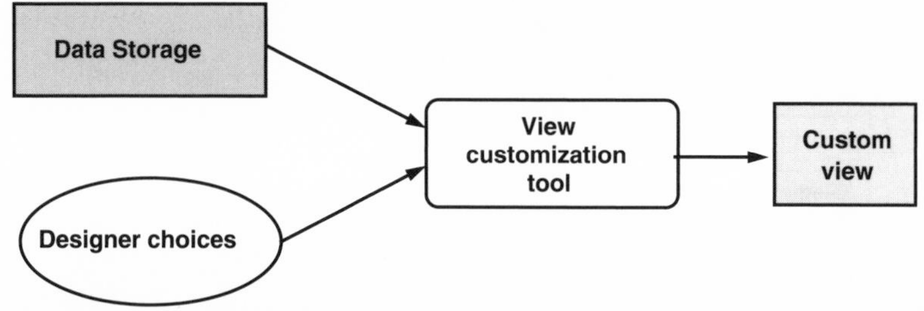

Figure 3.2 View customization

Figure 3.2 illustrates how a view customization tool is used to create specialized views. `TableView`'s customization tool is called Table Builder. This chapter discusses `TableView` and Table Builder in detail, and argues that by combining a powerful application framework with view building blocks and a data model architecture, ViewBuilder increases the percentage of an application that can be handled automatically and decreases the work required by the application developer.

The data model architecture serves as an application programming interface (API) that defines a communication protocol between views and the data they manage, see Figure 3.3. This architecture functions as an insulating layer between the actual data and the views that display them. It ensures that views are reusable, because they do not rely on a specific underlying data organization.

Data Storage stores the actual data and supports the addition and deletion of data objects. It also supports access to each data object's fields. The Data Manager manages the Data Storage components. It forwards all data access requests from the Document to the appropriate Data Storage component.

The Document is the central component of the data model. It passes data access requests on to the Data Manager. It also performs change

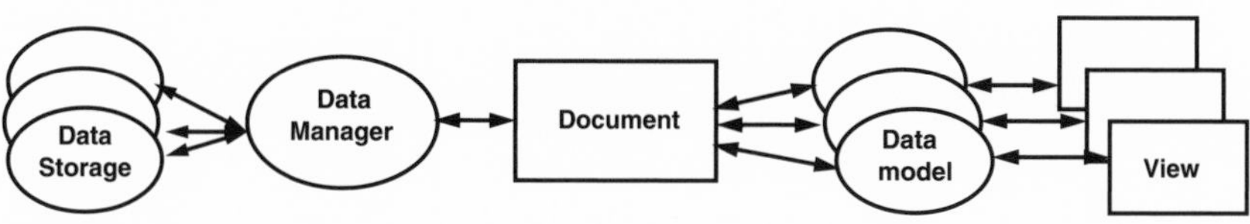

Figure 3.3 ViewBuilder data model architecture

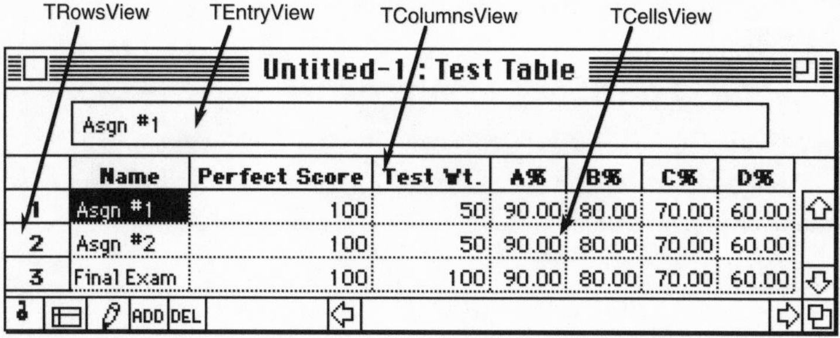

Figure 3.4 `TableView`

propagation by notifying all views when data have changed. This change propagation feature allows several views to display and manipulate the same data, while ensuring that all views are kept up to date.

Each view has a matching Data Model which contains a description of the data being displayed by the view. In the case of a table, Data Model contains a list of the records currently in the table and a list of the fields within each record to be displayed.

Data wrappers are used to pass data from one component to another in a format-independent fashion. Each data wrapper can be queried about the data it contains and whether it can convert them from one format to another. This allows views to extract the form of the data they can best handle, without requiring them to know ahead of time what format the data are in.

The ideas of components and tools to manage components are not new. The OLE/COM (Object-Linking Environment from Microsoft, and the Common Object Model from Microsoft and Digital Equipment Corporation) and the OpenDoc/SOM (OpenDoc and System Object Model by IBM, Lotus, Apple, and Novell) are commercial implementations of this idea. The introduction of components gives rise to the need to create a standard way to handle views and the underlying data. Hence, the technology described in this chapter is not entirely fictional.

3.2 TableView

A `TableView` is a window containing rows and columns of text as shown in Figure 3.4. The window can be scrolled, opened, closed, moved, resized, and in general, manipulated as any other window. The contents of the window can be selected, inserted, deleted, and rearranged in size, color, and style.

The objective of `TableView` and Table Builder is to automate the creation of tables in any application. Because tables are frequently used, their reusability can pay off handsomely in greater programming productivity and quality. It is worthwhile to incorporate the ideas of others when designing such a universal component.

Let's review the state of the art in view component research to date. This will provide a good background for our new design, which will address the strengths and weaknesses of current technology.

3.2.1 ViewEdit

ViewEdit, developed by Apple Computers Inc, allows developers to design and customize MacApp view resources [Apple91]. It is a powerful interface builder, but because it has no notion of the data that will be contained within the views, it is unable to simulate the view's behavior. Instead, ViewEdit provides only a static picture of views: it does not allow the designer to try out the view during the designing process. However, ViewEdit was used as a role model when designing `TableView`.

3.2.2 Garnet

Garnet [Meyers89b] is an integrated environment consisting of a constraint system, a toolkit, debugging tools, and an interface builder that allow designers to rapidly prototype graphical applications. The interface builder, Lapidary, is notable for its use of *programming by example*, in which the developer demonstrates how the interface should behave and then writes the necessary code.

Garnet is written entirely in Lisp, and therefore inherits all of that language's strengths and weaknesses. Specifically, each tool is customizable if the developer is willing to write some additional Lisp code. Garnet's appeal to developers may be limited by their concern over issues of speed, efficiency, and maintainability.

Garnet's primary weakness is its lack of a common data model which would allow designers to integrate the interface components with the data they manage.

3.2.3 ACEKit

Nardi and Zarmer [Nardi91] describe an application construction toolkit called ACEKit which includes a table view and builder very similar to `TableView` and Table Builder. But, ViewBuilder differs from ACEKit in two fundamental ways. First, ACEKit's table does not define a method of providing table customization tools to the end user. `TableView` implements a runtime architecture that allows the user to add customization options to the running table. Second, ACEKit does not provide a common data model. This means that there is no means of connecting one view to another, and that prevents the developer from quickly composing an application from several views. Furthermore, the lack of a data model means that the table builder tool does not allow the table designer to establish the mappings between the data and their representation within the table.

Clearly, in order to allow developers to concentrate on their primary task of developing an application, we must provide them with the means to rapidly create application components such as tables. Until these tools are available, time constraints will force developers to choose between cutting back on the feature set of a table or of an application itself. Whichever choice is made, the application's ability to effectively interact with the user is adversely affected.

3.3 The TableView Approach

`TableView` is a specialized view which manages tabular data. It implements the following table-specific features:

- It displays textual data in a format-independent fashion.
- It supports the addition and removal of records and fields.
- It allows cell editing via a spreadsheet-style interface.
- It allows formatting of all textual elements. Font, font size and text styles are fully configurable both at design time and runtime.
- It supports fixed and controllable sorting of records by the user.
- It includes an *OptionsView*, which can be used at run time to access the formatting and sorting features mentioned above.
- It allows customization of the initial field data mappings.

- It implements a runtime *Data Pivot* that toggles between the standard mapping of records to rows and fields to columns, and the inverse mapping.
- It supports data selection and table navigation by mouse or keyboard.

Table Builder is used to customize these options. The list below highlights its features:

- It visualizes all available options, which means that designers need not understand the `TableView`'s internal structure to customize it.
- It demonstrates all customizations in realtime via a sample table which allows the table designer to "try before you buy."
- It allows designers to add, remove, or edit table fields and their mappings to application data.
- It makes available options that allow control over both the table's appearance and its behavior.
- Import/Export Options feature allows a designer to customize tables in existing, compiled applications.

3.4 ViewBuilder Data Model Architecture

In this section, we will describe the implementation of the data model architecture and describe how `TableView` fits into this architecture.

Each type of data object is given a unique class identifier to distinguish it from other data objects. In addition, each field is accessed via a unique key identifier. We can uniquely specify an individual data field value, called a *data item*, by combining a data object identifier with a field identifier.

Views can be chosen to display individual fields, data objects, or data items. For example, `TableView` renders data fields as table fields, data objects as table records, and data items as table cells, see Figure 3.5.

3.4.1 Communication Protocol

The communication protocol defines how the components of the Data Model Architecture interact with each other. The protocol supports a number of actions, each of which is illustrated below. Though for the purpose of illustration we will assume that these actions are initiated by a

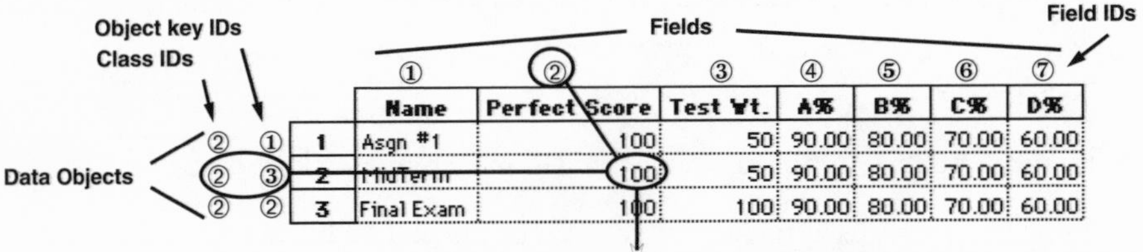

Figure 3.5 How data are accessed from data objects via object keys and field IDs

view, they can also be initiated by the document when it reads itself in from disk or during initialization.

Display Data Action

When a view needs a data item, it builds a `GetFieldValue` message and sends the message to its data model. The data model forwards the message to the document, which passes it on to the Data Manager. The Data Manager determines which data storage has the data and then passes the message on to that data storage. The data storage returns a data wrapper containing the actual data, which is then passed back to the View. The View extracts the data from the data wrapper and displays them, see Figure 3.6

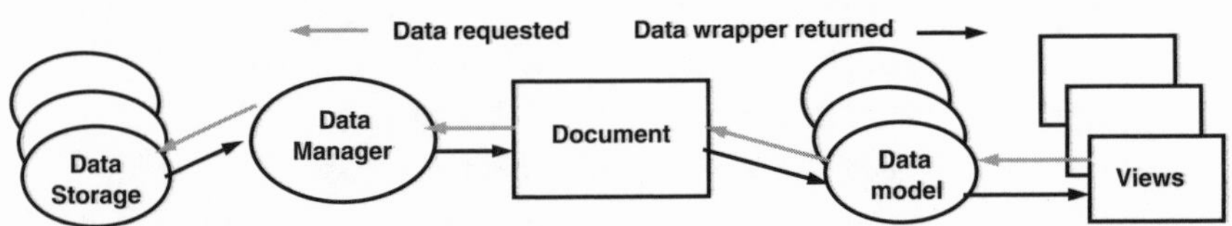

Figure 3.6 Displaying data

Change Data Action

When a data item is changed, the view places the changed data into a data wrapper and sends it with a `FieldValueChanged` message to the data model. The data model forwards the message to the document, which passes it on to the Data Manager. The Data Manager determines which data storage stores the data, and then passes the data on to that data storage, see Figure 3.7.

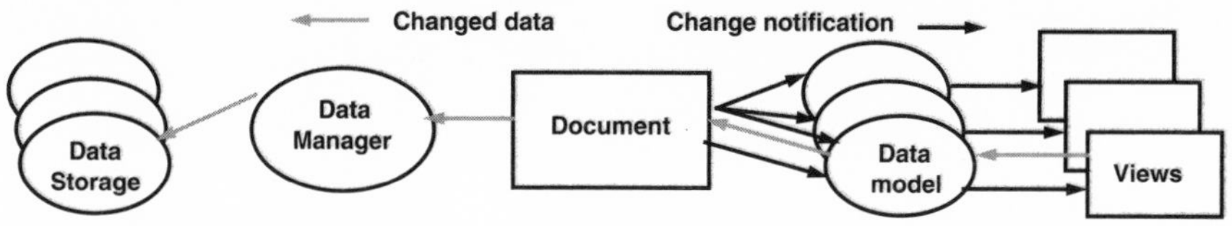

Figure 3.7 Changing data

The data storage changes the stored data to their new values. The document then sends a `DoFieldValueUpdate` message to each data model notifying them of the change. Each data model determines if its view is interested in the change, and if so, the view is instructed to update its display to reflect the data's new values. The protocol described above is used to handle the following field changes:

- Changing a field's classID or fieldID
- Changing a field's data type
- Changing a field's title
- Changing a field's default value
- Changing a field's current value

Change Selection Action

When the user changes the current selection in a view, the view sends a `SelectionChanged` message to the data model. The data model then forwards the message to the document, which sends a `DoSelectionUpdate` message to each data model notifying it of the change, see Figure 3.8.

Each data model determines if its view is interested in the change, and if so, passes it the selection change. The view receives this selection change notification and updates its display to reflect it.

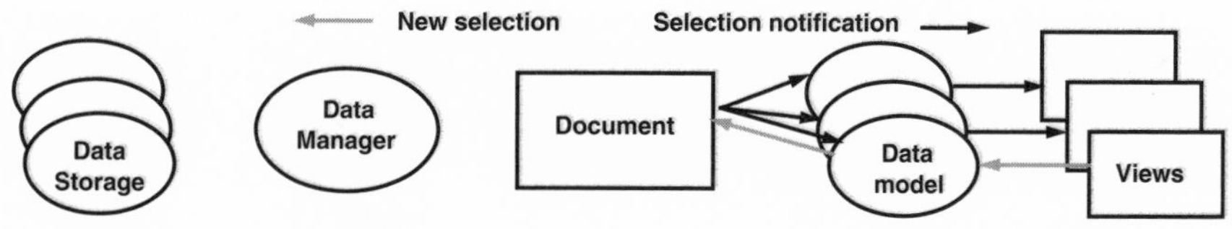

Figure 3.8 Changing selections

Add and Remove Field Actions

Data fields and their visual representations can be added and removed by views. When this occurs, the view sends an `AddFieldChange` or `RemoveFieldChange` message to the data model, which then forwards it to the document. The document passes the message on to the Data Manager, which determines which data storage stores the data and then passes the message on to that data storage, see Figure 3.9.

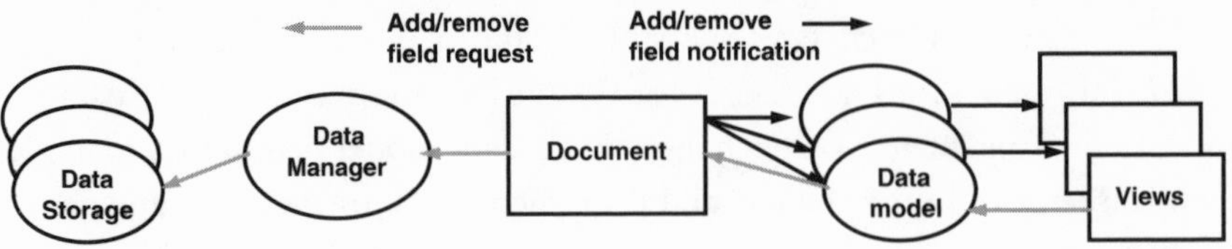

Figure 3.9 Adding and removing fields

The data storage adds or removes the field in question from its internal storage. After the addition or removal, the document sends a `DoAddFieldUpdate` or `DoRemoveFieldUpdate` message to each data model notifying it of the change. Each data model determines if its view is interested in the change, and if so, the view is instructed to update its display to reflect it.

Add Object Action

Views map data objects to some visual component. When a view adds a new data object it sends the `AddObjectChange` message to its data model. The message is passed to the document, the Data Manager, and eventually to the data storage, see Figure 3.10.

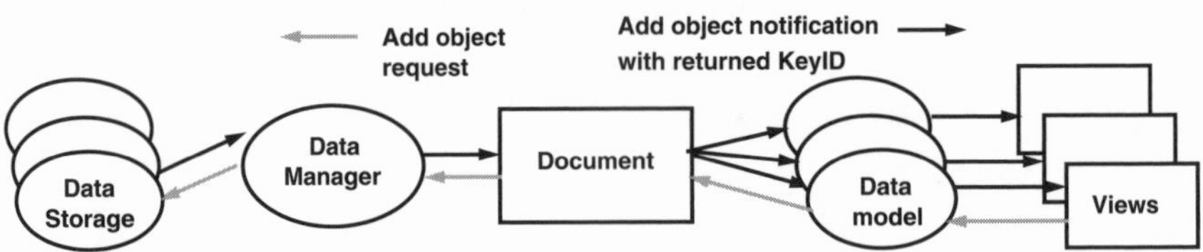

Figure 3.10 Adding objects

The data storage adds the object to its internal storage and assigns it a unique key identifier, KeyID. The Key is returned to the document, where it is included in the `AddObjectUpdate` message sent to each of the data models, and thus to each interested view.

Remove Object Action

When a data object is removed from a view, the view sends a `RemoveObject` message to its data model. The message is passed to the document, the Data Manager and eventually to the data storage, see Figure 3.11.

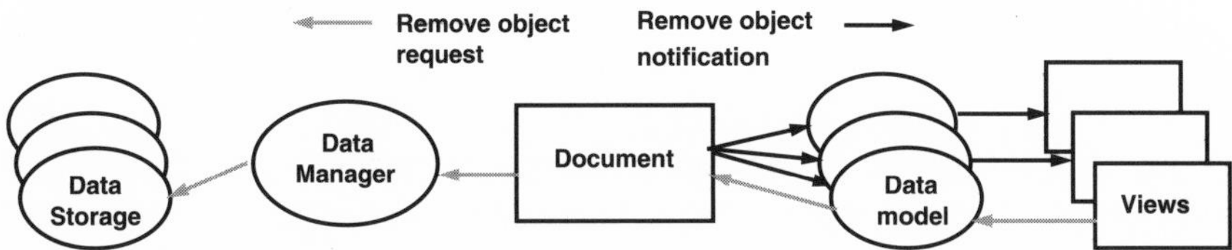

Figure 3.11 Removing objects

The data storage removes the object from its internal storage. The document then sends a `RemoveObjectUpdate` message to each of the data models, and thus to each interested view.

3.5 TableView Implementation

This section is divided into two parts. First, each of the major `TableView` components is described. Second, we describe the extensions made to `TableView` in order to provide dynamic control over `TableView`'s appearance and behavior at run time. Here is where we learn the nitty-gritty of framework construction. But, if you do not want to dive into the details of this architecture, skip to the next section.

TTableModel and Data Mapping

The `TTableModel` object is a subclass of `TDataModel` that maps conceptual records, fields, and field values to visual rows, columns, and cells. When the `TableView` receives a request to draw a cell, it passes that request to `TTableModel` to be translated or mapped.

`TTableModel` can do its mapping in two ways. First, it can map each record (internally, these are the `TObjectKeys` found in the data model's `fObjectKeyList`) to a row, and each field (internally, these are the `TFields` found in the data model's `fFieldMappingList`) to a column. This traditional mapping is called *row orientation.* Second, `TTableModel` can do the reverse, and map records to columns and fields to rows. This mapping is called *column orientation.*

View

`TView` provides support for drawing and clipping within its boundaries, and handling events from the mouse and keyboard, see Figure 3.12.

Figure 3.12 `TView` class hierarchy

TTableView

This is a view building block class responsible for displaying the table's data and allowing the user to interact with those data. In addition, it contains command creation methods that can be overridden by subclasses in order to specialize the table's behavior. Command objects are used to encapsulate actions in a fashion that allows the action to be easily undone.

These methods provide a convenient means of overriding the following table behavior:

- Adding and removing of records
- Handling of row, column, and cell mouse clicks and double-clicks
- Handling of keyboard navigation and selection
- Resizing of rows and columns

TGridView and TTextGridView

`TGridView` provides basic support for views that are composed of rows and columns of rectangular cells, see Figure 3.13. Rows and columns are of variable size, and can be inserted or deleted. `TGridView` does not implement a data structure to hold the data displayed within each cell; that is left to subclasses.

`TTextGridView` is a `TGridView` subclass that is specialized to handle textual data.

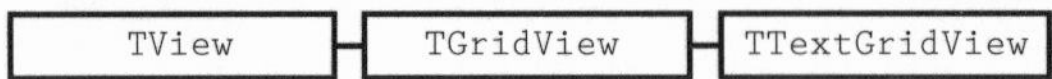

Figure 3.13 `TGridView` and `TTextGridView` class hierarchy

TOurTextGridView

This subclass of `TTextGridView` contains all the behaviors that are common to the `TextGridViews` used by `TableView`, see Figure 3.14. Included in this class is support for dim-highlighting, calculation of minimum widths and heights, and keyboard navigation.

Figure 3.14 `TOurTextGridView` class hierarchy

TCellsView

This class is responsible for drawing the table cells, see Figure 3.15. It passes all key and mouse events up to `TableView`, where they can be controlled by `TTableView` subclasses. This class provides support for keyboard navigation via the arrow keys, and `PgUp` and `PgDown` keys.

`TCellsView` also supports autosizing of rows and columns by providing methods that will measure the maximum height of a row's text or the maximum width of a column's text.

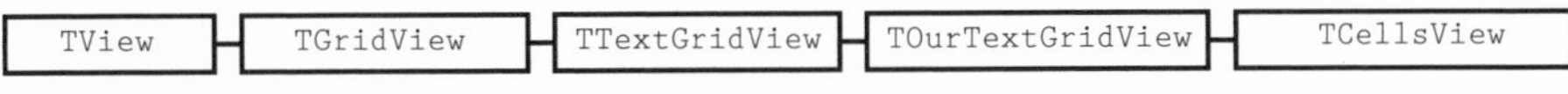

Figure 3.15 `TCellsView` class hierarchy

TRowsView

This class displays the list of row titles, see Figure 3.16. It synchronizes its scrolling with the scrolling of `TCellsView`. It supports selections by highlighting a row title and an entire row of cells. It allows the user to resize rows (if this option is turned on) by moving the cursor over the bottom edge of the row and dragging the border to a new position.

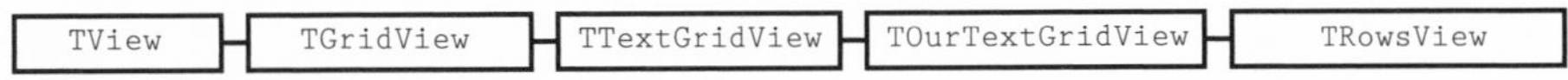

Figure 3.16 `TRowsView` class hierarchy

TColumnsView

The `TColumnsView` class manages the list of column titles, see Figure 3.17. It synchronizes its scrolling with the scrolling of `TCellsView`. It handles selections by highlighting a column title and an entire column of cells. It allows the user to resize columns (if this option is turned on) by moving the cursor over the right edge of the column and dragging the border to a new position.

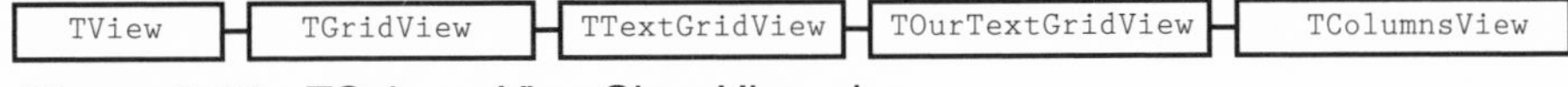

Figure 3.17 TColumnsView Class Hierarchy

TEntryView

This class provides a means of editing cell values. It communicates with `TCellsView` to determine which cell is to be edited, allows the user to edit the cell, and then passes the changed value back to `TCellsView`. It supports cut, copy, paste, and undo actions.

3.6 Dynamic Runtime Options Architecture

`TableView` was designed to allow customization of both its appearance and behavior. In this section we will describe the extensions made to `TableView` to allow this customization to take place dynamically from within a running application. First, we will provide definitions of the terms to be used in the following discussion:

- `TableOptions object`: an object which stores all of the customizable table options.
- `Options cluster`: a collection of one or more interface items that control one of the table options.
- `Object dependency`: a method of forming dependencies between objects in which objects may send messages to their dependents notifying them of changes.

In Figure 3.18, when the user changes the `CellsView` text style to bold, dependency is used to inform both the `TableOptions` object and the `TableView` that a change in the cell's text style has occurred. Next, the `TableOptions` object asks the Text Options cluster what the new cell text style is, and updates itself to store the new value. Finally, the `TableView` asks the `TableOptions` object what the new text style is, and updates the `CellsView`'s text style to match the new value.

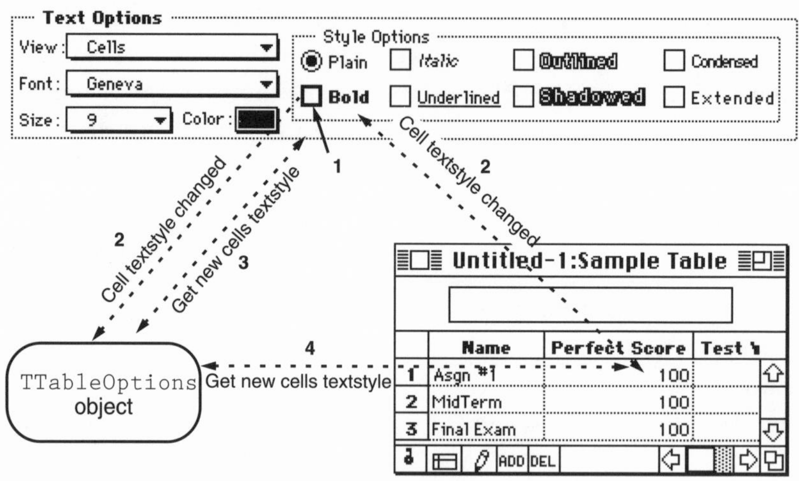

Figure 3.18 Runtime options architecture

3.6.1 Dynamic Runtime Options Classes

To implement the behavior described above, a number of `TableView` classes were subclassed. Figure 3.19 illustrates one example.

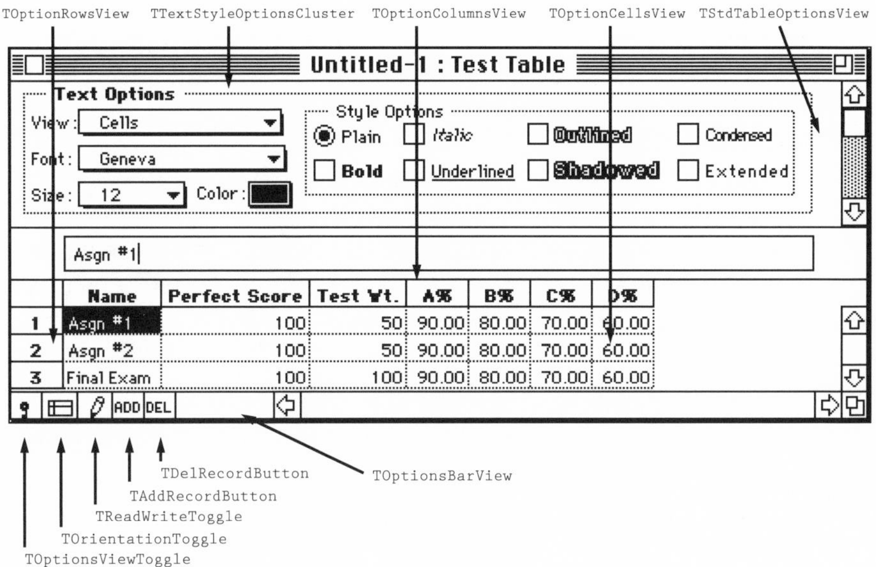

Figure 3.19 `TOptionTableView`-based table

TOptionsBarView

One of the most notable subclasses is the `TOptionsBarView` class, see Figure 3.20. An instance of this class is located in the lower lefthand corner of the table window. It contains a number of graphical toggles and buttons that allow the user to quickly perform table customizations or to initiate table actions such as adding or removing records. This subclass of `TDialogView` overrides `DoChoice`, and depending on which toggle or button is hit, sends the `TTableView` object the appropriate message.

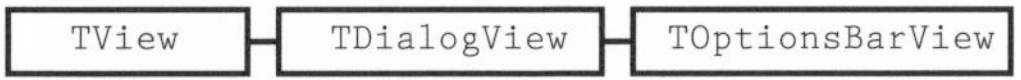

Figure3.20 `TOptionsBarView` class hierarchy

TOptionsCluster

`TOptionsCluster` is the abstract superclass of all option clusters, see Figure 3.21. It contains a field which stores the cluster's change ID. This ID is sent as part of the `Changed` message whenever the user makes a change to one of the cluster's controls.

Figure 3.21 `TOptionsCluster` **class hierarchy**

`TOptionsCluster` subclasses define methods `GetChoice` and `SetChoice`, which map data types to user interface controls. For example, the `TTextStyleOptionsCluster` maps a text-style record containing fields for the text font, size, and style onto two pop-up menus and a style cluster. The `TOptionsCluster` subclasses used in `TableView` are illustrated in Figure 3.22.

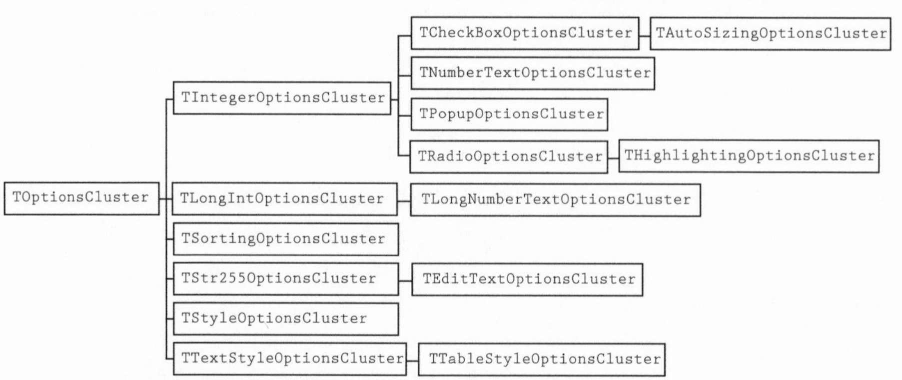

Figure 3.22 `TOptionsCluster` **subclasses**

TOptionsView

`TOptionsView` is an abstract class that defines the protocol between the option clusters, the `TableOptions` object, and the `TableView`, see Figure 3.23. `TOptionsViews` initialize the option clusters they contain and set up the dependencies required to implement the protocol described above.

Figure 3.23 `TOptionsView` **class hierarchy**

TStdTableOptionsView

The class `TStdTableOptionsView` is a specialized `TOptionsView` that contains three option clusters, see Figure 3.24.

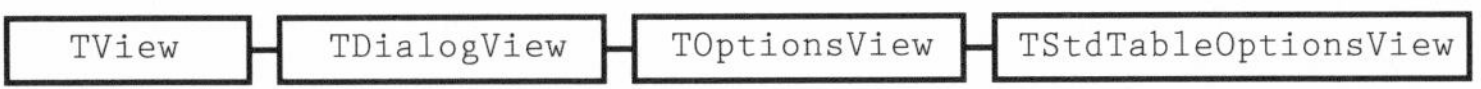

Figure 3.24 `TOptionsView` **class hierarchy**

The Text Options cluster allows the user to customize the text font, size, color and style of the `CellsView`, `RowsView`, and `ColumnsView`, see Figure 3.24. The Highlighting Options cluster controls whether highlighting is visible when the window containing the table is not frontmost. The Sorting Options cluster controls the sorting of records.

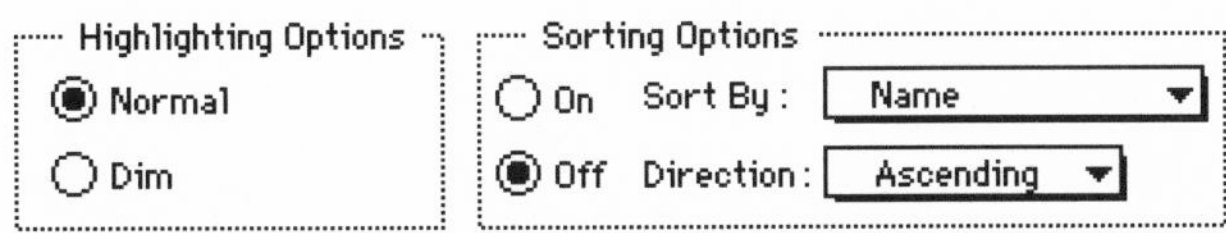

Figure 3.25 **Other option clusters in** `TStdTableOptionsView`

TOptionTableView

`TOptionTableView` is a subclass of `TTableView` whose primary responsibility is to provide support for the runtime options described above, see Figure 3.26. It overrides all of the command creation methods and performs the behavior that is appropriate, depending on the current option settings.

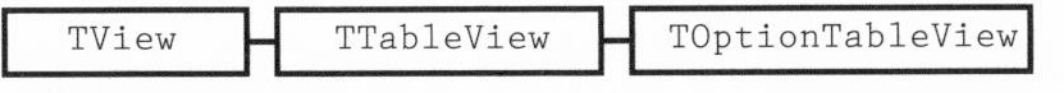

Figure 3.26 `TOptionTableView` **class hierarchy**

In addition, `TOptionTableView` overrides the `DoUpdate` method, which is called by its notifiers via object dependency whenever a runtime option is changed. This method responds to the change by altering the appearance of the table to match the new option setting. This class also handles the reading in, at initialization time, of the options resource generated by Table Builder.

TOptionCellsView

This subclass of `TCellsView` overrides the methods necessary to make runtime changes in the row and column autosizing option, the dim-highlighting option, and the keyboard navigation option, see Figure 3.27.

Figure 3.27 `TOptionCellsView` class hierarchy

TOptionRowsView

This subclass of `TCellsView` overrides the methods necessary to make runtime changes in the row resizing and autosizing options, see Figure 3.28.

Figure 3.28 `TOptionRowsView` class hierarchy

TOptionColumnsView

This subclass of `TCellsView` overrides the methods necessary to make runtime changes in the column resizing and autosizing options, see Figure 3.29.

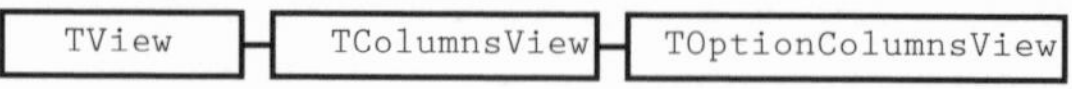

Figure 3.29 `TOptionColumnsView` class hierarchy

3.7 Table Builder Implementation

`Table Builder` is a stand-alone tool for customizing table views. In this section, we describe `Table Builder`, and explain how it can be used to both create and customize `TableView`-based tables.

When `Table Builder` is launched it first opens a new untitled document, see Figure 3.30. The document window contains four icons representing the four windows used by `Table Builder`. The first three buttons open the Option Windows, and the fourth button opens the sample table.

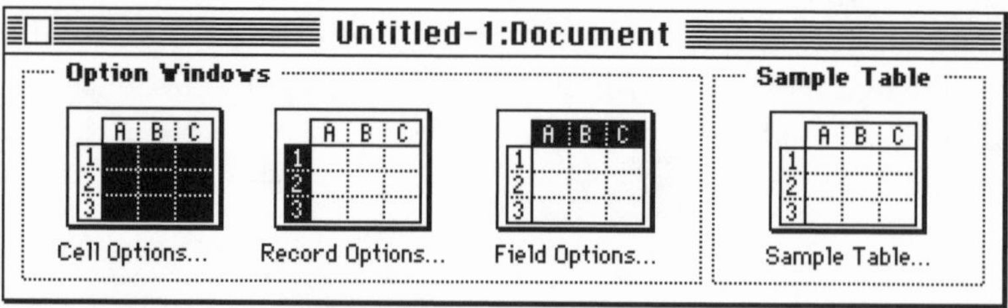

Figure 3.30 Document Window

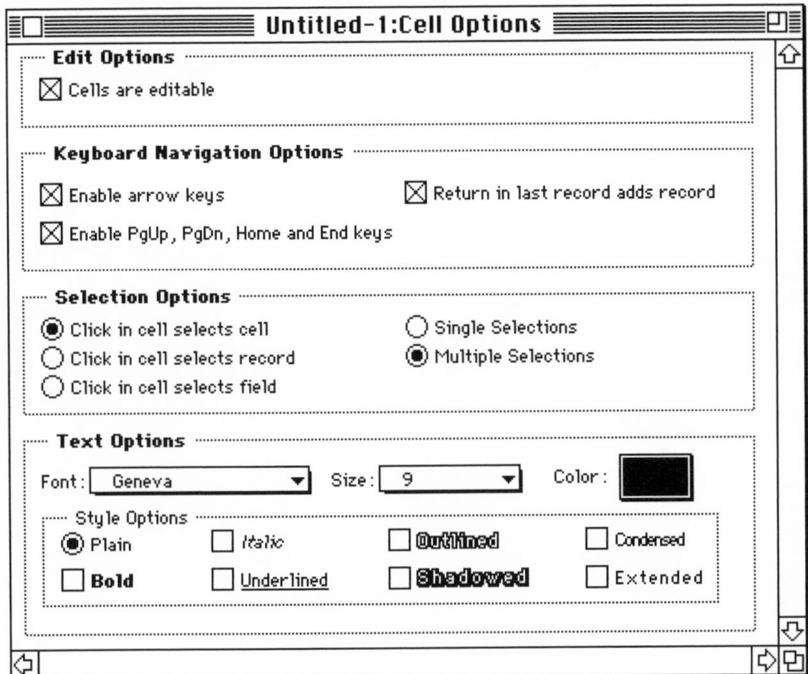

Figure 3.31 Cell Options Window

Cell Options Window

The Cell Options Window contains all the options that affect the table cells, see Figure 3.31. This window holds a number of option clusters, described below:

- Edit Options cluster: Controls whether the table is read-only or read-write. If the option is on, the sample table will contain an entry view.
- Keyboard Navigation Options cluster: Controls how the table will respond to key presses.
- Selection Options Cluster: Controls how the selections are handled when the user clicks on a cell.
- Text Options cluster: Controls how the cells will be displayed.

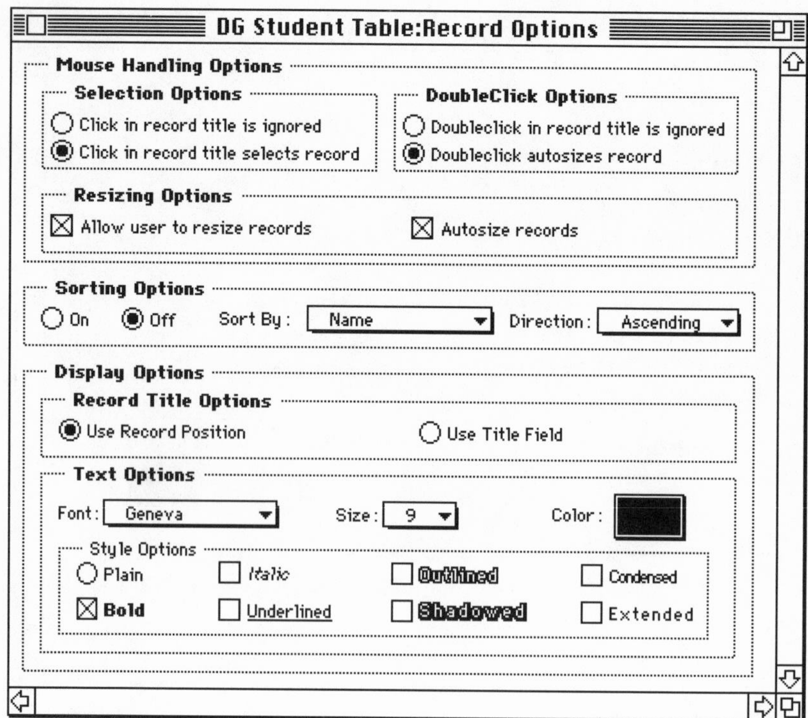

Figure 3.32 Record Options window

Record Options Window

The Record Options Window contains all the options that affect the table records, see Figure 3.32. This window is composed of a number of option clusters, described below:

- Selection Options cluster: Controls how the table will handle selections.
- DoubleClick Options cluster: Controls how the table responds to a double-click in the record title.
- Resizing Options cluster: Controls whether users are allowed to resize records. Controls whether or not records are automatically sized to fit their data.
- Sorting Options cluster: Controls sorting of records.

- Record Title Options cluster: Controls whether record title is based on the record's position or the record's title field.
- Text Options cluster: Controls how the record titles will be displayed.

Field Options Window

The Field Options Window contains all the options that affect the table fields, see Figure 3.33. This window is composed of a number of option clusters:

- Selection Options cluster: Controls how the table handles field selections when the user clicks in a field title.
- DoubleClick Options cluster: Controls how the table responds to a double-click in the field title.
- Resizing Options cluster: Controls whether or not users are allowed to resize fields. Controls whether or not fields are automatically sized to fit their data.

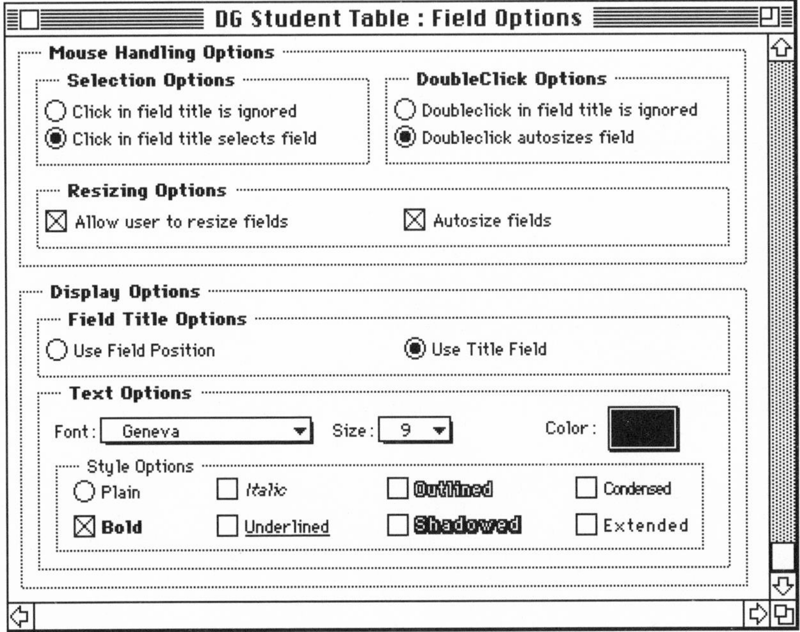

Figure 3.33 Field Options Window

- Field Title Options cluster: Controls whether field title is based on the field's position or its title.
- Text Options cluster: Controls how the field titles will be displayed.

Sample Table
The Sample Table is used to try out the table being designed, see Figure 3.34. It receives Change messages from the various option clusters, and responds by updating itself to match the new option settings.

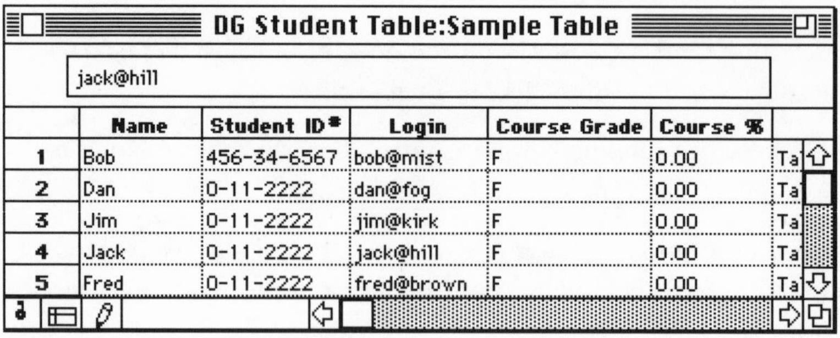

DG Student Table:Sample Table

jack@hill

	Name	Student ID*	Login	Course Grade	Course %	
1	Bob	456-34-6567	bob@mist	F	0.00	Ta
2	Dan	0-11-2222	dan@fog	F	0.00	Ta
3	Jim	0-11-2222	jim@kirk	F	0.00	Ta
4	Jack	0-11-2222	jack@hill	F	0.00	Ta
5	Fred	0-11-2222	fred@brown	F	0.00	Ta

Figure 3.34 Sample Table

The OptionsBar located in the bottom left-hand corner of the table window allows the table designer to use the table like an end user. It is important to note, however, that any changes made via the OptionsBar are not saved as permanent table options. Only the options made within the three option windows are considered permanent options. The OptionsBar is provided only to allow the designer to experiment with the same table that the end user will see.

3.8 Example: DreamGrader

DreamGrader is a simple classroom grading application that combines two `TableViews` with a three-dimensional chart based on `3DChartView` [Trognoh92], a previously created view building block, see Figure 3.35. DreamGrader has the following features:

- Course window: A main course window that stores the course name, instructor name, and course grade percentage breakdown.
- Test table: Each test "record" has fields for the test name, maximum score, test weight, and grade percentage breakdowns.

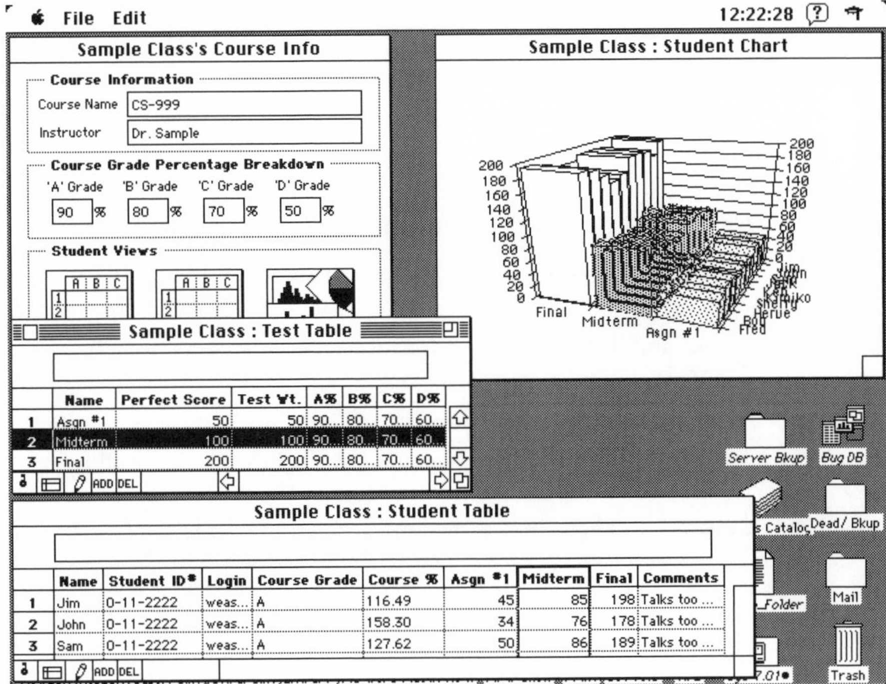

Figure 3.35 DreamGrader

- Student table: Each student "record" contains a student name field, a student ID# field, a login field, a course grade field, a course percentage field, a comments field, and a test score field for each test in the test table.
- Grade calculations: This feature calculates the course grade and overall percentage for each student. It updates whenever a score or test field is changed.
- Student chart: This feature maintains a three-dimensional bar chart of the student scores.
- Test table/student table link: This feature implements a link between each test record in the test table and its matching test score field in the student table.

- Student table/student chart link: This feature implements a link between each student score in the student table and its matching bar in the student chart.
- Data storage: The information entered into both tables should be storable and retrievable.

3.7.1 A Productivity Experiment

DreamGrader was created over the course of year as a test harness for successive versions of the `TableView` building blocks. When the work on `TableView` and Table Builder was completed, it was reimplemented in only two days.

Table 3.1 lists the breakdown of time and lines of code required to create the application with and without the ViewBuilder environment.

Table 3.1 DreamGrader implementation breakdown

Table feature implemented	Time	Lines of code with ViewBuilder	Lines of code without ViewBuilder
Main course window	2 hr	250	250
Test table	1 hr	50	≈20,000
Student table	1 hr	50	(Same as above)
Student grading	4 hr	300	300
3DChartView	1 hr	25	≈19,000
Test table/student table link	3 hr	200	500
Student table/student chart link	1 hr	100	500
Data storage	0 hr	0	5000
Total	15 hr	≈1,000	≈47,000

Though as a grading tool DreamGrader is limited, it is a fully functioning application with a powerful visual interface. The fact that it was developed in the short time described above strongly supports our earlier claim that by providing developers with high-level building blocks and a data model architecture, full-featured table-based applications can be created easily.

Further Reading

[Apple85] Apple Computer, *Inside Macintosh,* Volume 1–6, Addison-Wesley, Reading, 1985–1991.

[Apple91] Apple Computer, *MacApp 2.0 General Reference,* Addison-Wesley, Reading, May 1991.

[Apple87] Apple Computer, *Human Interface Guidelines: The Apple Desktop Interface,* Addison-Wesley, Reading,1987.

[Basili89] V. R. Basili, and J. D. Musa, The future engineering of software: A management perspective, *IEEE Software,* **7** (9) 1989.

[Cameron89] J. Cameron, A cognitive model for tabular editing, OSU-CICRC Research Report, June, 1989.

[Drogeson92] K. G. Drongesen, GraphView: A graphical application builder using the ViewBuilder common data model, 1992.

[Meyers89a] B. A. Meyers, User interfaces tools: Introduction and survey, *IEEE Software,* **6** (1), 15–23, 1989.

[Meyers89b] B. A. Meyers et al., Garnet: Comprehensive support for graphical, highly interactive user interfaces, *IEEE Computer,* **23** (11), 1989.

[Nardi91] B. A. Nardi, and Craig L. Zarmer, Beyond Models and Metaphors: Visual Formalisms in User Interface Design, Hewlett-Packard Laboratories, Palo Alto, CA 94303, 1991.

[Schmucker86] K. J. Schmucker, MacApp: an application framework, *Byte,* **11**, (8), 189–193, Aug. 1986.

[Trognoh92] H. R. Trognoh, Design and Implementation of a Reusable Specialized View for the ViewBuilder Environment, 1992.

[Wilson90] D. A. Wilson, Larry S. Rosenstein, Dan Shaffer, *Programming with MacApp,* Addison-Wesley, Reading, 1990.

[Sherry90] Y. Sherry, Beyond SpeedCode, presentation, computer science department, Oregon State University, Corvallis, OR 97331. 1990.

CHAPTER 4

Visual Programming With Frameworks

Preview

We will illustrate how to use a framework in the design of a program and then how to implement that design using high-level graphical tools, e.g., visual programming. Our framework (Objex) consists of a class hierarchy of reusable objects (storage, I/O, GUI, and graphics), and a generic model of interaction among the objects (cut/paste, multiview updates, document model) which preserves much of the design intrinsic to any application.

Reuse through inheritance yields dramatic programmer productivity. In fact, the approach described here renders much of the coding steps of traditional procedural programming as out of date as punched cards. To illustrate the power of inheritance, we will go on to show how to automate most of the programming using a graphical tool based on colored Petri Nets. Here is how it works: a new application is constructed from instantiations of the framework classes, followed by sequencing their behaviors by drawing a Petri Net on the screen. Finally, the actual code for the application is synthesized by simply traversing the Petri Net. Only the overridden methods need to be coded by hand.

This approach implements a rapid application development process based on reuse, specialization, and concurrent and incremental development. So much of this process can be automated that special tools can be written to do most of the work. The tools consist of a direct-manipulation user interface designer (RezDez), a graphical composition language, browser, and code generator (Petri Net Editor), and an application framework consisting of 430 reusable methods (Objex Framework). The Objex Framework consists of 19,000 lines of C++ source code and is tailored for graphical user interface applications.

Preliminary experiments with this development approach suggest a coding effort reduction of 10-to-1 for small application programs (under 1,000 lines), and 2-to-1 for medium-sized applications (under 6,000 lines). The source code for both Macintosh and UNIX workstations supporting X-Windows is available to the reader for research purposes.

4.1 What Is Objex?

Objex-by-Design is a method of incorporating reuse of design and code into an integrated software development process using an object-oriented class hierarchy of reusable code (Objex library), an object-oriented application framework which incorporates the design of a generic application (Objex framework), and a graphical language editor and code generator (Petri Network Editor). When wrapped together, we call this package *Objex* for short.

Table 4.1 summarizes code productivity improvements obtained in initial experiments with Objex. We make no claims concerning overall productivity improvements with this system, but speculate that further improvements will lead to reduced effort, improved quality, and quicker application development. Note in Table 4.1 that hand-crafted code is reduced by a factor of 2-to-1 for medium-sized applications, and by as much as 10-to-1 for small applications. Furthermore, using the graphical programming language based on Petri Nets, the programmer can enjoy as much as a 30-to-1 advantage over hand-coding techniques.

Table 4.1 Lines of code required to implement the applications using different tools. Each application was repeatedly designed and coded in the following: Macintosh Toolbox routines, Objex framework, and Petri Net graphical language

Tool Used	Macintosh Toolbox	Objex Application Framework	Petri Net Editor	Sum of Objex and Application
Application Built				
MVC Demo	3000	300	100	16330
MiniDraw	7000	300	0	16330
ExampleDraw	8000	300	0	16330
Petri Net Editor	6000	2500	—	18530
Browser	4700	2000	—	18030

The reusable design and code are inherited from the Objex framework to generate most of the new application. But, how does a programmer go about composing a large GUI application without a high degree of knowledge about the reusable design and code? In what follows, we will attempt to convince the skeptical reader that the productivity advantages claimed in Table 4.1 are not only possible, but actually conservative estimates of how great object-oriented frameworks are. First, we will build a case for why the application framework idea works, and survey a few earlier attempts to do the same thing.

4.1.1 Yet-Another-Framework

The framework approach is different from any procedural approach, because a framework is a complete application which derives its functionality by calling programmer-written code. A framework calls programmer-supplied routines rather than the other way around. This subtle reversal means that design and code reuse can be achieved with very little knowledge of the interaction mechanism of an entire class of applications.

In an object-oriented framework, the generic functionality of the framework is provided by a class library that is tailored to the domain of application. In other words, frameworks are generic applications which are made even more specific by specializing the base classes of the built-in class library. This part of the object-oriented paradigm can be partially automated, as we intend to show.

But, frameworks incorporate more than a class library. They also implement a design based on some interaction model. In fact, frameworks differ largely according to their interaction models. The simplest application that can be synthesized by a framework is an instance of the framework itself. Such an instance will compile and execute, but do nothing whatsoever. Therefore, it is up to the programmer to add functionality to the framework. MacApp for the Macintosh, and InterViews and ET++ for X-Window systems are good examples of first-generation frameworks [Alger90, Linton89, Reiss87, Schmuker86, Weinand88].

The problems and limitations of existing frameworks are shown in Table 4.2. We propose to adopt the framework approach, but in addition, we will propose a semiautomatic means of composing applications from such frameworks which overcomes many (but not all) of the problems listed in the table. The significance of this work is in the integration

Table 4.2 User interface development tools and systems: Problems and solutions. MVC refers to the Model-View-Controller model of interaction

Problems with existing tools and systems	Solution	Objex components	Other systems
A. Offer too little functionality and support only a small part of the development task: 1. Contents of application windows: • Do not help the programmer create application-specific graphics. • The programmer must handle all input events at a low level. • Intertwined interaction between the user interface and the application logic is not considered. (e.g., change propagation) 2. Common aspects of GUI applications: • Accessing documents • Undo/redo commands • Printing • Managing memory • Manipulating data structures	• MVC • Pluggable and adaptable domain-specific views • Reusable design (a model of interaction and control of flow among classes) • Reusable code	• MVC-based application framework with a rich set of domain-specific views • Class library (structured graphical objects and data structures)	• Garnet • Objex • NeXTStep • MacApp • ET++
B. Lack architectural models for large applications: • Do not help designers decompose and structure complex GUI applications • Hard to visualize the overall architecture of the entire GUI application • No abstraction mechanism	• Reusable design • MVC • Objex Petri Net • Net hierarchy (subnet)	• MVC-based application framework • Petri Net Editor • Browser	• Smalltalk • MacApp • ET++ • HyperCard
C. Representation of Control Sequences: • Hard to understand • Hard to edit • Hard to reuse	• Objex Petri Net • Net hierarchy (subnet)	• Petri Net Editor	• State Diagram Interpreter • Rapid/USE • UIMX • Objex • Trillium
D. Lack a single conceptual graphical model used for integrating: • Specification • Modeling • Design • Validation • Simulation • Rapid prototyping	• Annotated Petri Net	• Petri Net Editor • Code generator • Simulator • Reachability analysis tool	•Garden

of an object-oriented framework with a composition language based on Petri Nets. Objex-by-Design is not the first system to combine a visual means of programming-in-the-large with a framework of reusable design and code, but it is perhaps the most novel. This combination permits a programmer to ignore many low-level details of textual programming, thus increasing productivity, as shown in Table 4.1. In addition, the graphical Petri Net composition language provides both documentation and automatic code generation capabilities, which are not present when using a mere text-only framework.

4.1.2 Some Messy Details

Although *user interface toolkits*, such as the Macintosh Toolbox [Keh90] and Xt for the X Window System, hide much of the complexity of graphical user interface (GUI) programming, difficulties still arise due to the intertwined interaction between the application's direct-manipulation user interface and logic, see Table 4.2. For example, updating a view on the screen may require updating the underlying data structure and broadcasting changes to all other views whose graphical rendering depends on the same data structure. Also, the programmer must handle all low-level input events and draw graphical objects using the underlying low-level graphics package. Furthermore, toolkits may factor out user interface components, but provide no support for common tasks such as printing, undo and redo, accessing document files, and manipulating data structures. As a result, code that is common to most GUI applications is rewritten for each application. More importantly, toolkits do not make clear how to use the toolkit procedures to create a desired interface, because toolkits do not incorporate a model of the application.

Many user interface development systems (UIDSs) have attempted to correct these problems by providing a model, and hiding much of the details of GUI construction. Most UIDSs help the designer create GUI objects in a window or layout using predefined toolkit items. Several shortcomings which are common to most existing UIDSs have limited their success:

- They offer too little functionality, and support only a small part of the GUI software development task.
- They lack architectural models and abstraction mechanisms for large GUI applications.

- Representation of control sequences is difficult to understand, edit, and reuse.
- They lack a single conceptual, graphical model to be used as a medium for integrating specification, modeling, design, validation, simulation, and rapid prototyping.

We propose a new approach which combines the benefits of domain-specific frameworks with a graphical composition language to enforce the Objex-by-Design principles. It has the following features:

- It is capable of modeling both the static and dynamic aspects of GUI applications at a higher level of abstraction through the use of an object-oriented application framework that supports a modified MVC design methodology and that embodies most generic functionality required when constructing a GUI application.
- It benefits from known Petri Net analysis techniques to verify behavioral properties of the modeled system.
- It produces an executable specification which can be directly executed by a suitable interpreter to simulate the system being modeled, and it can be easily translated into almost any existing implementation language, such as Pascal, C, or C++.

Due to the fact that graphical rendering and user input are always tightly coupled in GUI applications, our modified MVC-based framework combines the functionality of the MVC view and controller into one object (view) [Knolle, Krasner]. Placing responsibility for input and output in the same object reduces the total number of objects and the communication overhead between them. Even though our framework is based on a model of interaction that is quite different than the original MVC paradigm, we will still call it an MVC paradigm.

The proposed Petri-Net-based object-oriented conceptual modeling approach provides solutions to many problems encountered in the development of GUI applications:

- The underlying MVC-based object-oriented application framework offers much more functionality than a user interface toolkit, and supports a significant part of the GUI software development task.

- It provides a solid architectural model and abstraction mechanism.
- The representation of control sequences is easy to understand, edit, and reuse.
- It is able to integrate the phases of specification, modeling, design, validation, simulation, and rapid prototyping of GUI applications according to the Objex-by-Design principles, which have been successfully employed by the operational software paradigm.

The design of object-oriented application frameworks is probably the most far-reaching use of object-oriented programming in terms of reusability, because it supports not only the reuse of code but also the reuse of design. As in MacApp and ET++, the design and implementation of common aspects of most GUI applications, such as handling windows, undo and redo, saving and opening files, and printing, are already available in a reusable form.

The change propagation mechanism provided by the MVC approach helps the programmer deal with the intertwined interaction between the user interface and the application logic. It permits multiple views of the same data to be displayed simultaneously, such that data changes made through one view are immediately reflected in the others. With the support of a rich set of domain-specific views in the application framework, the programmer can easily create and manage the application-specific graphics, even without writing any code. In situations where the developer must write unique code to derive new subclasses, they are easy to create because the developer can reuse both the design and implementation from their abstract and concrete superclasses.

4.2 The Objex System

Objex consists of the following:

- The application framework, including extensive classes for data storage, graphics, and documents, see Figures 4.1–3
- The visual programming language for composing applications as Petri Nets.
- The code generator: C++ code is synthesized from the application framework, annotated Petri Net, and programmer-supplied routines.

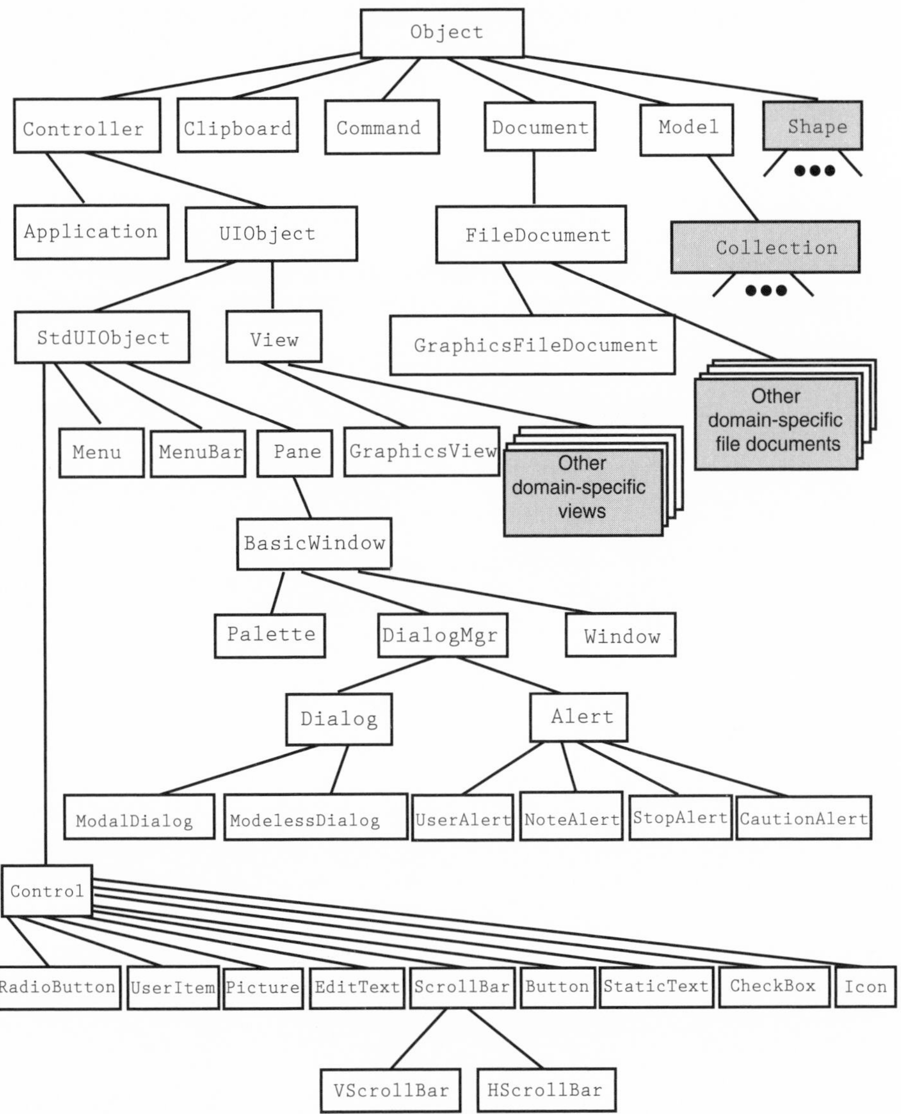

Figure 4.1 The Objex application framework class hierarchy

- RezDez: Yet another resource editor for constructing GUI objects by direct manipulation. With RezDez, a rapid prototype of the GUI can be constructed without programming.

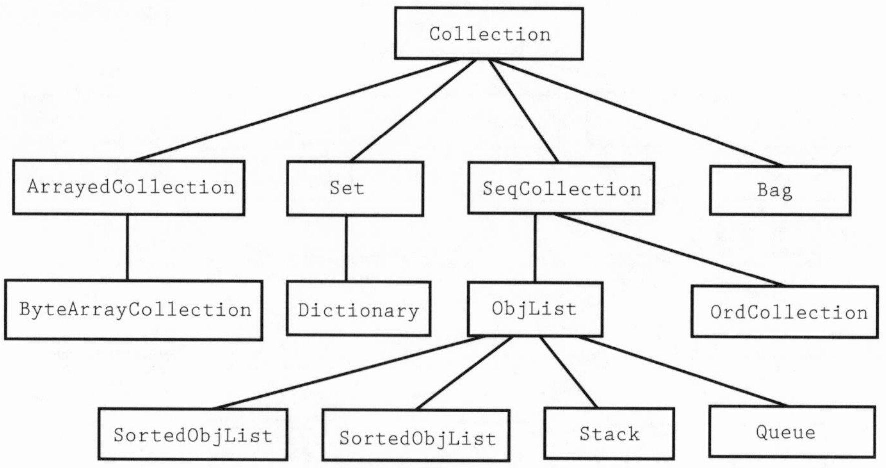

Figure 4.2 The storage structure class hierarchy

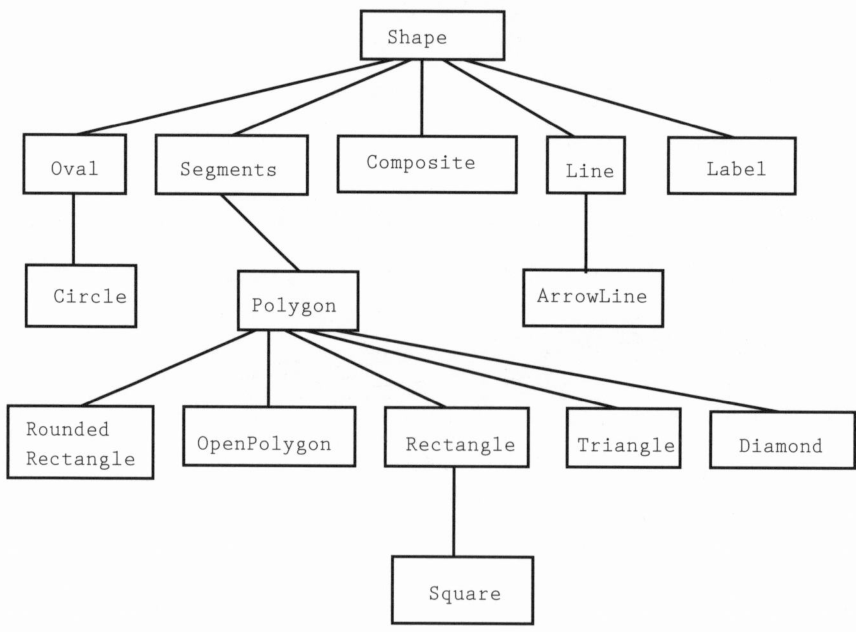

Figure 4.3 The graphics support class hierarchy

A top-level view of these class hierarchies and the way in which they interact with an implementation is shown in Figure 4.4. The entire framework rests on top of the GUI toolbox of the Macintosh in one

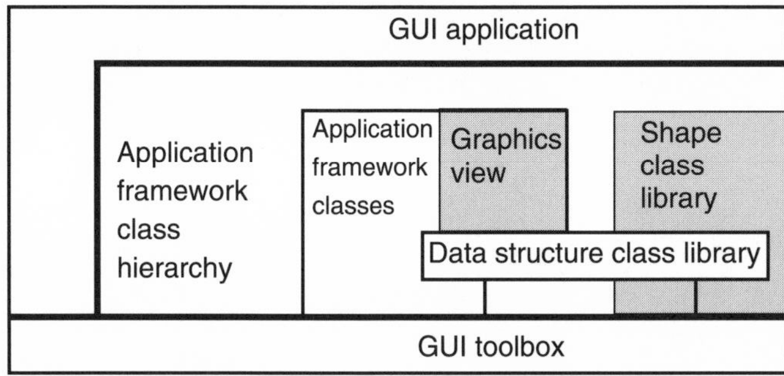

Figure 4.4 General Structure of the Objex framework and its relationship to a particular system

implementation, and on top of the Xlib toolbox in another implementation. Hence, the framework approach is independent of a particular development platform.

Applications developed within the Objex framework are insulated from the low-level toolboxes of any host machine. However, portability is valid only for applications that do not step outside of the framework.

4.2.1 The Framework

The Objex framework borrows from many existing frameworks. Table 4.3 summarizes Objex and compares it to two of the most similar frameworks: MacApp and ET++ (See later chapters on each of these other frameworks). Many other frameworks exist which have not been compared here.

The design goals of Objex were to produce a compact (19,000 source lines of C++), useful (data storage and graphics are included) framework that incorporated a strong model of interaction. Objex supports cut/copy/paste, documents on file, printing, automatic iteration of data storage operations, and a number of features which need not be reinvented by its users. Currently, the Objex framework supports Macintosh and X-Windows (UNIX) GUIs.

4.2.2 Petri Networks

Recall that a Petri Network is formally a graph containing two kinds of nodes and connecting arcs. The nodes called *places* correspond to program states. The nodes called *transitions* correspond to actions that can be single instructions, or an entire procedure. Arcs connect places to transitions, and

Table 4.3 Summary of Objex and related application frameworks

Framework	Objex	MacApp	ET++
Feature			
Implementation language	C++	Object Pascal C++	C++
Window system	Macintosh	Macintosh	SunWindows, X, NeWS
Data structures	Support	Basic support	Support
Graphics library	Support	No support	Basic support
Application class	Small	Big	Small
Menu class	Yes	No	Yes
Menu handling	Direct message	Target chain	Target chain
MVC	Modified	Modified	Modified
Separation of view and other UI objects	Yes	No	Partial separation
Undo/redo	Multiple levels	Single level	Single level
Graphical specification	Yes	Partial	No
Composite objects	No	No	Yes

transitions to places. Labels on arcs signify passage of data. The basic idea of visual or graphical programming with Petri Nets PNs is to specify the actions of an application by diagramming all possible execution paths through the application. Annotations are added to permit translation of the net into a useful program. An example of an annotated Petri Net representation for a GUI application is shown in Figure 4.5.

In Figure 4.5, icons represent places; thus each menu, dialog box, window, or alert has a unique icon. Rectangles represent transitions, and arcs connect places to transitions and transitions to places.

The programmer selects an appropriate tool from the tool palette on the left, and draws the diagram as shown. Double-clicking on a place, transition, or arc brings up a dialog containing additional information.

Places in the PN Editor

Places are classified as either *modal* or *modeless.* A modal place represents an interface object which puts the user in a state or mode. For Macintosh, modal dialogs and alerts constitute modal user interface objects. In

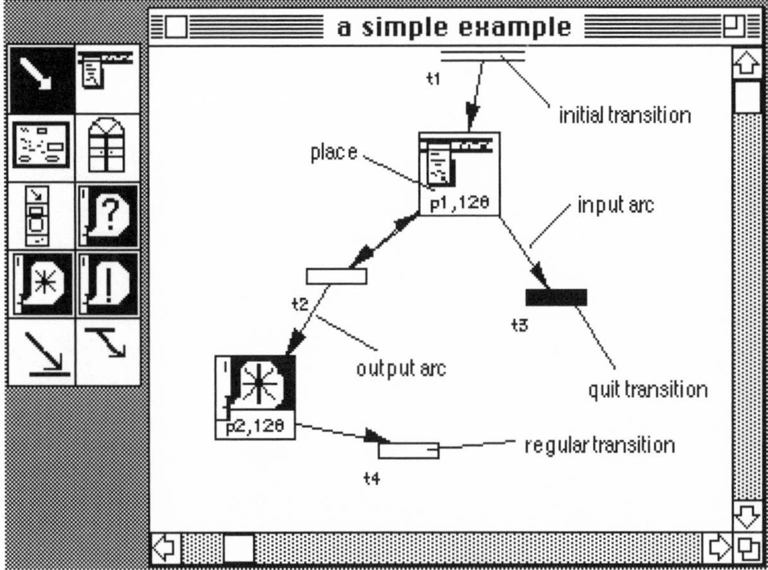

Figure 4.5 Petri Net representation for a simple example

turn, a modeless object does not require the user to respond before doing something else.

Each place is labeled with a unique name (e.g., p1) and a resource ID. Resource IDs are used to retrieve static descriptions of user interface objects from an application's resource file. Menus, palettes, and window places are modeless, whereas stop alert, caution, and note alert places are modal; however, the modes for dialog places can be specified by the user through the selection of radio buttons.

Transitions in the Editor

Each transition represents a mouse action performed on a selectable area of a GUI object. The GUI object place for which the action is performed is called the owner of the transition, and is connected to the transition by an input arc. Thus, a transition must be connected to at least one place by an input arc, each of which describes transition input conditions for enabling that specific transition. For example, the transition *Save* will not be performed in the *File* menu in the absence of an opened window displayed on the screen.

Within the net, transitions are drawn as boxes, each labeled with a unique name (e.g., t1). There are two types of special transitions, INIT and QUIT. The former is represented as a double bar, which when fired initiates (i.e., starts) an application. In turn, QUIT transitions are displayed as black rectangles, and the firing of a QUIT transition represents quitting an application. Note that INIT transitions do not have input places, whereas QUIT transitions lack output places.

Arcs in the PN Editor

Places and transitions are connected by directed arcs: places connect to transitions by *input arcs* and transitions connect to places by *output arcs.* Input arcs may be annotated with a predicate which determines if an action is allowed. For instance, a transition, representing the Save item of the File menu, cannot be selected in the absence of either a window or a File menu displayed on the screen. Moreover, the Save item cannot be selected if a modal object, such as a modal dialog box or an alert box, is displayed on the screen.

Annotations may include messages, Boolean preconditions, or sequence numbers. Predicates are Boolean expressions whose values (either *true* or *false*) depend on the current state of the net, permitting the specification of conditional flows within the net. Sequence numbers are integer constants which can be used to determine the execution order of concurrently activated objects at the moment of firing a transition.

Example: A Personal Query System

Our first illustration is a personal query system which holds names and addresses of business acquaintances. The main GUI objects consist of a query dialog with three editable boxes and four buttons, and a file menu for controlling the application, see Figure 4.8.

Each time the *Prev* button is selected, the file backs up one record. Each time the *Next* button is pressed, the file advances one record. To update the record, the user types in new data and selects the *Change* button to confirm the update.

The first step after constructing these two GUI objects with Rez Dez is to determine the GUI classes that are to be subclassed to handle the menu and dialog. Clearly, the menu and dialog classes from the Objex framework fit this requirement. But, in addition, we need a document to hold the records of the file, and an *about dialog* to tell the user about this application. Taken together, this totals 5 GUI objects, as shown in Figure 4.7.

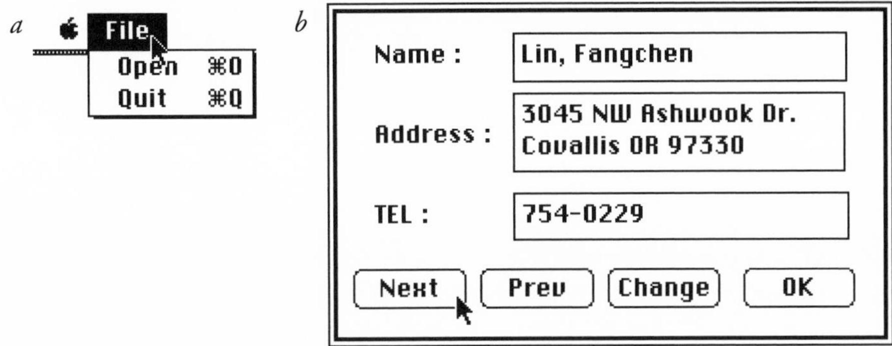

Figure 4.6 (*a*) Menu for controlling the application. (*b*) Dialog for displaying record contents

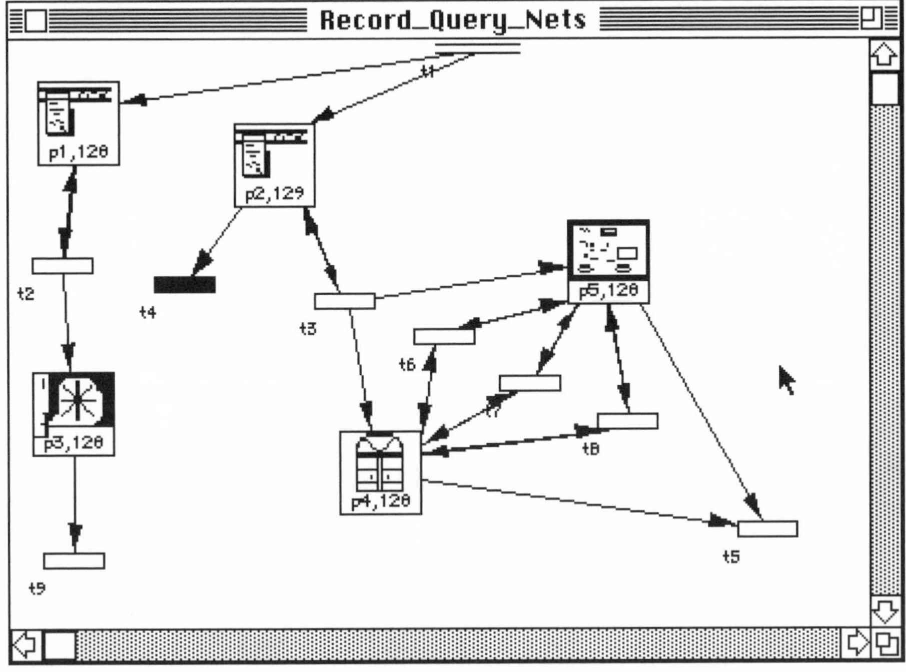

Figure 4.7 Petri Net representation for a record query application

The value of an instance variable is specified next by double-clicking the dialog place icon, see Figure 4.8. Actually, the instance variables specialize the class for a particular application. In effect, this causes the code

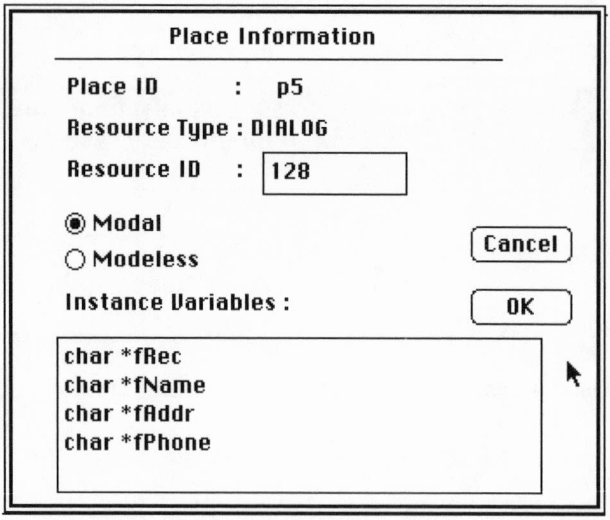

Place Information

Place ID : p5

Resource Type : DIALOG

Resource ID : 128

Modal

Modeless

Instance Variables :

Cancel

OK

char *fRec
char *fName
char *fAddr
char *fPhone

Figure 4.8 Dialog box for request of dialog place details

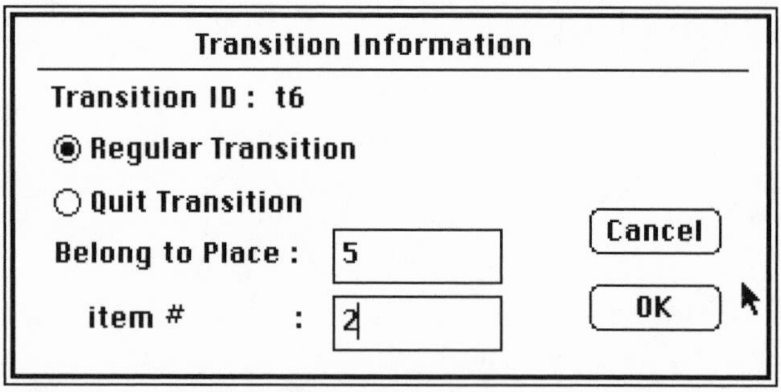

Transition Information

Transition ID : t6

Regular Transition

Quit Transition

Belong to Place : 5

item # : 2

Cancel

OK

Figure 4.9 Dialog requesting transition attributes

synthesizer to specialize the framework by subclassing and inheriting. That is, a GUI class is customized by adding new application-specific data (i.e., instance variables) and behaviors (i.e., methods).

There are four buttons in the query dialog which will initiate messages when they are clicked with the mouse. Thus, there are four transitions connected by input arcs from the dialog place in Figure 4.7 (t5, t6, t7, and t8). For example, after drawing the transition for the *Next* button, we must enter the attributes of the *Next* button transition, see Figure 4.9. In this dialog box, the user specifies the item number of the *Next* button

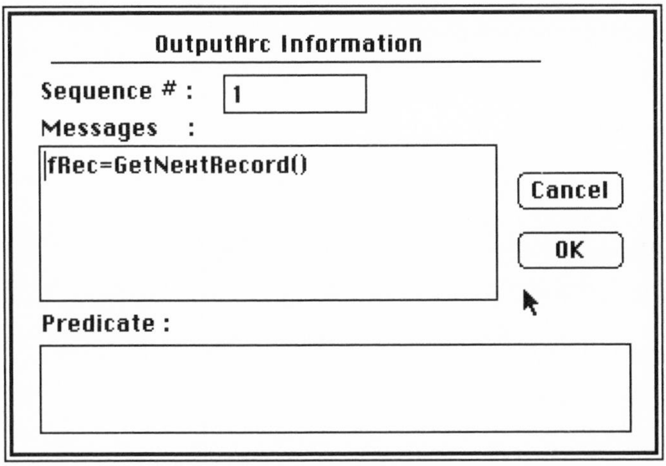

OutputArc Information

Sequence # : 1

Messages :

fRec=GetNextRecord()

Cancel

OK

Predicate :

Figure 4.10 A dialog for getting annotations for an output arc

in the dialog resource (see Figure 4.9) and declares the dialog place p5 to be the owner of the transition by entering the place ID of the dialog place.

The third step is to determine message connections between the various objects. We do this by drawing arcs connecting transitions to places representing message-receiving objects, and associating messages with each output arc. An object can be both the sender and receiver of a message, meaning that the object sends a message to itself.

After the *Next* button is pressed, the contents of the next record are displayed in the *editText* box of the query dialog. To specify this, the dialog place sends a message to the window place asking for the next record, which is then returned in the form of a string. The string is separated into tokens, which are then displayed in the *editText* boxes of the query dialog.

Two output arcs are drawn from the transition representing the *Next* button to the window place, and to the dialog place, see Figure 4.7. To specify the message sent to the window place, the user double-clicks the output arc connecting transition t6 to place p4, then provides the information shown in Figure 4.10.

The message `fRec=GetNextRecord()` is entered. The sequence number of the output arc is set to 1 to assure that the messages are sent in the proper order.

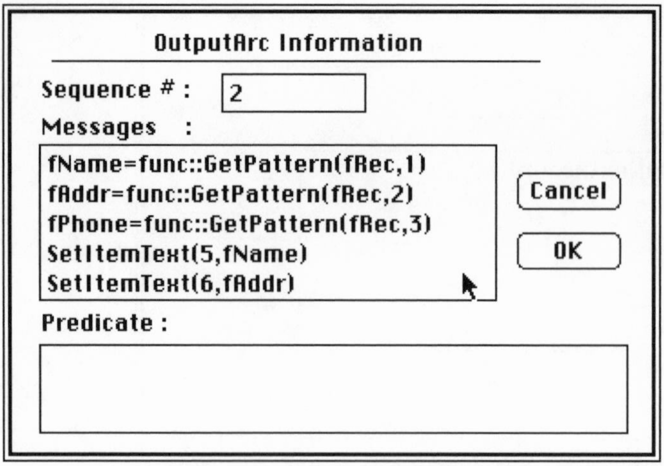

OutputArc Information

Sequence # : 2

Messages :

fName=func::GetPattern(fRec,1)
fAddr=func::GetPattern(fRec,2)
fPhone=func::GetPattern(fRec,3)
SetItemText(5,fName)
SetItemText(6,fAddr)

Cancel

OK

Predicate :

Figure 4.11 Dialog requesting annotation for an output arc

Since the query dialog is still on the screen after the *Next* button is clicked, an output arc is drawn back to the dialog place. To analyze and display the record string obtained from the file, the following messages are inscribed on the output arc, and the sequence number of the output arc is set to 2, see Figure 4.11:

```
fName=func::GetToken(fRec,1)
fAddr=func::GetToken(fRec,2)
fPhone=func::GetToken(fRec,3)
SetItemText(5, fName)
SetItemText(6, fAddr)
SetItemText(7, fPhone)
```

The contents of each record are derived from `fRec` and stored in three variables: `fName`, `fAddr`, and `fPhone`. The keyword `func` tells the Code Generator to connect a user-defined function to the framework instead of a member function (method).

Note that `GetToken` parses string `fRec` and returns its nth token. `SetItemText` is a method defined in the `CLDialog` class which displays a string within a dialog box.

When a transition is not connected to its input place through an output arc, a message, `DoClose()`, from a corresponding object to itself is implied. For example, transition t5, indicating the *OK* button, is not connected to its input places through output arcs, the dialog place, or the

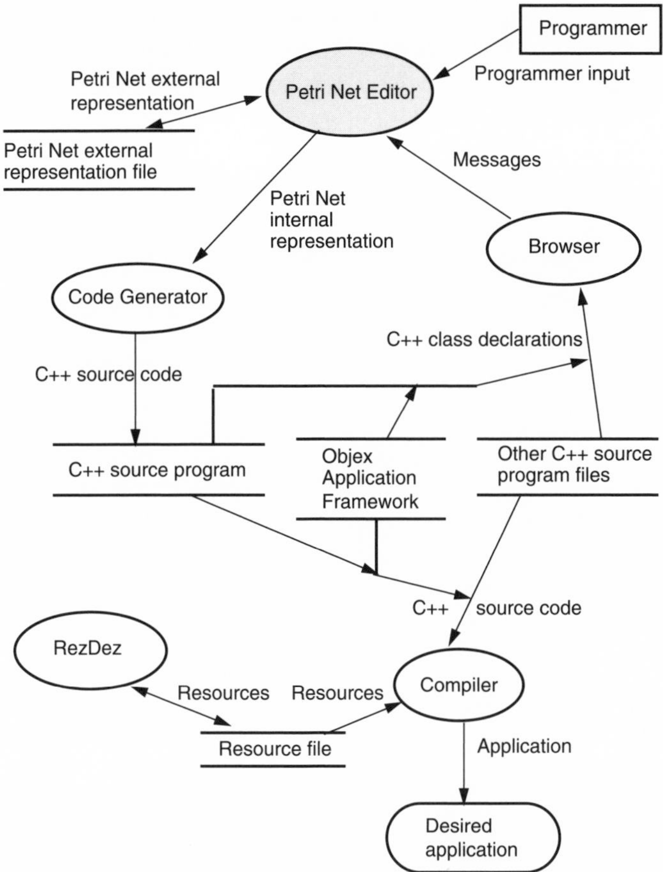

Figure 4.12 Dataflow diagram for the Petri Net tools

window place. Therefore the query dialog and the opened file are closed after the *OK* button is pressed.

4.3 Using the Petri Net Editor

Input to the Petri Net editor is shown in Figure 4.12:

- Specifications from the programmer: The Petri Net objects and message flows are specified by the programmer. The programmer enters the required information for an object (e.g., the resource ID of a GUI object).

- Reusable messages selected from the Browser: The Browser parses C++ source programs, builds the class hierarchy tree chart, displays the methods (i.e., messages) for the classes, copies the methods selected by the user, and sends the list of messages to the editor.
- Petri Net external representation: Petri Net external representation is saved by the editor as a text file according to the internal Petri Net representation. The programmer can open existing files as editor input.

The editor interacts with the programmer, processing the input and converting it to an internal Petri Net model. The editor output includes:

- Internal Petri Net representation: This model becomes the input for the Code Generator, which in turn generates C++ source code as output.
- External Petri Net representation file: As noted above, the editor converts the internal representation file into an external representation file for subsequent use.

The output of the Code Generator (i.e., C++ source code) becomes the input for the C++ compiler, which in turn compiles the source code, links the source code to the Objex framework and to other C++ source program files, loads resources from the resource file, and generates the desired application.

Syntax Checks

Syntax checks are performed to assure that the Petri Net has a legal structure and observes syntax rules. Syntax restrictions may be either built-in or compulsory. Build-in restrictions are properties that are automatically enforced by the editor, since the editor is unable to violate them. Built-in syntax restrictions include the following:

- A transition must be connected by at least one input arc.
- An arc can only be drawn from a place to a transition.
- A quit transition cannot have an output arc.
- An initial transition cannot have an input arc.
- Every net must have exactly one initial transition.

The first restriction cannot be violated since a transition cannot be created in the absence of an input arc. The editor does not allow an initial transition to be copied, cut, or pasted. Thus, the final restriction given above cannot be violated.

Compulsory syntax restrictions are properties that are not automatically guaranteed by the editor, but which must be fulfilled in order to run the Code Generator. The system can also perform a syntax check for compulsory restrictions when *Check Syntax* in the *Tools* menu is invoked. The compulsory syntax restrictions include:

- Each place should be connected to at least one output arc.
- The initial transition should have at least one output arc.

4.4 Design and Implementation of the Petri Net Editor

The Petri Net Editor was constructed within Objex-by-Design by subclassing and instantiating classes of the Objex framework. In Figure 4.13, the derived classes are indicated by a number. They can be classified as follows:

- GUI objects (items 1–13)
- Petri Net storage structures derived from the CLModel class and the data structure library, and Petri Net storage objects derived from the CLObject class (items 15, 16, and 17)
- Graphics objects derived from the shape library (item 18)
- Petri Net domain-specific view (item 14)

Appending * to the end of a method name indicates an override of an Objex framework method.

4.4.1 User Interface Classes

The user interface classes are standard, and can be implemented through the Objex framework. Objects derived from these classes must be modified to override certain standard methods (specialization).

PNApp
The class `PNApp` implements the main event loop. It has a member, `fBrowser`, which is responsible for the initialization of the Browser,

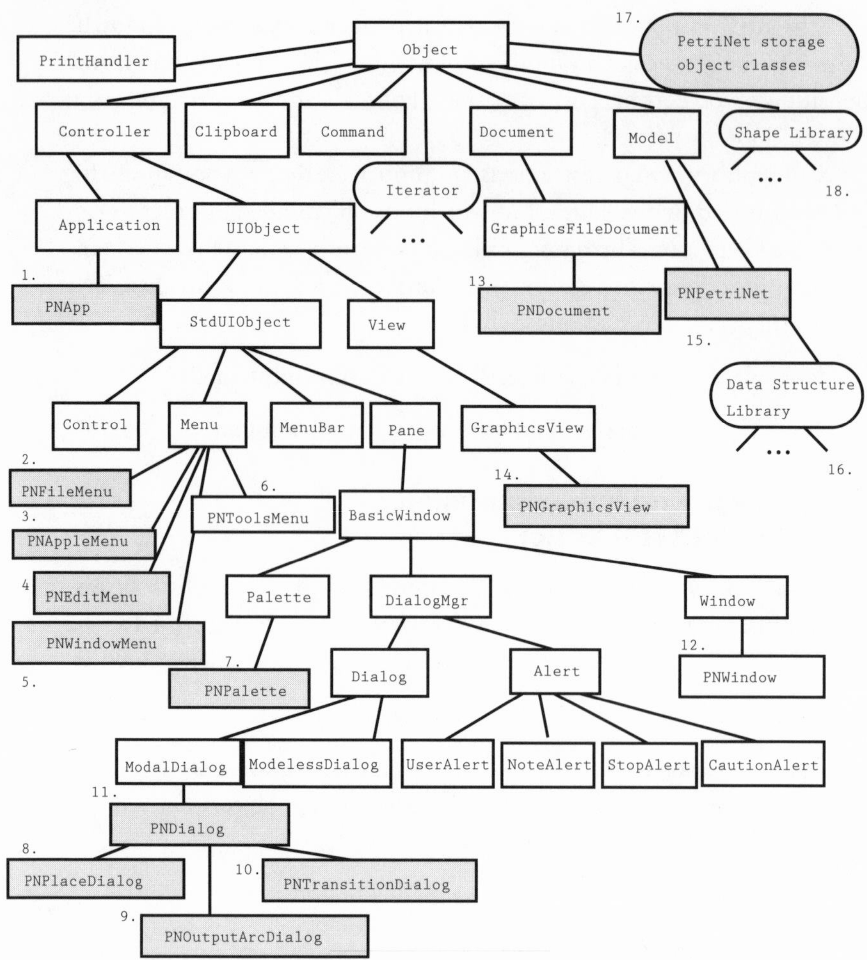

Figure 4.13 PN editor classes derived from the Objex framework

obtaining lists of selected methods, closing the Browser window, and removing selected methods from the lists [Li91].

`CreateMenus*` and `Initialize*` are overridden. The first is used to create the menu bar objects and objects which are specific to the editor; the second, which is an abstract method from the CLApplication class, is overridden to perform additional application initializations. These tasks include the creation and initialization of palette objects and the `fBrowser` member.

PNDialog

The class PNDialog is responsible for displaying all dialogs requiring a user response before proceeding with further tasks. This is an extended subclass which provides two additional methods, HandleRadioGroup and DrawDLine, that are not provided in the framework. The first is used to manipulate the radio group, and the second is responsible for line drawing within dialog boxes.

Other Dialog Classes

PNPlaceDialog requests place information, PNTransitionDialog requests transition information; and PNOutputArcDialog requests output arc information. For each of these dialog classes, DoMouseDown* is the only method which is overridden.

PNDocument

This class is used to override CreateModel*, DoRead*, DoWrite*, and DoSetUpMenu*. The first creates an instance of the class PNPetriNet class; the second and third are used to read/write the attributes of Petri Net data elements and their corresponding shapes from or to files; and the fourth is overridden to set up the application's menus.

Menu Classes

The classes PNAppleMenu, PNFileMenu, PNEditMenu, PNToolsMenu, and PNWindowMenu are responsible for menu commands. Each overrides the method DoMenuCommand* to perform tasks in accordance with a menu item selected by the user.

PNPalette

The method DoMouseCommand* is overridden to highlight icons from the palette, as selected by the user, and notifying the view of the current shape tool.

PNWindow

The PNWindow class implements standard window manipulation tasks, including resizing and zooming. DoNew* is overridden for performing those tasks required each time a window is created, including calling the initialization method of the view or setting up menu status (e.g., enabling Close or Save As in the File menu).

DoOpen*, DoClose*, and DoSaveAs* are overridden for purposes of specialization. DoOpen* and DoSaveAs* call parental class versions of DoOpen and DoSaveAs and change their own menus. DoClose* calls a parent class version of DoClose, and checks to determine if the current window is the Petri Net window. If the response is positive, the palette is hidden since there can be no window on the screen after DoClose is performed.

Code for DoClose* is provided to illustrate some details, as follows:

```
Boolean PNWindow::DoClose(void) {
    Boolean success=CLWindow::DoClose(); // call parental
    if(success) {//if the window is closed successfully
        if(gApplication->GetWindowCountByName("PNWindow")) {}
        else {// window list is empty now
                // set up menu status
            gApplication->fMenuBar->DisableMenuItem(FILE_ID,SAVE);
            gApplication->fMenuBar->DisableMenuItem(FILE_ID,SAVE_AS);
            gApplication->fMenuBar->DisableMenuItem(FILE_ID,CLOSE);
            gApplication->fMenuBar->DisableMenuItem(TOOL_ID,1);
            gApplication->fMenuBar->DisableMenuItem(TOOL_ID,2);
            gApplication->fMenuBar->DisableMenuItem(EDIT_ID,0);
            gApplication->fMenuBar->DisableMenuItem(WIND_ID,PNWIND);
            CLBasicWindow *aPalt; aPalt=gApplication->
                                    GetWindowByName("PNPALETTE");
            if (aPalt) ShowHide(aPalt->fWindPtr,false);//hide the palette
        }
    }
    return success;
}
```

4.4.2 Storage Structure Classes

PNPetriNet

PNPetriNet is used for the storage of the Petri Net structure, derived from CLModel since this structure is not a standard data structure as defined in the Objex framework. PNPetriNet uses two lists to store pointers for places and transitions, as shown in Figure 4.14. placeList and transitionList are instances, respectively, of PNPlaceList and PNTransitionList, each of which are subclasses of CLObjList.

For each place or transition there is a unique ID: placeID or transitionID. The instance variables, placeCount and transitionCount, are used to record the IDs for the most recently created places and transitions. When a new place or transition is created, the value of placeCount or transitionCount, respectively, is increased, as is the ID of the new place or transition.

4.4.3 Hierarchy of Petri Net Storage Object Classes

The class hierarchy of the Petri Net storage object classes is constructed as shown in Figure 4.15. There are three major branches, PNPlace, PNTransition, and PNArc, each of which is derived from the

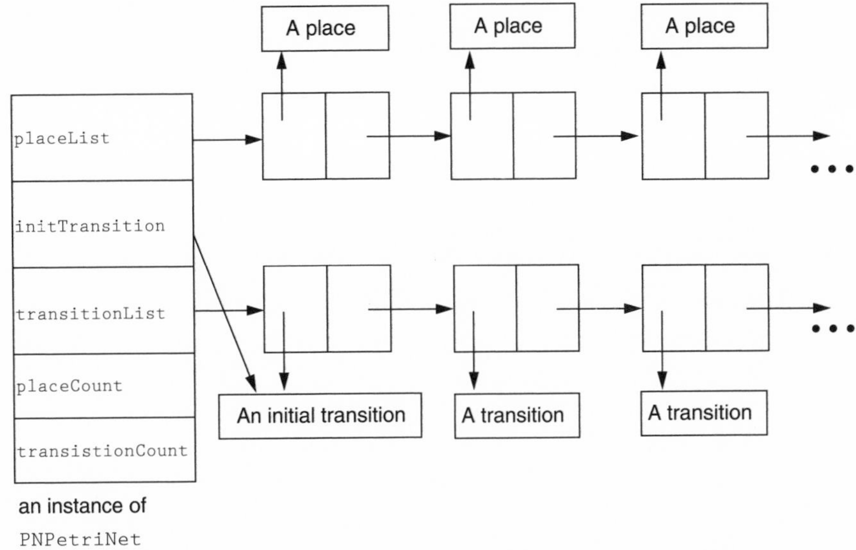

Figure 4.14 An Instance of `PNPetriNet`: Storage of the Petri Net model

`CLObject` class. The design of these classes is based on the principle of code sharing, to the greatest degree possible without compromising logical relationships among classes.

`PNPlace` is an abstract class responsible for maintaining the attributes and common behaviors of place objects. The following classes are responsible for object behaviors:

- `PNMenuPlace`, for the behavior of a menu place
- `PNWindowPlace`, for the behavior of a window place
- `PNPalette`, for the behavior of a palette place
- `PNDialogPlace`, for the behavior of a dialog place
- `PNAlertPlace`, for the behavior of an alert place
- `PNStopAlertPlace`, for the behavior of a stop alert place
- `PNCautionAlertPlace`, for the behavior of a caution alert place
- `PNNoteAlertPlace`, for the behavior of a note alert place.

PNTransition

`PNTransition` is an abstract class responsible for maintaining common information among all transition objects.

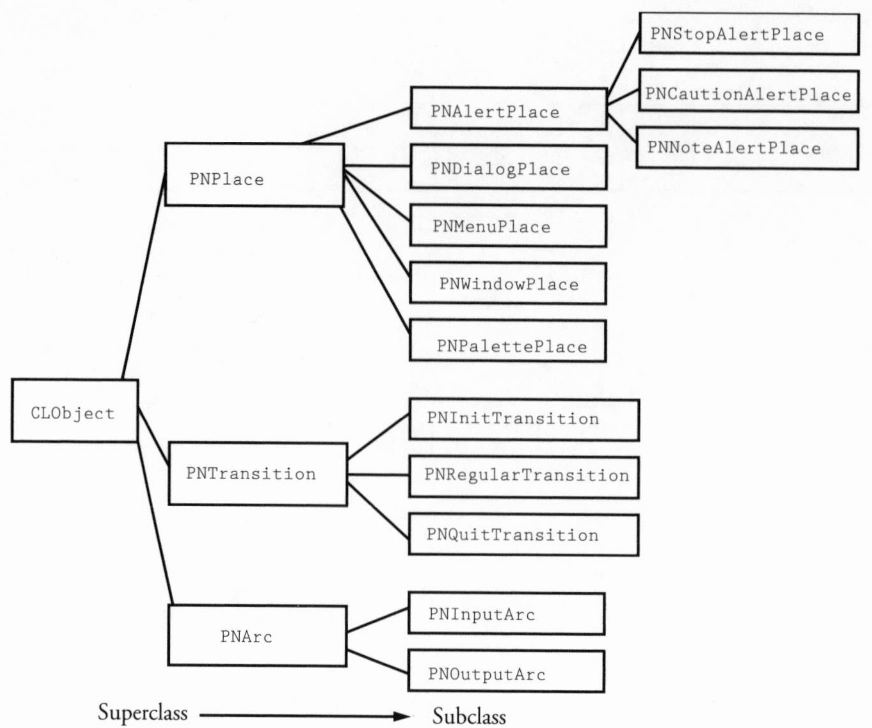

Figure 4.15 Class hierarchy of Petri Net storage object classes

PNInitTransition

`PNInitTransition` is responsible for storing and maintaining information regarding initial transitions.

PNRegularTransition

`PNRegularTransition` is responsible for storing and maintaining information for regular transitions. As shown in Figure 4.16, a regular transition has a list of pointers to output arcs and maintains a pointer to the place which owns the transition.

`inputPlaceArcs` is a list of pointers to input place arcs, which in turn stores pointers to the input places for this transition. `inputPlaceArcs` is used by the Code Generator to generate Boolean statements to check for the existence of certain objects. `itemNumber` is the number of the item represented by the transition within a GUI object.

PNQuitTransition

`PNQuitTransition` is responsible for storing and maintaining information regarding QUIT transitions.

PNArc

`PNArc` is a subclass of `CLObject`, and is an abstract class which maintains common information on arc objects.

PNInputArc

`PNInputArc` is responsible for maintaining information for an input arc.

PNOutputArc

`PNOutputArc` is responsible for maintaining information and behaviors for output arcs.

4.4.4 Graphics Object Classes

The graphics classes maintain graphic representations of Petri Net objects that are derived from the Objex framework shape library, see Figure 4.17. Behaviors are inherited from the parent classes. Each object maintains a pointer to its corresponding Petri Net object.

PNIcon

`PNIcon` is a subclass of `CLIcon`, used for the representation of a graphics view of a place.

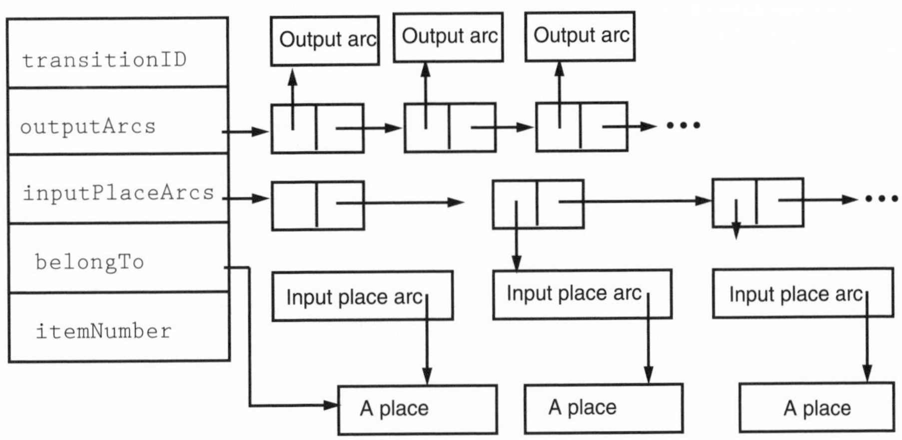

Figure 4.16 Instance of `PNRegularTransition`

PNArrowLine

`PNArrowLine` is a subclass of `CLArrowLine`, used for the graphic representation of input or output arcs.

PNTwoLines

`PNTwoLines` is a subclass of `CLSegment`, and draws a pair of lines to represent an initial transition.

PNRect

`PNRect` is a subclass of `CLRectangle`, used to represent the graphics view of a regular or a QUIT transition.

PNLabel

`PNLabel` is a subclass of `CLLabel`. It shows the ID of a transition and keeps a pointer to the graphics object which is labeled.

PNGraphicsView Class

The `PNGraphicsView` class is responsible for the manipulation of shapes displayed in the editing window. The storage structure shown in Figure 4.18 as `fShapeList` contains a list of pointers to shapes. `CLGraphicsView`

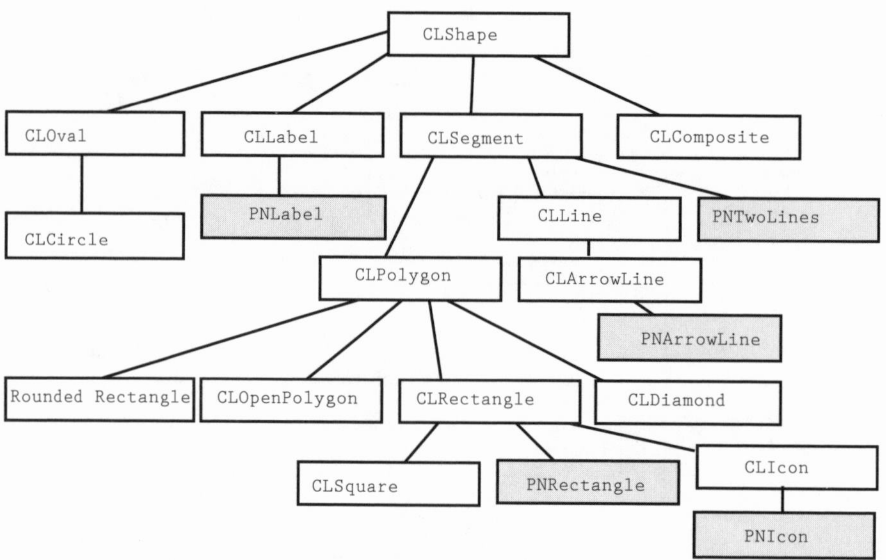

Figure 4.17 Class hierarchy of graphics classes. White boxes represent classes of the shape library, while shaded boxes represent classes derived for the Petri Net Editor

navigates these shapes by iterating its storage structures, based on the following algorithm:

```
CLIter nextDataStructure(fShapeList);
CLCollection *aDataStructure ;
CLShape *aShape;
while (aDataStructure = (CLCollection *) nextDataStructure())
{
    CLIter next(aDataStructure);
    while (aShape = (CLShape *) next())
        ......
};
```

4.5 Experience with the Petri Net Editor

To illustrate the utility of the editor, two extremely different applications are implemented: MiniDraw, and MiniCalculator. In addition, we want to measure the degree to which use of the editor can reduce programming time and effort.

4.5.1 MiniDraw

The MiniDraw application supports multiple concurrently displayed windows, cut-and-paste editing operations, reading and writing of data to and from document files on disk, undo and redo of multiple commands, and setting patterns for drawing a variety of shapes. Figure 4.19 shows a basic screen dump for this application.

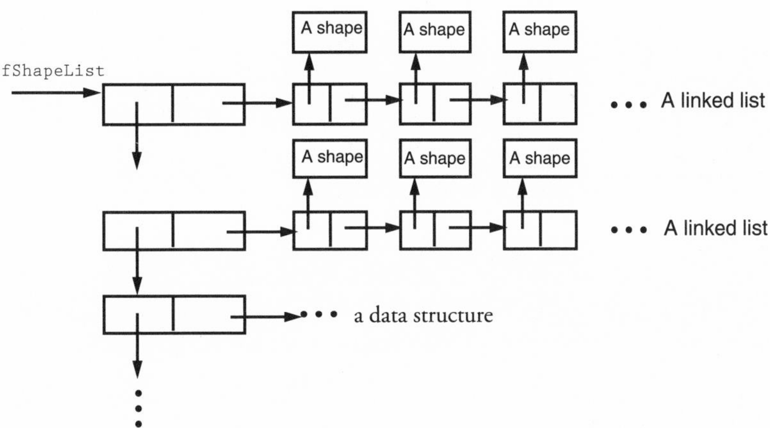

Figure 4.18 Storage structure (`fShapeList`) of `CLGraphicsView`

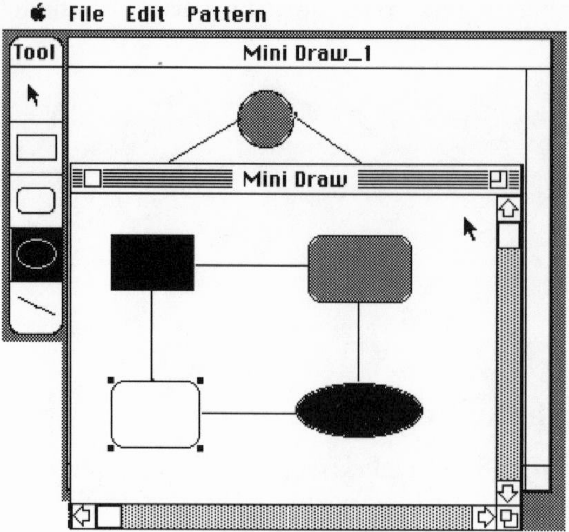

Figure 4.19 Basic screen for Mini Draw

The visual program for this example is specified in Figure 4.20. Messages inscribed on output arcs are methods inherited from the Objex framework, and `DoCut`, `DoPaste`, `DoCopy`, `DoSelectAll`, `SetPattern`, and `CLSetCurrentShapeTool` are `CLGraphicsView` methods.

The Objex framework prevents the bypass of the MVC model of interaction, so a `CLGraphicsView` object cannot be directly accessed. Thus, to send a message to the view within a window, `GetViewByName` is sent to the window place to obtain a pointer for the `CLGraphicsView` object. The returned pointer is stored in a variable, `aView`, which can then be declared a local variable for the method generated for that transition, or it can be declared as an instance variable for the place sending the message.

The Petri Net editor automatically generated 529 lines of code. In addition, it was necessary to add 16 lines of code to provide the necessary `include` statements, and a statement declaring `aView` as a local variable.

4.5.2 MiniCalculator

MiniCalculator consists of a modeless dialog box with buttons for accepting user input, and an editText box in which results can be displayed, see Figure 4.21. The Petri Net representation for this application is shown in Figure 4.22.

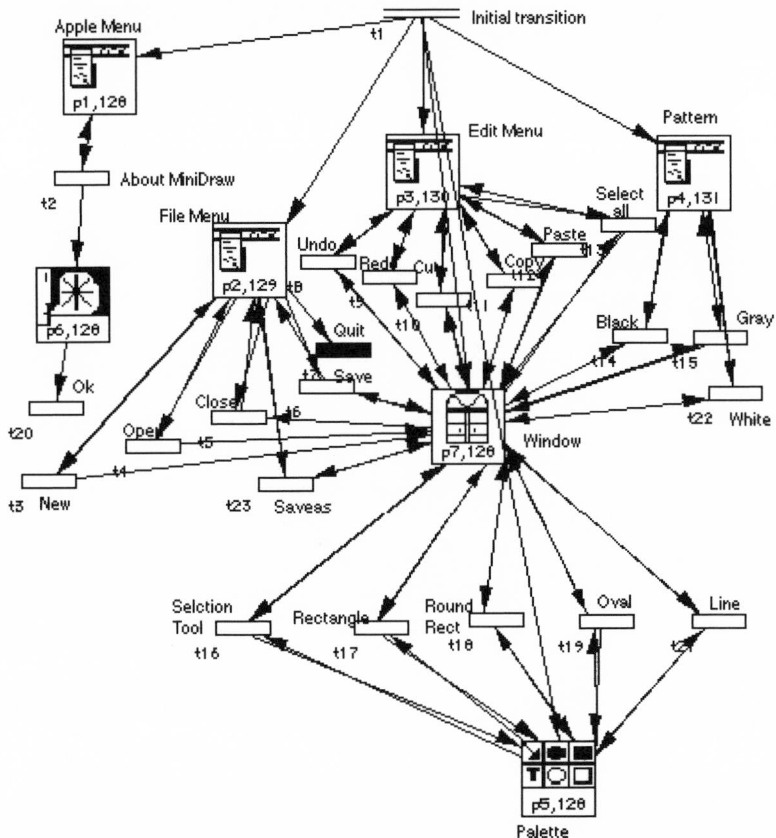

Figure 4.20 Petri Net representation for MiniDraw example (screen dump with added textual explanations of entities)

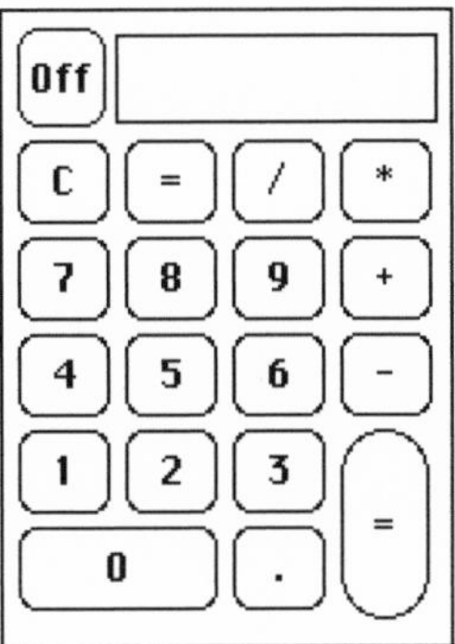

Figure 4.21 MiniCalculator As Dialog

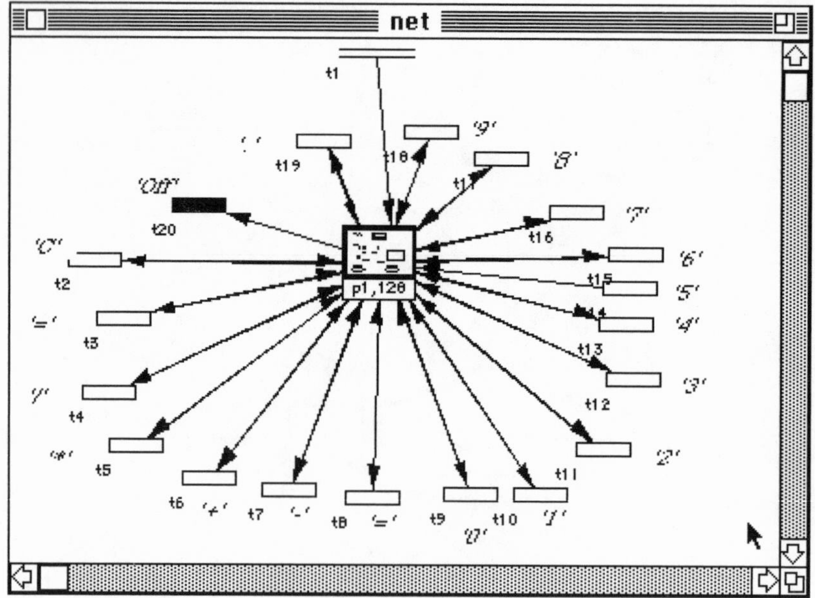

Figure 4.22 Petri Net representation for a calculator

A dialog place is drawn for the derivation of a subclass from the `CLModelessDialog` class. Five instance variables are declared for saving application-specific data:

- `double fOperand` stores the current value of the operand.
- `double fResult` stores the result of an operation.
- `char fOperator` stores the arithmetic operator.
- `char *fStr` stores a number in the form of text.
- `Boolean hasDecPt` indicates if there is a decimal point within the current operand.

As shown in Figure 4.22, 19 transitions were created to represent digital buttons, the decimal point button, the arithmetic operation buttons, and the `Off` button of the calculator. Transition t20, which represents the `Off` button, is a QUIT transition that terminates the execution of this application.

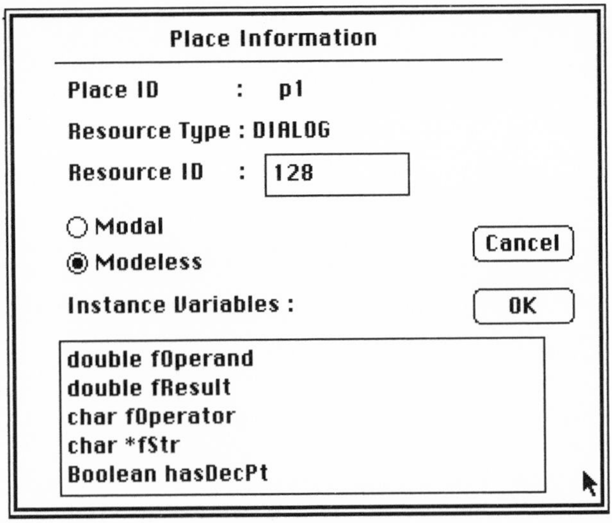

Place Information

Place ID : p1

Resource Type : DIALOG

Resource ID : 128

Modal

Modeless

Cancel

OK

Instance Variables :

double fOperand
double fResult
char fOperator
char *fStr
Boolean hasDecPt

Figure 4.23 Dialog requesting information on a dialog place

The dialog place is connected by an output arc from the initial transition, indicating that a modeless dialog object is created after the application is started. The message `DoClear()` is sent to the modeless dialog, initializing the instance variables for a new modeless dialog object. This method is also called when the *C* (clear) button is pressed.

When a digit button is selected by the user, the digit is appended to `fStr`, which is then converted to a number. The value of `fStr` is then displayed in the editText box, which is item #1 in the modeless dialog resource representation of the calculator. The messages inscribed on the output arc from transition t10 to place p1 are:

```
GetDigit("1")
fOperand=func::atof(fStr)
SetItemText(1,fStr)
```

`GetDigit` is a new member function of the dialog place, atof is a string convert function defined in the C library, and `SetItemText` is a method from the class `CLDialog` used to display a string in the `editText` box, see Figure 4.24.

When the first decimal point is entered, `'.'` is appended to `fStr`, which is then displayed in the editText box. If a decimal point already exists, then nothing is done when the '.' button is selected. The messages

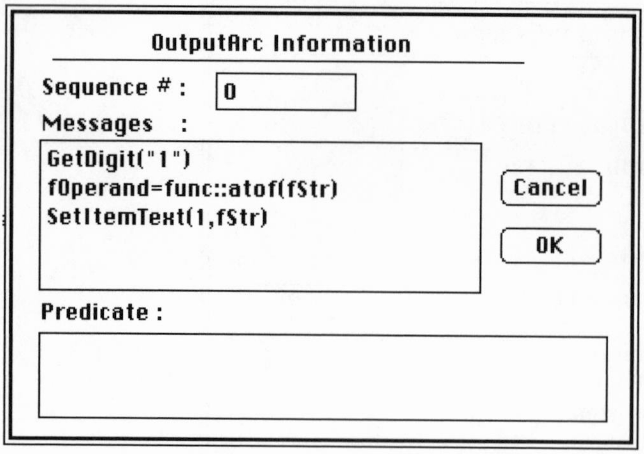

OutputArc Information

Sequence # : 0

Messages :

GetDigit("1")
fOperand=func::atof(fStr)
SetItemText(1,fStr)

Cancel

OK

Predicate :

Figure 4.24 Messages inscribed on the output arc drawn from t10 to p1

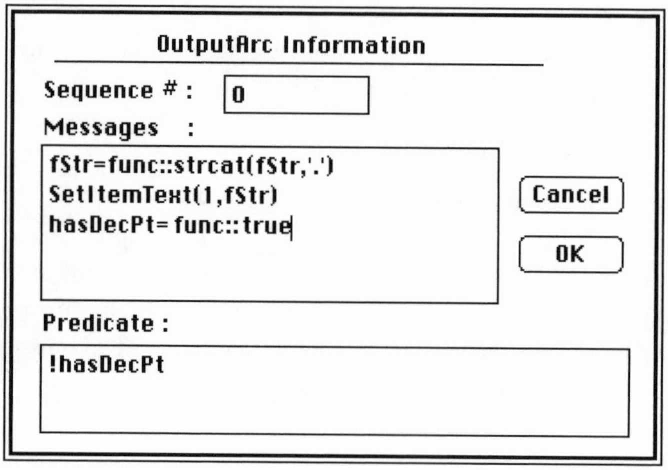

OutputArc Information

Sequence # : 0

Messages :

fStr=func::strcat(fStr,'.')
SetItemText(1,fStr)
hasDecPt= func::true

Cancel

OK

Predicate :

!hasDecPt

Figure 4.25 Messages and predicate inscribed on the output drawn from t19 to p1

`fStr=func::strcat(fStr,".")`, `hasDecPt=true`, and `SetItem-Text(1,fStr)` are inscribed on the output arc from t19 to p1, see Figure 4.25. The predicate !`hasDecPt` is entered by the user.

The statements generated for the transition t20 are as follows:

```
If (!hasDecPt) {
        fStr=strcat(fStr,'.');
        SetItemText(1,fStr);
        hasDecPt=true;
}
```

When an operation button is selected, the operation is performed, the result of the operation is displayed in the editText box, and the operator is saved. This is done by sending messages back to the modeless dialog box, see Figure 4.26. For instance, the following messages are inscribed on the output arc from transition t6, which represents the `'+'` button, to p1:

- `PerformCalculation()` does the calculation according to the old value in `fOperator`.
- `func::num2str(fResult,fStr)` converts the result to a string.
- `SetItemText(1,fStr)` shows the result value.
- `fOperator=func::'+'` saves the operator for later use.
- `func::strcpy(fStr,"0")` sets the string to "0".
- `hasDecPt=func::false` sets the value of `hasDecPt` to FALSE.
- `fOperand=func::0` resets the value of `fOperand`.

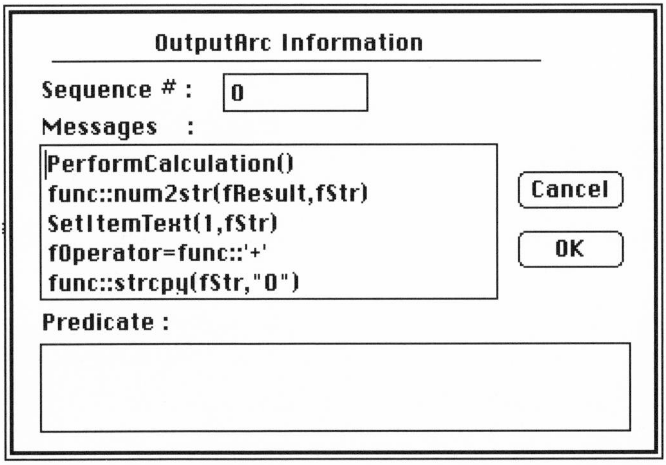

OutputArc Information

Sequence # : 0

Messages :

PerformCalculation()
func::num2str(fResult,fStr)
SetItemText(1,fStr)
fOperator=func::'+'
func::strcpy(fStr,"0")

Cancel

OK

Predicate :

Figure 4.26 Messages inscribed on the output arc drawn from t6 to p1

Note that `num2str` is a user-defined function which converts a number type `double` to a string. This demonstrates how to attach functionalities to user interface objects through the use of messages inscribed on output arcs. The message `PerformCalculation` is an application-specific method written by the user. The code for `PerformCalculation` is:

```
switch(fOperator) {
    case '+':
        fResult=fResult+fOperand;
        break;
    case '-':
        fResult=fResult-fOperand;
        break;
    case '*':
        fResult=fResult*fOperand;
        break;
    case '/':
        fResult=fResult/fOperand;
        break;
    case '=':
        break;
}
```

Redundant segments of generated code might be abstracted into separate procedures to improve program readability. For example, the following code segment appears in the methods for performing operation buttons, and can be abstracted into a single module for subsequent recall:

```
PerformCalculation();
num2str(fResult,fStr);
SetItemText(1,fStr);
fStr=strcpy(fStr,"0");
hasDecPt=false;
fOperand=0;
```

Most of the code added by hand deals with key down events. The method `DoKeyDown` was overridden to convert the keycodes for pressed keys to the number of items in the modeless dialog box. This example demonstrates one of the limitations of the Petri Net Editor. That is, an action taken for a key down event cannot be specified with the editor.

This program resulted in 395 lines, of which 285 lines of code were automatically generated and 110 lines were added by hand. Recall that the underlying framework consists of over 16,000 lines of reusable design and code.

4.6 An Evaluation

Effort

The time and effort required to implement these examples and two others is summarized in Table 4.4. The MM (work months) and TDEV (development time) estimates are based on the well-known CoCoMo method of cost estimation, which is a nonlinear law relating lines of code to effort and time [Lewis 90]. We conclude that the Petri Net tool vastly improves productivity of programmers. But, these results apply only to small, simple applications. The gains are not nearly as great for larger applications.

Table 4.4 Time and effort results for four sample applications

	MiniDraw	Help system	Calculator	Query record
Lines of codes generated	529	327	285	283
MM (effort)	0.58	0.35	0.30	0.30
TDEV (time)	2.03	1.67	1.59	1.58
Total lines of codes	545	330	395	549
MM (effort)	0.6	0.35	0.42	0.6
TDEV (time)	2.05	1.68	1.81	2.06
%saving in effort	96%	99%	71%	50%
%saving in time	99%	99%	87%	76%
Number of places	7	7	1	5
Number of transitions	20	18	20	9
Number of arcs	66	26	38	25
Number of messages	50	0	61	30

Reuse

Table 4.5 shows how many objects in the Objex framework were reused, how many subclasses were added, and how many methods in the Objex framework were reused in each example.

The implementation of the Petri Net Editor demonstrates the reusability of the Objex framework classes, thus reaffirming the basic principle of reusable design. Also, because the reusable components are used in so many different applications, they become thoroughly tested, adding to the reliability of new applications. Only a few errors in the framework classes were uncovered through their reuse in these small examples, leading to a low defect rate.

Table 4.5 Reuse of Objex classes in the sample applications

	MiniDraw	Help System	Calculator	Record Query
Framework objects reused	31	15	10	19
Number of subclasses added	8	8	2	8
Number of methods reused	276	71	64	109

The Petri Net Editor provides a favorable environment for the construction of GUI application prototypes, saving considerable programming time and effort. Since a graphical editor provides programmers with a useful application overview, this approach avoids the possibility of losing programmers in a confusing mass of statements.

Limitations

The major limitation of the Petri Net Editor is that interactions among objects within a place cannot be specified. For example, the interactions among a view, a model, and a document, each of which are within a window object, cannot be specified. In the case of deriving subclasses from these classes, it is necessary for the developer to step beyond the use of the Petri Net Editor to create domain-specific classes by hand. However, the newly derived classes are relatively easy to create, since they can reuse both design and implementation from the framework.

A second problem is the separation between framework, editor, and resource. Unless the programmer is knowledgable in these three areas, it is unlikely that the Petri Net Editor can be used effectively. These tools are not suitable for novice or inexperienced experts. A higher degree of coupling is needed to reduce the level of detail needed to specify a complete application.

Finally, some types of statement structures cannot be derived from the specifications of output arcs, messages, predicates, or the sequence numbers currently provided by the editor. For example, an `if..else` statement cannot be correctly described solely using predicates. In addition, a loop structure cannot be represented by any means currently available within the editor.

Further Reading

[Alger90] J. Alger, Using model-view-controller with MacApp. *Frameworks, The Journal of Macintosh Object Program Development,* **4** (2), 4–14, 1990.

[Bruno86] G. Bruno and G. Marchetto, Process-translatable Petri Nets for the rapid prototyping of process control systems. *IEEE Trans. Software Eng.* **SE-12** (2), 590–602, 1986.

[Gamma89] E. Gamma, A. Weinand, and R. Marty, ET++—An object oriented application framework in C++. In *proceedings of ECOOP '89*, ed. C. Stephen, Cambridge University Press, 283–297.

[Genrich81] H. J. Genrich, and K. Lautenbach, System modeling with high-level Petri Nets. *Theoretical Computer Science* **13,** 109–136, 1981.

[Keh90] Huan-Chao Keh and T. G. Lewis, Direct-Manipulation User Interface Modeling With High-Level Petri Nets, *Tech. Report 90-60-17*, Dept. of Computer Science, Oregon State University, Corvallis, OR, 1990.

[Knolle89] N. T. Knolle, Variations of model-view-controller. *Journal of Object-Oriented Programming,* **2** (3) 42–46, 1989.

[Krasner88] G. E. Krasner and S. T. Pope, A cookbook for using the Model-View-Controller user interface paradigm in Smalltalk-80. *Journal of Object-Oriented Programming,* **1** (3), 26–49, 1988.

[Linton89] M. A. Linton, J. M. Vlissides, and P.R. Calder, Composing user interfaces with InterViews. *IEEE Computer,* **22** (2) 51–60, 1989.

[Reiss87] S. P. Reiss, Working in the Garden environment for conceptual programming. *IEEE Software,* **4** (6) 16–27, 1987.

[Schmucker86] K. J. Schmuker, MacApp: An application framework. *Byte* **11** (8) 189–193, 1986.

[Urlocker89] Z. Urlocker, Abstracting the user interface. *Journal of Object-Oriented Programming,* **2** (4), 68–74, 1989.

[Biljon88] W. R. Van Biljon, Extending Petri Nets for specifying man-machine dialogues. *Int. J. Man-Mach. Stud.* **28** 437–455, 1988.

[Weinand88] A. Weinand, E. Gamma, and R. Marty, ET++—An object-oriented application framework in C++, In *proceedings of OOPSLA '88*, San Diego, CA, 46–57, Sep. 1988.

PART

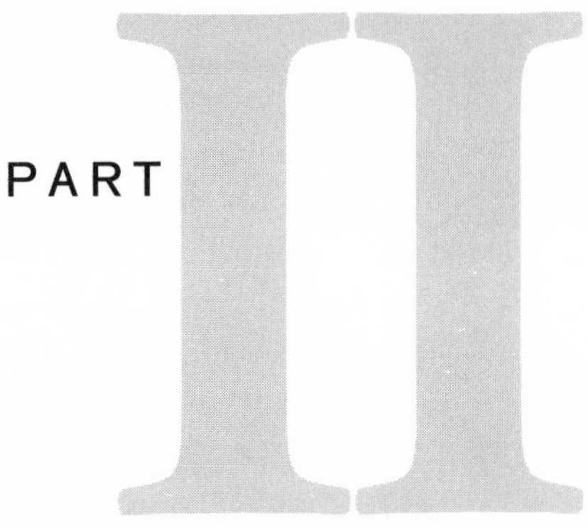

Off-The-Shelf Designs

Larry Rosenstein, in Chapter 5, provides a knowledgeable tour of MacApp, the first widely used and commercially available application framework. MacApp encapsulates not only the Macintosh toolbox routines, but also automates many of the routine operations found in almost all Macintosh applications, e.g., File I/O, Editing (Cut/Copy/Paste). But better still, this chapter exposes how MacApp evolved into a sophisticated framework over years of experience and feedback from users. This is something that few frameworks can boast.

We give Wolfgang Pree, Chapter 6, a chance to get even with the Macintosh crowd. He describes the fledgling steps toward framework technology on the Microsoft Windows platform. MFC (Microsoft Foundation Classes) is really a class library with a few basic framework capabilities. But, we think it is fair to toss this example into a book about frameworks because MFC is doomed to become a widely used class library, and over time, will evolve into a powerful framework.

In an attempt to keep the UNIX crowd happy, we invite André Weinand and Erich Gamma to tell the story of their application framework, ET++, in Chapter 7. Developed on UNIX for a Swiss Bank, this elegant framework incorporates a very strong model of interaction, and has ambitions to become a portable application development framework. You might think of ET++ as a second generation MacApp, but one that is evolving toward platform independence.

In Chapter 8, Paul Calder describes the design principles and implementation of InterViews, which is a GUI-domain framework for X-Windows. Interviews is aimed at developing GUI parts and so is really more of a tool kit.

Chapter 9 introduces the frameworks of Taligent, a company formed by Apple and IBM to reset the desktop computing software agenda. Joined later by Hewlett Packard, this small company is trying to rejuvenate the software industry by changing the rules. Instead of writing large monolithic applications which are tied to one GUI platform, the Taligent strategy is to make it not only possible, but economically attractive to write small, highly leveraged applets (small applications) that are easily ported to many platforms. A challenging task, given that the computer industry has more or less become calcified by lack of innovation and progress in the software development realm. Can Taligent do it? Read and decide for yourself.

CHAPTER 5

MacApp: First Commercially Successful Framework

LARRY ROSENSTEIN

Preview

The purpose of this chapter is not to explain how MacApp works internally, which is of interest only to programmers using MacApp. (Even then, most MacApp programmers don't need to know how it works internally). What you should take away from this chapter is a better understanding of how frameworks operate.

First, we will give a short history of MacApp and explain how it evolved. One important point about designing a framework is that it takes more than one iteration, and possibly several years, to get it right.

Then, we will develop a small sample application built from MacApp components, walking you through the steps of an icon editor. This tour is divided into two parts: the development of classes and subclasses, and then the development of interactions among the classes and subclasses.

5.1 Background

MacApp® is a framework intended for writing full-featured Macintosh® applications [MacApp, Wilson90]. It implements the common structure that all Macintosh applications share, thereby allowing the application developer to concentrate on the application-specific parts of the program.

The Macintosh is known for its consistent user interface across all applications. But implementing that user interface requires a fair amount of work on the part of the developer. Even though the Macintosh ROM contains hundreds of useful functions [Apple92], the burden is on the programmer to call the appropriate function when needed.

For example, all Macintosh applications include a main event loop that processes events. Some events, such as a click in the menu bar, are handed off to the Macintosh Toolbox. Other events, such as a click inside a window, must be handled by the application itself. The Toolbox doesn't provide the application's basic control flow. Programmers either implement this from scratch, or more likely, copy the basic structure of an existing program.

MacApp simplifies Macintosh application programming by implementing the common application structure (e.g., the main event loop and menu handling). Sure, you could do this by copying a sample program and editing in changes. But unlike a sample program, MacApp can be customized by subclassing the classes it contains and overriding specific member functions to provide application-specific behavior.

For example, MacApp provides the main event loop and dispatches mouse clicks in the menu bar to the Macintosh Menu Manager, without the programmer having to write a line of code. But MacApp can't possibly provide the application-specific code that processes a chosen command. Instead, it calls a member function, which developers override to implement a specific command.

MacApp 1.0 was shipped in January, 1987, and is currently in its third major revision. MacApp was one of the first commercially available object-oriented frameworks, and to date, several hundred applications written using MacApp are on the market.

5.2 Design Evolution

It is useful to review the process by which MacApp was designed and how a design evolved over time. This summary may be helpful as you begin writing your own object-oriented frameworks.

An application framework embodies the ideal application structure in a form that is reusable in many specific applications. If you adopt this viewpoint, then your framework design process must include two tasks, both of which were incorporated into MacApp's design process.

First, the framework designers must become knowledgeable about the application's domain. Otherwise, it will be difficult to embody the key concepts of the application domain in the framework's design and implementation.

Second, the design team must obtain feedback from the application's clients, and revise the framework based on that feedback. You cannot really claim to have a reusable framework until it has been used in a variety of cases.

The MacApp project was begun in the Fall of 1984. The initial design was created by examining the Macintosh programmer's documentation and the source code of early Macintosh applications written at Apple Computer. In addition, the MacApp designers consulted with the developers of those applications. The goal was to learn the "correct" structure for Macintosh applications and to become expert at writing them.

The next step was to design MacApp's class hierarchy and the runtime interaction between the objects of those classes. In general, choosing the classes was straightforward. MacApp was an application framework, so it was natural to include an application class. And since most Macintosh applications deal with documents and windows, MacApp included document and window classes.

Choosing the classes in this way was more of a guideline than a strict rule. For example, Macintosh applications also deal with the menu bar, menus, and menu items, but MacApp does not include classes that represent these concepts. In these areas, MacApp programmers designed a procedural interface that is closer to the underlying Macintosh Toolbox.

Designing the framework interactions was not as straightforward. The Macintosh Toolbox defines how the application's main event loop should be implemented and how to respond to certain events, such as a click in a window's title bar. Mapping this application structure onto MacApp's object structure was relatively easy. For example, MacApp's class `window` was called to process a click in the title bar.

But, the Toolbox does not define how an application organizes information inside its windows, how it processes menu commands, etc. MacApp's design for these interactions was based on examining existing applications and trying to generalize the application structures they implemented.

MacApp's design has evolved over time, based on feedback from programmers. Client feedback is an important part of framework design, in order to validate the framework's reusability. Programmers associated with the framework developers can provide some feedback, but it is also important to get feedback from outside developers.

The first MacApp distribution to outside developers occurred in the Spring of 1985, and Apple has continued to provide early versions to developers. Soliciting feedback from outside developers not only helps you refine the framework design, but also encourages a user community to develop.

A good example of evolution in the MacApp design is the mechanism for organizing the contents of windows. MacApp 1.0, embodied two separate concepts: *frames* and *views*. Windows (which were also frames) could contain a number of frames, and each frame contained a view.

MacApp 2.0 generalized the concept of views to support subviews. The window became the root of a view hierarchy. This eliminated the need for a separate frame concept, and simplified the architecture. In addition, MacApp 2.0 included many predefined view classes that could be laid out graphically using a view editor. Instead of writing lines of code to create a view hierarchy, the programmer could create the hierarchy from a resource generated by the view editor.

MacApp 3.0 refined the architecture introduced in version 2.0. A view could have associated *adorners* and *behaviors*. An adorner modifies the visual appearance of a view: for example, it may draw a border around a view. A behavior modifies the way the view responds to events.

Besides these kinds of architectural changes, MacApp has changed to incorporate new Macintosh features. For example, Macintosh System 7 introduced features such as Apple events and Publish/Subscribe. Supporting these features required changes to MacApp.

Any significant change to a framework causes a dilemma for the framework designer. Is it better to improve the framework, even though it may require clients to recompile programs that use the framework, and possibly, to modify their source code? Or should the designer preserve the framework interface and forgo the improvement?

There is no hard-and-fast answer. Sometimes it is possible to change the framework in a way that's compatible with older versions. Or new features can be added alongside existing features.

For example, Apple could have maintained the frame concept from MacApp 1.0, and just added the new view class as a parallel feature. Instead, it made an extensive change to MacApp which required clients to modify their source code. Nevertheless, MacApp 1.0 users were generally in favor of Apple making improvements to MacApp.

But as the number of MacApp users, and the sizes of their applications, grew, the sentiment turned toward preserving the interface. You are likely to see a similar effect as your frameworks evolve.

5.3 Classes

MacApp consists of about 180 classes. To get started using MacApp, however, you need to understand only four classes: `TApplication`, `TDocument`, `TView`, and `TCommand`. A partial class hierarchy looks like:

```
TObject
   TEventHandler
       TCommandHandler
           TApplication
           TDocument
               TFileBasedDocument
           TView
               TWindow
               ...
   TEvent
       TCommand
           TTracker
           ...
```

Many of the other classes are specific subclasses of `TView` and `TCommand` that provide useful functionality. There are also several utility classes that implement simple collections, manipulate files, etc.

`TApplication`, `TDocument`, and `TView` are all subclasses of `TCommandHandler`, which in turn is a subclass of `TEventHandler`. `TEventHandler` represents an object that can respond to various events. These events include user input such as mouse clicks and keystrokes, as well as events defined by the MacApp architecture. An example of the latter is responding to a menu command.

`TCommandHandler` adds to `TEventHandler` the concept of a command context. Commands in a MacApp program, whether initiated by a menu item, keystroke, or mouse click, are defined by a command object. Each command object has an associated command handler that is responsible for managing the command object. As we will see later, each command handler processes the commands that directly affect it.

The first class that you need to understand when programming with MacApp is `TApplication`. `TApplication` implements the standard event loop found in every Macintosh application, and distributes events to the appropriate event handler (application, document, view, etc.). The application object also handles application-level menu commands such as `Open`, `New`, and `Quit`.

`TDocument` represents the user's document. It manages the user's data in memory as well on disk, and processes commands that read, write, and change the data. At runtime, there is one document object for each opened document.

`TDocument` defines the general behavior of documents. Most applications, however, store their documents' data in a single disk file. `TFileBasedDocument`, which is a subclass of `TDocument`, provides explicit support for this storage mechanism, which makes it easier to implement the document class.

`TView` implements a drawing canvas. Each view defines its own local coordinate system, and all drawing is clipped to the view's rectangular boundary. These properties allow the view to draw graphics without knowing where the view is positioned and without interfering with other views.

Each view contains a list of contained views, or subviews. The set of views in a window form a hierarchy with the window object (which is also a view) at the root. `TWindow` implements window-specific behavior, and is the interface between MacApp's view hierarchy and the Macintosh Window Manager.

MacApp comes with a library of predefined view classes that you can use in your application's windows. Most of these implement buttons, scroll bars, and other kinds of controls that you would expect to find in a Macintosh application. There are also views that implement simple tables and lists, and that interface with the built-in Macintosh text-editing package.

The final class you need to deal with initially is `TCommand`. `TCommand` represents a change to the application (usually to the document). The command object encapsulates the steps needed to perform a command, as well as the steps needed to undo it. The command object is also responsible for saving enough information so that the command can be undone.

An important subclass of `TCommand` is `TTracker`, which implements a particular mouse action. MacApp passes to the tracker a series of mouse coordinates. The tracker follows the mouse and provides feedback to the user. When the user releases the button, the tracker usually performs the action specified by the mouse gesture. Since `TTracker` is a subclass of `TCommand`, it inherits the command functions responsible for performing and undoing a command.

5.4 Interactions

The best way to understand how MacApp works is to look at the steps required to create an application using MacApp. Because of the way MacApp is architected, it is relatively simple to create an application that displays some data on the screen, and to add features to the application step by step.

As an example, we will use a simple icon editor application that it shipped with MacApp. The icon editor displays a magnified view of a black and white icon. (See Figure 5.1) The user can draw in the icon with a pencil tool and invert the entire icon. The program follows the Macintosh human interface guidelines and supports cut, copy, and paste; open and save; print; etc.

5.4.1 Getting Started

The first step is to create the application's foundation, on which we can implement other features. The result of this stage is an application that can open one or more untitled documents, as well as implement most of the behavior common to all Macintosh applications.

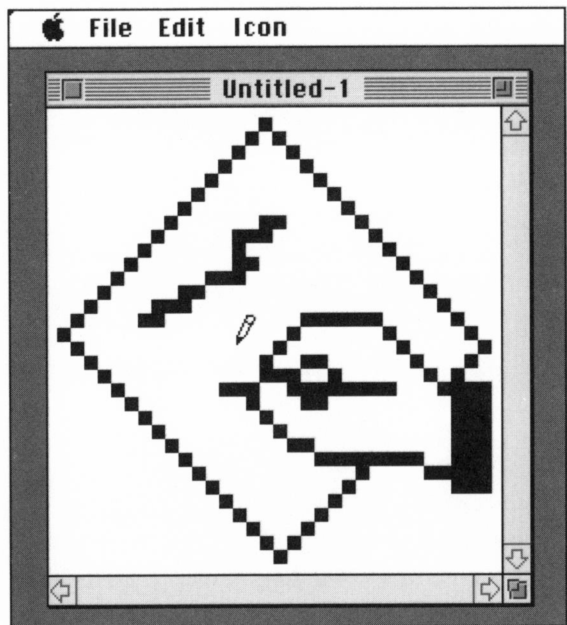

Figure 5.1 `IconEdit` in action

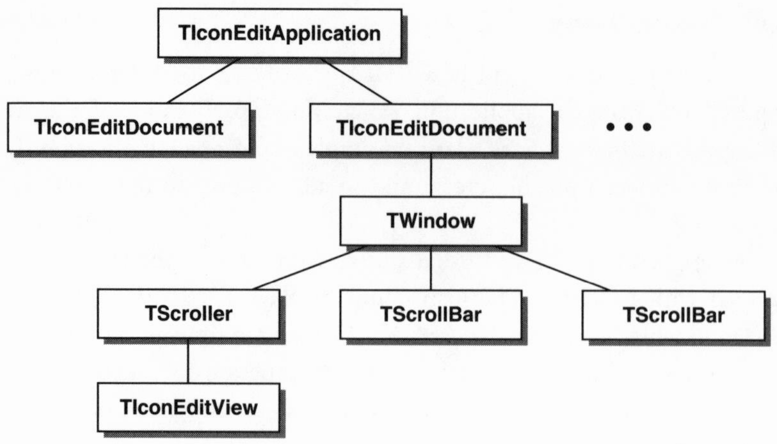

Figure 5.2 `IconEdit` runtime object structure

To begin writing the icon editor, we create three subclasses: `TIconEditApplication`, `TIconEditDocument`, and `TIconEditView`. These fit into the MacApp class hierarchy as follows:

```
TObject
   TEventHandler
       TCommandHandler
           TApplication
               TIconEditApplication
           TDocument
               TFileBasedDocument
                   TIconEditDocument
           TView
               TIconEditView
```

The class hierarchy shown above represents only the inheritance relationship between the classes. Another important relationship is the runtime relationship, which forms the basis for how the objects interact with one another at runtime.

At runtime, the icon editor objects relate to one another as shown in Figure 5.2.

The lines between classes represent a *container* or *has-a* relationship. The application contains a list of opened documents. MacApp supports multiple simultaneous opened documents.

Each document contains a list of the windows associated with it. In the icon editor, each document has exactly one window. The window forms the root of a tree of views that defines the appearance of the window.

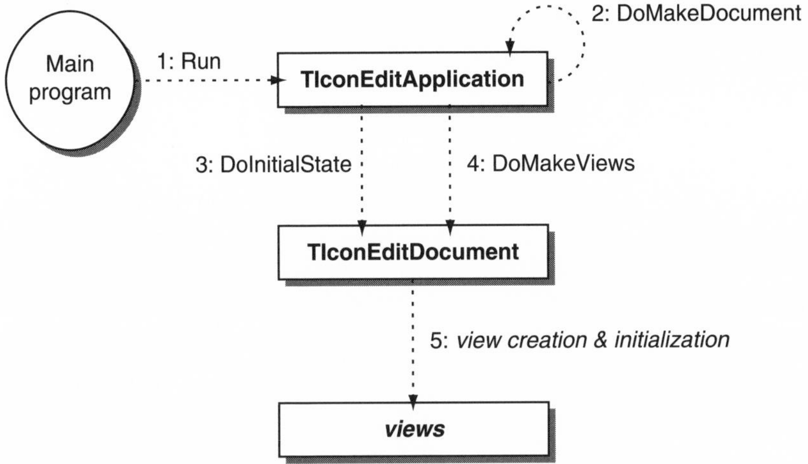

Figure 5.3 Messages sent during application initialization to create a new document

The icon editor window is a typical Macintosh window. It contains a scrollable area and horizontal and vertical scroll bars. Each of these elements is implemented by a separate view object.

`TScroller` is a view that implements horizontal and vertical scrolling. The image that it scrolls is defined by its subviews, and in this example is just a `TIconEditView`. The scroller translates the drawing done by its subviews according to the current scroll position. The scroll bar views provide the standard Macintosh scrolling behavior and communicate the scroll position to the scroller.

An important part of any framework is how its objects are created and hooked together. The icon editor program begins by initializing the Macintosh Toolbox, and MacApp. Figure 5.3 depicts the important messages that are sent during the initialization. Then the icon editor program creates an instance of `TIconEditApplication`, and calls the application's Run member function, which is implemented in MacApp's `TApplication` class.

`TApplication::Run` enters the application's main event loop. The first event the application receives will be an Apple event from the Macintosh Finder® that tells the application what to do. The three choices are: open a new, untitled document; open one or more existing documents; or print one or more documents.

Regardless of which Apple event it receives, `TApplication` next creates an appropriate document object. To do this, it calls its `DoMakeDocument` member function; see step 2 in Figure 5.3. You override `DoMakeDocument` to create an instance of your document class. In the icon editor, this is an instance of `TIconEditDocument`.

The document object contains the data associated with the document. `TIconEditDocument` contains an instance of the class `TIconBitmap`, which contains the actual bitmap and provides useful function for manipulating it.

At this point, we have created the application and document objects. In this scenario, we will assume that the user has opened the icon edit application, which means that the application should open an untitled document. To initialize the document's data, `TApplication` calls the document's `DoInitialState` member function, which is shown as step 3 in Figure 5.3. `TIconEditDocument` overrides this function and initializes its bitmap to a default image.

At this point, the document object is fully initialized. The next step is to create a set of views, including a window, that can display the contents of the document. MacApp does this by calling the document's `DoMakeViews` member function, see step 4 in Figure 5.3. `TIconEditDocument` overrides this member function and creates a window that contains two scroll bars and a scroller. The scroller, in turn, contains an instance of `TIconEditView`. The latter is the only view the icon editor programmer has implemented; the window, scroll bars, and scroller are provided as part of MacApp and are used as-is.

One way to create the view hierarchy is to write code to create each view object, and to hook them together. But MacApp also provides a mechanism to read a view hierarchy from a Macintosh resource (A resource is a piece of data associated with the application, but separate from the application's code. The resource contains parameters for defining windows, buttons, dialogs, icons, and strings of text, sounds, etc.).

This approach has two advantages. First, it reduces the overall application size. The MacApp designers found that the view resource size was significantly less than the code to create the equivalent view hierarchy.

Second, a view resource can be edited to change the appearance of the window without recompiling the application. MacApps shipped with a `ViewEdit` program that can create and modify view resources, and third parties also ship similar editors.

In this scenario, the only member function that `TIconView` implements is `Draw`. The `Draw` function is responsible for drawing the contents of the view. Each view has its own local coordinate system, so the `Draw` function doesn't have to be aware of the view's location in the hierarchy. In addition, drawing within a view is clipped to the view's boundary. Before calling `Draw`, MacApp sets up the drawing environment appropriate for the view's local coordinate system and boundary.

`TIconEditView::Draw` is very simple. It calls `TIconBitmap::Draw`, which in turn uses the QuickDraw call `CopyBits` to copy the bitmap stored in the `TIconEditDocument` onto the screen.

MacApp does not define an object-oriented graphics interface; instead, programmers use the normal QuickDraw API implemented in the Macintosh Toolbox [Apple94]. The advantage of this approach is that it doesn't introduce another level of software on top of QuickDraw, but it also means that MacApp programmers do not use a pure object-oriented API.

At this point, the application is fully initialized and continues processing events.

The application startup seems involved, but it only requires that you create three subclasses and override four member functions, shown in Table 5.1.

Table 5.1 MacApp `IconEdit` application setup

Classes	Member functions
`TIconEditApplication`	`DoMakeDocument`
`TIconEditDocument`	`DoInitialState`
	`DoMakeViews`
`TIconEditView`	`Draw`

This doesn't include the class `TIconBitmap` and its member functions, which is code that would have to be implemented whether you were using MacApp or not.

Even though we have implemented only four functions, the application has quite a few features at this early stage of development. The user can move, resize, close, etc. its window, scroll the contents of the window, and choose commands from the menu. Many menu commands, such as `New`, `Quit`, and even `Print` are completely implemented.

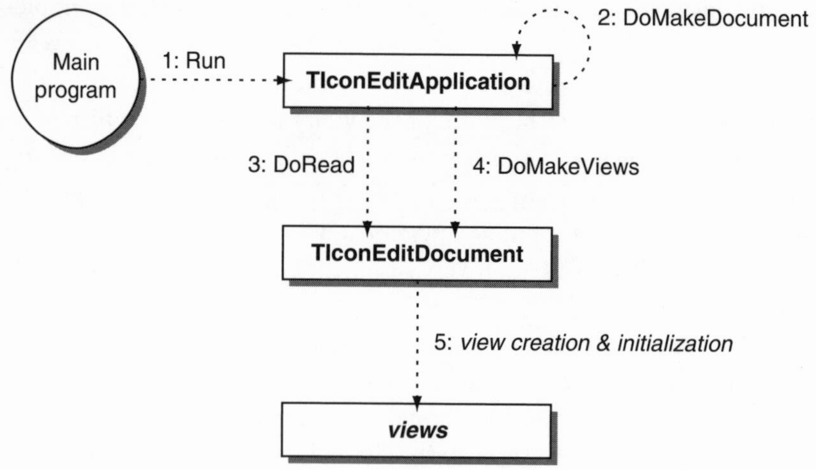

Figure 5.4 Messages sent during application initialization to open an existing document

This demonstrates the value of an object-oriented framework such as MacApp. The programmer implements only a few functions, and inherits considerable functionality from the framework.

5.4.2 Opening and Saving a Document

The preceding scenario described the case where the user opens the application to create a new, untitled document. The case where the user opens an existing document is very similar, see Figure 5.4. Instead of the document initializing its internal data to a default state (in the `DoInitialState` function), the document reads its data from a disk file.

This is done by the document's `DoRead` member function. MacApp's `TFileBasedDocument` class, from which `TIconEditDocument` inherits, takes care of opening the appropriate file, and passes a `TFile` object to `DoRead`. `TFile` provides member functions to read from and write to the file, and to access properties of the file.

`TIconEditDocument` overrides `DoRead` to read the bitmap data from the file (Actually, it calls a member function of `TIconBitmap` to do this.). It also calls the inherited `DoRead` function, which reads generic information such as that needed for printing.

It doesn't matter whether the user opens a document from the Macintosh Finder or by choosing `Open` from the menu. In the former case,

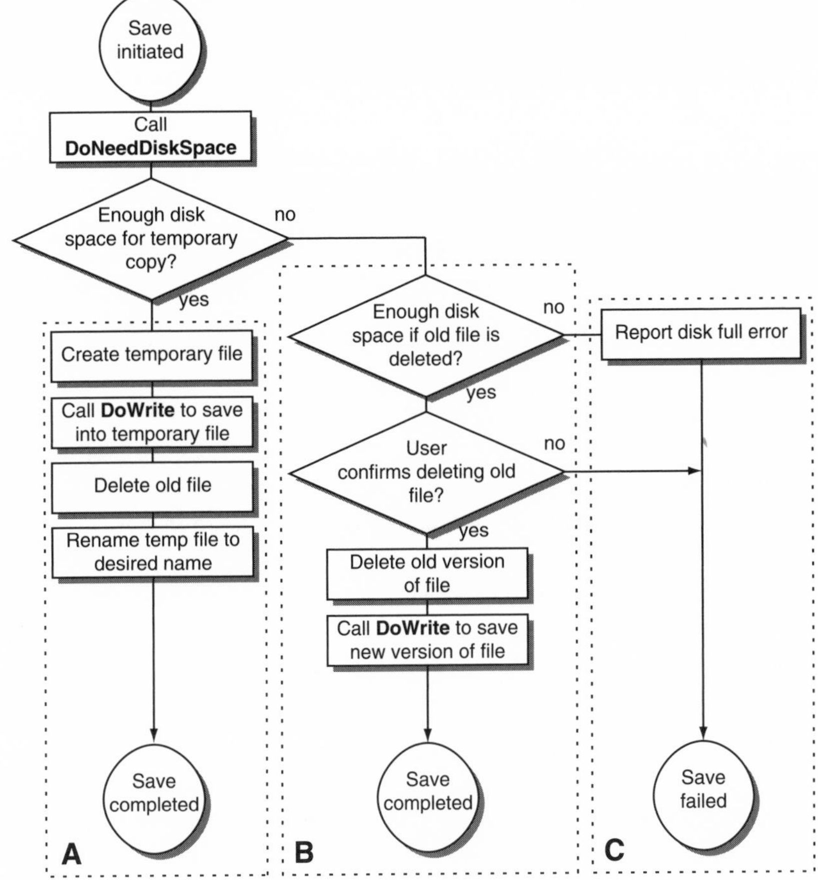

Figure 5.5 Flow of control for saving a file

MacApp takes care of processing the Apple event sent by the Finder that contains the name of the document. In the latter case, MacApp uses the standard file selection dialog to obtain the name. In addition, implementing `DoRead` allows MacApp to implement the standard `Revert` command.

Saving a document is done in much the same way as opening one. `TFileBasedDocument` defines a `DoWrite` member function, which `TIconEditDocument` overrides. The code for `DoWrite` mirrors that of `DoRead`, the only difference is the direction of the data transfer.

Behind the scenes, MacApp does quite a bit of work to ensure the document is saved safely, see Figure 5.5. Instead of saving the document's new version over the old, MacApp creates a temporary file and passes that to `DoWrite`. This is shown as path A in Figure 5.5. After `DoWrite` saves the new version of the document, MacApp deletes the old version and renames the temporary document to the desired name. The existence of the temporary file is transparent to the document object; the `DoWrite` function simply writes into whatever file is passed to it.

MacApp also handles situations where the free disk space is low. At the start of the save process, MacApp checks that there is enough free disk space to contain the temporary file. To find out the disk space requirements of the document, MacApp calls the document's `DoNeedDiskSpace` member function, which you override to return the amount of disk space needed to save the document.

If there isn't enough disk space to create the temporary file, MacApp checks whether deleting the original would free up sufficient space. If so, it asks the user whether to go ahead. This is path B in Figure 5.5. Otherwise, it reports that the disk is full, and allows the user to save to a different disk. See path C in Figure 5.5. Saving to a different disk is done with the `Save As` command, which MacApp implements (calling `DoWrite` and `DoNeedDiskSpace` as needed).

For space reasons, Figure 5.5 does not show what happens if either `DoWrite` call fails. In such cases, MacApp deletes the partially saved file and reports an error to the user. Note that if the user has chosen to save over the existing file, then the existing file has been lost. (But the user was warned of this possibility). The document's data is still in memory, however, and the user can try to save to another disk.

At this point, the icon edit program includes the member functions shown in Table 5.2. (The newly added functions appear in boldface.):

Table 5.2 MacApp `IconEdit` application incorporating file saving

Classes	Member functions
`TIconEditApplication`	`DoMakeDocument`
`TIconEditDocument`	`DoInitialState`
	`DoMakeViews`
	`DoRead`
	`DoWrite`
	`DoNeedDiskSpace`
`TIconEditView`	`Draw`

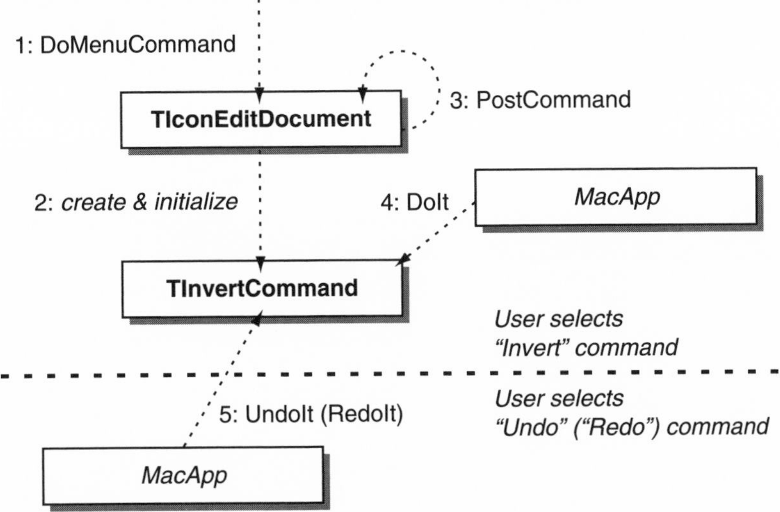

Figure 5.6 Basic command handling

5.4.3 Command Handling

Even though the icon editor has quite a few features at this stage, it's not a very interesting application, because the user can't change the document. In this section, we add a command to invert the bits in the icon.

In the MacApp architecture, all undoable commands are implemented by a subclass of `TCommand`. As we mentioned earlier, the command object is responsible for implementing the command, as well as saving enough information so that it can undo the command if necessary.

The upper part of Figure 5.6 shows the messages sent when the user chooses `IconEdit`'s `Invert` menu command. In this case, the `TIconEditDocument` object creates the command object in its `DoMenuCommand` member function. It then calls its own `PostCommand` function to start command processing, as step 3 of Figure 5.6 indicates.

Once MacApp receives the command object, it calls the object's `DoIt` member function (Step 4), which in this case inverts the pixels in the icon. MacApp also modifies the name of the undo menu item to include the name of the command (in this case, `Undo Invert`).

If the user selects the `Undo` command, MacApp calls the command object's `UndoIt` member function; see the lower part of Figure 5.6. The same command object is used for undo as was used originally. The

TInvertCommand's UndoIt function restores the document to its original state. As before, MacApp changes the undo menu item to Redo (in this case, Redo Invert).

If the user selects Undo a second time, MacApp calls the command's RedoIt function to perform the command again. Although DoIt and RedoIt both perform the command, DoIt usually does some extra work to save the information needed for undo.

MacApp implements only one level of undo. When the user selects the next menu command, the program creates another command object and returns it to MacApp. MacApp frees the first command object before calling the new command's DoIt function.

The icon editor's invert command is very simple to implement. Since inverting the bitmap twice results in the same image, it isn't necessary for the command object to save any state in order to be able to undo the command. Instead, inverting the icon a second time is sufficient to restore it to its original state.

Also, the actual bitmap manipulation is implemented in the TIconBitmap object. The invert command simply calls the document's InvertIcon function, which in turn calls TIconBitmap::Invert. This design eliminates the need for the command to directly change the document's data.

TInvertCommand's DoIt, UndoIt, and RedoIt member functions each just call the InvertIcon function defined in TIconEditDocument. InvertIcon modifies the bitmap and causes the window to be redrawn. (How the latter happens is the subject of the next section.)

There is one more step in the process of implementing the invert command; namely, creating the command object and returning it to MacApp. MacApp defines a number of member functions that you override to process commands. In this case (and as Figure 5.6 shows), Invert is selected from a menu, so the proper function is DoMenuCommand. (We'll discuss other ways of processing commands below.)

DoMenuCommand is called when the user selects a command from the menu. Each menu command has an associated command number, which MacApp passes to the DoMenuCommand function.

TCommandHandler defines the DoMenuCommand function, and the application, document, and view classes all inherit DoMenuCommand. The intent is that each object handle the commands that apply to it. In this

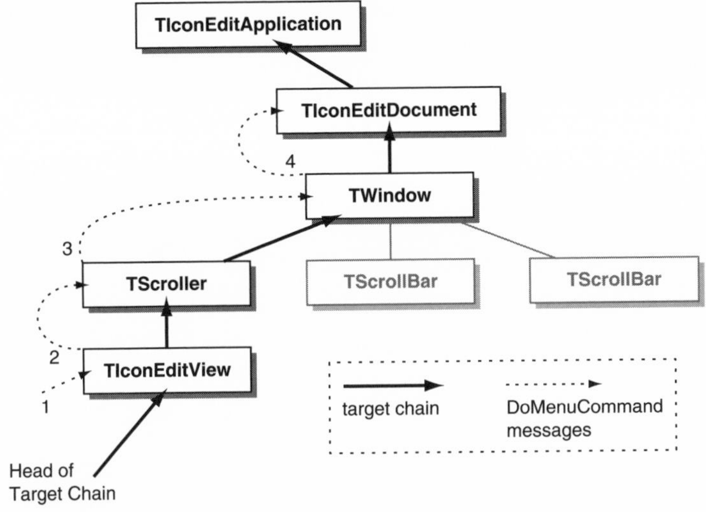

Figure 5.7 `IconEdit` target chain

case, since the invert command changes the document's data, the document should handle the command.

The mechanism MacApp uses to process menu commands is the target chain. The application maintains a target command handler, which gets the first chance to process a menu command. Usually the target is the view in the active window on which the user is focusing. If there are no open documents, then the application object will be the target.

Each command handler points to the next handler in the chain; see Figure 5.7. The chain normally goes up the view hierarchy until it reaches the window, which is the root of the view hierarchy. The window then points to the document object, which, in turn, points to the application. In the icon editor, each window contains only one main view, and that view is the head of the target chain when its window is active.

To process a menu command, MacApp calls the `DoMenuCommand` function of the target object, which in this case is an instance of `TIconEditView`. If the command is handled by the target, then the target creates a command object and returns it to MacApp. Otherwise, the target calls the `DoMenuCommand` function of the next handler in the chain. This continues until the proper handler is found for the command, or the process reaches the end of the chain (The latter shouldn't happen in practice, for reasons we'll explain below.).

In the case of the Invert command, `TIconEditView` gets the first chance at processing the command. Since it doesn't handle the invert command, it calls the scroller's `DoMenuCommand`, which calls the window's `DoMenuCommand`, which calls the document's `DoMenuCommand`. Since the document handles the command, its `DoMenuCommand` function creates an instance of `TInvertCommand` and returns it to MacApp. At that point, MacApp calls the command's `DoIt` function, as described earlier.

In theory, it's possible that no object in the target chain handles the command. In that case, MacApp displays an alert to the user. This doesn't happen in practice, and is really a program error, because such menu commands are normally disabled and cannot be selected.

Menu commands are enabled and disabled using the target chain as well. Each command handler implements a `DoSetupMenus` member function, which is responsible for enabling the commands that the handler can perform (The same member function also adds check marks to menu commands where needed.).

MacApp first disables all the menu commands, and then calls the target's `DoSetupMenus` function. The `DoSetupMenus` function begins by calling the `DoSetupMenus` function of the next handler in the chain. Then it enables the menu commands that it can perform.

The net result is that the only enabled menu commands are ones that some handler has enabled, presumably because the handler can process the command.

The Invert command can be performed any time there's an open document. Therefore, the `DoSetupMenus` function in `TIconEditDocument` always enables the Invert menu item. If there's an open document, then the document object will be in the target chain and the `Invert` command will be enabled. If no document is open, then the command will be disabled by MacApp and never enabled.

The enabling test for other menu commands can be more complicated. For example, the icon editor supports pasting an icon into the document. `TIconEditDocument` enables the menu command only if the clipboard contains data that it can import.

At this point, the icon editor program includes the classes and member functions: shown in Table 5.3.

The icon edit application that comes with MacApp includes two other command classes: `TIconEditCommand`, which implements `cut`, `copy`, and

Table 5.3 MacApp `IconEdit` application incorporating `Invert`

Classes	Member Functions
`TIconEditApplication`	`DoMakeDocument`
`TIconEditDocument`	`DoInitialState`
	`DoMakeViews`
	`DoRead`
	`DoWrite`
	`DoNeedDiskSpace`
	`InvertIcon`
	`DoMenuCommand`
	`DoSetupMenus`
`TIconEditView`	`Draw`
`TInvertCommand`	**`DoIt`**
	`UndoIt`
	`RedoIt`

`clear`, and `TIconPasteCommand`, which implements `paste`. These classes are implemented in exactly the same way as `TInvertCommand`.

Also, the program supports enlarging and reducing the size of the bitmap displayed on the screen. These commands do not affect the document, only the way the bitmap is drawn. Therefore, `TIconEditView` handles these commands.

In addition, the `enlarge` and `reduce` commands are intentionally not undoable. The reason is that MacApp only supports one level of undo, and it isn't worthwhile to "waste" the undo on a command that doesn't change the document. For example, if the user has made a change to the document and has enlarged the view to get a better look, it should still be possible to undo the actual change.

Commands that are not undoable can still be implemented with command objects. A command object has an internal flag that indicates whether the command changes the document. If the command does not change the document, then MacApp will not free the previous command when performing the new, non-undoable command.

It's also possible to perform a non-undoable command in the `DoMenuCommand` function itself, without creating a command object at all. In fact, this is how the icon editor implements the `enlarge` and `reduce` menu commands.

5.4.4 View Updates and Change Propagation

At any point in time, the views of a document should reflect the current state of the document. Whenever the document changes, for example as a result of a menu command, the views must be updated to reflect the change. MacApp uses a form of MVC (see Chapter 2) to implement change propagation.

Normally, view updating is done by invalidating the appropriate parts of the view. Invalidation is a feature provided by the Macintosh Toolbox. The program can designate a region of a window that needs updating. The Toolbox will then send the application an update event. The application processes the update event by refreshing the window's contents.

MacApp builds on this process by supporting invalidation on a view-by-view basis. The base class `TView` implements several member functions that invalidate all or part of a view. MacApp converts the invalid areas from view-relative to window-relative coordinates, and calls the appropriate Toolbox invalidate functions.

Figure 5.8 shows the basic messages sent when invalidating part of a view (upper half of the figure) and processing an update event (lower half). The figure uses the Invert command as an example. MacApp calls the `DoIt` function of the `TInvertCommand` object (step 1), which calls the `InvertIcon` function of `TIconEditDocument` (step 2).

After modifying the icon, `TIconEditDocument` calls the `TIconEditView`'s ForceUpdate function (step 3). This isn't a direct function call; the exact mechanism is described below. `ForceUpdate` is defined by MacApp in the base class `TView`. It invalidates the entire view by converting the view's bounds to a window-relative rectangle and calling the appropriate Toolbox function (step 4).

The Macintosh Toolbox sends an update event to the application if any of its windows has an invalid area that needs updating (Step 5). MacApp processes the update by calling the window's `Update` function (step 6). This traverses the view hierarchy, calling the `Draw` function for views that require updating (step 7).

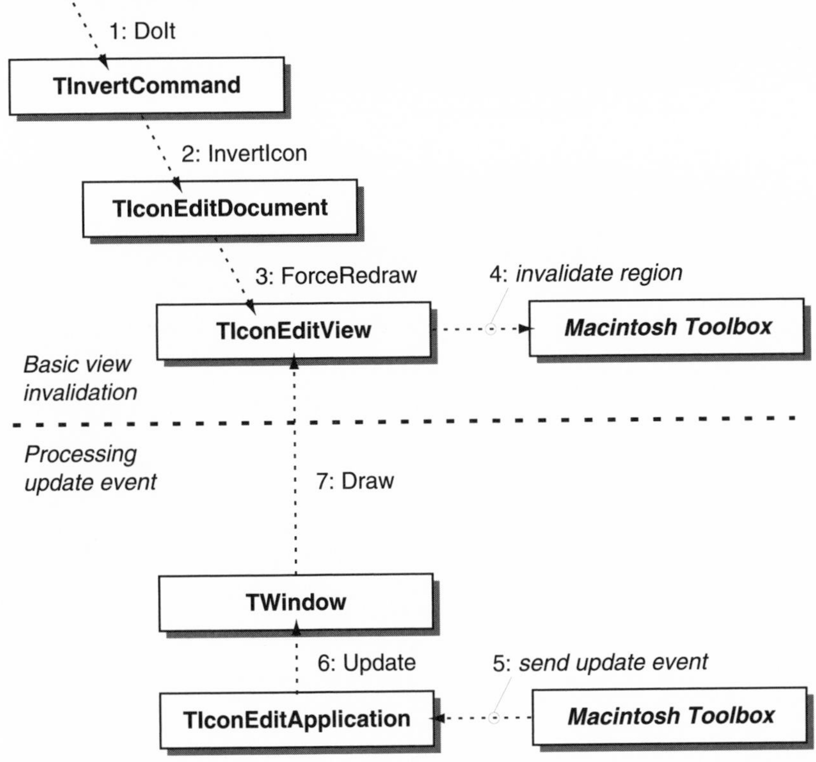

Figure 5.8 Messages sent during basic view invalidation and update processing

Figure 5.8 shows the document object directly invalidating the view. Although this implementation works, it is not very extensible. If you wanted to modify the application to show more than one view of the same document, you would have to modify the document object to invalidate the additional views. This change would have to be made in each place the document changed its data.

Instead, it is better for the document to indirectly update its view. That way, it doesn't have to be aware of all the views that may be displaying its data.

MacApp provides a general dependency mechanism that solves this problem. Any object in the application can be a dependent of another object. When an object changes, all its dependents are notified of the change. In the case of documents and views, the view registers itself as a document dependent when it is created. Then when the document changes, the view will be notified and can invalidate itself.

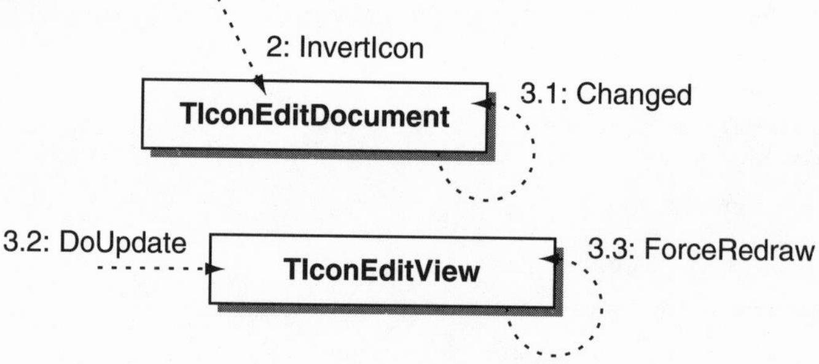

Figure 5.9 Messages sent during change propagation (expanding step 3 of Figure 5.8)

Figure 5.9 elaborates step 3 of Figure 5.8 to show how this works. To signal a change, the document calls its own `Changed` function (step 3.1). You do not have to override `Changed`. To distinguish between different kinds of changes, the `Changed` function accepts a change ID and the object that caused the change.

The `Changed` function finds all the dependents of the document, and for each calls the dependent's `DoUpdate` function for each (step 3.2). Since the process of finding dependents is implemented in MacApp, there's no direct "connection" between the document and view objects (That's why Figure 5.9 doesn't show the `DoUpdate` message as coming from `TIconEditDocument`.).

You must override `DoUpdate` and take whatever action is appropriate. `DoUpdate` is passed the change ID, the object being changed, and the object that caused the change. In this case, `TIconEditView` overrides `DoUpdate` and responds by invalidating its entire extent (step 3.3). In a more sophisticated application, the view would try to minimize the invalidated area based on what part of the document actually changed. In that case, the change ID would indicate the kind of change made to the document.

Using the dependency mechanism decouples the document from its views. This makes it easier to modify the icon editor to support multiple views of the same document (e.g., at different magnifications).

MacApp's MVC mechanism is not tied to views and documents. It can be used between any two objects in MacApp. For example, a complicated document may be implemented using several objects which synchronize with one another by using the dependency mechanism.

Table 5.4 lists the classes and member functions contained in the icon editor at this point

Table 5.4 MacApp `IconEdit` application incorporating updates

Classes	Member functions
`TIconEditApplication`	`DoMakeDocument`
`TIconEditDocument`	`DoInitialState`
	`DoMakeViews`
	`DoRead`
	`DoWrite`
	`DoNeedDiskSpace`
	`DoSetupMenus`
	`DoMenuCommand`
	`InvertIcon`
`TIconEditView`	`Draw`
	`DoUpdate`
`TInvertCommand`	`DoIt`
	`UndoIt`
	`RedoIt`

5.4.5 Mouse Tracking

Selecting items from a menu is only one way of making a change to a document. Another way is to use the mouse to directly change the document. In the case of the icon editor, we want to allow the user to draw directly within the view.

MacApp defines a `TTracker` class that you subclass to implement a mouse-based command. `TTracker` is a subclass of `TCommand`, which means it inherits the `DoIt`, `UndoIt`, and `RedoIt` functions defined in `TCommand`. In addition, it adds functions specifically for tracking the mouse. The two important tracker functions are `TrackMouse` and `TrackFeedback`.

`TrackMouse` is responsible for updating the state of the tracker based on the current mouse position and the anchor point, which is the point at which the user initially clicked. `TrackFeedback` is responsible for giving the user visual feedback on the state of the tracker.

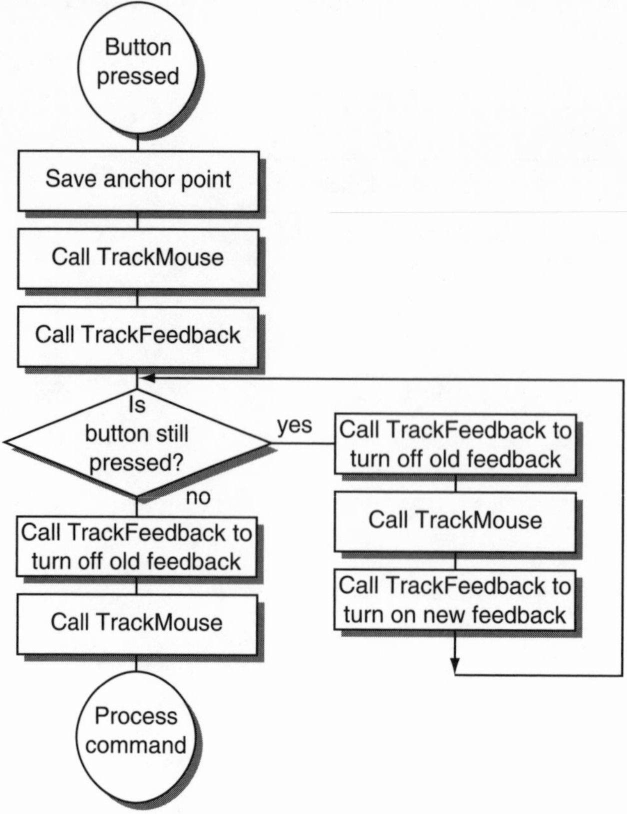

Figure 5.10 Mouse tracking flow of control

MacApp calls these functions from within a tracking loop. The loop starts when the user presses the mouse button, and finishes when the user releases the button. A flowchart of the loop is shown in Figure 5.10.

Note that MacApp calls `TrackFeedback` twice each time through the loop: once to turn off the old feedback and once to turn on the new feedback.

At the end of the tracking loop, `TrackMouse` returns a command object that encapsulates the change to the document. MacApp processes this command object as described earlier. In most cases, this command object is the same one that did the tracking (Recall that `TTracker` is a subclass of `TCommand`.).

The icon editor defines the `TIconDrawCommand` class that allows the user to draw directly into the icon. The class starts by creating a copy of the icon, which it can modify. The `TrackMouse` function updates the appropriate bit in this icon, while the `TrackFeedback` function draws the update bit in the view.

When the user releases the mouse button, MacApp calls the tracker's `DoIt` function, which installs the modified icon in the document and saves the original icon. `UndoIt` and `RedoIt` simply swap between the original and modified icons.

Adding this mouse-based command requires implementing the tracker class as well as overriding `DoMouseCommand`, as shown in Table 5.5.

Table 5.5 MacApp `IconEdit` application incorporating mouse tracking

Classes	Member functions
TIconEditApplication	DoMakeDocument
TIconEditDocument	DoInitialState
	DoMakeViews
	DoRead
	DoWrite
	DoNeedDiskSpace
	DoSetupMenus
	DoMenuCommand
	InvertIcon
TIconEditView	Draw
	DoUpdate
	DoMouseCommand
TInvertCommand	DoIt
	UndoIt
	RedoIt
TIconDrawCommand	TrackMouse
	TrackFeedback
	DoIt
	UndoIt
	RedoIt

5.4.6 Summary

You've seen how MacApp provides the basic skeleton of a standard Macintosh application. Any function that is application-specific is implemented by a member function that one of the application's classes overrides. For example, MacApp handles the details of calling the Macintosh Toolbox to invalidate part of a window, and of processing the subsequent update event. But when it comes time to draw the contents of the window, it calls the view's `Draw` function, which you must override.

Frameworks that you design and implement will take the same approach. Your goal is to implement the common parts of your problem in the framework, while giving the framework clients the flexibility to customize it to their needs. These seem like conflicting goals (standardization and flexibility), but object-oriented languages help satisfy both at the same time.

You may not see the benefit of frameworks immediately. It requires more care to design a reusable framework than it does a single application. But once you have a second project and can reuse the framework design and implementation, you should begin to see the advantages.

Further Reading

[Apple94] Apple Computer, Inc., *Inside Macintosh: Imaging with QuickDraw*, Addison Wesley, 1994.

[Apple92] Apple Computer, Inc., *Inside Macintosh: Macintosh Toolbox Essentials*, Addison Wesley, 1992.

[MacApp] MacApp is available from APDA, Apple Computer, Inc., P.O. Box 319, Buffalo, NY 14207-0319.

[Wilson90] D. A. Wilson, L. S. Rosenstein, and D. Shafer, *C++ Programming with MacApp*, Addison Wesley, 1990. Covers MacApp 2.0.

CHAPTER 6

Reusing Microsoft's Foundation Class Library—A Programmer's Perspective

WOLFGANG PREE

Preview

Microsoft's Foundation Class Library®*(MFC; Microsoft 1994) constitutes a GUI application framework implemented in C++ for the development of Windows applications. Its principal architecture builds on the lessons learned from other GUI frameworks such as MacApp [Apple89; Wilson90; see Chapter 5 in this book], ET++ [Weinand88 and 92, Gamma92; see Chapter 7 in this book] and Interviews [Linton89; see Chapter 8 in this book].

A sample application for analyzing capital gains is used to illustrate how to use MFC. A user of this application enters an initial amount, the interest rate, and monthly payments or withdrawals. The application plots a curve that reflects the implied effects over the years. Figure 6.1 shows a snapshot of this application.

We point out MFC's core architecture and mechanisms, and demonstrate how the framework specialization is reduced by appropriate tools. A discussion of MFC's design concludes this chapter.

6.1 Features of the MFC Framework

MFC applications can perform the following functions:

- Manage an arbitrary number of windows, together with their data and the visual representation of these data.
- Take care of windows (moving, resizing, activation on clicking, and so on) and their contents (invalidating regions when windows are brought in front of others, etc.).

* This contribution is based on MFC Version 2.5 and Microsoft's Visual C++ Development System 1.5

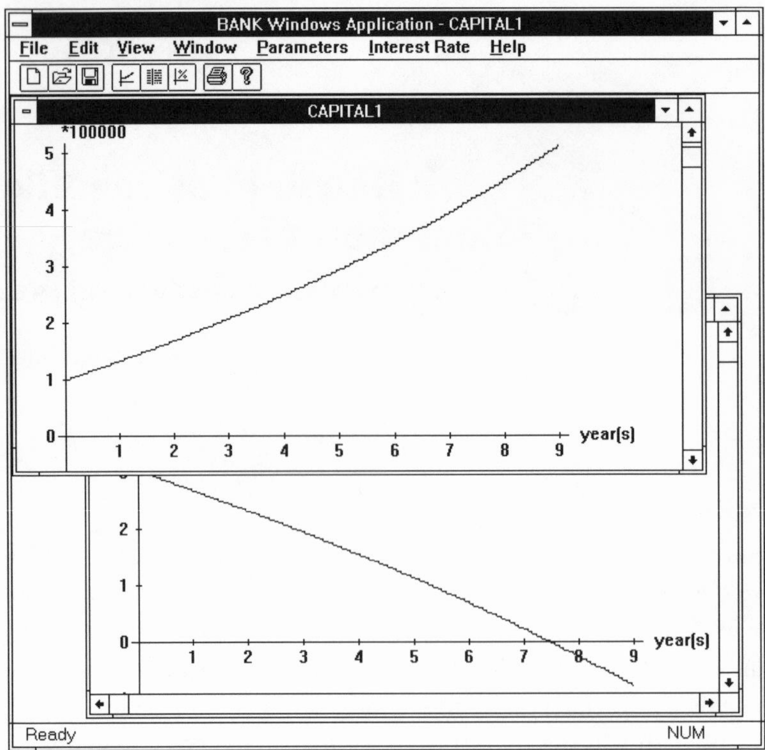

Figure 6.1 Sample application built with the MFC framework

- Handle the File menu commands `Open`, `Save`, `Save As`, `Print`, and `Print Preview` via the corresponding default dialogs. These commands can also be invoked by pressing buttons on the tool bar.
- Process input data of control items in dialog boxes.

Supporting the following features of Windows applications requires specialization of MFC reusable components:

- Event handling: in order to make possible the selection of objects by means of the mouse, MFC provides mechanisms for handling events (mouse movements, mouse clicks, menu selection, keyboard input, and so on).
- Access to relational databases: MFC database classes allow the programmer to manipulate data relying on the Open Database

Connectivity (ODBC) standard. So a high degree of database management system independence is achieved.

- Object Linking and Embedding (OLE)
- Context-sensitive help

6.2 A MFC-Friendly Environment

The minimum set of tools required to adapt the MFC framework are a text editor and a suitable C++ compiler and linker. Fortunately, a much more powerful tool suite is offered, for example, by Microsoft's Visual C++ development system. Since the tools AppWizard and ClassWizard are specifically tailored to MFC, we will describe them in more detail (see Section 6.3). AppWizard and ClassWizard directly support the adaptation of MFC classes and mechanisms. AppWizard is used only once during application development, to generate all necessary classes forming a "blank" Windows application having default menus, window handling, etc. ClassWizard eases the task of reacting to specific events. It also allows the user to generate new classes and to map instance variables to control items in dialogs. ClassWizard is used during the whole development cycle of an application.

Furthermore, the development system smoothly integrates the following tools:

- A resource editor called AppStudio
- A source editor tailored to C++ sources
- A class browser and query tool
- A debugger
- A project manager
- And last but not least, a C/C++ compiler and linker

6.3 MFC's Cornerstones

This section focuses on principal mechanisms and concepts incorporated in the MFC framework. The MFC framework provides elementary user interface building blocks (for example, buttons and menus), basic data structures (for example, the classes `CObList`, `CObArray`, `CDate`, and

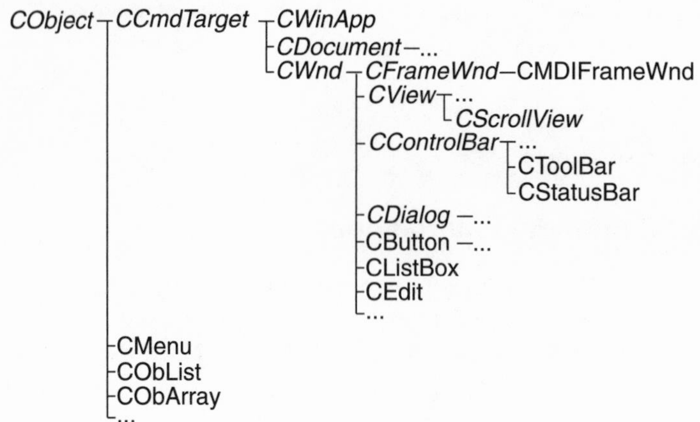

Figure 6.2 Core classes of the MFC framework

`CString`) and high-level application components such as the classes `CWinApp`, `CDocument`, `CView` and `CWnd`. Together with the elementary building blocks, the high-level application components predefine, as far as possible, the look and feel of MFC-based applications.

Figure 6.2 shows the inheritance relationships of MFC classes that are relevant in this context. Abstract classes are written in italics. According to MFC's naming conventions, class names start with *C*.

Root class

Almost all MFC classes are derived from class `CObject`, and so inherit its behavior. The abstract class `CObject` defines and partially implements the protocol for *meta-information* and object serialization.

Meta-information is a generic term for information about objects and classes. C++ does not allow inquiries about an object, such as its class. Due to this deficiency, many C++ libraries implement a mechanism to provide meta-information. Like other class libraries, MFC uses macros to extract the necessary information out of a class in header and implementation files. MFC offers only rudimentary access to meta-information, by the method `IsKindOf(classname)`. This method returns `TRUE` if the receiving object is an instance of `classname` or one of its subclasses.

Serialization by means of method `Serialize` allows the user to write and read the contents of an object, i.e., the values stored in the instance variables, to and from a file.

Data Structure Classes

The MFC framework offers classes to store objects in lists, arrays, and dictionaries (called *maps* in MFC; they store key/value pairs). These components are typically used without any modifications.

Classes Defining a Generic Windows Application

In general, GUI applications are *event-driven,* and try to avoid modes. As a consequence, the user of an event-driven application ideally can enter commands in any order via input devices such as a mouse or keyboard. A GUI application has to process incoming events accordingly. For example, clicking with the mouse on the title bar of a window should be handled by a GUI application in such a way that the window can then be moved by the mouse. Clicking on the menu bar should cause the corresponding menu to open. The user should be able to select an item by moving the mouse over the menu and releasing the mouse button over the desired item. While the mouse is moved over a menu, the corresponding menu items have to be highlighted.

In MFC, a `CWinApp` object gathers incoming events and dispatches them to the various components of the application. Each running application has exactly one `CWinApp` object. After a Windows application is started, MFC's `WinMain` function is called and sends the messages `Init-Instance` and `Run` to the particular `CWinApp` object—actually to an instance of a subclass of the abstract class `CWinApp`. Invoking method `Run` starts the *event loop,* a loop that constantly processes incoming events (see Figure 6.3).

Many GUI applications are document-oriented; i.e., they manage documents. For example, any number of spreadsheets can be handled by a spreadsheet application. The data constituting one spreadsheet (its numbers, formulas, and the text contained in the cells) are handled by a subclass of the abstract class `CDocument`.

MFC directly supports document-oriented applications. Its core architecture is a derivative of MVC (see Chapter 2).

The MFC classes `CDocument` and `CView` correspond to the model and view components of MVC. The fact that a `CDocument` object can have several `CView` objects to display its data (i.e., model) closely resembles the MVC concept. How the controller aspect of MVC is handled in MFC is discussed below in the next section.

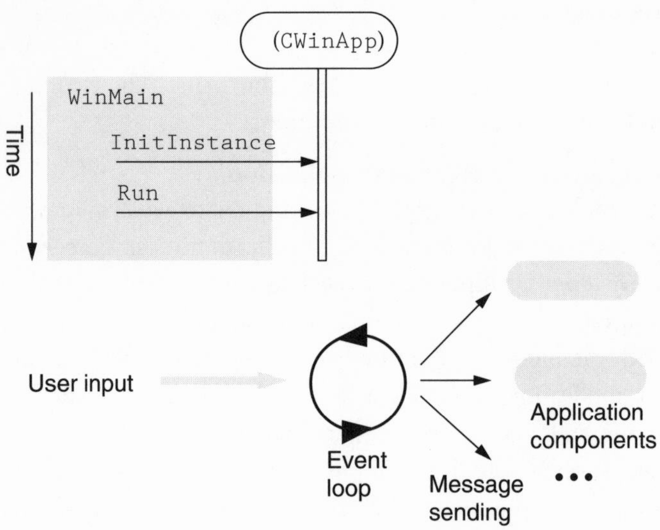

Figure 6.3 Starting the event loop in a MFC application

Another property of class `CWinApp` is that a `CWinApp` object conceptually manages any number of `CDocument` objects. (The actual MFC implementation deviates slightly from this conceptual view. Since this detail is irrelevant in this context we will not discuss it.) Figure 6.4 applies the OMT notation [Rumbaugh91] to depict the object structure of a MFC-based application. In the figure, the upper `CDocument` object refers to one `CView` object, through which the end user views and edits its data. The contents of the other `CDocument` object are displayed and edited by

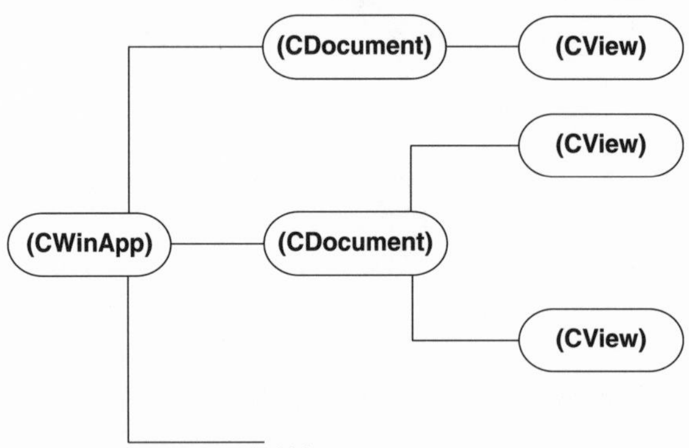

Figure 6.4 Principal object relationships in a MFC-based application

two CView objects. The CWinApp objects takes care of all CDocument objects. For example, if the user quits the application, the CWinApp object asks the CDocument object to check whether changes in their data should be saved or not.

If the initial MFC adaptation is generated by AppWizard, the programmer can choose whether the application manages exactly one document (Single Document Interface, SDI) or an arbitrary number of documents (Multiple Document Interface, MDI). The class CWinApp can also be used to implement nondocument-oriented applications such as desktop calculators.

Event handling

The way events are handled in MFC is pretty close to the conventional C function library called Windows Software Development Kit (SDK). The SDK library supports a callback style of programming: the library functions read events and call out to various functions which the application programmer has previously registered with the library functions. These callback functions are invoked with an event identifier and parameter values, with details regarding a particular event. So applications based on SDK usually have functions with extensive switch statements determining which particular event happened. Depending on the event identifier, the additional parameter values have to be type cast. This way of handling events is error-prone—break statements might be forgotten, inappropriate type casts can cause subtle runtime errors, etc.

MFC alleviates this problem a bit by encapsulating the identification of incoming events. Depending on the identified event, certain methods are called with the corresponding parameters.

Unfortunately, these event handling methods are not declared as dynamically bound methods in the MFC classes. Dynamic binding is reimplemented (for efficiency reasons?!) via clumsy macro statements. Let us illustrate this by an example. When the left mouse button is pressed over a CSampleView object (CSampleView being a subclass of CView), MFC calls method OnLButtonDown of the CSampleView object only if

- This method is overridden in CSampleView.
- The overridden method is marked as a special event handling method by the add-on afx_msg in the class definition, see Figure 6.5.

- The macro `DECLARE_MESSAGE_MAP` is called in the class definition, see Figure 6.5.
- The macro `ON_WM_LBUTTONDOWN()` is contained in the message map declaration of the implementation file, see Figure 6.5.

Though this significant overhead for implementing event handling methods can be generated by the ClassWizard tool, the readability of header and implementation files suffers.

If an object does not react to a Windows event, MFC forwards the event to other objects. This forwarding mechanism is based on Windows-specific strategies which we will not discuss here.

```
header file with class definition:
    class CSampleView: public CView {
    public:
        . . .
        afx_msg void OnLButtonDown(UINT nFlags, CPoint point);
        DECLARE_MESSAGE_MAP()
    protected:
        . . .
    };

implementation file:
    . . .
    BEGIN_MESSAGE_MAP(CSampleView,CView)
        //{{AFX_MSG_MAP(CSampleView)
        . . .

        ON_WM_LBUTTONDOWN()
        . . .
        //}}AFX_MSG_MAP
    END_MESSAGE_MAP()
    . . .
    void CSampleView::OnLButtonDown(UINT nFlags, CPoint point)
    {
        . . .
    }
    . . .
```

Figure 6.5 MFC-specific reimplementation of dynamic binding for event handling methods

6.4 Adaptation Support

AppWizard, ClassWizard, and the resource editor AppStudio strongly support the adaptation of the MFC framework to a specific application. In effect, an application is produced by a combination of program generation and overriding, plus some coding. Microsoft's Visual C++ development system integrates these tools into an environment.

In order to demonstrate adaptation we develop a capital gain analysis application, a part of which is shown in Figure 6.1.

Generation of the Application Skeleton

AppWizard is used once in the adaptation process. A programmer specifies various options via a dialog, for example, whether the application should handle exactly one document (SDI) or any number of documents (MDI). If the user chooses MDI, AppWizard generates the corresponding subclasses of `CWinApp`, `CDocument`, `CView`, and `CMDIFrameWnd` (see Figure 6.6).

Viewing a document's data

According to the MVC-related separation of data and their graphical representation, we add the required instance variables and access methods to `CCaptialDoc`: for this simple capital gain analysis, a `CCapitalDoc` object stores the initially invested amount, the monthly payment, the interest rate, and the date when the capital is invested. The corresponding values can be entered by the application user via a dialog box whose implementation is sketched in the next section.

In order to display the data, a grid consisting of a time axis and a capital axis as well as the capital gain curve, has to be drawn. For this reason, the programmer overrides `OnDraw` of class `CView` in the subclass `CCaptialView`. The framework calls `OnDraw` to draw on the screen and the printer. MFC takes care to redraw views, for example, if windows are brought in front of others. If the data change, the document causes a

```
CObject ┬ CCmdTarget ┬ CWinApp ─ CCaptialApp
        │            ├ CDocument ─ CCaptialDoc
        │            └ CWnd ┬ CFrameWnd ─ CMDIFrameWnd ─ CMainFrame
        │                   ├ CView ┬ ...
        │                   │       └ CScrollView ─ CCaptialView
        │                   └ ...
        └ ...
```

Figure 6.6 Classes generated by AppWizard (written in bold face)

```
void CCapitalView::OnDraw(CDC *pDC)
{
    CPen penStroke,
    penStroke.CreatePen(.........);
    . . .
    pDC->MoveTo(CPoint(......));
    pDC->LineTo(CPoint(......));
    . . .
    // access to document's data
    ...= GetDocument()->GetInterestRate();
        // GetDocument() is a method generated by AppWizard
        // in class CCapitalView; it returns a CCapitalDoc pointer
    . . .
    pDC->TextOut(xPos, YPos, ". . .");
    . . .
}
```

Figure 6.7 Fragments of CCapitalView's OnDraw method

redraw operation of all associated views by invoking its method `UpdateAllViews`.

MFC encapsulates SDK-specific functions for producing graphical output by classes such as `CDC` (for drawing context), `CPen`, and `CFont`. Figure 6.7 shows some fragments of the `OnDraw` method.

Menu and Dialog Handling

This section explains how the resource editor AppStudio and the ClassWizard tool automate the adaptation of the MFC framework.

Remember that a document's data should be entered via a dialog box. The application user should be able to open this dialog by choosing a menu item. We assume that the menu item Initial Parameters opens the corresponding dialog box, see Figure 6.8.

In order to implement this behavior, a programmer simply "draws" the menu with AppStudio. AppStudio works like other user interface building tools to create and rearrange items in menus, dialog boxes, and the tool bar, in a direct-manipulation interface style. A programmer defines user interface element properties in dialog boxes. Besides these item-specific properties, AppStudio assigns an identifier to each item and relates unique integer numbers to these identifiers. The identifier names can be changed by the programmer. Figure 6.9 illustrates that we chose the identifier `ID_INIT_PARAMS` for the Initial Parameters menu item.

Figure 6.10 shows how to implement the handling of the Initial Parameters menu item using the ClassWizard tool. In the upper left

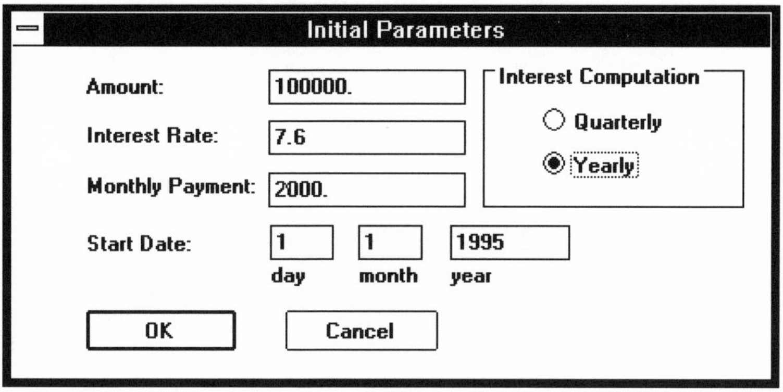

Figure 6.8 Snapshot of the Initial Parameters dialog box

combo box of ClassWizard, the class `CCapitalDoc` is selected as the message handler.

In connection with menu items, a programmer can do the following:

- Handle the actual menu item selection.
- Enable or disable a menu item.

In order to react to a menu item selection, `COMMAND` has to be chosen in the right hand message list, see Figure 6.10.

By pressing the Add Function button, the necessary changes are accomplished in the header and implementation files of class `CCapitalDoc`, analogous to the description in Section 6.2 on event handling. The programmer only has to provide the application-specific code then. Figure 6.11 lists the code generated by ClassWizard in bold face.

In order to implement `OnInitialParameters`, an appropriate `CDialog` subclass has to be implemented first. AppStudio and ClassWizard allow the programmer to generate this class. Using AppStudio, a

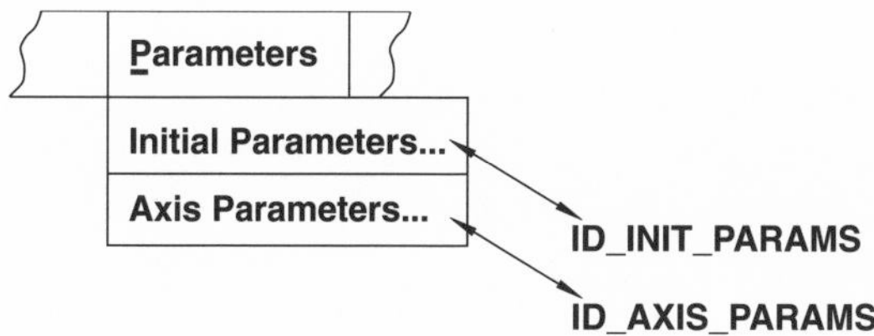

Figure 6.9 Menu specification with AppStudio

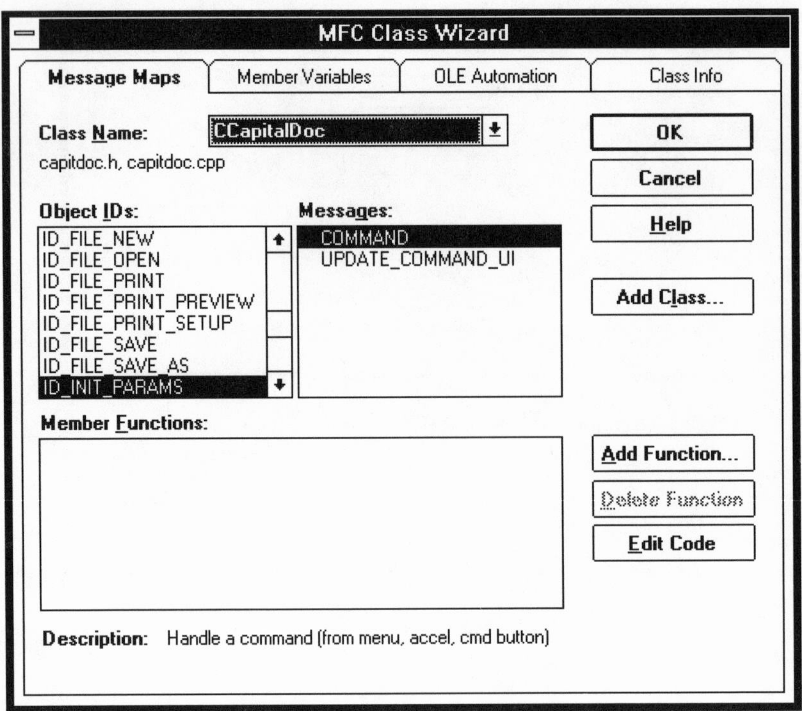

Figure 6.10 Snapshot of the ClassWizard tool

programmer can quickly create the dialog box. Similar to menu items, dialog controls such as buttons and edit fields have unique identifiers.

The `CDialog` subclass that deals with the corresponding resource is created simply by invoking ClassWizard from AppStudio. ClassWizard automatically prompts an Add Class dialog where the programmer can change the proposed class and file names. After the `CDialog` subclass is generated, the programmer can add instance variables that correspond to dialog controls, see Figure 6.12.

ClassWizard declares these instance variables in the class definition and initializes them in the constructor. Depending on the type of an instance variable, a value range can be specified, too. In this case, ClassWizard generates the necessary code in the dialog class to ensure the entering of valid data. For example, the instance variable `InterestRate` should accept only values between 0 and 20.

The generated class `CInitParamsDlg` can now be used in the method `OnInitialParameters`, see Figure 6.13. The method `DoModal` opens the

```
header file with class definition:
    class CCapitalDoc: public CDocument {
    public:
        . . .
        afx_msg void OnInitialParameters();
        DECLARE_MESSAGE_MAP()
    protected:
        . . .
    };

implementation file:
    . . .
    BEGIN_MESSAGE_MAP(CCapitalDoc,CDocument)
        //{{AFX_MSG_MAP(CCapitalDoc)
        . . .
        ON_COMMAND(ID_INIT_PARAMS, OnInitialParameters)
        . . .
        //}}AFX_MSG_MAP
    END_MESSAGE_MAP()
    . . .
    void CCapitalDoc::OnInitialParameters()
    {
        // TODO: Add your command handling code here
    }
    . . .
```

Figure 6.11 Code generated by ClassWizard

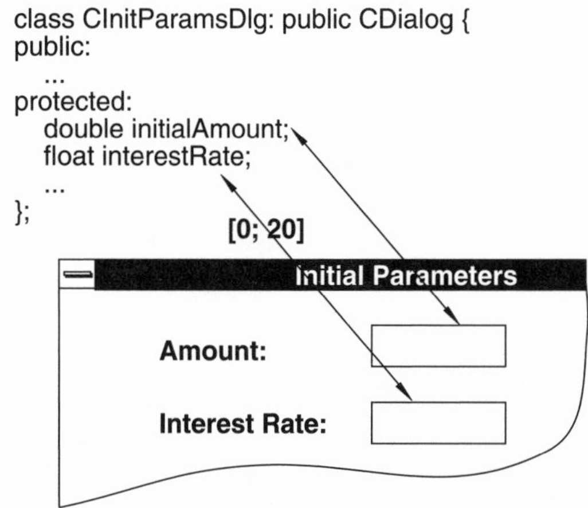

Figure 6.12 Mapping between dialog controls and instance variables of a CDialog subclass

```
void CCapitalDoc::OnInitialParameters()
{
    CInitParamsDlg initParamsDlg;
    // dialog controls <- values of document instance variables
    initParamsDlg.initAmount= initAmount;
    . . .
    if (initParamsDlg.DoModal() == IDOK) {
        // document instance variables <- values displayed
        //                                  in dialog controls
        initAmount= initParamsDlg.initAmount;
        . . .
        UpdateAllViews(...);
    }
}
```

Figure 6.13 Handling of the Initial Parameters menu item

dialog as a modal dialog (i.e., the user has to close the dialog before continuing to work with the application) and returns `IDOK` after the OK button is pressed.

Figure 6.14 illustrates the interaction between the principal components of the capital gain analysis application after the user has chosen the Initial Parameters menu item.

6.5 Design Issues

The tool support for adapting MFC substantially eases application development. On the other hand, we recognize some shortcomings when taking a look at the design of the MFC framework.

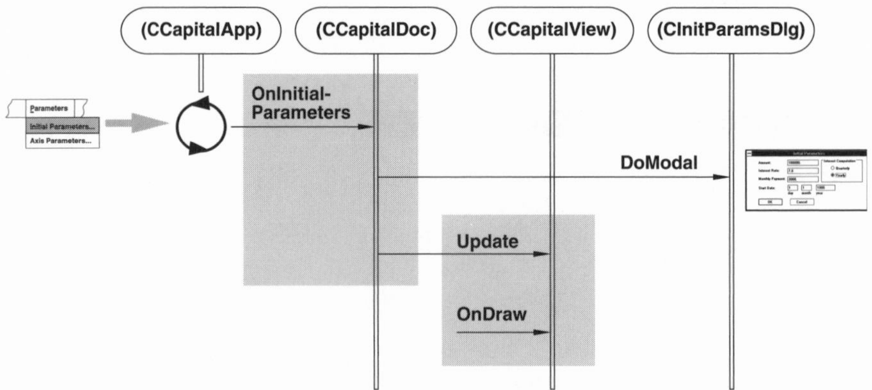

Figure 6.14 Dynamic aspects of the capital gain analysis application

Several GUI frameworks have gone through an evolutionary development process. For example, early versions of MacApp (see Chapter 5) constituted a thin layer above the conventional Macintosh toolbox. Experience with a GUI framework that "wraps" a conventional library has corroborated that it takes time to smoothly integrate advanced abstractions of the GUI domain that significantly ease the implementation of sophisticated features. MFC lacks support for features that are often essential in the GUI domain. In general, MFC is apparently a GUI framework in its early development stages for several reasons:

- MFC programmers are often confronted with SDK-related details. The MFC framework is still a thin layer on top of SDK. For example, MFC programmers have to know Windows message identifiers in the realm of event handling. Another example is that programmers deal with the Windows-SDK-specific device context when coding graphical output. Though SDK-pitfalls are avoided, MFC programmers have to be familiar with SDK-specific mechanisms. (This can also be advertised as an advantage: SDK programmers can transfer their know-how when using MFC.)
- Besides numerous spots where the MFC programmer strongly feels the Windows SDK pulse, there are various features that are essential in the GUI domain but are not adequately addressed by MFC:
  - MFC does not incorporate a miniframework for undoable commands. Each MFC-based application has to implement this aspect on its own.
  - MFC does not support the implementation of direct-manipulation features (e.g., feedback the in case of mouse tracking).
  - Scrolling or splitting of the window contents still requires too much implementation effort compared to state-of-the-art GUI frameworks (such as ET++ and MacApp). Zooming is not supported at all in MFC.

Due to these deficiencies, enormous effort would, for example, be attached to the implementation of a MFC-based hypertext system which allows a user to edit hypertext documents (including a text drag-and-drop functionality) and to edit the graph that shows how the hypertext documents are linked.

A reason for the last two deficiencies might be that the abstraction CWnd is inappropriate. CWnd represents too heavyweight an abstraction for "visual objects." All subclasses, such as control items, inherit, for example, the clipping property. Thus, it would be inefficient to base other components—such as a collection view that displays a list of items—on CWnd. For example, ET++ offers a lightweight abstraction called VObject instead of CWnd, see Chapter 7. Many other ET++ components, such as Menu, CollectionView, TreeView, GraphView, Scroller, Splitter, and Zoomer are based on VObject, so that these deficiencies can be avoided elegantly.

As far as language-related implementation details are concerned, MFC confuses the programmer. Dynamic binding works in C++ only if objects are generated dynamically (new). Since MFC circumvents this C++ feature in the realm of message handling and reintroduces it via macro calls, the programmer can declare variables statically and still have the dynamic binding flavor. But other (C++) dynamically bound methods won't work then because of the static variable declaration.

6.6 Summary

Despite MFC's deficiencies, it turns out to be significantly easier and less error-prone to develop Windows applications using MFC, compared to the conventional C function library SDK.

Though MFC does not directly address the development of sophisticated GUI applications (e.g., applications relying on an easy-to-use and intuitive direct-manipulation user interface style), MFC is well suited to produce applications with numerous dialogs. Many traditional commercial applications apply dialogs for entering parameters for database queries and displaying their results. The enhancements of the latest versions of MFC and the Visual C++ development system focus on access support to relational databases and thus corroborate this point of view.

The MFC framework benefits enormously from the well-integrated framework adaptation and development environment. Beginners might even be confused—what's in the framework and what is provided by the environment?

Further Reading

[Apple89] Apple Computer, *MacAppII Programmer's Guide, 1989.*

[Gamma92] E. Gamma, *Objektorientierte Software-Entwicklung am Beispiel von ET++: Design-Muster, Klassenbibliothek, Werkzeuge,* doctoral thesis, University of Zürich, 1991; published by Springer Verlag, 1992.

[Krasner88] G. E. Krasner and S.T. Pope, A cookbook for using the model-view-controller user interface paradigm in Smalltalk-80, *Journal of Object-Oriented Programming,* **1** (3), 1988.

[Linton89] M. A. Linton, J. M. Vlissides, and P. R. Calder, Composing user interfaces with InterViews, *Computer,* **22** (2), 1989.

[Microsoft94] Microsoft Corporation, *Visual C++ and Microsoft Foundation Class Library Manuals,* 1994.

[Rumbaugh91] J. Rumbaugh, M. Blaha, W. Premerlani, F. Edd., and W. Lorensen, *Object-Oriented Modeling and Design,* Prentice Hall, Englewood Cliffs, 1991.

[Weinand88] A. Weinand, E. Gamma, and R. Marty, ET++ —An object-oriented application framework in C++ OOPSLA'88, Special Issue of *SIGPLAN Notices,* **23** (11), 1988.

[Weinand92] A. Weinand, *Objektorientierter Entwurf und Implementierung portabler Fensterumgebungen am Beispiel des Application-Frameworks ET++,* doctoral thesis, University of Zürich, 1991; published by Springer Verlag, 1992.

[Wilson90] D.A. Wilson, L.S. Rosenstein, and D. Shafer, *Programming with MacApp,* Addison-Wesley, 1990.

CHAPTER 7

ET++ — a Portable, Homogeneous Class Library and Application Framework

ANDRÉ WEINAND AND ERICH GAMMA

Preview

This chapter presents the design, architecture, and construction of ET++, an object-oriented application framework implemented in C++ for a UNIX environment and various standard window systems. ET++ 3.0 and its tools and documentation are distributed in the public domain. It is available by anonymous ftp from `ftp.ubilab.ubs.ch` in the directory `pub/ET++`. The current release of ET++ runs under X11, SunWindow, and the Macintosh.

ET++ incorporates a portable and homogeneous object-oriented class library integrating user interface building blocks, basic data structures, and high-level application framework components. ET++ eases the building of highly interactive applications with consistent user interfaces following the direct manipulation principle.

The ET++ class library is implemented in C++, and can be used on several operating systems and window system platforms. Since its conception, the class library has been continuously redesigned and improved. It started with an architecture which was close to MacApp. Over several iterations a new and unique architecture evolved.

A by-product of the ET++ project is a set of tools which were designed to support the exploration of ET++ applications at runtime. This chapter covers the design philosophy and some of the tools associated with the ET++ framework.

7.1 From Toolbox to Application Framework

Making computers easier to use is one of the reasons for the interest in interactive and graphical user interfaces that present information as pictures instead of text and numbers. They are easy to learn and fun to use. Constructing such interfaces, on the other hand, often requires considerable effort because they must not only provide the functionality of conventional programs, but also have to show data as well as manipulation concepts in a pictorial way. Handling user commands from input devices such as a mouse or a keyboard in order to build an event-driven application complicates the programmer's task even more. Commonly, up to 50–80% of the code is devoted to user interface aspects.

Much of the user-friendliness of applications comes not only from an iconic user interface but also from a uniform user interface across applications. This leads to a significant amount of development redundancy, because most of the code required by the user interface has to be reengineered for every new application.

A first solution to reduce this complexity has been the invention of so-called toolboxes, rich collections of library functions that implement the low level components of the user interface like windows, menus, and scrollbars. Modern toolbox implementations like the *Motif toolkit* for the X Window System [Berlage91] use object-oriented programming techniques to improve flexibility and extensibility by dynamic binding and inheritance.

Much of a typical application's main program built on top of a toolbox is merely program *glue* that manages the calling of toolbox subroutines, or in object-oriented toolboxes, implements the callbacks invoked by the toolkit. The major drawback of the toolbox approach is that it does not define an overall structure for an application. In addition, toolboxes can only ensure user interface consistency at the level of individual user interface widgets, and not at the application level. A partial solution is to provide developers with a program skeleton which can be copied and modified to fit the application's requirements. But skeletons are not the optimal solution, because they duplicate code which should go into a library, and because they make the application code more complex and less manageable.

A promising solution is that of an (object-oriented) framework in general, and an application framework in particular. While the framework approach is useful for the development of any software, it is especially attractive if a standard user interface should be encouraged, for it is possible to completely define the components that implement this standard and to provide these reusable components as building blocks to other developers. This is an advantage over the toolbox approach, where user interface *look-and-feel* guidelines are by prescription rather than implementation.

7.2 An Example of an ET++ Application

Figure 7.1 shows a screen dump of ET++Draw to give an idea of what kind of applications ET++ supports. ET++Draw is a classical drawing program. The following list highlights some tasks ET++ takes care of without any special effort by the programmer when building applications such as ET++Draw:

- Editing of several drawings in several windows.
- Scrolling of the window contents (including autoscrolling and real-time scrolling).
- Displaying disconnected portions of the drawing by using several panes.
- File and dialog management for loading and storing a document.

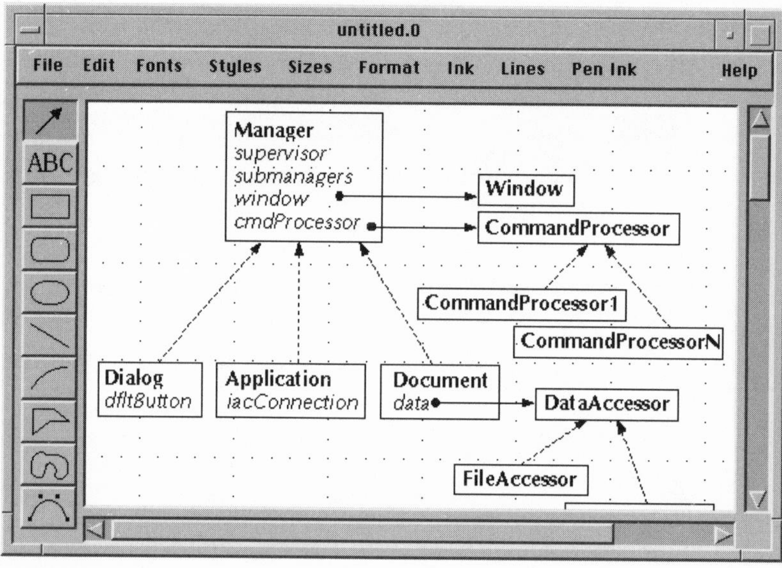

Figure 7.1 ET++Draw an example of an ET++ application

- Incremental flicker-free screen update based on double buffering.
- Device-independent hard copy output of the drawing, for example, in PostScript. The printing of the drawing can always be previewed on the screen.
- The application runs on all window systems supported by ET++.
- The appearance of user interface widgets like scrollbars and buttons can be switched dynamically at runtime. Currently, Motif- and Macintosh-inspired ET++ looks are supported.

Other parts of the implementation that are not handled automatically but are supported by components of ET++ include:

- Data structures underlying the draw application (lists, sets, dictionaries, etc.).
- A powerful text-building block which supports editing of rich text, that is, text with different character and paragraph attributes.
- Input/output of the data structures used in the application (even data structures containing cycles, because ET++Draw supports arbitrary visual connections between shapes).
- Undoable commands (multilevel).
- A notification mechanism for maintaining dependencies among objects. ET++Draw uses this mechanism to implement the visual connections between shapes. A connection depends on the positions of the shapes it connects.
- Support for transferring a selection of shapes to the clipboard or to duplicate any shapes, a feature which substantially simplifies the implementation of undoable commands.
- Import and export of graphics, images, and text in standard exchange formats (e.g., TIFF, PICT, PBM, RTF) is facilitated by a converter framework.
- Automatic layout of a group of graphical objects, for example in dialog boxes.

7.3 Architectural Overview

The backbone of the ET++ architecture is a layered class hierarchy with about 300 classes, see Figure 7.2. This hierarchy is organized as a "mostly" single-rooted class library, that is, most of the classes descend from a common base class `Object`. While this organization is not very popular in C++, it has proven to be well suited for our needs. It enabled the implementation of some valuable infrastructure inherited by all descendants of `Object`, while also allowing us to step away from the root class when appropriate. For example, runtime access to information about the classes of an application (meta information) could be smoothly integrated into the class library by defining the corresponding infrastructure at the root class, yet geometric shapes in a drawing program can be defined as descendents of nonroot objects.

The *Toolkit layer* contains the most important low-level building blocks of the ET++ class hierarchy: the class `Object`, the root of the overall class hierarchy, implements the common behavior for all ET++ classes. *Data Structures* are general purpose classes, like arrays, lists, sets, etc.,

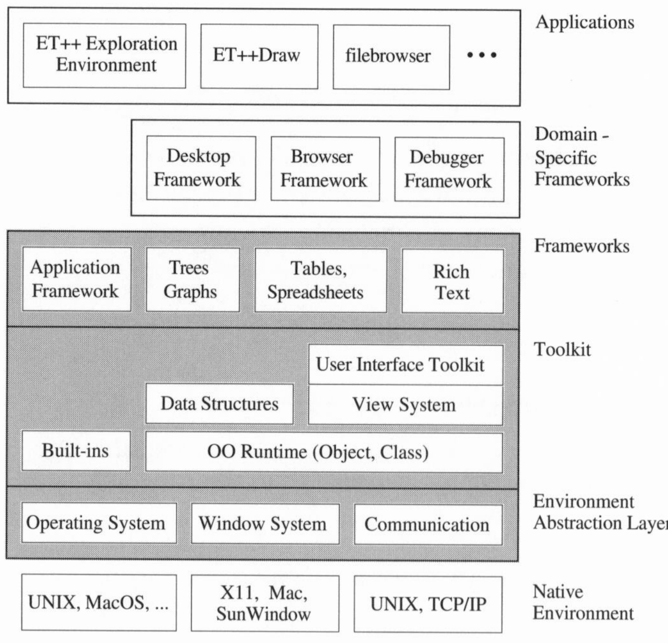

Figure 7.2 E++ architecture

which are used heavily in the implementation of ET++ itself. *View System* contains a small number of graphical building blocks which implement the common behavior of all graphical classes, and defines a framework to easily build new components from existing ones. *User Interface Toolkit* contains all the graphical and interactive components found in almost every user interface toolbox, such as menus, dialogs, or scrollbars.

The *Framework layer* contains a small number of high-level frameworks. The *Application Framework* classes are high-level abstract classes that factor out the common control structure of applications running in a graphic environment. They define the abstract model of a typical ET++ application, and together form a generic ET++ application. The other frameworks provide high-level and extensible building blocks for rich text, tables and spreadsheets, and trees and graphs.

On top of this core system are more domain-specific frameworks. These are part of the ET++ distribution, but are not the topic of this chapter.

ET++ Exploration Environment is a set of exploration tools which are automatically included in every application. The tools allow one to inspect the running application, to better understand the program.

The *Environment Abstraction layer* provides its own hierarchy of abstract classes for operating system services, interapplication communication, window management, input handling, and drawing on various devices. Subclasses exist for implementing the system interface layer's functionality for various native window and operating systems.

7.4 The Toolkit

7.4.1 Built-in Classes

ET++ is not strictly single-rooted, and not all classes descend from `Object`. Classes which are used like built-in types do not descend from `Object`. Examples are the geometry classes `Point` and `Rectangle`, or the class `String`. These classes are not used in a polymorphic way, and are treated as built-in types.

7.4.2 The Class Object

However, most classes of ET++ are derived from `Object`. `Object` defines protocols (abstract methods) for comparing objects, for notification between objects, and for object I/O, to name just the most important ones.

The ET++ object I/O facility supports the transfer of arbitrarily complex polymorphic data structures from memory to an ET++ stream and vice versa. This functionality is based on the abstract methods `PrintOn` and `ReadFrom`, which are overridden in subclasses to stream an object's instance variables. The power of the ET++ object I/O facility lies in the fact that the programmer does not have to distinguish between transmitting a pointer to an object and an ordinary scalar typed variable. Moreover, circular structures are linearized, and multiple references to the same object are restored properly. Storing pointers is implemented by a map per stream, which assigns a unique identifier to each transmitted instance. This identifier can be transferred to other address spaces or to permanent storage.*

Object I/O needs some information about the type of an object at runtime, because not only the state of an object but also its corresponding class have to be transmitted. ET++ runtime support would even provide enough information about an object's instance variables to implement the `PrintOn` and `ReadFrom` methods generically in the class `Object`. But we preferred the approach of a programmer selectively deciding which instance variables should be written to disk. Instance variables caching some state of an object that can easily be reconstructed in the `ReadFrom` method do not even have to be transferred to disk. Another example is a hash table that compacts itself, i.e., ignores empty slots, when it is saved.

The case of encountering an unknown class while reading back an object structure leads to the discussion of *dynamic loading and linking*. To handle this case gracefully, ET++ includes a mechanism to load a new class and link it to a running application. The implementation of dynamic linking in ET++ exploits the virtual function mechanism of C++ to provide type-safe incremental linking [Stroustrup87]. This dynamic linking support can be further used to extend a running system. In the ET++Draw application, e.g., a new kind of shape can be implemented and incrementally linked while the application is running.

The object input/output facility, together with the flexible stream classes of ET++, allowed the implementation of a generic `DeepClone`

---

* It is interesting to see that a pointer does not identify an object uniquely, because an object can be deleted after a transfer and another one allocated at the same address. Consequently, some precautions have to be taken to handle this case properly; otherwise, the same identifier would be assigned for different objects.

method for objects in the class `Object`:* The stream classes support object transfer not only to disk files but also to a buffer in memory. To do so, the `PrintOn` method is simply invoked to write an object to a dynamically growing buffer in memory; it is followed by `ReadFrom`, which creates the duplicate object by reading the buffer. Experience with ET++ has shown that `DeepClone` is hardly ever overridden in subclasses.

The object input/output facility is also used as the standard format for transferring arbitrary data structures to other ET++ applications via the clipboard. The transparent integration of dynamic linking into the object input/output mechanism allows the copying of instances of classes from the clipboard that are not known in the running application.

Another general mechanism provided by `Object` is *change notification*. The basic idea is to give some support to the synchronization of objects, for example, a model with its associated view in an MVC-design. Providing this mechanism at the root class of ET++ allows the synchronization of completely independent objects. Notification is modeled after Smalltalk-80's support for dependencies [Goldberg83]. `AddObserver` is the method for registering an object as dependent on another object. Modifications of the state of an object are announced with a `Changed` method, triggering a call of the `DoObserve` method for all dependent objects. To react to a change notification, `DoObserve` has to be overridden. The default implementation of notification in `Object` uses a space efficient global dictionary to store the Object's observers. Subclasses are free to provide implementations with better performance.

Notification has proved to be a very useful mechanism, and is not used only in MVC-designs. ET++Draw, for example, uses notification to maintain visible connections between arbitrary graphical elements.

7.4.3 Portable Runtime Support for C++

Even with the upcoming *runtime type information* standard for C++ (RTTI), the runtime system does not provide any information about the class structure or the instance variables of an object. Consequently, an additional mechanism has to be introduced to gather this information, in order to support an `IsKindOf` method and for the object I/O facility.

---

* A deep clone of an object consists of its instance variables plus a deep clone of all objects referenced by it.

ET++ uses the approach of associating with each class a special object describing its structure. These descriptors are instances of the class `Class` which is itself a subclass of `Object`. In analogy to Smalltalk-80, they are called *metaclasses.* (Strictly speaking this is a misnomer because these descriptors are not classes but only instances). Metaclasses store the following information about a class:

- The name of the class.
- The size of an instance in bytes.
- Its superclass.
- The names and types of its instance variables.
- A source code reference to the definition and implementation part of the class.

The types of the instance variables and the source code reference were introduced in order to give support for the ET++ exploration environment.

Because the C++ runtime system gives no access to type and structure information, the programmer must provide some of this information manually. Nevertheless the principle *do not bother the programmer* was always a consideration in designing the metaclass mechanism. For this reason, preprocessor macros extract as much as possible automatically from the source code [Gamma89].

7.4.4 Container Classes

The basic building blocks of ET++ include abstract data types often referred to as *container classes.* Included are `OrdCollection` (dynamically growing arrays), `ObjList` (linked lists), `Set` (hash tables), and `Dictionary`, to name a few. See Figure 7.3. They are more or less modeled after the *Smalltalk collection classes.*

The container classes deal with any instance derived from the class `Object` which excludes more specific type checking at compile time. Recent implementations of C++ support parameterized types (templates) as an alternative approach, allowing more type checking at compile time. But because the support for templates and maturity varies between different compilers, the authors are still reluctant to use templates.

```
Object
    Container
        Collection
            SeqCollection
                ObjArray
                ObjList
                    SortedObjList
                OrdCollection
            Set
        Dictionary
```

Figure 7.3 The container classes

Robust Iterators

Container classes require mechanisms often referred to as *iterators* [Liskov86] to inspect their elements one by one. One way to implement iterators is to store the state of the traversal in the container class itself. The disadvantage of this approach is that only one iterator can be active for an instance of a container class at any time. For this reason, ET++ implements a companion class for each container class, storing the traversal's state in instances of it. This approach allows several iterators to be active at the same time.

A problem that has to be considered is what happens when the underlying collection of objects is modified during a traversal. CLU, a language with built-in support for iterators [Liskov86], requires that the collection not be modified while an iterator is active. It is up to the implementor of an iterator to handle this case properly. This restriction cannot be enforced when working with an application framework, because a lot of the control flow resides in the framework. A client can hardly decide whether an iterator is active at a certain point and whether it is secure to remove an object from a collection. ET++ container classes take care of this problem by introducing robust iterators. The basic idea is that deletion of an object is delayed until no more iterators are active. Due to this change, some hidden bugs and memory leaks have been eliminated from ET++. Their implementation of the robust iterators profited from the fact that a lot of the code has been factored out and realized in the common superclass of all container classes (`Container`). Kofler gives a detailed description of the design and implementation of robust container classes for ET++ [Kofler89].

7.4.5 The View System

`VObject` (visual object) is the most general graphical class in ET++. It defines a protocol for drawing graphical objects on the screen, for input event handling and distribution, and for managing their sizes and positions.

A design goal for instances of `VObject` was to keep them small and lightweight. This means that visual objects have very little memory or performance overhead, even when using thousands of them (for example as leafs and nodes in a large tree view). Consequently, instances of `VObject` have no built-in coordinate transformation and establish no clipping boundary. Our experience shows that this is an asset rather than a burden because most of the simple graphical objects (e.g., the items in a menu, or buttons) do not need a clipping boundary anyway and gain no benefit from having their own coordinate system [Weinand92].

The relatively large interface of `VObject` mirrors the fact that it should be possible to design all high-level algorithms dealing with graphical objects in terms of the abstract protocol of `VObject` alone. This approach automatically results in the algorithms working on any kind of graphical object. As an example, in addition to its origin and extent, `VObject` defines the abstract protocol to maintain a baseline, which is essential for the alignment of instances of `VObject` representing text.

Most of the interface of `VObject` is composed of simple utilities which are implemented in terms of a few dynamically bound methods; this is a so-called *bottleneck interface*. In order to create a new subclass, it is necessary to override only a small number of methods. `VObject` provides quite a number of methods to change its origin and extent or the *x* or *y* components thereof (`SetExtent`, `SetOrigin`, `SetContentRect`, `SetWidth`, `SetHeight`, `Align`, and `Move`). It would be bothersome if all these methods had to be overridden in every subclass. But with the bottleneck interface, it is in fact necessary to override only `SetOrigin` and `SetExtent`.

Besides its rendering on the screen, every graphical object must include a mechanism to react to input events. `VObject` defines methods for various input events, like key and mouse button presses, which are called when the corresponding input event occurs. In order to react to a specific event, the corresponding method must be overridden. The default implementation of these methods is to propagate the event to another `VObject` referenced by an instance variable.

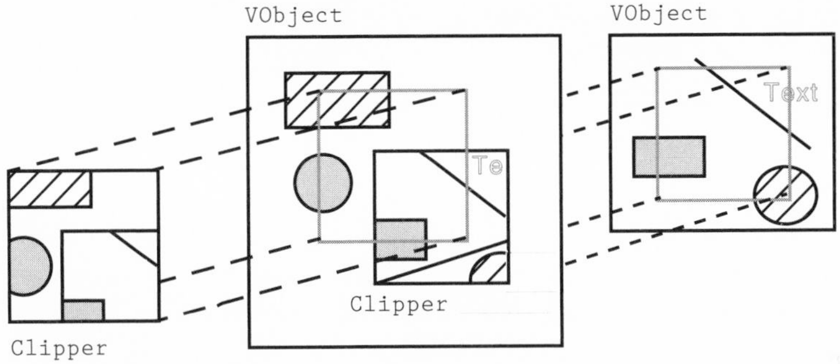

Figure 7.4 A hierarchy of nested clippers

An interesting mechanism of the graphical foundation classes is their ability to combine several instances of `VObject` (e.g., a `Collection`) into a single, composite object which can be treated as one `VObject`. The abstract class `CompVObject` applies methods executed on itself to all of its components, and forwards input events to one of them. The layout management of a composite `VObject` is the responsibility of a subclass. With the introduction of the `CompVObject`, the instances of `VObject` are most easily arranged in a treelike fashion, which allows a reasonable default implementation of all event-handling methods: the event is dispatched downwards, and the calls to handle an event are by default propagated up to its container.

The class `Clipper` is a subclass of `VObject`. It defines an independent coordinate system and clips the graphical output of a `VObject` to a rectangular area. It is kind of a "hole" through which another `VObject` or a part of it can be seen and scrolled. The implementation of scrolling is based on this class. Because `Clipper` is a subclass of `VObject`, a `Clipper` can again be installed within a `Clipper`. This results in the concept of hierarchies of independently scrollable `VObject` objects nested to arbitrary depth, see Figure 7.4. Applications for this will be given later in the general discussion of the graphic building blocks.

It is sometimes hard to determine when it is necessary to redraw an object in order to update its image on the screen in response to changes in its internal state. This is due to the fact that visual objects may be obscured partly or completely by other objects which have to be redrawn as well. The ET++ view system makes use of an indirect drawing scheme (*invalidation*) which makes it completely unnecessary to call the `Draw` method of a `VObject` directly because all control flow is factored out into the framework. An ET++ application simply announces which `VObject` objects (or part thereof) must be redrawn by calling a method which adds the region occupied by the `VObject` to a single update region per window. Whenever ET++ is idle, it requests the application to redraw the update region by calling the `Draw` method of the topmost `VObject` (e.g., a view installed in a window). Because invalidation is cheaper than redrawing, this delayed update mechanism optimizes the redrawing on the screen without further help from the application.

Since redrawing is completely under the control of the view system framework, it is possible to integrate further optimizations that are transparent to the application. *Double buffering*, for example, provides for flicker-free screen update by collecting the output of a sequence of drawing requests in a memory (shadow) buffer, which is copied to the screen in a single operation. This substantially simplifies the implementation of the text-handling classes because it is no longer necessary to minimize the screen flicker by sophisticated incremental update strategies.

This indirect synchronous drawing scheme works very well with most classical application types, but has its limitations when dealing with *animation* or *digital motion video* because it is not feasible to invalidate and redraw regions of the screen at real-time video rates. However, Shnorf [Schnorf93] shows how support for motion video can be integrated into ET++ with very little modification.

User Interface Elements

Graphic building blocks, like menus, buttons, scrollbars, and editable texts, are the "Lego blocks" of an interactive user interface, and are available in almost any user interface toolbox. But usually there is only a fixed set of them, and no simple way to modify existing ones or to construct new ones from predefined lower-level components.

Inheritance is one possibility for modifying existing components or adding behavior to them. An example is adding a borderline by overriding the `Draw` method of a `VObject`. But if all predefined items should have a borderline, it becomes necessary to override all corresponding draw methods, which results in duplicated code. As another example, a button may consist of an image or text, a single or double borderline, and a special behavior to react to mouse clicks. A scrollbar typically consists of an up and a down button together with an analog slider, which itself may be a filled rectangle, an image, or even a number reflecting its current value. All these parts may be useful for other kinds of dialogs, or even in a completely different context.

At first sight, multiple inheritance or mix-ins seemed to be a possible way to combine various kinds of basic classes to form the complex items mentioned above. But on second thought, it became obvious that multiple inheritance was not the ultimate solution. As an example, multiple inheritance does not allow the combination of a `TextItem` and two `BorderItems` in order to get a `DoubleBorderedTextItem`.

Another observation was that dialog items most often come in groups. The Macintosh printing dialog, to take just one complex dialog box, consists of about 30 different items which are placed nicely in a dialog window. On the Macintosh the placement of dialog items can be handled interactively with the resource editor. But if the size of a single item changes, the overall layout of the dialog has to be redone. Moreover, the precise horizontal and vertical alignment of text items is a tedious task if done by hand. This led to the integration of some automatic layout management in ET++ which is based on a hierarchical and high-level layout description rather than on the explicit placement of items.

An almost perfect approach for two-dimensional hierarchical composition of visual elements is the UNIX text processing tool `eqn`, a troff-preprocessor for typesetting mathematics [Kernighan75]. `eqn` translates a simple description of a formula into a sequence of typesetting commands. The basic items of `eqn` are characters or strings which can be pieced together with a number of layout operators to form more complex items. Repeated grouping of items finally leads to a tree representation of the formula.

As a result, a design idea emerged for all kinds of user interface building blocks. ET++ provides a small number of basic items which can be pieced together with a number of layout operators to form more complex items. All graphical elements visible on the screen are bound into a tree of `VObject` objects, whose root is installed in a `Window`.

The simplest items, such as the classes `TextItem`, `LineItem`, and `ImageItem`, are direct subclasses of `VObject`. In contrast to more complex components, they do not have a separate model and view, because the underlying data structure and its rendering are very simple, and interaction behavior (e.g., editing) is typically not needed. Figure 7.5 shows some of the user interface components of the class hierarchy.

```
VObject
    TextItem
    ImageItem
    PictureItem
    Clipper
        Window
        Zoomer
    CompVObject
        Slider
        Matte
        BorderItem
        Box
            Expander
            Form
            OneOfGroup
            ManyOfGroup
        Button
            ActionButton
            RadioButton
            ToggleButton
```

Figure 7.5 User interface components

The layout operators, as subclasses of `CompVObject`, are responsible for controlling both the communication among their components and the relationships among the locations of these components, i.e., the layout management.

`BorderItem`, for example, draws a borderline around its contents and displays an optional title aligned above its contents in a number of ways. The contents, as well as the title, are in turn instances of `VObject`.

`Box` implements a tabular layout of its component `VObject` items. The commonly used horizontal or vertical lists of items are special cases of a general layout: Each `Box` item can be aligned horizontally as well as vertically in a number of ways (left, right, center, top, bottom, or base). `Box` implements a very powerful mechanism which fits the needs of most complex dialog layouts without having to position items explicitly, as shown in Figure 7.6.

`OneOfGroup` (`ManyOfGroup`) is a subclass of `Box` that implements the one-of (many-of) behavior of several on/off buttons. Any single item in the statement of Figure 7.6 could be replaced by an arbitrarily complex composite item. Because this generality is not needed, convenience constructors exist for often-used dialog patterns. This allows a much simpler description, as shown in Figure 7.7.

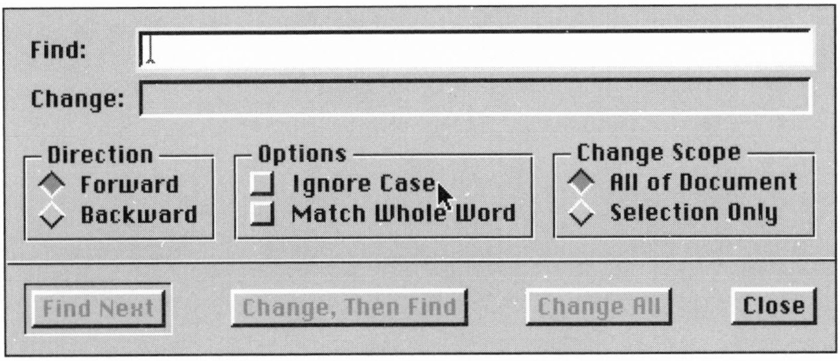

```
new VBox(
    new Form(
        new TextItem("Find:"),new TextField,
        new TextItem("Change:"), new TextField,
    0),
    new HBox(
        new BorderItem("Direction",
            new OneOfBox(eLeft,
                new HBox(eBase,
                    new RadioButton,
                    new TextItem("Forward"),
                0),
                new HBox(eBase,
                    new RadioButton,
                    new TextItem("Backward"),
                0),
            0)
        ),
        new BorderItem("Options",
            new ManyOfBox(eLeft,
                new HBox(eBase,
                    new ToggleButton,
                    new TextItem("Ignore Case"),
        // ...
    0),
    new LineItem,
    new HBox(
        new ActionButton("Find Next"),
        new ActionButton("Change, Then Find"),
    // ...
    0)
0);
```

Figure 7.6 Part of a dialog box and its defining statement

```
new VBox(
    new Form(
        "Find:",new TextField,
        "Change:",new TextField,
    0),
    new HBox(eCenter,
        new BorderItem("Direction",
            new OneOfBox("Forward", "Backward", 0)),
        new BorderItem("Options",
            new ManyOfBox("Ignore Case", "Match Whole Word", 0)),
    // ...
0);
```

Figure 7.7 Building a dialog using convenience constructors

7.5 Application Framework

The application classes define the application's natural components and how they interact. This interaction is the main difference between an application framework and a collection of abstract but not strongly related classes. The former allows the factoring of much of the control flow into the class library, while the latter requires that the developer know exactly when to call which method.

7.5.1 Managing Presentations

The ET++ Application Framework centers around a hierarchy of *presentations.* A presentation is a collection of (mostly) visual components, like menubars and menus, dialogs, views, and windows that make up one aspect of an application. Every presentation is managed by an instance of class `Manager` or a subclass thereof.

An application consists of a hierarchy of `Manager` instances: the top-level `Manager` is an instance of the specialized subclass `Application`, which controls the application as a whole and manages any number of subclasses of `Manager`.

Figure 7.8 shows an example (snapshot) of the dynamic relationship between instances of `Manager` and their subclasses. The small circles denote methods (*factory methods*) clients have to override in order to create specific `Manager` objects. After their creation, ET++ takes care of them.

The most important subclass of `Manager` is `Document`. In addition to its responsibilities as a subclass of `Manager`, `Document` encapsulates the

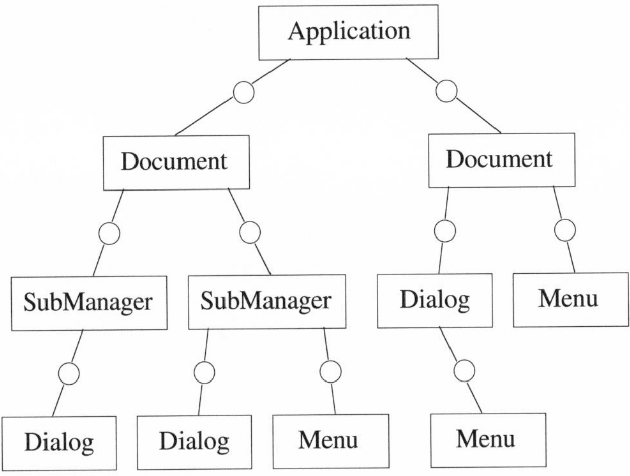

Figure 7.8 Typical manager instance hierarchy

data structure (the model) of an application and collaborates with another abstraction (`Data`, see below) in order to load, and later store and close the model.

The implementation of loading and closing documents is a good example of factoring out the common control flow: consider, for example, an end user who intends to open a new file without saving the old modified file to disk. The abstract class `Document` manages all necessary dialogs to ask the user if and where to save the old file and what file to open next.

If a presentation is not document-based but, for example, a database front end or a simple control panel or dialog, it is sufficient to just create a subclass of `Manager`. ET++ dialogs, and even menus, are subclasses of `Manager`. See Figure 7.9.

`Dialog` implements a standard behavior for modal or modeless dialog boxes. A single method must be overridden to create the dialog's

```
Manager             // manages a presentation
    Application     // manages an application as a whole
    Document        // manages model-based presentation
    Dialog          // manages dialog box presentation
    Menu            // a presentation of a one-of-many selection
```

Figure 7.9 Manager classes

`VObject` tree, another to set up the initial state, and another to react to all dialog interactions.

`Manager` is a good example of a simple yet powerful abstraction that is applied in different areas and greatly reduces the number of concepts a developer has to learn.

7.5.2 Data and Converter Framework

The abstract class `Data` defines an interface for transparently accessing and converting external or remote data, like files, components embedded in documents or databases, or the clipboard. Clients typically use subclasses of `Data` to extract an object that will be used as a model. The `Data` abstraction tries to hide details like the source and original format of the external data by always providing an object that is convenient for the client to work with. A text editor, for example, will ask a `Data` object to convert the data source to a subclass of `Text`; a graphics editor will try to get a `Picture`. After the client is done with the object, the object can be converted back to its original form and saved in its original place.

The most important subclass of `Data` is `FileData`, a data source connected to a file stream of the underlying file system. Another subclass is `ObjectData`, which wraps a given `Object`. It is used for implementing the ET++ clipboard and drag-and-drop mechanism.

The implementation of the `Data` uses the *converter framework* of ET++. This framework first uses `TypeMatcher` objects to determine the type of an external data source. It then tries to find a `Converter` object from the set of available `Converter` objects which can convert the external data to a requested class type. If more than one conversion sequence is possible a selection dialog is presented to the user.

The converter framework can be easily extended by clients with new `TypeMatcher` and `Converter` objects. Because existing and new applications work on `Data` only, they automatically profit from any new `Converter` objects by being able to exchange and import data formats previously unknown to them. `Converter` objects are provided for Rich Text (RTF), Macintosh PICT2, TIFF, Encapsulated PostScript (EPSF), X11 Bitmap Format (XPM), and Portable Bitmap Format (PBM).

7.5.3 Viewing

The main task of graphical applications is rendering the document's data structures on the screen. `VObject` objects or subclasses thereof are the basic components for implementing the entities of the model as graphical elements.

In addition, interactive applications have the notion of a current selection on which some operation triggered by the user will be performed. The class `View`, another subclass of `VObject`, represents an abstract and possibly arbitrarily large drawing surface. Its main purpose is to factor out all control flow necessary to manage rendering and printing, as well as maintaining a current selection. A `Document` can have any number of `View` objects, all showing the same model in various representations. This closely corresponds to the MVC model of Smalltalk.

In addition, a `View` adds the ability to be visible in multiple `Clipper` objects; that is, different portions of the same `View` can be shown in different places on the screen. This powerful concept is used in ET++ for the implementation of the classes `Splitter` and `PageView`. A `Splitter` shows disconnected portions of an underlying `View` in several panes. A `PageView` breaks an underlying continuous `View` into separate pages and displays each of them with a border and an optional header and footer as a matrix of pages. Because this functionality is totally transparent to the original `View`, `Splitter` and `PageView` can be used with any existing and future `View` subclass.

7.5.4 Undoable Commands

An important issue for user-friendly applications is the ability to undo commands because this allows novice users to explore applications without the risk of losing data. Implementing undoable commands, unfortunately, is difficult unless there is some support from a framework. One approach for their implementation is to collect enough state before executing the command in order to be able to reverse its effect when the user selects `undo`. For a single level `undo` this state can be discarded whenever the next command is performed. Clearly, it is difficult to build a totally automatic but efficient framework for undoable commands without further support by the programmer. But it is possible to design a framework that factors out the flow of control, leaving to the programmer only the decisions regarding what state to save and how to `do` and `undo` a command.

The abstract class `Command` defines the protocol, while subclasses of the abstract class `CommandProcessor` implement the control flow, for executing and undoing a command. Simple nonmodel-based `Manager`-like `Dialog` objects have an `SingleCommandProcessor` which allows a single-level undo. Documents typically have an `UnboundedCommand-Processor` which keeps all command objects since the last load or save operation.

To implement an undoable command, a subclass of `Command` has to be derived. Such a subclass defines the necessary state variables and methods for doing and undoing the command. ET++ applications never perform commands directly, but simply instantiate command objects and pass them to ET++. The framework calls their methods and frees command objects when they are no longer undoable.

Command classes, which were first introduced in EZWin [Lieberman85], are a very elegant example of the reuse of an abstract design, and not only ease the implementation effort substantially, but also help to modularize complex applications into small and more manageable pieces.

7.6 High-Level Building Blocks

In addition to the basic user interface elements described above, ET++ provides higher-level building blocks for textual, tabular, and hierarchical data.

7.6.1 Rich-Text Building Block

A text-building block has to support a spectrum of different applications. At the lower end are text entry fields in dialog boxes. A drawing editor uses editable text for annotations. A program editor needs efficient text for editing and displaying pretty printed source code. Finally, at the higher end are on-line documents which require support for multiple character and paragraph styles with embedded graphics and hypertext links.

To cover this entire spectrum, text-building is not implemented as a monolithic object but as a separate framework. The key abstractions of this framework and their responsibilities are:

- `Text` maintains the text data structure and sends out a notification whenever the text changes.
- `TextView` renders the text, handles input, and change notifications from its `Text` object. It maintains the text composition, that is, how the text is broken into lines. The responsibility for finding

the breaks is delegated to a `TextFormatter` object. The rendering of a single line of text is delegated to a `TextPainter` object.

- `TextFormatter` finds the line breaks in a paragraph.
- `TextPainter` renders a single line of text, and is responsible for handling typographic effects like justification and ligatures.

Each abstraction is implemented by a family of classes. To create an editable text object the client selects a `TextView` class and combines it with `Text`, `TextFormatter`, and `TextPainter` objects. This approach enables the creation of editable text objects with different functionality by combining different text objects in different ways. `TextView` acts as the controller of an editable text object and mediates between the other objects.

Figure 7.10 illustrates the hierarchy of `TextView` classes. `StaticTextView` renders text, while `TextView` also handles input and implements text editing operations. `CodeTextView` further adds autoindenting, *find-matching-bracket* features, and pretty printing of program text to the functions provided by `TextView`. A `ShellTextView` object is connected to a shell and supports the ability to enter commands and to log their outputs.

```
Object
    View
        StaticTextView
            TextView
                CodeTextView
                ShellTextView
```

Figure 7.10 `TextView` hierarchy

Following the goal of using uniform mechanisms wherever possible, the implementation of the class `TextView` uses the same mechanism for invalidating a region of a view in order to update the screen as described in a Section 7.4.5. Due to double buffering, the screen is updated flicker-free, even for text displayed against arbitrary backgrounds.

The separation of the text storage from the `TextView` and the use of notification to communicate changes enables one to view the same `Text` object in multiple `TextView` objects.

Classes for managing the data structures of a text are descendants of the abstract class `Text`, see Figure 7.11.

```
Object
    Text
        CheapText
        GapText
            StyledText
                VObjectText
```

Figure 7.11 `Text` hierarchy

Text defines a bottleneck interface for its subclass. Editing operations like `Cut`, `Copy`, and `Paste` are implemented in terms of a `ReplaceRange` primitive. Subclasses have to implement only this method. Efficient access of the text contents is achieved by iterators which retrieve a subsequence of text, character by character, word by word, or paragraph by paragraph.

`CheapText` is the simplest implementation of a text data structure, and is primarily used for testing purposes. The underlying data structure is a dynamic character array. `GapText` is used for larger texts, and implements the text abstraction as a character array with a gap as known from the text package of the *Andrew system* [Hansen87]. The class `StyledText`, supports the assignment of different character and paragraph attributes to a text range.

Another subclass of `Text` is `VObjectText`. `VObjectText` enables one to embed arbitrary objects into a text which behave as ordinary characters. The protocol for such character-like objects is defined by the class `VisualMark`. It defines the interface for measuring and rendering character-like objects. An example is the subclass `VObjectMark`, which implements the `VisualMark` interface for `VObject` items. It enables the embedding of arbitrary `VObjects` into text. Figure 7.12 shows the ET++Write application. It uses `VisualMark` objects to embed pictures and the running clock.

`TextFormatter` is responsible for finding the line breaks in a text. The line-breaking functionality is factored into its own object to enable the use of different line-breaking strategies. ET++ provides two implementations, `SimpleTextFormatter` and `FoldingTextFormatter`. `SimpleTextFormatter` breaks the text only at explicit line breaks, whereas `FoldingTextFormatter` breaks the text into lines of a given width.

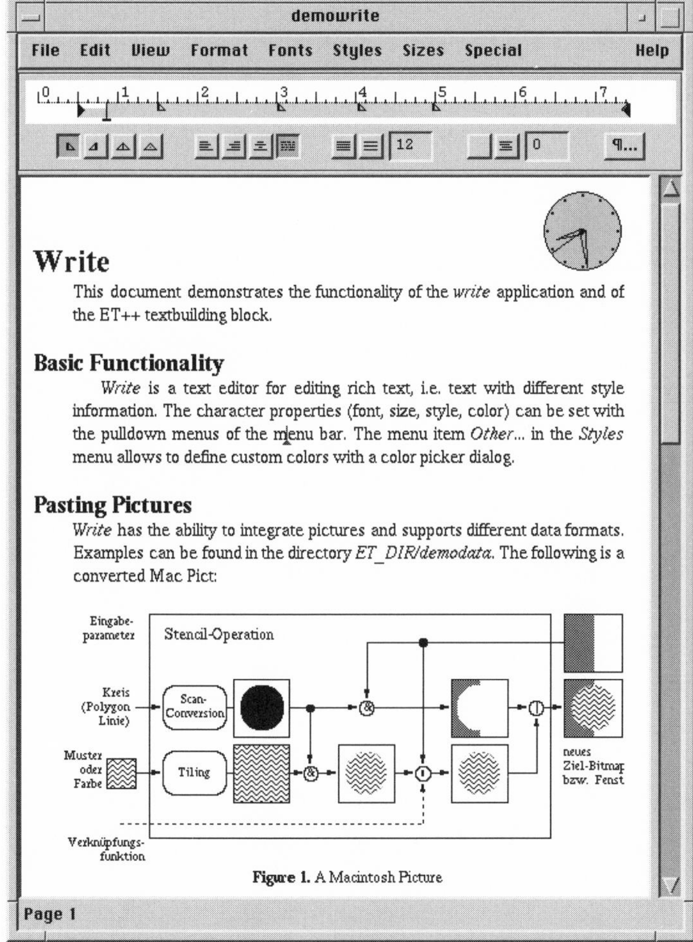

Figure 7.12 ET++Write

`VisualMark` objects turned out to be a powerful extension mechanism for text, as they are not limited to embedding pictures. In ET++Write, `VisualMark` subclasses were used to implement:

- *Markers* Zero-width characters with a symbolic name, they are used to define *sticky* targets for hypertext links.
- *Hypertext links* The link target is referenced as a <document name, marker name> pair.

- *Action links* These display a little icon and store a shell script which is executed when the user clicks on the icon.
- *Annotations* These are shown as an icon, and when clicked pop-up a dialog for entering an annotation.
- *Counters* for headings and figures Counters look like ordinary characters, but they are objects with the additional behavior to update a counter.

Another example is the *FileBrowser* application, which uses `VisualMark` objects to enable the inclusion of pictures as comments in source code.

The text-building block has proven to cover a wide range of application needs. For example, ET++Write uses a custom `TextView` subclass with `VObjectText` and `FoldingFormatter`. Simpler text-entry fields use the standard `TextView` class with `GapText` and `SimpleTextFormatter`. More specialized text entry fields which need to support data validation are covered by a family of `TextField` classes. Multiple `TextField` classes share the same `TextView`, and thereby reduce the memory requirements.

In addition to the core text classes described above, the text-building block includes several `Command` classes for manipulating text in an undoable way.

The text-building block leverages the converter architecture for supporting import and export of text in different formats, like the RTF interchange format.

7.6.2 Grid Views for Tabular Data

Another important class derived from `View` is `GridView`. `GridView` is a flexible framework for displaying cells in a matrix and forwarding input to them. It also takes care of selecting and deselecting single cells, as well as contiguous and noncontiguous areas of cells. `GridView` is a basic building block for many user interface objects which have to present a collection of selectable cells.

`GridView` makes no assumptions about the underlying data structure of a cell, but clients are required to override at least a `DrawCell(`column, row, rectangle`)` method to draw a cell's content. The fact that a cell is not an object appears to be not very object-oriented, but our experience has shown that in many cases it is much easier to implement a single method

```
View
    GridView
        CollectionView
        ObjectGridView
        StringGridView
```

Figure 7.13 `GridView` **hierarchy**

by accessing an existing data structure than to convert the data structure to a class `GridView` requires. A benevolent side effect is that not every element in a table has to be allocated as an object, which can result in a major performance improvement for larger tables.

A typical example from the ET++ exploration environment is a scrolling list containing the names of all available classes. The ET++ runtime system already maintains a collection of metaclasses. Converting them to `TextItem` objects (a subclass of `VObject`) would be much more cumbersome than to override `DrawCell` and access the `Name` method of the metaclass.

`StringGridView` is a subclass of `GridView` for manipulating a matrix of cells containing `String` objects. Again, `StringGridView` makes no assumption about where the `String`s are stored; clients have to implement `GetString(`column, row`)` and `SetString(`column, row`)` methods. In the same way as `TextField`, `StringGridView` maintains a single instance of a `TextView` for implementing a memory-efficient floating string editor. Whenever keyboard focus is transferred to a cell (e.g., by clicking into it) the cell is overlaid with `TextView`, which in turn allows editing of the cell's contents.

Another specialized `GridView` is `CollectionView`, which displays any collection of `VObject` items as provided by the foundation classes in a tabular format. `CollectionView` items are used for displaying tables with heterogeneous contents which require some polymorphic cell behavior, as in Figure 7.13.

7.6.3 Tree Views for Hierarchical Data

`TreeView` renders a tree data structure (in fact a `VObject` tree) and implements simple editing operations, for example, moving nodes and collapsing or expanding subtrees. Different layouts are supported. Each layout is represented as a separate object which can be plugged into a

```
Object
    TreeLayout
        TopDownLayout
        LeftRightLayout
        IndentedLayout
        CollapsedLayout
        OptimizedLeftRightLayout
```

Figure 7.14 `TreeLayout` hierarchy

`TreeView`, see Figure 7.14. The `TreeView` class itself can be easily adapted to show any kind of hierarchical data. To do so, a client overrides the `MakeChildrenIterator` and the `NodeAsVObject` methods. `MakeChildrenIterator` is used to traverse the hierarchy. `NodeAsVObject` defines the visual representation of a node in the hierarchy.

`GraphView` is a subclass of `TreeView`. It adds support for the layout of acyclic graph structures. It uses a simple layout algorithm which builds on top of `TreeView`. `GraphView` allows the user to interactively rearrange a generated layout.

7.7 Object-Oriented Modeling of System Dependencies

Portability was a major issue in the design of ET++. In order to be independent of a specific environment, all environment dependencies were encapsulated by introducing an abstract system interface defining a minimal set of low-level functionality necessary to implement ET++. These functions can be subdivided into the following categories:

- Window management and input handling
- Graphic system, and graphic resource management (fonts, images, cursors)
- Interapplication communication
- Operating system services and resources

Every category is defined as an abstract class which has to be subclassed for a specific environment or output device. These subclasses are considered the *environment abstraction layer* of ET++. As a consequence, ET++ classes and applications do not contain any operating or window system-specific calls, which makes it possible to port ET++ to other environments with a minimum of effort.

The two abstract classes `System` and `WindowSystem` define the entry point into the system interface layer. Their responsibility is to instantiate new objects representing operating system resources like files and directories, or window system resources like ports (windows), font managers, images, and cursors.

In addition, `System` defines an abstract interface for multiplexing system events coming from different sources. In a terminal emulator, for example, it is necessary to send and receive data to or from another process as well as from the window system.

Due to the clean and abstract interface between `System` and `WindowSystem`, they are completely decoupled, which allows the combination of any window system with any operating system.

The hierarchy of port classes and their interfaces is another illustration of appropriate object-oriented modeling of system dependencies, see Figure 7.15.

```
Port
    PicturePort
    PrinterPort
        MacPictPort
        PostScriptPort
        // ...
    WindowPort
        XWindowPort
        SunWindowPort
        MacWindowPort
        // ...
```

Figure 7.15 Port hierarchy

The root of this hierarchy is the abstract class `Port`, which defines the graphical output primitives common to all output devices. Subclasses of `Port` override the abstract output primitives with a device-dependent implementation, or they add device specific methods.

`PicturePort` collects all drawing requests in a compact data structure which represents the standard ET++ exchange format for structured graphics.

`PrinterPort` adds abstract methods for dealing with an abstract printing device. Its subclasses `MacPictPort` and `PostScriptPort` are implementations for generating Macintosh PICT2 files and PostScript.

The abstract class `WindowPort` extends the output interface of `Port` with methods for input handling and window management. In essence, every instance of `WindowPort` represents a single window of the underlying window system.

The subclass `XWindowPort` is an implementation of `WindowPort` for X11; `SunWindowPort` is for SunWindows, Sun's now obsolete library-based window system; and `MacWindowPort` for the Macintosh. Due to dynamic binding of the device dependent methods, ET++ is able to run applications on different window systems.

Usage of the port classes is straightforward: ET++ maintains a current output port to which all drawing requests are automatically directed. Because updating of this port is completely under the control of the application framework, application-transparent printing is just a matter of switching the current port to a printer port.

The design of ET++'s imaging model was influenced by two conflicting goals: it had to be sophisticated enough to ease its use in ET++ applications considerably, but at the same time simple and sufficiently device-independent to allow an implementation on top of various window systems with minimum effort.

A consequence of the second goal was the decision not to support the inherently device-dependent and nonportable raster operations found in most current window systems. These operations are difficult to emulate (for example on a printing device like a PostScript printer), and their visual effect on color systems is often unpredictable or unsatisfactory. Therefore, a subset of the stencil/paint model found in the PostScript imaging language was adopted. This model can be emulated on most window systems with little effort.

In PostScript, all drawing is performed by first constructing an arbitrarily shaped path which is then used for filling and stroking with a color, pattern, or more complex graphics. ET++ uses a subset of this general concept.

This imaging model is embodied in 35 primitive methods which must be implemented for any particular output device. The (stateless) interface to these primitives is cumbersome to use because they all take their drawing attributes as parameters. A second (stateful) interface has been added which maintains attributes such as fill and stroke pattern, pen position, etc., thereby providing an alternative set of graphic functions with fewer parameters. Other interfaces exist to further reduce the number of parameters for common usages. But, in the spirit of bottleneck interfaces, all these alternative interfaces are based on the primitives defined in the abstract class `Port`, and thus do not enlarge the device interface.

A problem with the implementation of this simple and abstract device interface is that it is sometimes difficult to use functions provided by an underlying window system suitable for optimizing special cases. Passing every single character through the device interface and the clipping machinery of the window system just to get displayed, for example, is inefficient. This is why most window systems provide special functions for drawing more than one character at a time (a *batch*) in order to internally use a single optimized operation to clip and display the entire batch. Because such optimizations are inherently window system-dependent and cumbersome to use, ET++ provides methods to output only a single character, but implements an abstract mechanism to collect all characters in a window system-dependent data structure, which automatically is flushed by ET++ at appropriate times.

7.8 Runtime Object Inspection*

The runtime structure of an ET++ application bears little resemblance to its static code structure. The static code structure is frozen at compile time, and consists of fixed inheritance relationships. The runtime structure consists of a network of communicating objects. It is difficult to understand the dynamic structure based on the static class hierarchy. Understanding the dynamic structure is even more complicated in ET++ applications, due to the heavy use of object composition.

To address this problem, we implemented exploration tools to support the analysis of the dynamic object structure of an ET++ application. Every ET++ application has these tools optionally built in; they execute in the same address space as the application.

* ET++ also includes some browsers for the static analysis of an application, that is, the source code and the class hierarchy. However, since this functionality is currently subsumed by Sniff, we focus on the runtime object inspection support.

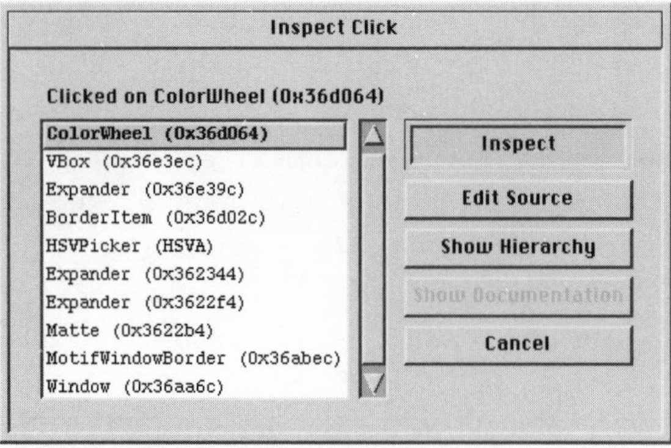

Figure 7.16 Inspect click dialog

7.8.1 Inspect Clicking

When exploring an application at runtime, the first problem is how the user can define the focus of interest. In other words there has to be a convenient entry point into the object network. A graphical application can profit from the fact that a lot of interesting objects are visible on the screen. We therefore added a so-called *inspect click* feature. An inspect click is just a mouse click together with some modifier keys. It allows you to click on any visible object on the screen to inspect it. An inspect click helps you to answer the question "what is this object on the screen?" from an implementation point of view.

Figure 7.16 shows the dialog displayed after inspect clicking an object in an color picker dialog box.

The list on the left shows the path up the visual hierarchy, starting at the clicked object and ending at the window object of the dialog. An object is identified by its class name and an optional identifier which defaults to the object's address. Enumerating the chain of parent objects enables you to easily navigate to an object's parent. Clicking the `Inspect` button brings up the inspector on the selected object.

7.8.2 The Inspector

The inspector has five panes, as shown in Figure 7.17. The top left pane shows the list of the application classes. The number in parenthesis shows a snapshot of the number of allocated instances. Selecting a class name in this pane fills the middle pane with the instances of the class. An object is identified by its class name and an optional identifier, which defaults to its address.

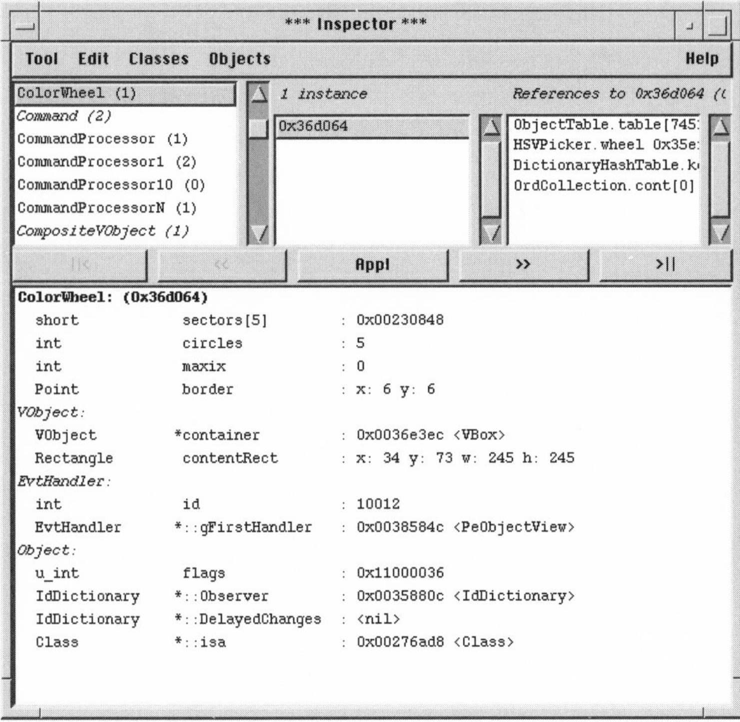

Figure 7.17 Inspector

Selecting an object shows the object's state in the bottom pane. This pane shows the instance variables, including the ones inherited from base classes. Pointer variables indicate their static type. If the dynamic type differs from the static type, this is shown as well. (See for example, the `container` instance variable in Figure 7.17.) Clicking on a pointer variable dereferences the pointer and shows the corresponding object. The buttons between the top and the bottom panes allow you to navigate back and forth along the path of visited objects.

Another interesting feature of the inspector is the possibility to query for other objects having a reference to the currently inspected one. The result of such a query is shown in the top right pane. Selecting an object from this list shows its state in the bottom pane.

The Inspector is a helpful tool for navigating back and forth in the object network. However, it can only give you a keyhole view, since it can only show one object at a time. To get a better understanding of the objects and their relationships, the exploration environment also includes an object structure browser.

7.8.3 The Object Structure Browser

The *object structure browser* visualizes runtime relationships between objects. It shows an object's part-of hierarchy. For example, Figure 7.18 shows the part-of hierarchy of a color picker dialog. A node represents an object and the thin lines connect the object with its parts. The object structure browser can be invoked from the inspector on the inspected object. Double clicking a node in the object structure browser shows the corresponding object in the inspector.

The part-of hierarchy serves as a starting point for additional queries on object relationships. The *Points To* and *Referenced From* menu items can visualize the outgoing and incoming references of a selected object. The references are shown as additional (colored) lines between the objects. The object structure has also some built-in knowledge of the ET++ class library and it can also display event distribution paths and notification relationships.

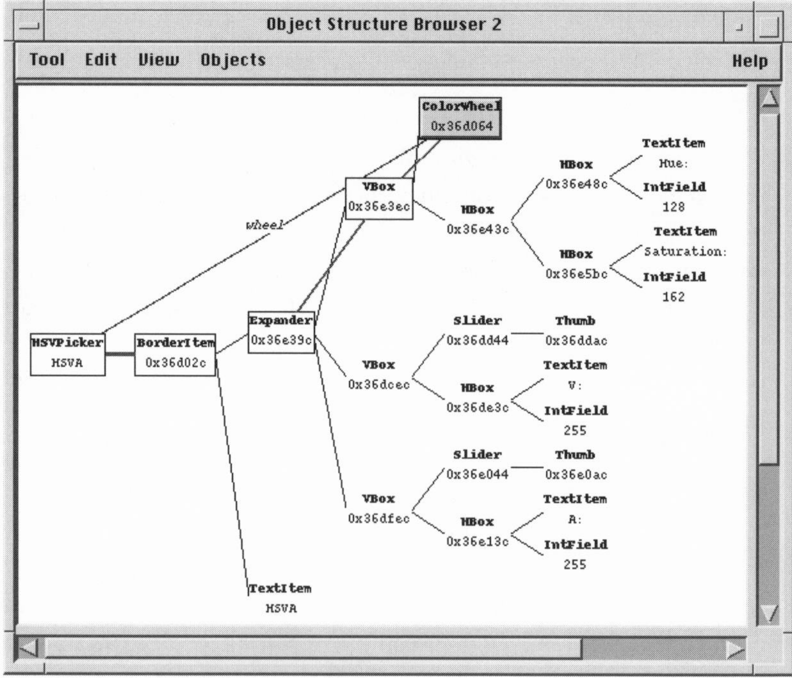

Figure 7.18 Object structure browser

7.8.4 Runtime Support for the Exploration Environment

The exploration tools described above require some additional runtime support. The functionality to find all the instances of a class is based on an object table. This table is maintained by the root class `Object`. Its constructor adds an entry to the table, and its destructor removes an entry. The maintenance of the object table can be turned off for applications which are in production use. The object table is also used to find objects pointing to a specific object.

The determination of an object's parts requires some help from the class implementor. The root class `Object` defines a `CollectParts` method which can be overridden by subclasses to let the tools know which object references point to an object's parts. Another instrumentation method is `InspectorId`, which is overridden to define an additional textual identifier for the instances of a class. This identifier is derived from the values of an object's instance variables. It is shown in both the inspector and the object structure browser.

7.9 ET++ Applications

A class library in general, and a framework in particular have to be validated by real applications. During the development of ET++ we switched back and forth between the roles of class library developers and class library clients. The result of this is a set of samples which are distributed together with ET++. This section gives a short overview of the samples, followed by two more comprehensive applications.

7.9.1 Samples

The samples address two different needs. First, they were used by us to validate the design of the class library, and second, they are used by developers to learn the class library.

The samples include both simple entry-level applications and more comprehensive ones. It was an important goal of ET++ to cover the entire spectrum. During the evolution of the class library we always focused on making the applications simpler and reducing their code bulk.

The entry-level applications include:

- *Nothing*, the minimal ET++ application
- *Hello*, a graphical Hello World program

- *Calculator*, a simple calculator
- *TwoShapes*, and *ThreeShapes*, minimal drawing applications
- *Miniedit*, a simple text editor

The more advanced applications are:

- *FileBrowser*, a program editor combined with support for navigating in the directory hierarchy
- *Spreadsheet*, a simple spreadsheet which uses the TCL interpreter [Ousterhout94] for expression evaluation
- *Er*, a simple diagram editor for entity-relationship diagrams
- *IconEdit*, an icon editor which understands a large number of image formats
- *Draw*, a drawing application
- *Write*, a simple word processor

7.9.2 Sniff

Sniff is a pragmatic C++ programming environment providing browsing, cross-referencing, design visualization, documentation, and editing support. The main goal in developing Sniff was to create an efficient and portable C++ programming environment which makes it possible to edit and browse large software systems textually and graphically with a high degree of comfort, and without using large amounts of system resources [Bischofloerger92]. See Figure 7.19.

Sniff also integrates a front-end for the *gdb* debugger. The integration of etgdb was achieved by using the ET++ provided interapplication-communication services. See Figure 7.20.

7.9.3 SwapsManager

The SwapsManager project [Eggenschwiler92] used ET++ to implement a custom application which helps a trader in pricing a financial instrument called a *swap*. The application is built around the notion of a *domain-specific desktop*. In contrast to more conventional desktop environments which present icons only for documents and folders, this desktop consists of iconic presentations from the trading domain. The top right

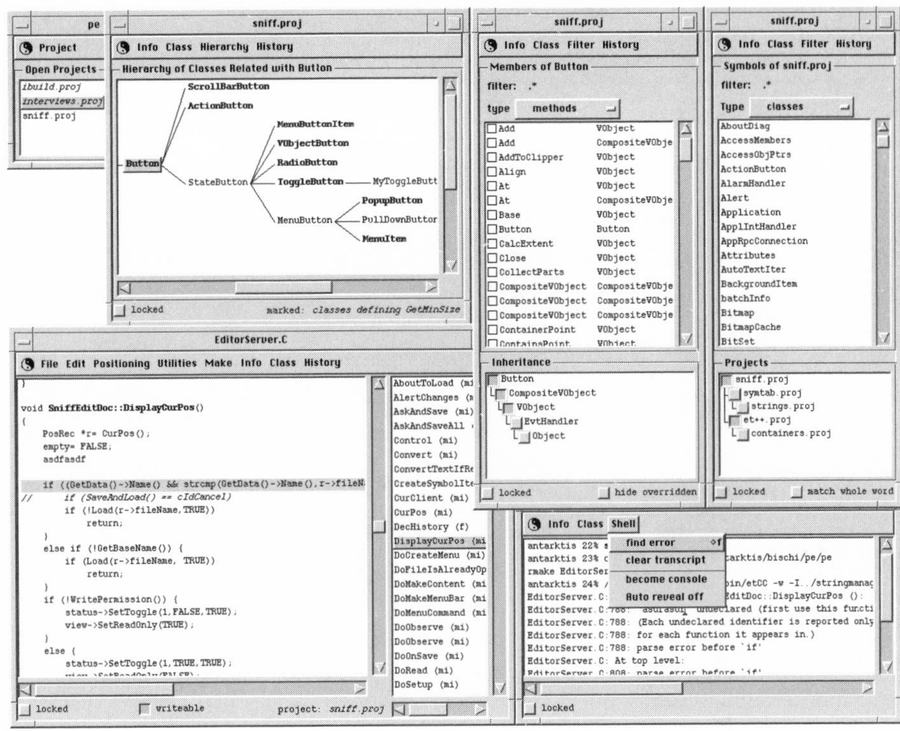

Figure 7.19 Screen showing different windows of the C++ Programming Environment Sniff

window in Figure 7.21 illustrates the iconic representations for swaps, portfolios (collections of swaps), yield curves (yields for a set of maturities), and scenarios (possible interest changes applicable to a yield curve). The icons can be manipulated by drag-and-drop. For example, to add a swap to a portfolio, the trader drags the scenario icon onto a yield curve.

As in common desktop environments, an iconic representation can be opened and inspected in a window. The bottom right window shows a more conventional form-based interface for editing the data of a swap object. The left window shows a graphical editor opened on a yield curve object. This editor provides a palette of tools for changing and inspecting the curve. Manipulating the curve creates an interest-rate scenario object which shows up on the desktop. In addition to changing the curve, the trader can also apply any existing scenario by dragging a scenario icon

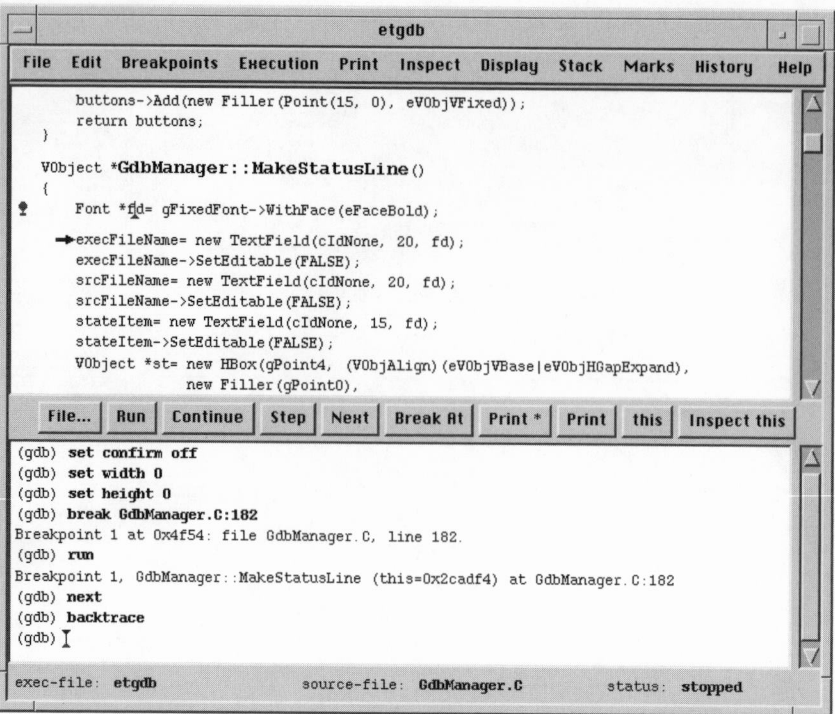

etgdb
File Edit Breakpoints Execution Print Inspect Display Stack Marks History Help
buttons->Add(new Filler(Point(15, 0), eVObjVFixed));
return buttons;
}
VObject *GdbManager::MakeStatusLine()
{
Font *fd= gFixedFont->WithFace(eFaceBold);
execFileName= new TextField(cIdNone, 20, fd);
execFileName->SetEditable(FALSE);
srcFileName= new TextField(cIdNone, 20, fd);
srcFileName->SetEditable(FALSE);
stateItem= new TextField(cIdNone, 15, fd);
stateItem->SetEditable(FALSE);
VObject *st= new HBox(gPoint4, (VObjAlign)(eVObjVBase|eVObjHGapExpand),
new Filler(gPoint0),
File... Run Continue Step Next Break At Print * Print this Inspect this
(gdb) set confirm off
(gdb) set width 0
(gdb) set height 0
(gdb) break GdbManager.C:182
Breakpoint 1 at 0x4f54: file GdbManager.C, line 182.
(gdb) run
Breakpoint 1, GdbManager::MakeStatusLine (this=0x2cadf4) at GdbManager.C:182
(gdb) next
(gdb) backtrace
(gdb)
exec-file: etgdb
source-file: GdbManager.C
status: stopped

Figure 7.20 ET++ Front-end for gdb

onto a yield curve icon. Each of these manipulations triggers a recalculation of all dependent data, which enables the trader to easily perform a risk analysis for different scenarios.

A swap is just one of many financial instruments. However, each of these instruments requires a similar calculation engine to analyze prices and values. A framework for building calculation engines has evolved [Birer93] to cover more than one of these instruments.

7.10 Conclusions

ET++ is a comprehensive class library that provides a rich set of functionality. To avoid the increased complexity that this rich functionality implies, we have always tried to apply uniform mechanisms wherever possible. For example, ET++ applies the concept of recursive composition for managing `VObject` items and `Manager` objects. In general, object composition was used to support customization of complex objects. A good example is the

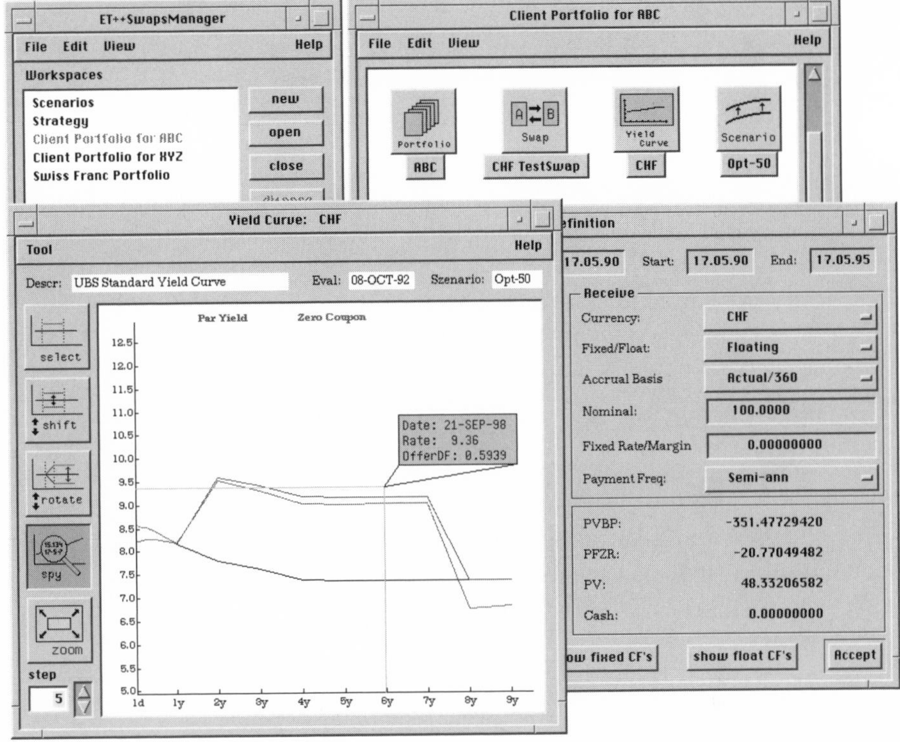

Figure 7.21 Swaps trading workspace of the ET++SwapsManager

text-building block, but the same concept was also applied to customize `Manager` objects with different command processors, and `Document` objects with different data sources. Another example for applying uniform mechanisms is updating the screen. In ET++, all screen updates are done with the same invalidation mechanism.

Our focus on unifying mechanisms enabled us to discover some recurring object-oriented design structures. This was a starting point for working on *design patterns* [Gamma92, Gamma94]. A design pattern names, abstracts, and identifies key elements of a common object-oriented design structure. The goal is to capture these structures in a succinct and easily applied form.

Another means of reducing the complexity of ET++ was to use C++ features in a conservative way. For example, we avoid virtual base classes and multiple inheritance altogether. Learning a comprehensive class library is already hard enough, and using all possible language features increases its complexity.

Finally, the small size of our project team (the two authors) was quite helpful in reducing code redundancies and constructing a homogeneous system.

We consider the ET++ core architecture to be mature. However, ET++ is still actively maintained and refined. For example, a recent addition consists of improved international support. The Unicode character set can be used to store text. There is also support for different keyboard input methods [Dürst94]. Keyboard input methods provide a mechanism for converting keyboard input to ideograms such as those found in Japanese or Chinese.

7.11 Availability

ET++ 3.0 and its tools and documentation is distributed in the public domain. It is available by anonymous ftp from `ftp.ubilab.ubs.ch` in the directory `pub/ET++`. The current release of ET++ runs under X11, SunWindow, and the Macintosh.

Further Reading

[Berlage91] T. Berlage, *OSF/Motif™: Concepts and Programming*, Addison-Wesley, Wokingham, England, 1991.

[Birer93] A. Birrer and T. Eggenschwiler, Frameworks in the financial engineering domain: An experience report, In *Proceedings ECOOP '93 (Kaiserslautern, Germany, July 26–30)*, LNCS 707, O. (Nierstrasz, ed.), Springer-Verlag, Berlin, 21–35, 1993.

[Bischfloerger92] W. R. Bischofberger, Sniff—A pragmatic approach to a C++ programming environment, In *USENIX Proceedings C++ Conference (Portland, OR)*, USENIX Assoc., El Cerrito, 67–81, 1992.

[Dürst94] M. J. Dürst, and A. Weinand, Introducing Unicode into an application framework, *Proceedings Unicode Implementers' Workshop 6*, Santa Clara, September 1994.

[Eggenschwiler92] T. Eggenschwiler and E. Gamma, ET++SwapsManager: Using Object Technology in the Financial Engineering Domain,

In *OOPSLA '92 Conference Proceedings* (October, Vancouver, Canada), published as *OOPSLA '92,* Special Issue of *SIGPLAN Notices*, **27** (10), 166–177, October 1992.

[Gamma89] E. Gamma, A. Weinand, and R. Marty, Integration of a programming environment into ET++—A case study, In *Proceedings ECOOP '89 (Nottingham, UK, July 10–14),* S. Cook, ed. Cambridge University Press, Cambridge, 283–297, 1989.

[Gamma92] E. Gamma, *Objektorientierte Software-Entwicklung am Beispiel von ET++—Design Muster, Klassenbibliothek, Werkzeuge*, (in German) Springer-Verlag, Berlin 1992.

[Gamma94] E. Gamma, R. Helm, R. Johnson, and J. Vlissides, *Design Patterns—Elements of reusable object-oriented software,* Addison-Wesley, Reading, 1994.

[Dürst94] M. J. Dürst, and A. Weinand, Introducing Unicode into an Application Framework, *Proceedings Unicode Implementers' Workshop 6*, Santa Clara, CA, September 1994.

[Goldberg83] A. Goldberg and D. Robson, *Smalltalk-80, The Language and its Implementation*, Addison-Wesley, Reading, 1983.

[Hansen87] W. J. Hansen, Data Structures in a bit-mapped text editor, *Byte Magazine*, **12** (1), 183–189, 1987.

[Johnson88] R. E. Johnson and B. Foote, Designing reusable classes, *The Journal Of Object-Oriented Programming*, **1** (2), 22–35, 1988.

[Kernighan75] B. W. Kernighan and L. L. Cherry, A system for typesetting mathematics, *Comm. Assoc. Comp. Mach.*, **18**, 151–157, 1975.

[Kofler89] T. Kofler, Robust iterators in ET++, *Structured Programming*, **14** (2), 1993.

[Lieberman85] H. Lieberman, There's more to menu systems than meets the screen, *ACM Computer Graphics (San Francisco, July)*, **19** (3), 181–189, 1985.

[Liskov86] B. Liskov and J. Guttag, *Abstraction and Specification in Program Development*, McGraw-Hill, New York, 1986.

[Myers87] B. A. Myers, Gaining general acceptance for UIMSs, *ACM Computer Graphics*, **21** (2), 130–134, 1987.

[Ousterhout94] J. K. Ousterhout, *Tcl and the Tk Toolkit*, Addison-Wesley Professional Programming Series, Addison-Wesley, Reading, 1994.

[Rosenstein86] L. Rosenstein, K. Doyle and S. Wallace, Object–oriented programming for Macintosh applications, In *ACM Fall Joint Computer Science Conference (Dallas, Texas, November 2–6)*, 31–35, 1986.

[Schmucker86] K. J. Schmucker, *Object-Oriented Programming for the Macintosh*, Hayden, Hasbrouck Heights, 1986.

[Schnorf93] P. Schnorf, Integrating video into an application framework, In *Proceedings First ACM International Conference on Multimedia (Anaheim, CA, August 1–6)*, ACM Press, New York, 411–417, 1993.

[Stroustrup87] B. Stroustrup, Possible Directions for C++, In *USENIX Proceedings and Additional Papers C++ Workshop (Santa Fe, NM, 1987)*, USENIX Assoc., El Cerrito, 399–416, 1987.

[Vlissides89] J. M. Vlissides and M. A. Linton, Unidraw: A framework for building domain-specific graphical editors, *Technical Report: CSL-TR-89-380*, Stanford University, Computer Systems Laboratory, July 1989.

[Weinand92] A. Weinand, *Objektorientierte Architektur für grafische Benutzungsoberflächen*, (in German) Springer-Verlag, Berlin 1992.

CHAPTER 8

InterViews: A Framework for X-Windows

PAUL CALDER

Preview

InterViews is a framework for building applications that interact with their users via a graphical interface. This chapter describes how InterViews fits into the spectrum of interface-building tools, and how interface programmers can use it to construct their creations. It also outlines some lessons that we learned about object-oriented programming and interface tools while designing and using InterViews.

The current version of InterViews, Version 3.1, is implemented on the X11 Window System [Scheifler86] under UNIX, although implementations for other operating system and window system platforms have been developed by various groups. InterViews is available in the public domain from ftp sites worldwide, and it is distributed with the X11 Window System in the contributed library.

8.1 InterViews History

The InterViews project began in late 1985 at Stanford University's Computer Systems Laboratory. Our goal was to make it easier to build applications with the kinds of graphical interfaces that users were beginning to demand for the new generation of graphics workstations; our catch cry was to make "easy-to-use" interfaces "easy-to-build."

At that time, there were few tools available to help programmers (the Apple Macintosh Toolbox [Apple85] and Smalltalk MVC [Krasner88] were notable exceptions). In particular, there were few tools for the new UNIX-based graphics workstations that we wanted to use. Early versions of InterViews [Linton87, 88, 89] were similar to other concurrently developed toolkits in that they defined heavy-weight interface objects (we called them *interactors*, although they are popularly called *widgets*) that represented complete interface components such as push buttons, scrollbars, and menus. However, even from those earliest versions, InterViews differed from other toolkits in two important aspects:

- It made a significant effort to extend the support for interface objects to a finer grain than the widget level.
- It emphasized mechanisms for the composition of components.

These early decisions had a direct influence on the kinds of objects that InterViews provides. In particular, InterViews objects are lightweight so that they can be used in large numbers to define the fine structure of application views, and they use a sophisticated geometry composition model based on the boxes-and-glue model used by the $\TeX$ document preparation system [Knuth84].

8.1.1 The InterViews Repertoire

Since InterViews uses object-oriented programming techniques, InterViews components are represented as class definitions. Application programmers use InterViews objects in two ways: *composition* and *extension.* Composition is the process of creating instances of predefined classes and incorporating them into the application's structure; extension is the process of defining new classes by subclassing from existing classes and adding or overriding class methods. The InterViews reference manual [Linton92] provides an overview of the key classes and their uses.

Chief among the InterViews classes is the `glyph` class [Calder90]. `glyph` represents the visible structure of the application: they manage the geometry of the interface, and they define its appearance. `glyph` subclasses represent visible data of various kinds. For example, `Character` represents an individual character in a piece of text; `Line` and `Circle` represent primitive elements in a drawing; `Border` adds decoration around another `glyph`; and composite `glyphs` arrange their components by tiling, stacking, or overlaying. An application defines its appearance by choosing primitive `glyphs` that display its data, and composite `glyphs` that compose the data in appropriate arrangements. Tables 8.1 and 8.2 list selected predefined primitive and composite `glyphs` and their usual uses.

One characteristic of `glyphs` that distinguishes them from similar components in other toolkits is that they are sharable. That is, a particular

Table 8.1 Predefined primitive `glyphs`

`glyph`	Attributes	Use
`Figure`	Path, brush, stroke color, fill color	Geometric graphics
`Character`	Character code, font, color	Text
`Glue`	Dimensions	Spacing
`Image`	Raster	Image graphics
`Label`	String, font, color	Text label
`Rule`	Dimensions, color	Visible separator
`ShapeOf`	`Glyph`	Spacing
`Space`	Horizontal dimensions, font	Text space
`Stencil`	Bitmap, color	Stencil graphics
`Strut`	Font	Text

Table 8.2 Predefined composite `glyphs`

Composite	Uses
`Box`	Tiling, aligning
`TBBox`	Top-to-bottom tiling
`LRBox`	Left-to-right tiling
`Overlay`	Overlaying
`Deck`	Stacking
`Page`	Explicit placement
`Aggregate`	Nonhierarchical layouts
`Composition`	Textual layouts

`glyph` instance can be used more than once in an application's views. This property can result in substantial reductions in application memory usage, since it reduces the number of `glyph` instances that applications need create. A good example of this sharing is evident when building views of textual data. A document editor, for example, need create only a single `glyph` to represent the letter *e*; it can use that same `glyph` wherever the letter appears in the text. For views of large documents, sharing can dramatically reduce the number of `glyph` instances needed; for example, the editor need only create hundreds of `glyphs` to display a document that might contain hundreds of thousands of characters.

`glyphs` define their appearance by drawing on a *canvas*, a two-dimensional (2D) drawing surface. The base class Canvas defines a PostScript-like protocol [Adobe85] for 2D drawing; subclasses implement the protocol for specific output devices such as X11 windows and PostScript files.

A *window* makes a canvas visible on a workstation screen and allows it to be manipulated via a window manager. A window contains a `glyph` (usually a composite `glyph`) that defines its appearance, and a hierarchy of *handlers* that respond to user input events directed to the window. The InterViews event distribution model is top-down; window events are passed to a top-level handler, which may pass them to nested handlers. Most handlers are associated with specific `glyphs` in the window; they implement interactive objects (widgets) in the interface. For example, a push-button object is represented as a `glyph` that defines the appearance of the button, and a handler that defines its behavior when pushed.

Finally, a *session* defines the context within which an application executes. Each application creates a single session object, which handles command-line processing, connects to the user's workstation display, coordinates component customization according to user preferences, initializes the toolkit objects, and runs an event dispatching loop. Normally, a session manages a connection with a single display; applications can attach additional *display* objects for programs that use multiple displays.

Most InterViews objects are not created directly. Instead, they are created by object factories, called *kits*. InterViews defines kits for various kinds of objects. For example, a *widget kit* creates interactive widgets such as buttons, menus, and scrollbars, a *dialog kit* creates predefined dialogs such as file choosers and type-in strings, and a *layout kit* creates formatting components that arrange `glyphs` using techniques based on the TEX geometry model.

This indirect way of creating objects insulates applications from the specific implementation details of the components they create; the application simply calls a kit method that returns an object of generic type. For example, to create a push button, a programmer calls the widget kit `push_button` method with parameters that specify a label and action. The application does not care whether the object returned is a Motif-like push button or an OpenLook-like push button; it just incorporates the component into the structure of the application. Indeed, InterViews provides several kinds of widget kits, each producing widgets that conform to different look-and-feel standards, and it allows the choice of kit to be deferred until run time. Thus, application users can specify the look and feel of the application in a preferences file or on the command line.

8.2 Composition: Assembling Predefined Components

The InterViews composition mechanism centers around `glyphs`. The `glyph` class protocol includes methods for building hierarchies of objects, for managing the sizes and positions of the `glyphs` in the hierarchy, and for drawing the assemblage on a canvas.

8.2.1 The Composition Model

Determining a suitable size for a graphical component such as a `glyph` is often a compromise; a component's preferred size is what it needs to best display its contents, but its actual size must reflect the practical considerations of the total amount of space available and the competing demands of other components.

Donald Knuth introduced an elegant geometry model in his TEX document preparation system [Knuth84]. The TEX model was specifically designed for formatting text, but the same ideas also work well for user interface components. TEX represents each character in a document by an appropriately sized rectangular box, and each space between characters by a piece of flexible glue. Then it composes these primitive objects into composites that arrange their components. For example, an `hbox` abuts its components left to right along a common horizontal axis, and a `vbox` abuts top to bottom. TEX typesets each line of type as an `hbox` containing characters and glue; then it collects the line boxes into `vboxes` that represent pages.

The power and simplicity of the TEX model stems from the way it supports changes in size. In addition to its preferred size, each component also defines a flexibility, represented by a stretchability and a shrinkability. When a composite calculates the sizes and positions of its components, it uses the flexibility of the components to take up any extra available space or to absorb any shortfall. Composites apportion extra space among their components according to the relative stretchabilities. For example, if one component is twice as stretchable as another, then it will receive twice as much additional allocation. Similarly, shortfall distribution depends on relative shrinkabilities.

`glyphs` support the $\TeX$ model by defining a preferred size and a willingness to stretch or shrink if the preferred size cannot be allocated. Composite `glyphs` calculate their own needs from those of their components, and they apportion their allocated space among their components according to the components' needs and the composite's layout strategy. For example, a `Box` calculates its components' space allocations so that they are tiled side-by-side, whereas an `Overlay` aligns them on top of each other.

`Boxes` are the most commonly used composite `glyphs`. Applications use `boxes`, often in combination with glue, to build structures that implement many common arrangement strategies. For example, Figure 8.1 shows screen images of a simple dialog box. When the window's size is changed, the message remains horizontally centered, the button remains aligned with the right edge of the message, and the vertical space remains equally distributed.

Figure 8.2 shows how the dialog box could be built with boxes and glue. The `LRBox` at the outermost level works like a $\TeX$ `hbox`—it arranges its components from left to right. Together with equally stretchable glue (represented by the zigzag lines) at the left and right sides, the `LRBox` ensures that the message remains horizontally centered. Similarly, the `TBBox` (which arranges components top to bottom) and glue maintain equal vertical spacing. Finally, the button is pushed to the right-hand side of the inner `LRBox` by a piece of infinitely stretchable glue to its left. The behavior of the layout could be modified by varying the geometric properties of the glue. For example, the glue that represents the vertical space between the message and the button could be made to stretch more

Figure 8.1 Simple dialog box

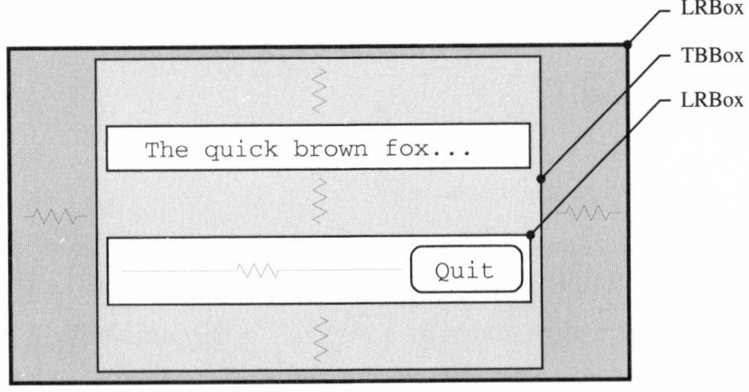

Figure 8.2 Dialog layout with boxes and glue

slowly than the top and bottom spaces by making its stretchability less than that of the other components.

8.2.2 Wrappers: Modifying A Glyph's Behavior

An important group of predefined `glyphs` are designed as *wrappers* that allow application programmers to modify the appearance or behavior of other `glyphs`. For example, a wrapper might embellish another `glyph` by drawing a border around it, or it might override some aspect of the `glyph`'s geometry. This approach considerably simplifies the toolkit because it allows programmers to compose the functionality they need from simple pieces.

Table 8.3 Predefined wrapper `glyphs`

Wrapper	Attributes	Uses
`Background`	Color	Solid backdrop
`Border`	Color, thickness	Simple border
`Margin`	Dimensions	Blank margin
`Center`	Alignment	Override origin
`Shaper`	Geometry	Override shape

Table 8.3 lists selected predefined wrappers, their attributes, and their common uses. The wrappers can be used to compose many common arrangements and effects. For example, suppose an application needs to display a message surrounded by a border. The application programmer

Figure 8.3 Composing a shadow frame with Background and Border

can compose the required appearance as a `Label glyph` contained in a `Border` wrapper. If the application also requires a background of a certain color, the programmer can simply wrap the `Label` in a `Background` glyph, then wrap the combination in a `Border`. If the application calls for a drop shadow, then that too can be added as wrapper. Figure 8.3 shows the resultant effect.

8.2.3 TextView: A Simple InterViews Application

The InterViews composition mechanisms can also be used to build more complex structures, including the kinds of layouts typical in views of text. The text views illustrated here show how applications can assemble views of complex data structures, but they are not fully functioning text editors. A more complete description of the implementation of a practical document editor that uses these same techniques can be found elsewhere [Calder92].

A simple text view can be assembled using `Characters`, `LRBoxes`, and `TBBoxes`. Figure 8.4 shows the resulting object structure, and Figure 8.5 shows the code that builds the view. The code iterates through the text

Figure 8.4 Simple text view object structure

```
TBBox* page = new TBBox();
LRBox* line = new LRBox();

int c;
while ((c = getc(file)) != EOF) {
    in (c == '\n') {
        page->append(line);
        line = new LRBox();
    } else {
        line->append(new Character(c, font, color));
    }
}
```

Figure 8.5 Code to build the simple text view

(assumed to be stored in a file), creating a `Character` for each printable character, an `LRBox` to contain all the characters in each line, and a `TBBox` to contain all the lines in the file.

The simple view can easily be extended to add extra features. For example, Figure 8.6 shows a screen image of a text view that displays text containing EUC-encoded Japanese characters. Although the new feature requires that the view display text of different fonts (and different character encodings), Figure 8.7 shows that only two additional lines of code are needed to build the new view. For ASCII-encoded text the code creates

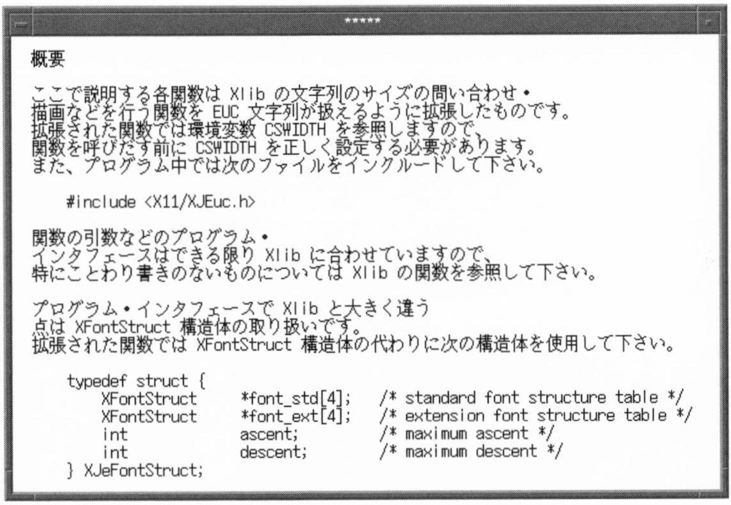

```
*****
概要

ここで説明する各関数は Xlib の文字列のサイズの問い合わせ・
描画などを行う関数を EUC 文字列が扱えるように拡張したものです。
拡張された関数では環境変数 CSWIDTH を参照しますので、
関数を呼びだす前に CSWIDTH を正しく設定する必要があります。
また、プログラム中では次のファイルをインクルードして下さい。

    #include <X11/XJEuc.h>

関数の引数などのプログラム・
インタフェースはできる限り Xlib に合わせていますので、
特にことわり書きのないものについては Xlib の関数を参照して下さい。

プログラム・インタフェースで Xlib と大きく違う
点は XFontStruct 構造体の取り扱いです。
拡張された関数では XFontStruct 構造体の代わりに次の構造体を使用して下さい。

    typedef struct {
        XFontStruct     *font_std[4];   /* standard font structure table */
        XFontStruct     *font_ext[4];   /* extension font structure table */
        int             ascent;         /* maximum ascent */
        int             descent;        /* maximum descent */
    } XJeFontStruct;
```

Figure 8.6 Text view containing EUC-encoded Japanese characters

```
while ((c = getc(file)) != EOF) {
    int (c == '\n') {
        page->append(line); line = new LRBox();
+   }   else if (!isascii(c)) {
+       line->append(
            new Character(tojis(c, getc(file)), kanji, color)
    );
    }   else {
        line->append(new Character(c, ascii, color));
    }
}
```

Figure 8.7 Code to build the EUC text view

`Characters` that use the 8-bit ASCII-encoded *ascii* font; for JIS-encoded text (kanji and kana characters) it creates `Characters` that use the 16-bit JIS-encoded *kanji* font.

Adding embedded graphics to the text view is also straightforward. Figure 8.8 shows a screen image of a text view that makes the whitespace characters in a file visible by drawing graphical representations of spaces, newlines, and formfeeds; Figure 8.9 shows the modified code that builds the view. A `Stencil` is a `glyph` that displays a bitmap, an `HRule` draws a horizontal line, and `VGlue` represents vertical blank space. The constructor parameters for `Rule` and `Glue` specify the object's size in printer's points.

Finally, the view can be extended to add text formatting. Figure 8.10 shows code for a version that formats text (or any other `glyphs`) into lines of specified width. The code uses an `LRComposition` to format its text

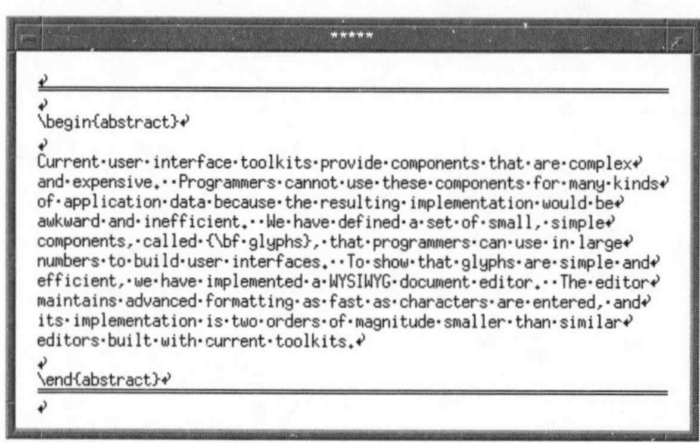

Figure 8.8 Text view with visible space characters

```
Bitmap* newline; Bitmap* space;

while ((c = getc(file)) != EOF) {
    if (c == '\n') {
        line->append(new Stencil(newline), color);
        page->append(line); line = new HBox();
    }   else if (c == '\f') {
        page->append(line);
        page->append(new HRule(color, 1));
        page->append(new VGlue(1));
        page->append(new HRule(color, 1));
        line = new HBox();
    }   else if (c == ' ') {
        line->append(new Stencil(space, color));
    }   else {
        line->append(new Character(c,font,color));
    }
}
```

Figure 8.9 Building the view in Figure 8.8

```
page = new LRComposition(
    new TBBox(), new TeXCompositor(), nil, linewidth
);
newline = new Discretionary(
    PenaltyGood, new HGlue(fil), new HGlue(), nil, nil
);
space = new Discretionary(
    0, new Character(' '), new HGlue(), nil, nil
);

int c;
while ((c = getc(file)) != EOF) {
    if (c == '\n') {
        page->append(newline);
    }   else if (c == ' ') {
        page->append(space);
    }   else {
        page->append(new Character(c));
    }
}
```

Figure 8.10 Building a formatted text view

components into lines, and it uses `Discretionaries` to represent possible formatting breaks.

The first parameter for the `LRComposition` constructor is the `glyph` into which the `Compositor` will compose its formatted lines. A typical editor might use another `Compositor` (most likely a `TBComposition`) to

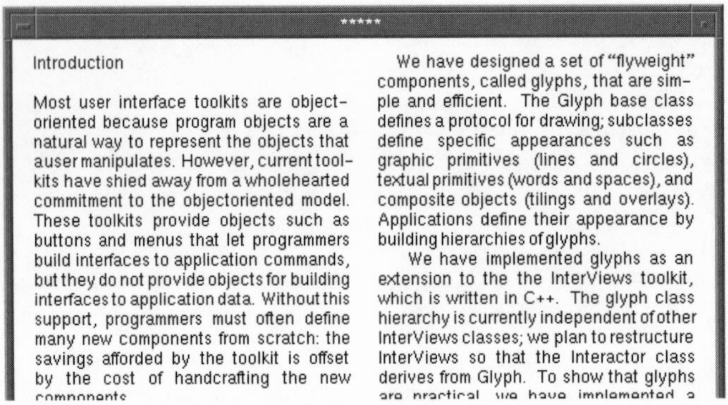

*****

Introduction

Most user interface toolkits are object-oriented because program objects are a natural way to represent the objects that a user manipulates. However, current toolkits have shied away from a wholehearted commitment to the objectoriented model. These toolkits provide objects such as buttons and menus that let programmers build interfaces to application commands, but they do not provide objects for building interfaces to application data. Without this support, programmers must often define many new components from scratch: the savings afforded by the toolkit is offset by the cost of handcrafting the new

We have designed a set of "flyweight" components, called glyphs, that are simple and efficient. The Glyph base class defines a protocol for drawing; subclasses define specific appearances such as graphic primitives (lines and circles), textual primitives (words and spaces), and composite objects (tilings and overlays). Applications define their appearance by building hierarchies of glyphs.

We have implemented glyphs as an extension to the the InterViews toolkit, which is written in C++. The glyph class hierarchy is currently independent of other InterViews classes; we plan to restructure InterViews so that the Interactor class derives from Glyph. To show that glyphs

Figure 8.11 Formatted text view

compose the lines into columns; here, a `TBBox` is sufficient. The second constructor parameter is a `Compositor` that tells the Composition how to find the formatting breaks; this example uses a `TEXCompositor` that implements a simplified version of the TEX optimum fit compositing algorithm [Knuth80]. The third parameter is a `glyph` that the `Composition` will insert between formatted lines. A typical editor might use `VGlue` to represent interline leading; here, a nil value adds no extra spacing. Finally, the last constructor parameter is the target width of the formatted lines.

The first constructor parameter for a `Discretionary` defines the formatting penalty that would be incurred if the break was taken; the remaining parameters define the appearance of the `Discretionary` in its unbroken and broken states. In this example, space characters are represented as `Discretionaries` with zero penalty (suitable places for a break). When a space is not selected as a break, it looks like a space character; when the break is taken, it looks like a zero-sized piece of `Glue`. The constant `PenaltyGood` in the constructor for the newline `Discretionary` represents the best possible place to break. This break, which marks the end of a paragraph, will always be taken.

More advanced formatting features can be added in the same way. For example, a view could use additional `Compositions` to format lines into columns, and columns into pages, it could specify possible hyphenation points by inserting `Discretionaries`, and it could justify the right margin by using stretchable `Glue` for space characters. Figure 8.11 shows part of a screen image of a text view that adds these features.

8.3 Extension: Defining New Components

Many aspects of an application's interface can be constructed by composing existing components. However, most nontrivial interfaces need at least a few components that are application-specific and hence must be defined by the application programmer. For example, a document editor application could build its menu bars and dialog boxes using predefined buttons and menus arranged in `boxes`, and it could represent the characters in the document using predefined `glyphs`, but it will probably need to define application-specific components to specify the way it responds to user events since that task is highly specific to the document-editing process.

8.3.1 Handlers: Responding to Events

Many application-specific components are new kinds of handlers that respond to input events in an application-specific way. To simplify the definition of such components, InterViews defines a `glyph` wrapper class, `InputHandler`, that hides the low level event-handling mechanism behind a higher-level protocol.

The `InputHandler` event model is suitable for many kinds of interaction, including those based on pointing, clicking, dragging, and typing. The model maps raw input events into calls on one of several class methods; Figure 8.12 shows the interface. The `press` and `release` methods are called in response to mouse button actions; `move` is called when the mouse is moved with no buttons pressed; `drag` is called for mouse motion with a mouse button down; and finally, `keystroke` is called when a keyboard event occurs. The base class methods do nothing; applications define their responses to events by subclassing from `InputHandler` and redefining the

```
class InputHandler : public MonoGlyph {
public:
    InputHandler(Glyph*, ...);
    ...
    virtual void move(const Event&);
    virtual void press(const Event&);
    virtual void drag(const Event&);
    virtual void release(const Event&);
    virtual void keystroke(const Event&);
    ...
};
```

Figure 8.12 Interface to the `InputHander` event methods

input methods as appropriate. For example, a text view would define the keystroke method to add printable characters to the document.

Like other `glyph` wrappers, InputHandler is derived from the base class `MonoGlyph`. A `MonoGlyph` is a `glyph` that implements the `glyph` protocol methods by simply delegating them to another `glyph`, called its *body*. Thus, wrapping a `glyph` in a `MonoGlyph` does not change the `glyph` in any way. However, the class is a convenient base class from which to derive wrappers that add extra methods to the `glyph` protocol, or that modify one or other of the `glyph` methods and inherit the remainder. For example, the `InputHandler` wrapper is implemented as a `MonoGlyph` that adds extra methods for responding to input events, the border wrapper is implemented as a `MonoGlyph` that redefines the draw method so that it draws a border around its body, and the `Margin` wrapper is implemented as a `MonoGlyph` that redefines the geometry management methods to add extra space around its body.

Defining `InputHandler` as a wrapper allows applications to easily add input handling behavior to `glyphs`. For example, an application could make a `glyph` in the interface sensitive to mouse clicks simply by defining an `InputHandler` subclass that redefines the `press` method, then wrapping an instance of the class around the `glyph`. Since the wrapper delegates all of the `glyph` methods to its body, the appearance of the interface does not change when the wrapper is added.

8.3.2 Glyphs: Defining Appearance

Applications may require new kinds of objects that cannot be represented using the predefined `glyphs`, or for which such a representation would be inefficient. Such applications define new primitive `glyphs` by subclassing from an existing `glyph` class. For example, an image, processing application might need a `glyph` to represent an editable image.

New `glyph` subclasses must reimplement the `glyph` class protocol methods so that the new object can be used in `glyph` hierarchies along with other `glyphs`; Figure 8.13 shows the class interface. In the figure, the `glyph` methods are grouped according to their function: the request and allocate methods are concerned with geometry management, the `draw`, `print`, and `pick` methods with appearance, and the remainder with implementing the `glyph` structure model.

The `request` and `allocate` methods define the `glyph`'s geometry management. The methods are complimentary: a `glyph`'s `request` method defines the space it wants; its `allocate` method defines how it distributes the space it finally gets. `glyphs` that represent primitive elements such as text and graphics typically define their requests in terms of the data they display. `Character`, for example, requests enough space to display a single `Character` shape in a particular font. Composite `glyphs` calculate their requests from the requests of their components. For example, the width of a horizontal tiling is the sum of the component widths.

Geometric data in InterViews are defined separately for each physical dimension because many geometry management algorithms operate identically in each dimension; the same algorithm can be used in any dimension if the dimension is specified as a parameter. For example, an algorithm that calculates geometry for a horizontal abutting arrangement is the same as an algorithm for a vertical abutting arrangement. If a general abutting algorithm is provided, the horizontal arrangement can be calculated by specifying the `X` dimension, and the vertical arrangement by specifying the `Y` dimension. Currently, `glyph` geometry is two dimensional. However,

```
class Glyph {
public:
    virtual void request (Requisition&) const;
    virtual void allocate (
        Canvas*, const Allocation&, Extension&
    );

    virtual void draw (Canvas*, const Allocation&) const;
    virtual void print (Printer*, const Allocation&) const;
    virtual void pick (
        Canvas*, const Allocation&, int depth, Hit&
    );

    virtual GlyphIndex count () const;
    virtual Glyph* component (GlyphIndex)
    virtual void insert (GlyphIndex, Glyph*);
    virtual void replace (GlyphIndex, Glyph*);
    virtual void remove (GlyphIndex);
    virtual void change (GlyphIndex);
    virtual void append (Glyph*);
    virtual void prepend (Glyph*);
};
```

Figure 8.13 `glyph` **class interface**

the same ideas appear to be useful in the third spatial dimension and even in the time dimension.

`glyphs` define two appearances: the `print` method defines an appearance suitable for final copy, such as on a printed page, and the `draw` method defines an appearance suitable for interactive display, such as on a workstation screen. For many `glyphs`, the appearance implied by drawing and printing is identical—as far as possible, the `glyph` looks the same on the screen as on the printed page. However, some applications display information on the screen that helps users interact with the application's view but that makes no sense in final form. For example, a text application might highlight the currently selected text on the screen, or a drawing editor might provide additional construction lines to help create graphics. `glyphs` that represent objects such as the highlighted text region or the graphics construction lines contribute to the drawn appearance, but they do not contribute to the printed copy.

The `draw` and `print` methods are passed a canvas (`printer` is a subclass of `Canvas`), which specifies the surface to draw on, and an `allocation`, which specifies the `glyph`'s geometry. Primitive `glyphs` define their `draw` and `print` methods in terms of rendering operations on the `Canvas`. Composite `glyphs` usually just recursively draw and print their components.

The class `Canvas` defines a PostScript-like rendering protocol; Figure 8.14 shows part of the class interface. The protocol uses a coordinate space in which dimensions are specified as floating point values measured in printer's points. The coordinate origin is at the lower left corner, and coordinate values increase toward the right and the top. This device-independent coordinate model simplifies the construction of applications that present a WYSIWYG interface because applications can use the same objects to produce visible output on several devices. For example, applications can use the same `glyphs` to generate both the visible output on a workstation display and a file-based representation suitable for printing, or they can portray views on workstations with displays that have different pixel densities.

The `new_path`, `move_to`, `line_to`, `curve_to`, and `close_path` methods define PostScript-like paths that can contain arbitrary combinations of straight and curved segments. The path construction methods build up a current path, which can subsequently be used to produce lines

```
class Canvas {
public:
    ...
    virtual void new_path();
    virtual void move_to(Coord x, Coord y);
    virtual void line_to(Coord x, Coord y);
    virtual void curve_to(
        Coord x, Coord y,
        Coord x1, Coord y1, Coord x2, Coord y2
    );
    virtual void close_path();

    virtual void clip ();
    virtual void stroke (const Brush*, const Color*);
    virtual void fill (const Color*);

    virtual void stencil (
        const Bitmap*, const Color*, Coord x, Coord y
    );
    virtual void image (
        const Raster*, Coord x, Coord y
    );
    virtual void character (
        const Font*, long code, Coord width,
        const Color*, Coord x, Coord y
    );

    virtual void transform (const Transformer&);
    ...
};
```

Figure 8.14 `Canvas` **class rendering methods**

and curves, solid areas, or as a graphics clipping region. The `stroke` method strokes the current path by tracing the path with a brush of specified characteristics dipped in paint of a specified color. The `fill` method fills the current path by spilling paint of a specified color into the area enclosed by the path.

The `stencil`, `image`, and `character` methods render fixed-geometry shapes at specified positions on the canvas. The `bitmap` method stencils the specified bitmap by painting the areas corresponding to the `1` bits in the specified color, and leaving areas corresponding to the `0` bits untouched. The `image` method copies the specified color raster to the canvas. The `character` method draws a single character from a specified font of type. The mapping from character codes into character shapes is font-specific, but fonts that encode characters intended for running text use the Adobe standard font encoding.

All canvas rendering is subject to graphics clipping defined by an arbitrary path, and to geometric transformation defined by a generalized 2D homogeneous transformation represented by a 2×3 matrix. The `transformer` method specifies the transformation to use; the `clip` method sets the clipping to a path previously defined by the path construction methods. Other methods (not shown) allow `glyphs` to save and restore transformations and clipping regions in a way similar to the PostScript `gsave` and `grestore` operations.

In addition to its rendering protocol, the class `canvas` also includes methods that help `glyphs` cooperate in efficiently redrawing the screen following changes to a view. The InterViews redraw model is based on the idea of *damage* regions. When a view changes, it does not redraw the changed region directly; instead, it registers the region for update. At some later time (usually when no input events are pending), InterViews will refresh the screen by drawing the entire `glyph` hierarchy with clipping set to the damage region. This mechanism ensures that the screen will be drawn correctly, even if `glyphs` overlap (as they often do), and it makes the update efficient since only the `glyphs` that intersect the damaged region need draw themselves.

8.4 Implementing InterViews Graphics on X11

The model that InterViews presents to application programmers is higher level than that presented by the X11 Window System platform on which it is implemented. In particular, InterViews defines a graphics model that supports device-independent coordinates with arbitrary geometric transformations, whereas X11 uses a screen-aligned pixel-oriented rendering model. This section outlines our approach to some of the issues we faced when implementing InterViews graphics on X11.

8.4.1 Painting Model

The implementation of the InterViews painting model under X11 is limited by the X11 painting model. InterViews color specifications include an alpha component that allows applications to draw semitransparent colors. However in X11, color can be applied only as a single solid color or by stippling one or two colors through a screen-aligned bitmap. X11 colors are represented by integer pixel values that index a color map, with pixel replacement rules restricted to bitwise binary operations on the

Figure 8.15 Transparent rendering with stippling masks

incoming (source) and existing (destination) pixel values. Thus X11 provides no direct support for semitransparent rendering. In the absence of a more powerful painting model, X11 exposes clients (such as InterViews) to some of the characteristics of the underlying hardware, which allows clients to choose the best strategy for mapping their graphics model on to the available capabilities.

If the available X11 server can accurately represent the red, green, and blue components of the paint (for example, if the machine supports a TrueColor or PseudoColor visual of sufficient depth), InterViews uses single-color stippling to simulate transparency. For example, if an application painted a black rectangle with a transparency of 0.5, InterViews would use a stippling mask with half of the bits on and half off, thus painting half of the pixels black and leaving the other half unmodified. The large diagram in Figure 8.15 illustrates the mechanism; the small figure in the upper left shows what it looks like on the screen.

However, if the X11 server cannot accurately represent a color (perhaps the machine supports only a small StaticGray or StaticColor visual), InterViews uses two-color stippling to synthesize extra shades of color, and it ignores the paint's alpha component. For example, on a monochrome display, InterViews synthesizes a 50% gray by using two-color stippling with equal proportions of black and white pixels.

8.4.2 Coordinate Conversion

InterViews components perform all geometric calculations using floating point `Coord` values. The X11 implementation must therefore convert `Coords` to the integer screen-pixel coordinates that the X11 graphics model needs. To avoid accumulating roundoff errors, InterViews postpones the conversion to screen coordinates until the final stages. However, even when conversion is done carefully, the rounding process can still produce visual anomalies in the final graphical display.

Consider, for example, a filled rectangle that is 2.4 pixels wide when transformed to screen coordinate space. Will the drawn rectangle be two or three pixels wide? Figure 8.16 illustrates the dilemma.

In the left half of the figure, the conversion to pixels is performed in *absolute* coordinates: the absolute `Canvas` coordinates of each corner are separately converted to screen coordinates. Thus the left edge of rectangle 1 (grey region), which is at 6.8 pixels, is rounded up to 7, while the right edge, at 9.2, is rounded down to 9. The result is a two-pixel drawn rectangle (black region). However for rectangle 2, which has its left edge at 13.3 and its right edge at 15.7, the same process results in a three-pixel drawn rectangle. Even though rectangles 1 and 2 are the same size in `Canvas` coordinates, the sizes of the drawn rectangles differ.

The righthand side of Figure 8.16 uses *relative* coordinate conversion. The coordinates of each point of the rectangle, relative to its origin, are converted to pixels. Then the coordinates of the origin are converted and added to the corner positions to give the final pixel positions. Assume that the origin of the rectangles is at the lower left corner. The right edge of rectangle 1 will then have a relative coordinate of 2.4 pixels, which will be rounded down to 2 pixels. Similarly the origin, which has an X coordinate of 9.3 pixels, will be rounded down to 9 pixels. Thus the left edge of the drawn rectangle will be at 9 pixels and the right edge at

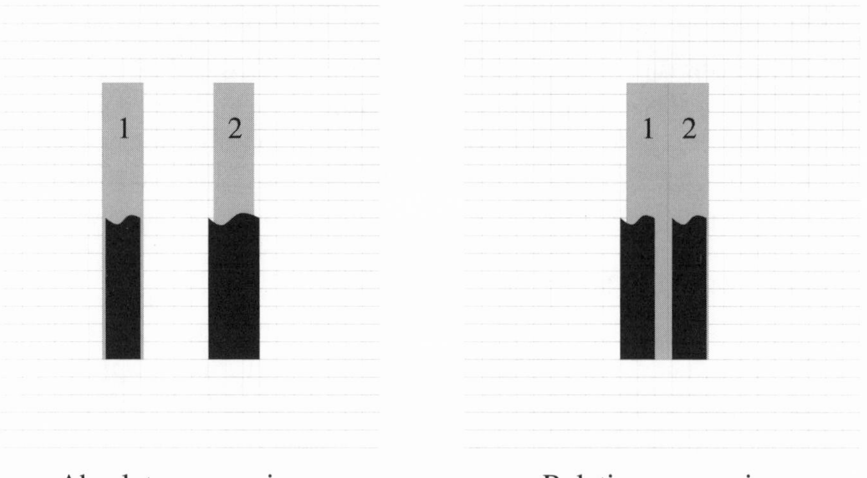

Figure 8.16 Pixel conversion anomalies

11 pixels. Converting coordinates in relative terms avoids size anomalies since the drawn rectangle will be 2 pixels wide no matter where on the canvas its origin falls.

However, the figure shows that relative coordinate conversion introduces a potential alignment anomaly. If two objects are aligned in `Canvas` space, then they may not appear aligned in screen space. Rectangle 2, for example, is positioned so that its left side is aligned to the right side of rectangle 1; both edges are located at 11.7 pixels. The left edge of the drawn rectangle for rectangle 2 will thus be rounded up to 12 pixels, whereas the right edge of the drawn rectangle for rectangle 1 was at 11 pixels. The result is an apparent 1-pixel gap between the two rectangles.

InterViews uses absolute coordinate conversion, since for most applications, the apparent gaps and overlaps caused by alignment anomalies are more visually disruptive than the varying sizes caused by size anomalies. An exception is that, when rendering stroked paths, the brush width is converted directly to pixels. Thus, a 2.4-pixel brush width will result in paths that are 2 pixels wide everywhere on the screen. Since stroked graphics are rarely used to create abutting objects, this concession improves the appearance of stroked graphics while generating few alignment anomalies.

8.4.3 Drawing Images and Text

X11 support for rendering images is limited to screen-aligned arrays of Boolean or pixel values. InterViews renders `Bitmaps` and `Rasters` by creating an XImage of the necessary size and populating the image from information in the `Bitmap` or `Raster`, taking account of any image transformation. Building an `XImage` and sending the image data to the X11 server is potentially slow, since the image might contain large quantities of data. To avoid incurring the cost each time the image is rendered, InterViews stores the rendered image as an `XPixmap` in the server, then uses `XCopyArea` to copy the pixmap to the window. If the image is rendered under several transformations, InterViews keeps separate `XPixmaps` for each transformation.

X11 text drawing support is limited to the `XDrawText` primitive, which draws one or more text strings that share a common horizontal baseline. (The protocol also includes the more limited `XDrawString` primitive and the specialized `XDrawImageString`.) Furthermore, with common versions of the X11 server, text drawing is supported for only a small collection of commonly used point sizes for which predefined character bitmaps are available. (Recently, X11 Releases 5 and 6 have improved the support for drawing transformed text.)

`XDrawText` draws a string of characters with successive character origins spaced by the character's format width. However, X11 uses integer-valued character metrics, whereas InterViews uses floating point character metrics. If a sequence of characters is aggregated into a long character string, cumulative roundoff errors can result in characters that are drawn at screen positions that differ significantly from their specified `Canvas` positions. To minimize character positioning errors, InterViews breaks long strings into smaller substrings, and it intersperses horizontal offset information to correct roundoff errors. This information maps naturally into the `XDrawText` protocol, which draws a list of `XTextItems` that begin at specified horizontal offsets from the end of previous items.

InterViews can use the `XDrawText` primitive only if the text is drawn with the identity transformation and if the text size corresponds to a point size that the X11 server supports. Otherwise, it builds a bitmap image of the character and renders it with techniques similar to the image-rendering techniques. As with images, the transformed bitmaps are stored in the X11 server as `XPixmaps` to improve rendering speed.

8.7 Conclusions: The InterViews Experience

Our experience building and using InterViews has taught us three key lessons:

- The object-oriented approach is a natural way to structure applications with graphical interfaces, but to be most effective it should be teamed with an object-oriented language.
- Even the fine-grained structure in an application interface can be represented as objects if the objects are cheap enough.
- A device-independent graphics model considerably simplifies the construction of graphical interfaces, and it can be efficiently implemented on standard workstation hardware.

An object-oriented approach is an effective way to build graphical interfaces because users naturally think of interfaces as composed of objects; representing user interface objects as program objects leads to straightforward implementations. Furthermore, an object-oriented model promotes the reuse of object definitions through subclassing or instantiation. Most current toolkits (if not all) use an object-oriented programming model, although many do not implement the model with an object-oriented language. (For example the X toolkit [McCormack88 and Swick88] uses C, as do its derivatives, such as Motif.) We have found that an object-oriented language such as C++ considerably simplifies the task of defining and using objects, because it frees the programmer from the need to manually implement subclassing and method-dispatch mechanisms.

Most user interface toolkits focus on components, such as buttons and menus, that programmers can use to provide interfaces to application commands, which typically need a relatively small number of components. However, such components are often too expensive to use to build views of application data, which may require many thousands of components. The InterViews `glyph` class is lightweight enough to represent the smallest components in application views and yet general enough to form the basis for more complex interface objects. The key to making `glyphs` lightweight is to make them sharable; a single `glyph` instance can be used to represent a data element wherever it appears in the view. This characteristic dramatically reduces the number of object instances needed to build views of many kinds of large and complex data structures.

Graphical components that are based on device-independent geometry and rendering models are more general (and hence more reusable) than those based on device-dependent models. Such components simplify the interface programmer's task because the same components can be used to define the appearance of the interface on a range of rendering platforms. Furthermore, InterViews shows that such a model can be efficiently implemented on top of a lower level protocol such as X11, even through the InterViews the model allows arbitrary graphical transformation of objects.

8.8 Acknowledgments

InterViews, like most large systems, was the result of a team effort. The team leader, Mark Linton, implemented key parts of the low level X11 code, and was responsibly for keeping the rest of us (mere PhD students at the time) on track. John Vlissides devised many of the key ideas that underlie the InterViews graphics model, and showed that they were practical by building the idraw drawing editor and the Unidraw application framework.

In particular, John developed the damage-based redrawing approach, and he started us thinking about lightweight graphical objects. Steve Tang built the ibuild interactive interface builder that caused us to think deeply about the role that different kinds of tools play in the user interface construction process. Other players, whose key focus was elsewhere but who nevertheless made substantial contributions, included John Interrante, Craig Dunwoody, and Doug Pan. The work at Stanford was supported in part by Fujitsu America, Inc, by a gift from Digital Equipment Corporation, and by a grant from the Charles Lee Powell Foundation.

Further Reading

[Adobe85] Adobe Systems Incorporated, *PostScript Language Reference Manual,* Addison-Wesley, Reading, 1985.

[Apple85] Apple Computer, *Inside Macintosh, Volume I,* Apple Computer, Inc, 1985. Also published by Addison-Wesley.

[Apple87] Apple Programmer's & Developer's Association, *MacApp: The Expandable Macintosh Application,* Apple Computer, Inc, 1987.

[Calder90] P. R. Calder and M. A. Linton, Glyphs: Flyweight objects for user interfaces, In *Proceedings of the Third Annual Symposium on User Interface Software and Technology,* ACM, Snowbird, UT, 92–101, October 1990.

[Calder92] P. R. Calder and M. A. Linton, The object-oriented implementation of a document editor, In *ACM OOPSLA '92 Conference Proceedings,* Vancouver, British Colombia, 154–165, October 1992.

[Cardelli87] Luca Cardelli, *Building User Interfaces by Direct Manipulation,* SRC Research Report #22, Digital Equipment Corporation Systems Research Center, Palo Alto, October 1987.

[Digital91] Digital Equipment Corporation, *DEC VUIT User's Guide,* Digital Equipment Corporation, Maynard, October 1991.

[Hardy91] E. J. Hardy and D. V. Klein, The Serpent UIMS, In *Proceedings of the Fourth International Conference on Human-Computer Interaction,* Elsevier Science Publishers, 265–269, 1991.

[Knuth84] D. E. Knuth, *The TEX book,* Addison-Wesley, Reading, 1984.

[Knuth80] D. E. Knuth and M. F. Plass, *Breaking Paragraphs into Lines*, Technical report STAN–CS–80–828, Stanford University, November 1980.

[Krasner88] G. E. Krasner and S. T. Pope, A cookbook for using the Model-View-Controller user interface paradigm in Smalltalk-80, *Journal of Object-Oriented Programming*, **1**(3), 26–49, 1988.

[Linton87] Mark A. Linton and Paul R. Calder, The design and implementation of InterViews, In *Proceedings of the USENIX C++ Workshop*, Santa Fe, NM, 256–267, November 1987.

[Linton88] M. A. Linton, P. R. Calder, and J. M. Vlissides, *InterViews: A C++ Graphical Interface Toolkit*, Technical report CSL–TR–88–358, Stanford University, July 1988.

[Linton89] M. A. Linton, J. M. Vlissides, and P. R. Calder, Composing user interfaces with InterViews, *Computer*, **22**(2), 8–22, 1989.

[Linton92] M. A. Linton, P. R. Calder, J. A. Interrante, S. Tang, and J. M. Vlissides, *InterViews Reference Manual, Version 3.1*, Stanford University, December 1992.

[McCormack88] J. McCormack, P. Asente, and R. Swick, *X Toolkit Intrinsics—C Language Interface*, Digital Equipment Corporation, March 1988. Part of the documentation provided with the X Window System.

[Myers89] B. A. Myers, User-interface tools: Introduction and survey, *IEEE Software* **6** (1), 15–23, 1989.

[Open89] *OSF/Motif Programmer's Reference, Revision 1.0*, Open Software Foundation, 1989.

[Palay88] A. J. Palay, W. J. Hansen, M. L. Kazar, M. Sherman, M. G. Wadlow, T. P. Neuendorffer, Z. Stern, M. Bader, and T. Peters, The Andrew Toolkit: An overview, In *Proceedings of the 1988 Winter USENIX Technical Conference*, Dallas, Texas, 9–21, February 1988.

[Scheifler86] R. W. Scheifler and J. Gettys, The X Window System, *ACM Transactions on Graphics*, **5** (2), 79–109, 1986.

[Schulert85] A. J. Schulert, G. T. Rogers, and J. A. Hamilton, ADM: A dialog manager, In *Proceedings of SIGCHI'85*, ACM, New York, 177–183, 1985.

[Sun90] Sun Microsystems, *OpenWindows Developer's Guide Users Manual*, Sun Microsystems Inc, 1990.

[Swick88] R. R. Swick and T. Weissman, *X Toolkit Athena Widgets—C Language Interface*, Digital Equipment Corporation, March 1988. Part of the documentation provided with the X Window System.

[Vlissides89] J. M. Vlissides and M. A. Linton, Unidraw: A framework for building domain-specific graphical editors, In *Proceedings of the ACM SIGGRAPH Symposium on User Interface Software and Technology*, Williamsburg, Virginia, 158–167, November 1989.

[Weinand88] A. Weinand, E. Gamma, and R. Marty, ET++—An object-oriented application framework in C++, In *ACM OOPSLA '88 Conference Proceedings*, San Diego, California, 46–57, September 1988.

Frameworks in Taligent's CommonPoint

GLENN ANDERT

Preview

This chapter defines the concepts and benefits of the framework approach to software architecture by examining a concrete example of a framework within the CommonPoint Input/Output (I/O) system. First, we give an overview of the Taligent system which is commercially sold as CommonPoint. CommonPoint is a large collection of frameworks; each one provides a layer of services to the application developer. Then we narrow down to the CommonPoint I/O System and the problems it solves. The SCSI framework is a reusable part within the larger I/O system of frameworks.

Study of the internal architecture of the SCSI framework illustrates how one framework can collaborate with other frameworks. This provides a concrete example of frameworks in action and illustrates the practical benefits of the framework approach to software architecture.

9.1 What Is CommonPoint?

A framework has two kinds of users: those who play the *client role* and those who play the *ensemble role*. A client is a body of code that uses the abstract services provided by the framework. The Consumer in Figure 9.1

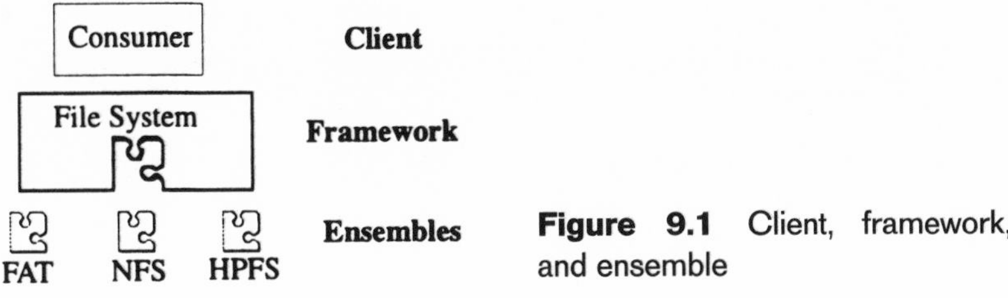

Figure 9.1 Client, framework, and ensemble

is an example of a client. An ensemble is a specialization of a client, which provides application-specific functionality, see Figure 9.1, again.

One or more of the framework's classes are considered public by its clients. The methods of these classes define the public interface of the framework. The File System in Figure 9.1 is an example of a framework. The top edge of the framework box represents the client interface. A framework might not be complete on its own. The puzzle-shaped bottom edge of the framework box represents the methods that the ensemble must provide in order to complete the framework, as well as the protected operations that the framework makes available to the ensemble's implementation.

An *ensemble* is a set of one or more classes that are derived from the framework and provide concrete implementations for the pure virtual methods declared by the framework, Together with the framework, an ensemble is a complete concrete implementation of the service offered by the framework's public interface. The NFS in Figure 9.1 is an example of an ensemble. The puzzle-shaped top edge of the ensemble box matches the slot in the framework box to indicate that the ensemble completes the framework.

A framework's public interface is typically used polymorphically by the client. In some cases, the client uses additional public operations exported by the ensemble. Clients typically instantiate the ensemble that they want to use. But in more sophisticated frameworks, the framework itself can provide mechanisms for automatically instantiating an ensemble for the client.

CommonPoint is the name of the Taligent framework. Its ensembles are written with the intent of providing client code with a rich and well-organized repertoire in the particular domain. They are also written with the intent of making it easier to create new ensembles on an ongoing basis. In the latter case, the framework has substantial default behavior. It often comes with one or more ensembles that allow it to "work out of the box." It is easy to customize. In C++, customization is typically done via *inheritance* and *overriding*. The ensemble can customize the framework without requiring modification of the framework's source code.

To provide the interaction protocols for key scenarios, the framework often embodies flow control, calling the ensemble's methods when the framework thinks that they we needed. This is much different than making calls to a library to make things happen.

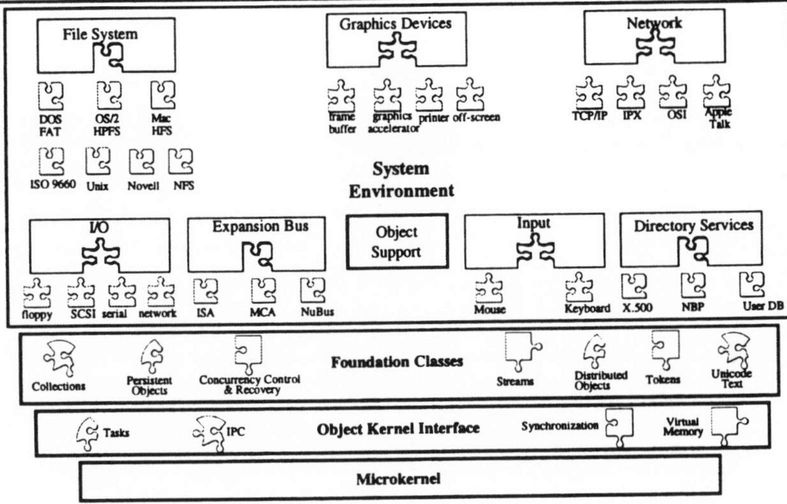

Figure 9.2 OS built from object frameworks

CommonPoint frameworks are composable. They can be layered, one on top of another. And a framework itself can be a specialization of a more abstract framework.

The objects in a CommonPoint framework vary in granularity. Some consist of large, complex objects. Others consist of lightweight, fine-grained objects.

CommonPoint uses frameworks at both the lowest levels in the system and the highest levels. Figure 9.2 is an abbreviated view of some of the frameworks in CommonPoint. Some examples of CommonPoint's use of frameworks include frameworks for the compound document architecture, window system, user interface, and development environment.

9.2 The Taligent I/O System

The Taligent I/O System is a highly reusable input/output architecture. It is composed of a number of collaborating frameworks. The I/O System could not meet its requirements without extensive use of frameworks.

Typically, the developer of a new device simply writes an ensemble for an existing framework. The framework takes on the responsibility for

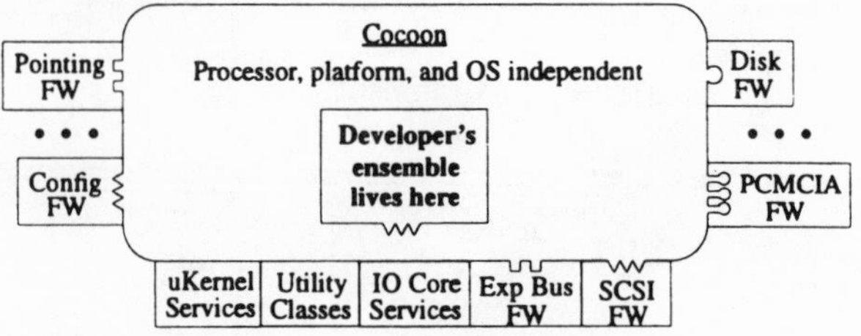

Figure 9.3 Developer code protected by cocoon

integrating the device into the rest of the system. It provides enough default behavior that the developer need only develop the hardware-specific code that is needed for the new device.

In the CommonPoint system, device configuration is done by an object known as a *Configuration Recorder.* The actual work of doing I/O to the device is performed by an I/O Service. These are different abstractions. I/O services do not embed I/O resources (such as I/O addresses) in their code. Therefore, an I/O service ensemble is independent of the physical location of the device. So, for example, a service that can operate a device integrated on the motherboard can operate the same type of device on an expansion card. Thus, board developers can often reuse drivers from the existing pool.

The CommonPoint system supports a wide range of devices, processors, and buses. But it also provides rigorous encapsulation of hardware dependencies. This allows the same I/O service code to work across different processors and buses. Hardware independence increases the potential reuse of I/O services.

Because of the fine-grained abstractions in the CommonPoint system, one I/O service is often layered on top of another, forming a stack of services. Each service exports a number of protocols for use by other services layered above. Each service demands a particular protocol of the service layered below. With this information, the framework can automatically instantiate service stacks. The service above uses the interface of the service below in a polymorphic fashion and does not know the identity of the concrete service below. This greatly increases the potential for reuse of the services above, and means that developers of new devices need only provide new ensembles for the lowest service.

Figure 9.3 shows the CommonPoint I/O System as a protective cocoon for an ensemble. The edge of the cocoon represents the services and frameworks available to the ensemble in the center. The cocoon also provides portability and release-to-release binary compatibility. This allows an ensemble written for a CommonPoint I/O framework to be processor- and platform-independent.

Because the cocoon also shields the ensemble from the host OS, a single I/O service ensemble can operate under CommonPoint as well as certain OSs produced by other vendors. Thus, instead of having to write a unique driver for each OS, the developer writes just a single I/O service ensemble that will work with multiple OS personalities.

9.3 Enabling Hardware Innovation

Extensive use of frameworks in CommonPoint results in a modular, open, extensible, and *fine-grain architecture. Modularity* allows easy assembly of a configuration of existing I/O service ensembles suitable for a custom piece of hardware. The architecture is layered via rigorous abstract service interfaces. There is clear separation of responsibility between the service provider and the service client. Applications do not directly access hardware— they just use the appropriate service interface. Therefore custom hardware can be built to take over the responsibility of virtually any I/O service, and as many layers as make sense the developer simply implements the new hardware; clients access it via a custom I/O service ensemble for the appropriate service framework. All of the higher-level services and applications still work. With the benefits of frameworks, developers can extend service interfaces with new features and capabilities. This architecture removes many barriers to hardware innovation.

9.3.1 Configuring Hardware Easily

Today's hardware systems cover the full spectrum from those requiring deep user involvement to configure the hardware, to those allowing automatic configuration by the OS. CommonPoint's I/O System supports this full spectrum. These are some of the mechanisms that the I/O System employs to provide as friendly a system as possible:

- When bus technology and I/O devices make it possible to detect the presence and nature of a device, the system does so automatically, even for dynamically installed hardware. I/O resources, such as interrupt levels and I/O registers, are automatically assigned when the device is capable of being programmed for different resources. This relieves the user of configuration chores.

- For devices that are incapable of automatic detection and/or configuration, user interaction is required. But, unlike conventional systems, the user does not edit configuration files. Rather, a direct manipulation graphical user interface is used to configure the hardware. In typical cases, all that is required is a simple drag-and-drop gesture. In other cases, the interface guides the user through the steps necessary for configuring that class of device, prevents the user from accidently creating an erroneous configuration, and provides quality feedback about configuration conflicts. This user interface is a CommonPoint OS personality feature. The I/O System's architecture makes it possible to construct such a user interface, without requiring the driver developer to write personality-dependent code.
- Device configuration information is stored in a persistent repository that is maintained automatically by the system. The repository is dynamically updated as devices come and go, freeing the user from manual configuration file maintenance.
- If the device supports it own storage of the required I/O software, then the system can download that software automatically, reducing software installation chores.
- Software is loaded into the running system dynamically, including kernel-level interrupt handlers. This eliminates the need for manual linking and system generation.
- Each new I/O device is assigned an identifier that is unique within the configuration. Because the assignment is automatic, the user is not required to give the new device a name. The identifier is hierarchical in nature and is computed from the hardware hierarchy itself; as a result, the system can give unique identifiers to arbitrary types and numbers of devices. A given device has the same identifier from boot to boot. As a result, these identifiers can in turn be embedded within objects on the desktop. This allows the user to use drag-and-drop gestures to direct 10 operations, without being required to know the name of the specific device, and get consistent behavior from boot to boot.

These identifiers are used as keys to manage user preference information, such as mouse speed. This allows the user to manage preferences for arbitrary configurations. For example, there can be three mice on one machine, each with a different mouse speed.

9.3.2 Maximizing Quality

When the developer writes an ensemble for an existing framework (rather than starting from scratch), numerous quality benefits ensue. Consider these advantages:

- Because the framework is reused, it is quite robust. New bugs are typically limited to new ensembles, greatly reducing the overall bug rate.
- CommonPoint's framework-based I/O architecture enables high performance. Because the ensemble typically provides just the hardware-specific details, the framework is responsible for most of the infrastructure, such as buffer management, queueing, and client thread control. The ensemble automatically benefits from the performance optimizations in the framework. Because the framework and ensemble are packaged in different shared libraries, the framework can be optimized independently of its many ensembles. And the framework can be optimized for specific platforms without impacting the ensembles. Together, these benefits greatly improve overall performance.
- The modular architecture, dynamic service installation, and use of frameworks together enable a smaller memory footprint.
- The architecture supports user-mode device drivers. A user-mode driver improves overall system robustness because it increases accountability and its bugs typically do not crash the whole system. But for certain devices with high bandwidth, low latency or real-time requirements, it can be necessary for significant portions of the driver to run in kernel mode in order to meet those requirements. The architecture supports these drivers as well. The trade-off is made on a per-framework basis, enabling an overall optimal balance between performance and system robustness.

- The Taligent OS is built on a microkernel architecture with *lightweight threads* and fast IPC. The I/O architecture performs I/O on a per-thread basis. This makes it easier for applications to ensure that they are always responsive to user action. Because IPC is fast, multiple address spaces can be used to provide bug isolation and accountability.
- The architecture is scalable across a wide range of platform performances. Multiprocessor support is built into the frameworks. Thus an ensemble that works on a uniprocessor also works on a multiprocessor, without any special attention by the ensemble developer. Multiprocessor support can be quite complex. Because the framework already provides it, ensembles are simpler, easier to write and understand, and have fewer bugs.
- Errors are reported by objects that contain information describing the nature of the error. They are delivered to clients as C++ exceptions. Because resources are managed by objects with destructors that free those resources, resources are properly reclaimed when no longer in use, even in the face of exceptions.
- Fine-grained abstractions and strong type checking at compile time result in code that has fewer bugs and is easier to read and understand.

9.4 Example: SCSI Services Domain

This section illustrates a SCSI Service framework that enables rapid construction of object-oriented SCSI device drivers. This gives a concrete example of the power of frameworks.

9.4.1 SCSI Background

SCSI, the Small Computer System Interface, specifies the mechanical, electrical, and functional requirements for a small computer input/output bus and command sets for peripheral device types commonly used with small computers.

Each SCSI bus can have zero or more SCSI devices attached. Each device is uniquely identified by its SCSI ID. Each device can have one or more logical units which can be of different types (a disk and tape can be two logical units of the same SCSI device).

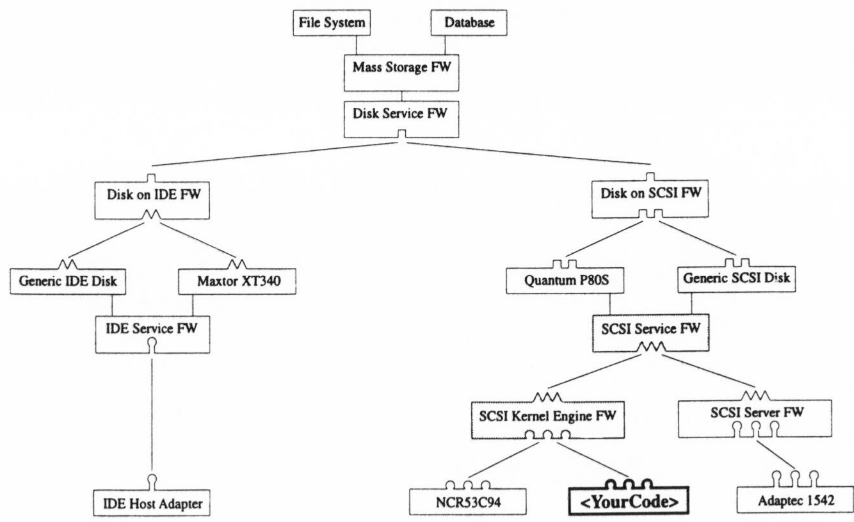

Figure 9.4 SCSI services context, clients, and implementation frameworks

9.4.2 Client View of the SCSI Service

How is the SCSI Service used? Consider Figure 9.4. The Disk Service framework provides the basic ability to read and write random-access, block-oriented storage devices. Disk On SCSI is an implementation framework for disk devices on SCSI buses. It provides default behavior for implementing the Disk Service Protocol for SCSI disks, and can be used out of the box for generic SCSI disks. Quantum P80S is a SCSI disk device. Quantum P80S ensemble specializes the Disk On SCSI ensemble with a small amount of vendor-specific logic.

The primary abstraction that the SCSI Service exports to its clients is the unit handle. A unit handle object represents the ability for one thread to send or receive SCSI commands and data to or from a single unit of some device on the SCSI bus. It provides methods for both synchronous and asynchronous I/O. The remaining objects and methods are beyond the scope of this chapter.

9.4.3 Overview of SCSI Implementation Frameworks

The SCSI Kernel Engine framework is responsible for managing client threads, queueing requests, buffer management, and DMA management. It provides considerable default behavior for SCSI service, but is not complete. The NCR53C94 ensemble completes the framework by providing low-level I/O register manipulation and adapter protocol. For a new SCSI adapter, the developer writes a <YourCode> ensemble, as shown in Figure 9.4.

The SCSI Kernel Engine framework keeps its queue in the kernel, handles I/O request state transitions at interrupt level, provides sharing of DMA channels, and synchronizes access to the adapter's I/O registers. This is an appropriate implementation framework for the NCR53C94 ensemble, because the NCR53C94 occasionally requires interrupts to be off when manipulating the adapter's registers and generates at least three interrupts for every client I/O operation.

In contrast, the SCSI Server framework keeps its queue in a user-level server task, communicates with its adapter via shared memory, does not use shared DMA channels, does not require synchronized access to adapter I/O registers, and under the right conditions, can produce fewer than one interrupt per I/O operation. This is an appropriate implementation framework for the Adaptec 1542 ensemble.

9.4.4 Instantiation of Composed Ensembles

The Disk Service framework supports multiple implementation frameworks and numerous concrete ensembles. Others are easily added. The same is true for the SCSI Service framework. Consider the Quantum P80S ensemble in Figure 9.4. It is dependent on the SCSI Service protocol. To achieve maximum reuse, its code should not know which concrete SCSI ensemble provides the service. To solve this problem, the stack of services is automatically instantiated, as follows: recall that each device has a unique identifier. The client (Mass Storage framework, in this example) supplies the name of the desired service protocol (Disk Service framework, in this example) and the identifier for the particular disk to the service stack mechanism, which in turn consults the service repository, selects appropriate services by protocol matching, and instantiates them. This allows the Quantum P805 ensemble to be instantiated on top of the NCR53C94 ensemble, without Quantum P80S's code even knowing about the existence of the NCR53C94 ensemble. This automatic composition of ensembles enables a high degree of reuse and greatly simplifies configuration.

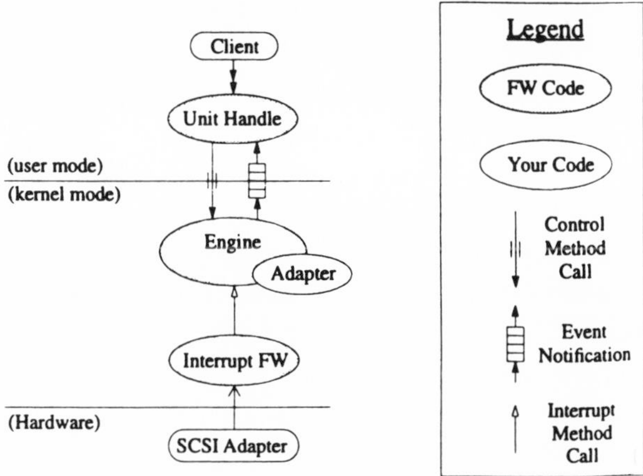

Figure 9.5 SCSI Kernel Engine components

9.4.5 Architecture or the Kernel Engine Framework

The SCSI Service framework defines the client protocol that allows clients to use SCSI services without regard for the particular adapter or style of implementation. The SCSI Kernel Engine framework inherits that protocol.

The SCSI Service framework defines, and provides default implementation of, a SCSI bus configuration. It provides the logic to scan the bus, recognize devices, and records configuration information. When appropriate, it can invoke device-specific objects to perform the device recognition and recording of configuration information. The SCSI Kernel Engine framework inherits this configuration implementation.

9.4.6 Fundamental Abstractions

Figure 9.5 illustrates the design of the SCSI Kernel Engine framework. There are two major objects of interest.

The first is a unit handle object, which represents the ability for one thread to perform I/O on a single unit or some device on the SCSI bus. A unit handle object is responsible for delivering I/O requests to the second object, the engine object for execution, and for waiting for completion events when appropriate. There may be more than one unit handle object for one unit. The engine object represents the controller for a single SCSI bus. The engine object contains a request queue for each active unit. It queues requests from one or more unit handle objects. It is responsible for executing the finite state machine that represents the sequence of atomic steps that must be taken in order to complete the I/O request. Each engine object is associated with many unit handle objects.

The unit handle object lives directly in its client's address space in user mode, and performs all of its work on within the client thread. The unit handles associated with a given engine can live in different address spaces. The engine object lives in kernel space. Some of its methods are known as control methods. These methods are called by the unit handle object and execute in kernel space on the client's thread of control. Invocation of these methods requires a user-to-kernel mode crossing. This mechanism is encapsulated in a control channel object that implements a synchronous procedure call model with *in* and *out* parameters. The mechanism is typically implemented using some sort of trap. So, a unit handle object has a control channel handle. It uses the control channel object to invoke control methods of its engine object.

9.4.7 Tailoring for the Specific Adapter

As seen in Figure 9.5, code is specific to the actual SCSI adapter that plugs into the engine object. This is how the engine is tailored to the specific adapter. The adapter object knows how to manipulate adapter registers to realize the actions necessary to make transitions in the finite state machine. It can contribute states, transitions, and actions to the finite state machine. It is relatively easy to implement because the unit handle and engine already take care of most of the work. The ensemble just fills in the hardware-specific details.

9.4.8 Unit Handle Responsibilities

The unit handle is responsible for keeping certain state. It shares a single engine object with other unit handles for the same SCSI bus. It might have a completion event queue. As indicated previously, the unit handle object is automatically instantiated on the client's behalf by the service stack mechanism. The set of unit handle objects for a given adapter collaborate to manage the lifetime of the engine that they share.

It is possible for the ensemble to override these behaviors. But the typical ensemble simply inherits a fully functional unit handle implementation that works out of the box.

9.4.9 Engine Responsibilities

The engine is responsible for keeping certain state. For each unit, it maintains a queue of requests, For each request, it maintains the finite state machine for the request, a handle on the buffer containing the data for the request, and the identity of the unit handle that issued the request. It maintains a proxy for each unit handle. For a unit handle with an event queue, it keeps the sender end of the unit handle's event queue object.

The engine is responsible for protecting the state with a critical section. It ensures that, at most, one thread is inside the critical section at a time. This includes both client threads executing control methods and a thread executing the interrupt method. Its synchronization works in the face of multiple processors.

The engine is not complete and cannot run out of the box because it does not know the low-level details of the adapter. Certain behaviors are left to the ensemble.

9.4.10 Ensemble Responsibilities

The ensemble manages limited state. Some adapters require the ensemble to cache copies of I/O registers. Some adapters require the ensemble to generate physical memory data structures shared with the adapter; in these cases the framework provides memory management services and the ensemble just fills in the appropriate fields.

The ensemble provides actions for starting and finalizing I/O requests. These typically manipulate the appropriate I/O registers or shared memory data structures. For adapters that generate several interrupts per I/O, the ensemble can augment the engine's finite state machine with additional states, transitions, and actions. The ensemble is also responsible for reporting errors to the engine.

The ensemble provides these behaviors by subclassing from the TSCSIKernelEngine class and supplying the required methods.

9.5 Conclusion

The I/O System provides numerous frameworks and hundreds of classes. Together, the SCSI Service framework and the SCSI Kernel Engine framework provide approximately 20 additional classes that utilize the I/O System frameworks in a fashion that is optimized for a certain style of SCSI adapter. The ensemble developer implements a single subclass, but gets the benefit of leveraging the others. This has the following benefits:

- Writing an equivalent driver for a conventional OS might require the developer to write five times as much code.
- Critical user benefits such as plug-and-play configuration and service activation are provided by default for all drivers.
- The framework provides an infrastructure that includes ready-for-production solutions to complex problems such as buffer management, queueing, client-server communication, synchronization, resource management, and error recovery. These solutions are optimized for the particular kind of device. The *N*th ensemble for a framework benefits from real-world testing by the *N*–1 previous ensembles. Because the framework can live in a shared library separate from the ensemble, when framework bugs are fixed, all ensembles can benefit. When performance enhancements are made to the framework, all ensembles can benefit. As a result, the quality benefits are enormous.

These benefits result in significantly lower cost and shorter time to market for developers. Furthermore, the open fine-grained object architecture will enable hardware and software innovation and provide the underpinning for tomorrow's highly adaptable software systems.

9.6 Acknowledgments

The CommonPoint I/O System is the result of years of hard work and would not have been possible without the contributions of many talented individuals, including Rick Auricchio, Chip Bering, Vicki Brown, Creed Erickson, Naresh Gupta, Brett Halle, Steve Lemon, George Norman, Patrick Ross, EU Sudhakaran, Eryk Vershen, and Shinzo Watanabe.

References

[Taligent93] *Leveraging Object-Oriented Frameworks,* Taligent Inc., Cupertino, CA, 1993.

[ANSI86] *ANSI X3.131-1986, Small Computer System Interface (SCSI),* American National Standards Institute, New York, 1986

[ANSI91] *Draft Proposed American National Standards X3.131-199x Small Computer System Interface (SCSI-II),* American National Standards Institute, Revision 10h, 10/17191.

[NCR89] *NCR 53C94/53C95/53C96 Advanced SCSI Controller Data Manual,* NCR Corporation, Santa Clara, CA, Rev 2.2, 1989.

[Adaptec 92] *AHA-1540C/1542C ISA to SCSI Host Adapter Technical Reference Manual,* Adaptec Corporation, Milpitas, CA, Revision A. September 1992, Stock number 510219-00.

PART III

Applications of Frameworks

In Chapter 10, John Vlissides describes Unidraw, which is an application of the best principles of object-oriented application frameworks. First, Unidraw reuses Interviews instead of reinventing a new GUI-based framework. Then, Unidraw extends InterViews into new domains, e.g., editors for graphical drawing, musical scores, and circuit design. John lets us in on the benefits of framework technology by sharing some size statistics gathered by real applications of Unidraw.

Chapter 11 shows how to merge a programming language with a framework to derive a powerful (visual) programming system, ProGraph CPX. In this exciting episode, Kurt Schmucker first surveys major features of ProGraph, and then illustrates how to write ProGraph applications from reusable framework components. ProGraph portends the future of software development, where end-user applications are quickly prototyped by reusing powerful underlying frameworks.

CHAPTER 10

Unidraw: A Framework for Building Domain-Specific Graphical Editors*

JOHN M. VLISSIDES

Preview

Unidraw is a framework for creating graphical editors in domains such as technical and artistic drawing, music composition, and circuit design. Unidraw simplifies the development of these editors by providing programming abstractions that are common across domains.

Unidraw defines four basic abstractions: *components* encapsulate the appearance and behavior of objects, *tools* support direct manipulation of components, *commands* define operations on components, and *external representations* define the mapping between components and the file format generated by the editor. Unidraw also supports multiple views, graphical connectivity, and dataflow between components. The Unidraw framework is implemented as a library of C++ classes built on top of the InterViews user interface toolkit and the X Window System.

This chapter describes Unidraw's design, implementation issues, and two domain-specific editors developed with Unidraw: a MacDraw-like drawing editor and a GUI builder. Our results indicate a substantial reduction in implementation time and effort compared with development on top of a user interface toolkit alone.

---

* This work reflects PhD research conducted at Stanford University and was underwritten in part by the NASA CASIS project under Contract NAGW 419, by the Quantum project through a gift from Digital Equipment Corporation, and by grants from the Charles Lee Powell foundation and Fujitsu America, Inc. Portions of this chapter appeared in *ACM Transactions on Information Systems,* Vol. 8, No. 3, July 1990, Copyright 1990, Association for Computing Machinery, Inc. Unidraw is distributed freely as part of the InterViews library. InterViews is available for anonymous ftp from `interviews.stanford.edu` in `pub/3.1.tar.Z`

10.1 What Is a Drawing Framework?

Graphical editors represent familiar objects visually and let a user manipulate the representations directly. Unfortunately, graphical editors are difficult to build with general user interface tools because such editors have special requirements. For example, user interface toolkits provide buttons, scroll bars, and ways to assemble them into a specific interface, but they do not offer primitives for building drawing editors that produce PostScript or schematic capture systems that produce circuit specifications (called *netlists*). Such applications provide direct-manipulation interfaces to graphical objects having diverse attributes, behaviors, and interdependencies.

We use the term *graphical object editor* for an application that lets users manipulate graphical representations of domain-specific objects and that generates one or more static representations. Most graphical object editors also feature:

- Noninteractive operations, usually invoked from menus, that affect the objects' state
- Structuring techniques for building hierarchies of objects
- Mechanisms for propagating information and maintaining graphical constraints between objects
- A way to store objects in nonvolatile form

We had three key goals in developing Unidraw:

- Support graphical object editing in a broad range of domains.
- Significantly reduce the time and effort needed to develop a domain-specific editor compared to implementation from scratch (that is, using just a conventional user interface toolkit).
- Create applications with performance and utility comparable to their from-scratch counterparts.

Take a schematic capture system, for example, which lets a circuit designer construct circuits interactively right on the computer screen. The designer can manipulate a schematic of a circuit element, such as a transistor or a logic gate, directly with the mouse; he or she can drag it to a particular location in a circuit and "wire" it up to other circuit elements.

The application maintains the illusion that the designer is manipulating real objects.

When the designer modifies the circuit, the application updates its internal representation so that it reflects the changes back to the designer. It detects when and where the designer clicks on a particular gate, and it responds appropriately. When the designer moves a gate to a new location, for example, the application can reroute connected wires so that they stay connected. It can analyze the circuit for illegal connections, thereby catching errors early. When the circuit is complete, the system can transform its internal representation into a standard netlist format from which a manufacturer can fabricate the circuit.

Clearly, traditional user interface toolkits don't support most of these capabilities, so developers must painstakingly design and implement them all. In contrast, Unidraw offers abstractions beyond the usual buttons, scroll bars, and menus; it offers abstractions that help developers build high-function applications like the schematic capture system. Unidraw frees developers from designing aspects of graphical object editors that are common across domains, like the need for an internal as well as a graphical representation, support for direct manipulation, connectivity maintenance, and generating new representations from the internal one. With Unidraw, developers focus on the aspects that are unique to a particular application domain.

Unidraw defines a reusable design for graphical object editor. Hence, it can reduce design implementation time dramatically. It won't do that for just any application, though: its abstractions don't help you implement, say, a word processor or an arcade game. But if you're developing a graphical object editor, Unidraw can be a big help. We'll see how in this chapter.

10.2 Unidraw's Design

10.2.1 Overview

Unidraw is designed to provide only the graphical editing portions of a larger application. Thus, in addition to providing the usual graphical editing functions, it must smoothly integrate with other parts of the application. Figure 10.1 depicts the dependencies between the layers of software that underlie a domain-specific editor based on Unidraw. At the lowest levels are the operating and window systems. Above the window

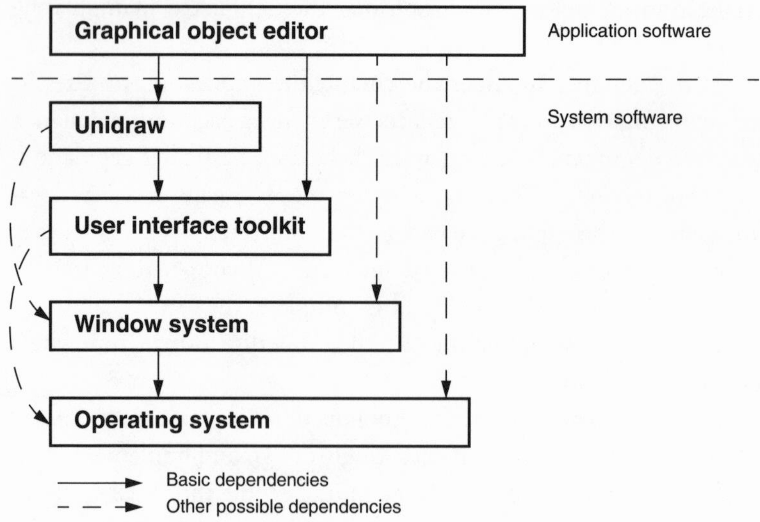

Figure 10.1 Layers of software underlying a domain-specific editor

system level are the objects provided by the user interface toolkit, including buttons, scroll bars, menus, and methods for composing them into generic interfaces.

In designing Unidraw, we focused on the common attributes of domain-specific editors. These attributes are supported by four classes of objects:

- *Components* represent the elements in a drawing. For example, elements might be geometric shapes in a technical drawing, schematics of electronic parts in circuit layout, or notes in written music. Components encapsulate the appearance and semantic properties of these elements. A domain-specific editor's main objective is to let the user arrange components to convey information in the domain of interest.

  Components have an MVC-like structure: the component *subject* corresponds to the model for the component, and the competent *view* corresponds to the component's view. (There is no object corresponding to an MVC controller.) The subject encapsulates the component's defining aspects, aspects that don't depend on presentation. As you would expect, the view defines a presentation for the component. However, in a twist on standard MVC, component views aren't necessarily visual, as we'll see shortly.

- *Tools* support direct manipulation of components. Tools employ animation and other visual effects for immediate feedback to reinforce the user's perception of dealing with real objects. Examples include tools for editing, rotating and translating, and for connecting components.
- *Commands* define operations on components and other objects. Commands are similar to messages in traditional object-oriented systems, in that components can receive and respond to them. Commands can also be executed in isolation to perform arbitrary computation, and they can reverse the effects of such execution to support `undo`. Examples include commands for changing the attributes of a component, duplicating a component, and grouping several components into a composite component.
- *External representations* convey domain-specific information outside the editor. Each component can define one or more external representations of itself. For example, a transistor component can define both a PostScript representation for printing and a netlist representation for circuit simulation; each is generated by a different class of external representation. An external representation object thus defines a one-way mapping between a component and its representation in an outside format.

Unidraw defines abstract classes for component, command, tool, and external representation objects. Subclasses implement domain-specific behavior in terms of the abstract class interfaces. For example, components define operations that let commands affect their internal state. This partitioning of graphical object editor functionality is the foundation of the framework's design.

10.2.2 Application Organization

Figure 10.2 shows the object structure of a typical domain-specific editor based on Unidraw. At the bottom level in the diagram are two component subjects, the leftmost containing subcomponent subjects. An entire domain-specific drawing is represented by a composite component subject that can be incorporated into a larger work. At the second level from the bottom are the corresponding views of the subjects. Note that the righthand subject has two views attached. Each component view is

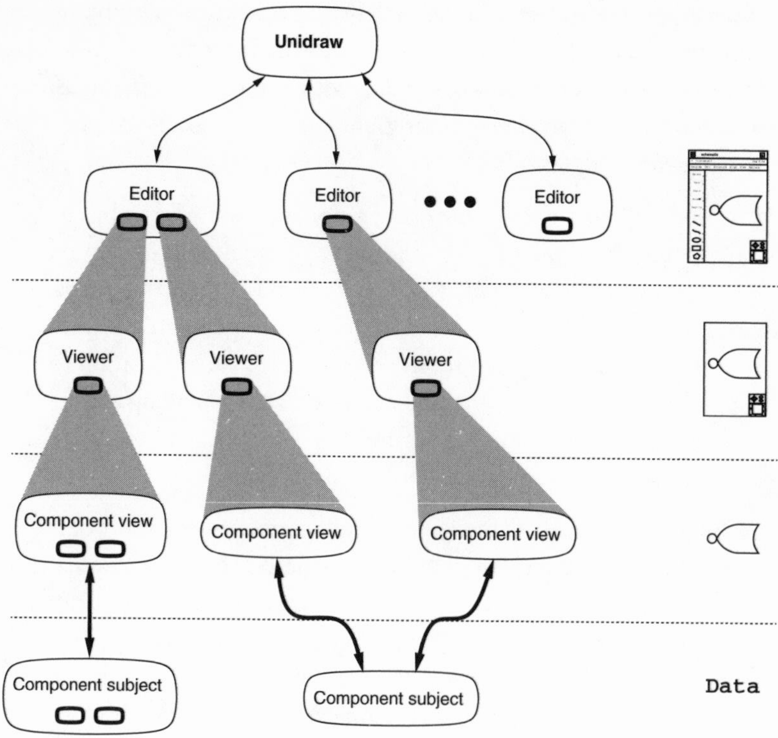

Figure 10.2 General structure of a domain-specific editor based on Unidraw

placed in a *viewer* at the third level. A viewer displays a graphical component view, most often the root view in a hierarchy. A viewer displays the view on the screen and supports scrolling and zooming it. Viewers also take events from the user interface toolkit and translate them into Unidraw protocol requests.

10.2.3 Editors

An *editor* associates tools and user-accessible commands with one or more viewers and combines them into a coherent user interface. An editor also maintains a *selection* object that manages component views in which the user has expressed interest. A Unidraw-based application can create any number of editor objects, allowing the user to work on multiple views of components. Operations requiring intereditor communication or coordination access the *unidraw object*, a one-of-a-kind object maintained by the application. For example, commands for opening and closing editors and quitting the application access this object. The unidraw object also maintains logs of commands that have been executed and reverse-executed to support arbitrary-level `undo` and `redo`.

Not shown in Figure 10.2 is the *catalog object*, which manages a database of components, commands, and tools. At minimum, a domain-specific editor uses the catalog to name, store, and retrieve components that represent user drawings. An editor could also access uninstalled commands and tools and incorporate them into its interface at runtime.

Note that Unidraw does not dictate a particular look and feel for a given editor object. A domain-specific editor may define editor objects that use separate windows for their commands, tools, and viewers. The framework specifies only how the editor mediates communication between components and the commands, tools, and viewers that affect them.

10.2.4 Components

A component defines the appearance and behavior of a drawing element.* The behavior has three aspects: how a component responds to commands and tools (subject/view interfaces), the component's connectivity; and how the component communicates with other components.

Subject and View Interfaces

Unidraw defines separate interfaces for component subjects and views. Tables 10.1 and 10.2 list the fundamental operations in these interfaces.

Component subjects define `Attach` and `Detach` operations to establish or destroy a connection with a component view. `Notify` alerts the subject's views to the possibility that their state is inconsistent with the subject's. Upon notification, a view reconciles any inconsistencies between the subject's state and its own. The `Update` operation notifies the subject of changes in state that *it* depends on. The subject is responsible for updating its state in response to an `Update` message.

A component subject can be passed an `Interpret` command to do some application-specific operation, and an `Uninterpret` command to cancel the effects of an `Interpret`. The subject might undo internal state

---

* Strictly speaking, a component in Unidraw comprises a subject and a number of views. However, a component is logically just one object in its domain. Hence we use the term *component* without specifying subject or view to refer to this logical component.

Table 10.1 Component subject interface

Return values	Operation	Arguments
	`Attach`	Component view
	`Detach`	Component view
	`Notify`	
	`Update`	
	`Interpret`	Command
	`Uninterpret`	Command
Transfer function	`GetTransferFunction`	
	(*child iteration and manipulation operations*)	
Graphic	`GetGraphic`	Mobility
	`SetMobility`	
Mobility	`GetMobility`	

Table 10.2 Component view interface

Return values	Operation	Arguments
	`Update`	
	`Interpret`	Command
	`Uninterpret`	Command
	(*child iteration and manipulation operations*)	
Graphic	`GetGraphic`	
	`Highlight`	
	`Unhighlight`	
Manipulator	`CreateManipulator`	Tool, Event
Command	`InterpretManipulator`	Manipulator

changes based on information in the command, or it might simply reverse-execute the command.

A component subject can contain other component subjects, allowing hierarchies of domain-specific components. Component subjects therefore define a family of operations for iterating through their child subjects (if any) and for reordering them.

The component view interface duplicates some of the subject interface, namely, `Update`, `Interpret`, `Uninterpret`, and those for child iteration and manipulation. By default, a subject's `Notify` operation calls `Update` on each of its views. `Interpret` and `Uninterpret` are defined on views because some objects deal with component views rather than their subjects. Hence it may be convenient to send a command to a view for (un)interpretation, which may in turn send the command to its subject (the default behavior). A component view may have a subcomponent view structure (which may or may not reflect its subject's structure), so the view interface also defines child iteration and manipulation operations.

Graphical Components

Graphical components are specialized components that use *graphic* objects in their subjects and views to define their appearance. A graphic contains graphics state and geometric information; it uses this information to draw itself and to perform hit detection. Graphical component subjects store their geometric and graphics state in a graphic, thereby delegating responsibility for low level graphics functionality. The `GetGraphic` operation returns the information in the subject's graphic. Graphical component subjects can also have a *mobility* attribute and define operations for assigning and retrieving it. Later we show how mobility affects the component's connectivity semantics.

Graphical components maintain a graphic that defines their appearance, so they provide a `GetGraphic` operation. `Highlight` and `Unhighlight` operations let views distinguish themselves graphically, for example, when they are selected.

`CreateManipulator` and `InterpretManipulator` define how a graphical component view reacts when it is manipulated by a tool, and how the tool affects the component after manipulation. Both operations use a *manipulator* to characterize the manipulation. Manipulators abstract and encapsulate the mechanics of direct manipulation; they are discussed further in Section 10.2.6.

Connectors

Unidraw supports connectivity constraints with the *connector* graphical component subclass. Since connectors are components, each consists of a subject and zero or more views, and can be manipulated directly. Hence connectors and other components can be treated uniformly.

A connector can be connected to one or more other connectors. Once connected, two connectors can affect each other's position in specific ways, as defined by the semantics of the connection. Connector subclasses support different connection semantics. A *pin* contributes zero degrees of freedom to a connection. A degree of freedom is an independent variable along a particular dimension, which for connectors is a Cartesian coordinate.

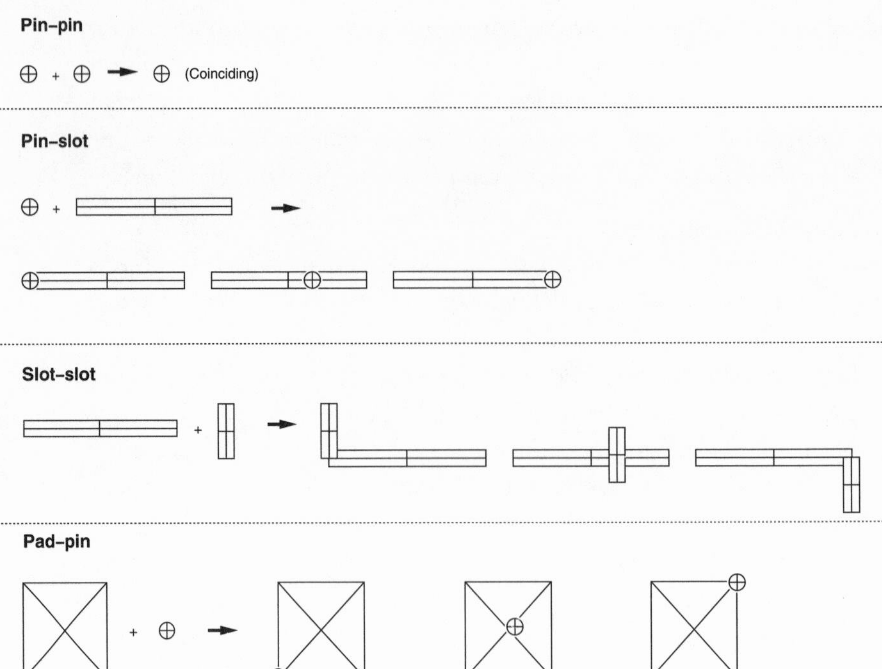

Figure 10.3 Several connections and their semantics

Slots and *pads* provide one and two degrees of freedom within certain bounds, respectively, and can undergo affine transformations.*

Figure 10.3 shows how different connectors behave in several connections, using the connectors' default graphical representations. The centers of two connected pins must always coincide (see Figure10.3(a)). A pin connected to a slot—Figure 10.3(b)—is free to move along the slot's major axis until it reaches either end of the slot; the pin cannot move in the transverse dimension. Two connected slots —Figure 10.3(c)—can move relative to each other as long as the center lines of their major axes share a point. Finally, Figure 10.3(d) shows how a pad–pin connection constrains the pin to stay within the confines of the pad.

A connector's mobility characterizes how the connector moves to satisfy connection constraints. The mobility attribute can have one of three

* Affine transformations are transformations in which parallel lines stay parallel. Translation, scaling, skewing, and rotation are affine transformations; perspective transformations are not.

values: *fixed, floating,* or *undefined.* In general, a fixed connector's position cannot be affected by a connection regardless of the connection's semantics, while a floating connector will move to satisfy the connection's semantics. Components other than connectors often have undefined mobility.

Mobility specifications help determine the placement of connectors. In Figure 10.3(b), for example, it is unclear which connector (the pin or the slot) actually moves. If, however, the slot's mobility is fixed and the pin's is floating, then the pin will always move to satisfy the connection constraints. If the slot is moved explicitly, then the pin will move to stay within it. An attempt to explicitly move the pin beyond the slot's bounds will fail; in fact, if the pin is also connected to another, orthogonal slot, *any* attempt to move it explicitly will fail. As a corollary, a connection can have no effect on two fixed connectors.

Connections involving pins, slots, and pads furnish a finite number of connectivity semantics. Additional semantics can be supported through subclassing. As an alternative to subclassing, however, the framework allows connections with a piece of *connector glue* interposed. Connector glue is characterized by a natural size, elasticity, and deformation limits (see Figure 10.4). Elasticity is specified in terms of independent stretchability (ε^+) and shrinkability (ε^-) parameters. Deformation limits are expressed as independent limits on the total amount the glue can stretch (λ^+) and shrink (λ^-). Elasticity is dimensionless; it determines how a deformation is apportioned to a collection of mutually dependent connections.

For example, Figure 10.5 shows three pins `P1`, `P2`, and `P3` connected *in series,* which implies the two connections share a connector. Glue is represented schematically (and in one dimension only) with resistor symbols. The elasticity (both shrinkability and stretchability) of glue `G1` is twice that of `G2`. Thus if `P1` and `P3` are pushed together or pulled apart, `G1` will shrink or stretch twice as much as `G2`. In general, ideal connector glue behaves like two nonlinear springs, one horizontal and the other vertical, each having independent spring constants and travel limits in tension (ε^+, λ^+) and compression (ε^-, λ^-).

Domain-Specific Connectivity

We have discussed connectors and their semantics, but we have not explained how they support connectivity between domain-specific components. For instance, how does one define a node in a graph whose arcs

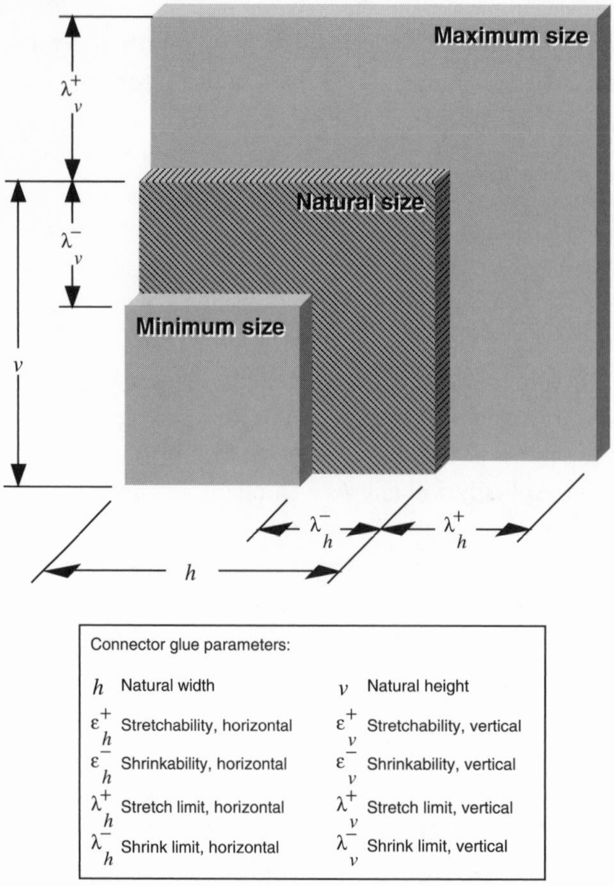

Figure 10.4 Connector glue characteristics

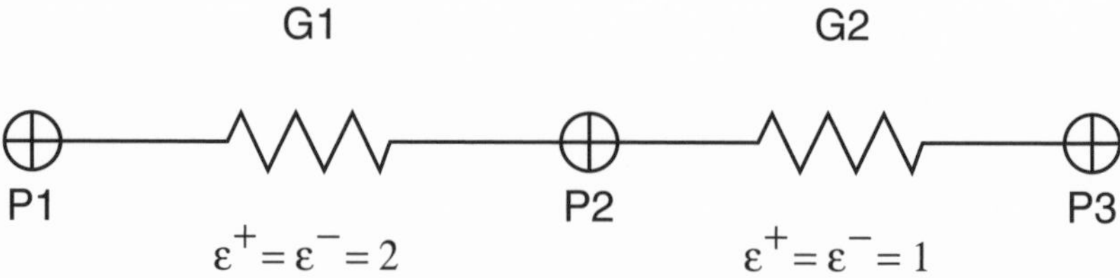

Figure 10.5 Three pins connected in series

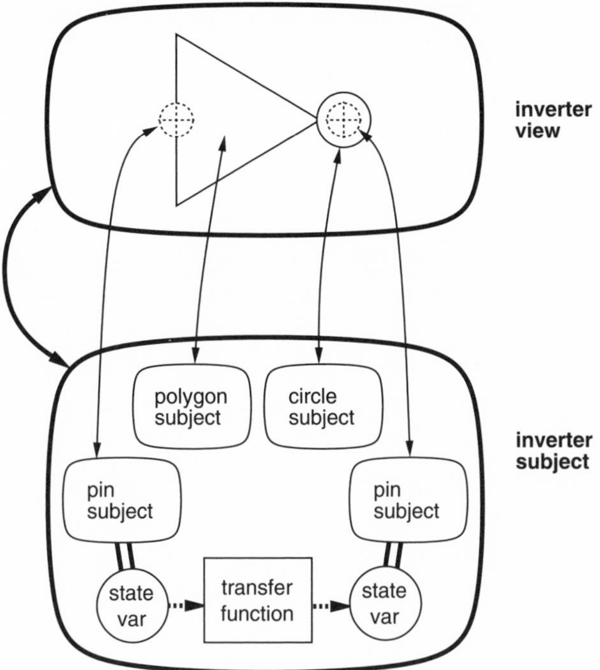

Figure 10.6 Possible composition of an inverter component

remain connected when the user moves it? Such domain-specific components are often compositions of simpler components.

Figure 10.6 shows how an electrical schematic for an inverter can be composed with polygon, circle, and pin subjects and views. Note that the pins are treated like any other component in the composition, but they have a special responsibility to define the inverter's connectivity semantics. The inverter sets their mobility according to the desired behavior. For example, it will fix both if their position should not be affected by any connections in which they participate. When the inverter interprets a command to move itself, it moves all its components accordingly, including the pins. Since the pins are fixed, they will not be affected by their connections; rather, any floating connectors that are connected to the pins will move according to the connection semantics.

Composite components can thus define connections between their internal connectors, and they can base their appearances on their connection semantics. This provides a simple way to support a variety of domain-specific connectivity constraints.

Dataflow and Transfer Functions

Unidraw supports dataflow for component–component communication. A component can have one or more *state variables*, each made up of a subject and views (MVC again). A state variable can be bound to a connector like an actual parameter is bound to a formal parameter in a procedure call. This lets the programmer define how information flows through a connection. Connectors define *parameter passing* semantics for any bound state variable, one of *in*, *out*, or *inout*. When connected, two connectors with bound state variables will pass their values accordingly.

For example, an *in* connector's state variable will receive the value of an *out* connector's variable. Passing a value between incompatible connectors (such as two *out* connectors) is an error; such connections should be disallowed by the tool or command making the connection.

Transfer functions complete the dataflow model by defining how the values of a component's state variables change as they flow "through" a component. For example, the inverter shown earlier could use an `Invert` transfer function to establish a dependency between the logic level state variables bound to its *in* and *out* pins: `Invert` assigns the inverse value of the input variable to the output variable.

The basic transfer function interface has a single operation, `Evaluate`, that instructs the transfer function to evaluate the dependencies on its state variables. A component can have an arbitrary number of state variables, but the interface allows for only one transfer function. Therefore transfer function subclasses normally add operations for specifying and distinguishing between different state variables. Components that require a combination of existing transfer functions must use a transfer function subclass that composes other transfer functions.

Figure 10.7 highlights the dataflow aspects of a circuit containing two inverters (as defined in Figure 10.6) connected in a feedback loop through a switched wire. Like the inverters, the wire is a component containing two connectors each having a bound state variable. A third state variable defines the position of the switch. The wire's transfer function assigns the value of one pin's state variable to the other's when the third state variable indicates that the switch is closed; otherwise the pin state variables are

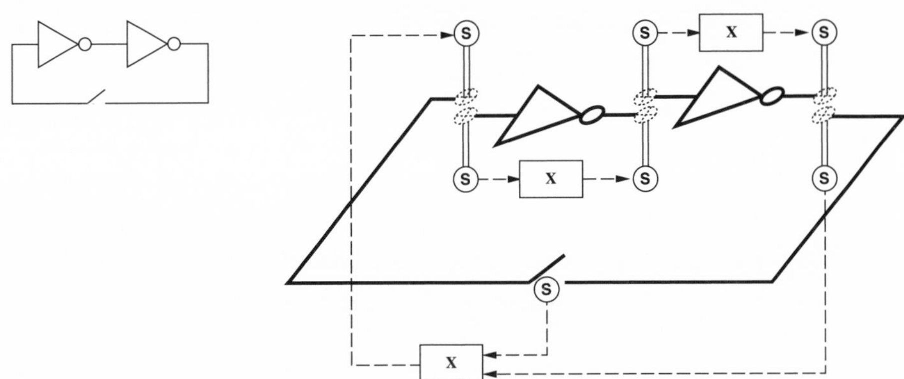

Figure 10.7 Dataflow elements in a circuit with two inverters and a switched wire

independent. The application might let a user flip the switch with a tool or through a dialog box containing a view of the third state variable.

Unidraw's dataflow model unites components, connectors, state variables, and transfer functions to make dataflow semantics easy to implement. The approach differs from more general attribute evaluation semantics, such as Higgens's [Hudson88], that propagate values automatically as soon as they are modified. In Unidraw, the programmer retains control over which values are propagated and when, independent of modification time or order. Problems arising from circularities are disallowed by default.

Table 10.3 Command interface

Return values	Operation	Arguments
	`Execute`	
	`Unexecute`	
Boolean	`Reversible`	
	`Store`	Comp. subj., Data
Data	`Recall`	Comp. subj.
	`SetClipboard`	Clipboard
clipboard	`GetClipboard`	
	(*child iteration and manipulation operations*)	

10.2.5 Commands

Table 10.3 shows the basic operations defined by the command interface. `Execute` performs computation to carry out the command. `Unexecute` performs computation to reverse the effects of a previous `Execute`, based on whatever internal state the command maintains. A command is responsible for maintaining enough state to reverse one `Execute` operation; repeated `Unexecute` operations will not undo the effects of more than one `Execute`. Unidraw supports multilevel `undo` by keeping an ordered list of commands to reverse-execute. In general, a Unidraw-based application will use command objects to perform undoable operations

Unidraw commands have an interpreted nature that sets them apart from commands in other frameworks: Components can interpret them like messages and uninterpret them to undo prior interpretation. Since a command can affect more than one component, a command must let components that interpret it store information that the components can use later to uninterpret it. A component uses the `Store` operation to store information in the command during its `Interpret` operation. The component can retrieve this information later with the `Recall` operation if it must `Uninterpret` the command.

Commands must also maintain a record of the component subjects they have affected and the order in which they were affected. Hence commands store a *clipboard* object, which can be assigned and retrieved with the `SetClipboard` and `GetClipboard` operations. A clipboard keeps a list of component subjects, and provides operations for iterating through the list and manipulating its elements. Typically, the clipboard is initialized with the component subjects whose views are selected when the command is first executed. Purely interpretive commands usually define their `Execute` and `Unexecute` operations to call `Interpret` and `Uninterpret` on the components in their clipboard.

It is often convenient to create *macrocommands*, that is, commands composed of other commands. The command interface includes operations for iterating through and manipulating child commands, if any. By default, (un)executing or (un)interpreting a macrocommand is semantically identical to performing the corresponding operations on each of its children. The framework includes a `MacroCommand` subclass that implements this functionality.

10.2.6 Tools

Unidraw-based editors use tool objects to let the user manipulate components directly. The user *grasps* and *wields* a tool to achieve a desired *effect*. The effect may involve a change to one or more components' internal states, or it may change the way components are viewed, or there may be no effect at all (if the tool is used in an inappropriate context, for example). Tools often use animated effects as they are wielded to suggest how they will affect their environment.

Making tools distinct from components lets programmers define direct manipulation semantics and component semantics independently, enhancing modularity and reusability. For example, general manipulation behavior can be defined in one Tool subclass and can apply to any number of components.

Tool Interface

The tool interface is shown in Table 10.4. Conceptually, tools are used on component views as they appear in viewers. Whenever a viewer receives an event, it asks the current tool (defined by the enclosing editor object) to produce a manipulator object.

Table 10.4 Tool interface

Return values	Operation	Arguments
Manipulator	`CreateManipulator`	Event
Command	`InterpretManipulator`	Manipulator
Component subject	`GetPrototype`	

A tool implements its `CreateManipulator` operation to create and initialize an appropriate manipulator, which encapsulates the tool's manipulation behavior by defining the three phases (grasp, wield, and effect) of the manipulation. A tool may modify the contents of the current selection object (also defined by the enclosing editor) based on the event. Moreover, a tool can delegate manipulator creation to one or more graphical component views (usually among those in the editor's selection object) to allow component-specific interaction.

A tool's `InterpretManipulator` operation analyzes information in the manipulator that characterizes the manipulation; then it creates a command that carries out the desired effect. If the tool delegated manipulator creation to a graphical component view, then it must delegate its interpretation to the same view.

The `GetPrototype` operation is defined by the *graphical component tool* subclass. Graphical component tools maintain a prototype component and define how that component is created and added to the drawing. The prototype is a graphical component subject that the tool copies and modifies to reflect the direct manipulation. The tool then inserts the copy into the component hierarchy with a `PasteCommand`.

Manipulator Interface

The manipulator interface (Table 10.5) is designed to reflect the grasp-wield-effect behavior of tools.

Table 10.5 Command interface

Return values	Operation	Arguments
	`Grasp`	Event
Boolean	`Manipulating`	Event
	`Effect`	Event
	(*child iteration and manipulation operations*)	

The `Grasp` operation takes a window system event (such as a mouse click or key press) and initializes whatever state is needed for the direct manipulation (such as animation objects). During direct manipulation, the `Manipulating` operation is called repeatedly until the manipulator decides that manipulation has terminated (based on its own termination criteria), in which case `Manipulating` returns FALSE. The `Effect` operation gives the manipulator a chance to perform any final actions following the manipulation.

Some kinds of direct manipulation may require several submanipulations to progress simultaneously. For example, the editor might let the user manipulate more than one component at a time. Therefore a manipulator can have children, and the manipulator interface includes operations for iterating through and manipulating them.

This simple interface can support direct manipulations ranging from text entry and rubber-banding effects to simulated real-world dynamics, such as imparting momentum to an object. The framework predefines manipulator subclasses for the most common kinds of manipulation.

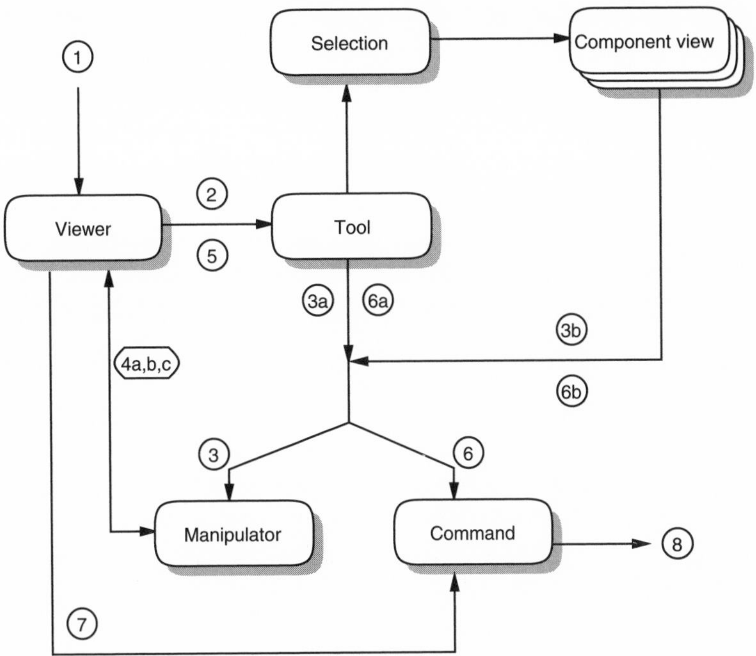

Figure 10.8 Communication between objects during direct manipulation

Since manipulators must keep information that characterizes the final outcome of a manipulation, subclasses usually augment the interface with operations for retrieving state that determines this outcome. For example, a manipulator that supports dragging the mouse to translate a graphical component will define an operation for retrieving the distance moved.

Object Communication During Direct Manipulation

Figure 10.8 diagrams the communication between objects during direct manipulation. The numeric labels in the diagram correspond to the transmission sequence:

1. The viewer receives an input event, such as the press of a mouse button.
2. The viewer asks the current tool to `CreateManipulator` based on the event.
3. Manipulator creation: the tool either: creates a manipulator itself (based on the selection or other information), or asks the

component views to create manipulators on its behalf. The tool must combine multiple manipulators into a composite manipulator. Each class of component view is responsible for creating an appropriate manipulator for the tool.

4. Direct manipulation: the viewer: invokes Grasp on the manipulator, supplying the initiating event; loops, reading subsequent events and sending them to the manipulator in a Manipulating operation (looping continues until the Manipulating operation returns FALSE); invokes Effect on the manipulator, supplying the event that terminated the loop.

5. The viewer asks the current tool to `InterpretManipulator`.

6. Manipulator interpretation: the tool either: interprets the manipulator itself, creating the appropriate command, or asks the component views to interpret the manipulators on its behalf. The views then create the appropriate commands. The tool must combine multiple commands into a composite (macro)command.

7. The viewer executes the command.

8. The command carries out the intention of the direct manipulation.

To illustrate this process, consider the following example of direct manipulation in a drawing editor. Suppose the user clicks on a rectangle component view (`RectangleView`) in the drawing area (viewer) with the `MoveTool`. The viewer receives a *mouse-button-went-down* event, and asks the current tool (the `MoveTool`, as provided by the enclosing editor) to `CreateManipulator` based on the event. `MoveTool`'s `CreateManipulator` operation determines from the event which component view was hit and adds it to the selection. More precisely, the selection object provided by the enclosing editor appends the view to its list.

If the selection object contains only one component view, then `MoveTool`'s `CreateManipulator` operation calls `CreateManipulator` on that component view. This gives the component view a chance to create the manipulator it deems appropriate for `MoveTool` under the circumstances. Since the user clicked on a `RectangleView`, the component view will create a `DragManipulator`, a manipulator that implements a downclick-drag-upclick style of manipulation. `DragManipulator` animates the dragging portion of the manipulation by drawing a particular shape in slightly different ways in each successive call to its `Manipulating` operation. The definition of DragManipulator parameterizes the shape, so that subclasses of DragManipulator are not needed to support dragging different shapes.

Once the viewer obtains DragManipulator from MoveTool, the viewer creates the illusion that the user is grasping and wielding the tool. First, the viewer calls Grasp on the manipulator, which lets the manipulator initialize itself and perhaps draw the first "frame" of the animation. Then the viewer loops, forwarding all subsequent events to the manipulator's Manipulating operation until it returns FALSE. Successive calls to Manipulating produce successive frames of the animation. Once manipulation is complete, the viewer invokes the manipulator's Effect operation, which gives DragManipulator a chance to finalize the animation and the state it maintains to characterize the manipulation. The viewer then asks the tool to InterpretManipulator; in this case, MoveTool in turn asks RectangleView to InterpretManipulator. In response, RectangleView constructs and returns a MoveCommand, which specifies a translation transformation. RectangleView initializes the amount of translation in the MoveCommand to the distance between the initial and final frames of the animation, which it obtains from the DragManipulator.

Tools Versus Manipulators

Early in the framework's design, there was no distinction between tools and manipulators—tools defined their own manipulation semantics. Then we found that many tools shared the same semantics, some shared similar ones, some could exhibit different semantics at different times, and others had unique (but potentially idiomatic) semantics. Tying distinctive behavior to individual tool subclasses was unsatisfactory, because we found no way to factor the classes so that different behaviors could be mixed and matched with different tools.

The solution was to encapsulate the manipulation semantics in an independent object, the manipulator. The more we experimented with this concept, the more apparent it became that it was a good solution. Manipulators package direct manipulation semantics nicely. Components can define independent manipulation semantics for the same tool, though even divergent semantics for a given tool should reflect the spirit of the tool.

The notion of allowing a component to create a specification of its manipulation semantics and later to produce a command based on the manipulation's outcome is hard to recast into a model that lacks manipulators. Manipulators also increase the chances for code reuse, because they can be used in many contexts and can be composed easily. For example, `DragManipulator` can be used by other component-modifying tools in addition to `MoveTool`. Thus we found it useful to abstract the mechanics of direct manipulation with tools in a separate manipulator object.

10.2.7 External Representations

An external representation of a component is generated by a non-graphical view of the corresponding component subject. Domain-specific external representation objects are derived from the *external view* subclass of the component view. This approach has several benefits:

- Since a component can have any number of views, it can also have any number of external representations, even simultaneously.
- Existing mechanisms for keeping a component view consistent with its subject can be used to keep the external representation consistent.
- Like other component views, external views can be composed to simplify generation of the external representation.

The external view interface defines two operations, `Emit` and `Definition`, that generate a stream of bytes constituting the external representation. `Emit` initiates external representation generation, and `Definition` is called recursively by `Emit`. Emit normally calls the external view's own `Definition` operation first. Then if the external view contains subviews, `Emit` must invoke the children's `Definition` operations in the proper order to ensure a syntactically correct external representation.

`Emit` is often used to generate "header" information that appears only once in the external representation, while `Definition` produces component-specific, context-independent information. For example, a drawing editor might use a `PostScriptView` external view subclass that defines `Emit` to generate global procedures and definitions. Component-specific subclasses of `PostScriptView` then need only define `Definition` to externalize the state of their corresponding component. Thus when `Emit` is invoked on an instance of any `PostScriptView` subclass, a stand-alone PostScript representation (known as *encapsulated* PostScript) will be generated. When the same instance is buried in a larger `PostScriptView`, only its definition will be emitted.

Unidraw predefines `preorder`, `inorder`, and `postorder` external views. These subclasses manage subviews, and support three common traversals of the external view hierarchy.

10.3 Summary of Unidraw Classes

Table 10.6 presents an overall breakdown of the framework in terms of both classes and lines of source code. As you can see, Unidraw is a relatively small framework.

Table 10.6 Unidraw code breakdown

		Code (lines)	
	Classes	**Interface**	**Implementation**
Components	38	1090	4810
Commands	42	900	2390
Tools/manipulators	16	500	1510
External representation	18	300	1150
State variables/transfer functions	20	410	1000
Application framework	5	460	2450
Creator	1	30	170
Toolkit-derived classes	22	390	1260
Utilities/globals	18	940	3260
Totals	180	5020	18000

In Tables 10.7 and 10.8, root classes appear in the leftmost column; subclasses appear in subsequent columns to the right. Classes that have subclasses are separated from their sibling classes by horizontal lines.

Unidraw includes classes for basic graphical components (such as lines and polygons), their views and PostScript external representations; commands for manipulating components and changing their attributes; commands that let the user access the catalog; tools for selecting, transforming, and otherwise modifying graphical components; manipulators supporting common direct manipulation such as *downclick-drag-upclick* interactions and text editing; state variables for basic graphical component attributes (such as color and fill pattern) together with sample views; and

Table 10.7 Predefined component subclasses

Component	GraphicComp	GraphicComps EllipseComp LineComp LinkComp RectComp TextComp			
		VerticesComp	SplineComp ClosedSplineComp MultiLineComp PolygonComp		
		Connector	PinComp PadComp		
			SlotComp	HSlotComp VSlotComp	
ComponentView	GraphicView	GraphicsViews EllipseView LineView LinkView RectView TextView			
		VerticesView	SplineView ClosedSplineView MultiLineView PolygonView		
		ConnectorView	PinView PadView		
			SlotView	HSlotView VSlotView	
	ExternView	InorderView PostorderView			
		PreorderView	PostScriptView	PostScriptViews PSEllipse PSLine PSLink PSRect PSText PSPin PSSlot PSPad	
				PSVertices	PSSpline PSClosedSpline PSMultiLine PSPolygon

transfer functions that support simple dependencies between an object's state variables.

The `Component` and `ComponentView` base classes implement the interfaces for component subject and views. `GraphicComp` and `GraphicView` subclasses add operations for graphics, e.g., geometric shapes like squares and circles. `GraphicComps` and `GraphicViews` subclasses implement MVC interactions among graphical objects. `ExternView` is a subclass of `ComponentView` that implements the external representation interface. `PreorderView`, `InorderView`, and `PostorderView` classes are

Table 10.8 Additional predefined subclasses

Command	AlignCmd, BackCmd, BrushCmd, CenterCmd, CloseEditorCmd, ColorCmd, ConnectCmd, CopyCmd, CutCmd, DeleteCmd, DupCmd, FontCmd, GravityCmd, GridCmd, GridSpacingCmd, MacroCmd, MobilityCmd, NewCompCmd, NormSizeCmd, OrientationCmd, PasteCmd, PatternCmd, PrintCmd, QuitCmd, RedToFitCmd, RedoCmd, ReplaceCmd, RevertCmd, RotateCmd, SaveCompAsCmd, SaveCmd, ScaleCmd, SlctAllCmd, UndoCmd, ViewCompCmd	
	StructCmd	GroupCmd, UngroupCmd
Tool	ConnectTool, GraphicCompTool, MagnifyTool, MoveTool, ReshapeTool, RotateTool, ScaleTool, SelectTool, StretchTool	
StateVar	BrushVar, ColorVar, FontVar, GravityVar, MagnifVar, ModifStatusVar, NameVar, PatternVar	
StateVarView	BrushVarView, ColorVarView, FontVarView, GravityVarView, MagnifVarView, ModifStatusVarView, NameVarView, PatternVarView	
TransferFunct	TF_2Port	TF_Direct
Manipulator	ManipGroup, TextManip	
	DragManip	ConnectManip, VertexManip

subclasses of `ExternView`. These act as base classes for three different approaches to generating external representations.

Classes `Connector` and `ConnectorView` and corresponding pin, slot, and pad subclasses implement connector semantics. The `Command` and `Tool` base classes implement the command and tool interfaces. These implement the layout and connectivity operations for nodes and arcs in graph structures such as circuit diagrams.

Also included are the classes `Catalog`, `Clipboard`, `Editor`, `Manipulator`, `Selection`, `StateVar`, `StateVarView`, `TransferFunct`, `Unidraw`, and `Viewer`, which define the interfaces for the elements we discussed in Section 10.2.

10.4 Applications

We have built several domain-specific editors with Unidraw [Vlissides90, Helm92, Vlissides91, and Stanford92]. In this section we will describe two of these editors: a drawing editor and a user interface builder. We have experimented with these editors to evaluate their utility and to discover their strengths and weaknesses relative to conventional implementations.

10.4.1 Drawing Editor

The drawing editor, called *Drawing*, is similar to MacDraw in that it provides an object-oriented, direct-manipulation editing environment for producing drawings and diagrams. It lets the user instantiate geometric objects, arrange them spatially, and compose them hierarchically. The user can apply affine transformations to the objects and specify graphical attributes such as color, font, and fill pattern. The user can also pan the drawing, and view it at different magnifications. Drawing generates a PostScript external representation for printing the drawing and incorporating it into larger works.

Unlike MacDraw, Drawing also supports multiple views. The user can edit in one view, say, at high magnification for detailed work, while the drawing is fully visible in another view for editing at low magnification. Unidraw ensures that changes to the drawing made in one view appear automatically in other views. Drawing also gives users considerable control over its interface, allowing them to include only the components, commands, and tools they need.

User Interface

Figure 10.9 shows a Drawing editing session and depicts the default interface schematically. The application presents one or more editor instances, each enclosing a viewer, pull-down menus containing *controls* that execute specific commands, controls for engaging the current tool, a *panner* for panning and zooming the viewer, and state variable views that display the values of state variables maintained by the editor. The controls, pull-down menus, and panner are defined by or derived from toolkit objects, while other objects are based on Unidraw classes.

Drawing creates a single editor instance initially. The user engages the current tool by clicking on the appropriate control along the editor's left edge. Two types of tools are available: graphical component tools for instantiating graphical components, and tools for manipulating components that have been instantiated already. Drawing provides graphical component tools for eight different components: text, simple lines, compound lines, ellipses, rectangles, polygons, open B-splines, and closed B-splines. Other

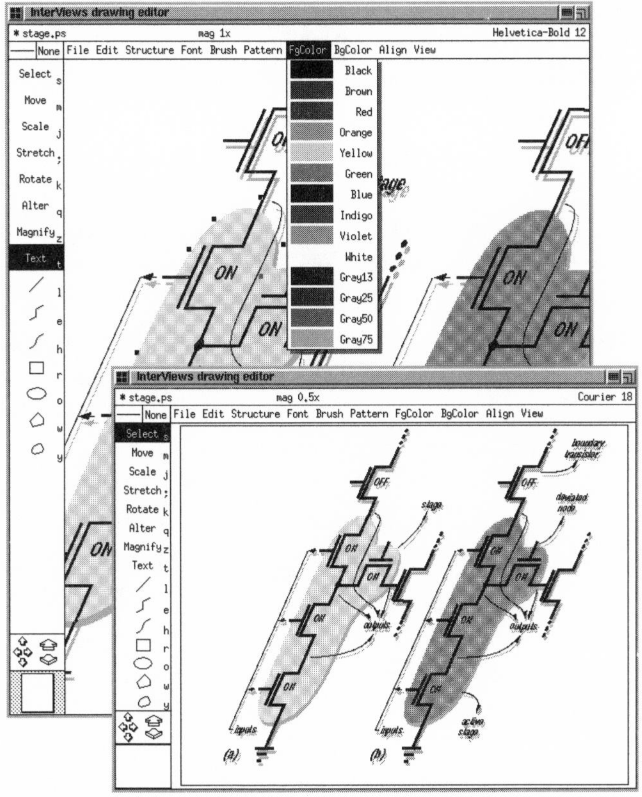

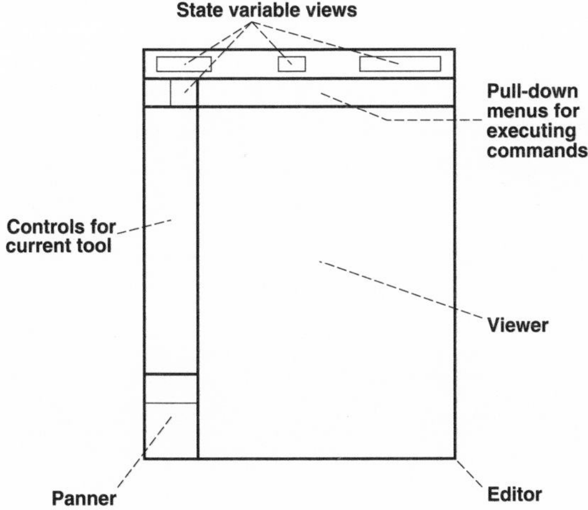

Figure 10.9 Drawing editor

tools include `Select`, for specifying components of interest; `Move`, `Scale`, `Stretch`, and `Rotate`, for applying affine transformations by direct manipulation; `Reshape`, for repositioning vertices and control points and for editing text components; and `Magnify`, which lets the user zoom in on a particular part of the drawing by dragging a rectangle around the area of interest.

Once a tool is engaged, the user wields it by clicking in the viewer. The tool's behavior thereafter varies with the type of tool and the components on which it is used, if any. All the tools provide dynamic feedback to show the consequences of their use. For example, the graphical component tools obtain a manipulator from their prototype component; the resulting component-specific animation supplies feedback that helps the user specify the new component's size and shape with ease. Transformation-applying tools such as the `Rotate` and `Stretch` animate the intermediate steps of the transformation before the user commits to the final transformation. The user can change the position of a spline's control point with `Reshape` and watch the spline's shape change in real time.

A pull-down menu contains a set of controls, each with an associated command. A control executes its command after the user selects the control through the pull-down menu. Most of Drawing's commands are predefined by the Unidraw library. These include commands for saving and restoring drawings via the catalog; modifying attributes such as line style and color; cutting, copying, and pasting components to and from a global clipboard; undo and redo commands; and structuring commands for grouping, ungrouping, and otherwise altering the component hierarchy.

To create a new view of the current drawing, the user invokes a command from the View menu that copies the editor, including its commands, tools, viewer, and other interface elements. The copy creates a new view of the component being edited, and places the view in its viewer. The user may then edit the component subject through either the original editor or the copy; changes made through one editor are reflected in the other. Any number of editors may be produced in this way. Once instantiated, they can be used to edit the original component subject or to edit other drawings. Each editor maintains its own selection object, allowing the user to select objects in one editor without disturbing selections in another, even if the editors contain the same subject.

Drawing's interface can be reconfigured at start-up time to include only those features a user requires. Through a command line option, the user can direct Drawing to write out a configuration file containing a list of individual strings and pairs of strings; the individual strings represent tool names, while the pairs associate a command name with the name of a pull-down menu. When the user starts Drawing with this file as an argument, the editor will incorporate into its interface only the commands and tools whose names it encounters in the file. The order in which the names appear dictates the arrangement of the controls in the tool palette and pull-down menus. By editing the configuration file, the user can exercise control over which commands and tools are included, and their arrangement.

Implementation

Drawing represents a lower bound of functionality and complexity for practical Unidraw applications. In general, drawing editors are the simplest graphical object editors in that most offer only:

- Graphical components with no underlying semantics
- Basic commands and tools for creating, manipulating, and modifying the components
- External representations that are straightforward mappings of their component structure onto a page description language such as PostScript

These elements are useful in many domains other than drawing, and most graphical object editors incorporate at least some drawing-editing capabilities in their own interfaces.

For these reasons, the framework predefines all the components, commands, and tools needed for basic drawing editing. Drawing's implementation assembles the predefined elements into a complete application with a minimum of new classes and code. Drawing does not exploit many of the framework's advanced features, such as support for connectivity and dataflow, but it does demonstrate multiple views and static interface customization. Drawing thus constitutes a bare-bones Unidraw application; it serves both as an example of a trivial (but useful) test case and as a tutorial for application writers unfamiliar with Unidraw.

Table 10.9 presents a breakdown of the Drawing implementation in classes and lines of source code. Since most of Drawing's functionality is inherited from the Unidraw library, the Drawing-specific code is dedicated mainly to defining the application's look and feel.

Table 10.9 Drawing code breakdown

	Classes	Code (lines) Interface	Implementation
Components	0	0	0
Commands	1	20	40
Tools/manipulators	0	0	0
External representation	0	0	0
State variables/transfer functions	0	0	0
Editors	1	80	890
Creator	1	20	30
Toolkit-derived classes	0	0	0
Globals	0	30	110
Totals	3	150	1070

Drawing defines three new classes, the largest being a subclass of editor called `DrawingEditor`. Each window shown in Figure 10.9 is a `DrawingEditor` instance that provides an independent interface for editing a drawing. Each `DrawingEditor` has its own component, command, and tool instances, and its own selection object. The lone command defined in Drawing, `NewViewCmd`, creates a new `DrawingEditor` instance by copying the original. Then it creates a new view of the component in the original editor, places it into the copy's viewer, and tells the unidraw object to Open the editor, making it visible on the screen. There is also a `DrawingCreator`, derived from the library's `Creator` class, that allows the catalog to recreate `NewViewCmd` from disk.

Experience

Of the applications we built with the Unidraw initially, Drawing gave us the best opportunity for comparison with existing editors. In designing Drawing, we tried to match the functionality and look and feel of idraw [Stanford92], an object-oriented drawing editor developed and distributed with InterViews.* idraw provides roughly the same functionality as MacDraw, but idraw is more appropriate for comparison purposes because

* Throughout this discussion, we refer to version 1.16 of idraw, which was included in the 2.6 release of InterViews.

it is a workstation-based application that runs in the X environment. idraw has a substantial following of users, and has established itself as one of the leading object-oriented drawing editors for X. We therefore used idraw as a benchmark in evaluating Drawing's performance.

idraw is implemented on top of InterViews, and since InterViews abstracts the underlying window system, idraw does not call X directly. idraw uses InterViews' predefined interactors* to compose its look and feel, and it uses the toolkit's structured graphics objects to support its graphical editing capabilities. Even with these assists, however, idraw still contains roughly 15,000 lines of source code. The difference in source code size between idraw and Drawing is considerable, but in fairness we should offer the following caveats:

- Drawing is particularly small, even compared to other Unidraw-based editors, because most of its functionality is provided by the Unidraw library. This follows our assertion that drawing editors represent the lowest-common denominator among graphical object editors.

- idraw and Drawing are nearly identical in functionality and appearance, but there are notable differences. Drawing provides multiple views and a customizable interface, features absent from idraw. On the other hand, idraw offers arrowheaded lines and operations for specifying graphical transformations numerically; Drawing does not support arrowheads, and provides only a direct-manipulation interface for transforming objects.

- idraw benefits from two years' refinement and user experience. We plan to replace idraw eventually with Drawing for our day-to-day drawing tasks, and doubtless this will yield improvements in both Drawing and the library that will affect their line counts.†

Despite these qualifications we can still conclude that Unidraw substantially reduced the size of the Drawing implementation, with an attendant decrease in implementation time. We also verified that Drawing is a

---

* *Interactor* is InterViews' term for *widget*, that is, user interface elements such as buttons, scroll bars, and menus through which the user controls the application.

† In fact, idraw version 2.1 (included in InterViews 3.1) is fully Unidraw-based and includes all the features of version 1.16. Version 2.1 is implemented in about 5000 lines of code.

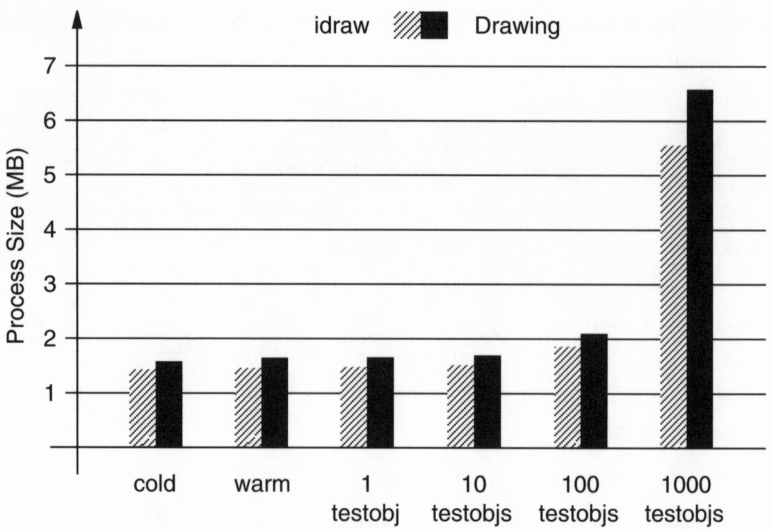

Figure 10.10 Runtime space requirements for idraw and Drawing

viable replacement for idraw by measuring the storage requirements and dynamic response of both editors. The measurements were made on an 8-plane DECstation 3100 using InterViews version 2.6 and the X11 Release 4 server and libraries.

To characterize the editors' runtime space requirements, we measured the size of their processes under six conditions:

- Immediately after startup ("cold")
- After having exercised their interfaces (pulling down menus, scrolling their drawing areas, etc.) but before creating any drawing objects ("warm")
- After having read in a `testobj`, a group of eight different geometric objects, one for each of the basic geometric objects the editors provide
- Displaying 10 copies of `testobj`
- Displaying 100 copies of `testobj`
- Displaying 1000 copies of `testobj`

Figure 10.10 shows that the Unidraw-based editor takes slightly more space to represent a drawing because of the overhead for maintaining

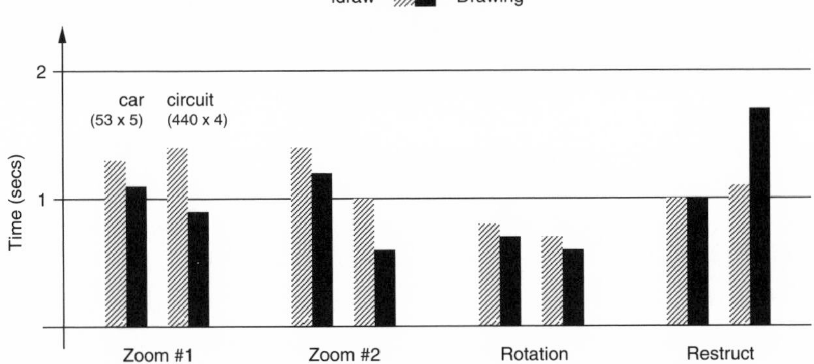

Figure 10.11 Comparison of idraw and Drawing runtime performance

multiple views. The predefined graphical components require almost twice as much storage as the corresponding idraw objects because the components maintain graphical information in their subject as well as their views. The added cost could be reduced if we treat the single-view case specially, but we have not applied such optimizations.

Another set of measurements relates idraw and Drawing's runtime performance. We measured how long it took idraw and Drawing to do each of four operations on two drawings, a sports car and a circuit diagram. These are representative of two common types of drawings: artistic drawings with complex, overlapping polygons and splines; and technical drawings consisting mainly of rectangles, lines, and text, with little or no overlap. We timed the following operations:

1. In the zoom #1 test, the drawing is zoomed from half size to quarter size and back. The drawing is fully visible throughout the test.
2. In zoom #2, the drawing is zoomed from half size to full size and back. The drawing is clipped at full size so that only half is visible.
3. In rotation, the top-level object in the drawing is rotated by 90°.
4. In restruct, the top-level object in the drawing is ungrouped and grouped again.

Figure 10.11 shows the average times for each test, based on twenty trials. Drawing performs at least as well as idraw in all but the restruct test. idraw uses InterViews' structured graphics facility to implement its graphical objects, and the framework uses the same structured graphics to represent the graphical attributes of components. Since the first three tests involve changes to graphical attributes, it is not surprising that the times for these tests are virtually identical. This proves that Unidraw-related overhead, such as subject-view communication and command interpretation and logging, does not measurably affect performance.

The Unidraw-based editor's performance does suffer slightly compared to the custom-built editor when a component is restructured. The overhead stems from the grouping operation: the multiview update algorithm discards the old views of the children that have been grouped, and then creates a view for the group, which includes views for the children. In contrast, idraw simply reparents the existing graphical objects without destroying or recreating them. The update overhead amounts to a constant factor, because the destruction and recreation of the views amounts to two extra traversals of the component hierarchy—both idraw and Drawing must perform similar traversals to draw the graphics following the grouping operations. In practice, it appears that this overhead is inconsequential. At any rate, the comparison is not entirely fair, since the Unidraw-based editor offers additional functionality in the form of a multiview editing environment in exchange for somewhat slower response in some cases.

From these findings and from hands-on experience with both editors, Drawing easily meets our goals in providing a viable replacement for its custom-built counterpart. Drawing offers essentially the same functionality and performance as idraw at a fraction of idraw's implementation cost, measured in lines of code. Since drawing editors reflect the basic capabilities of graphical object editors, these results imply that the basic operation and graphics performance of Unidraw-based editors will be comparable to conventional implementations—Unidraw incurs no significant space or time penalties.

10.4.2 User Interface Builder

User interface builders are designed to let the user specify the appearance of a user interface by direct manipulation instead of programming. The goals of such systems are threefold:

- Shorten the design time for a particular interface by eliminating the edit-compile-debug cycle from the design process.

- Shorten the implementation time by generating code from the graphical specification produced through direct manipulation.
- Allow nonprogrammers, especially those with graphic design and human factors skills, to design and implement user interfaces.

An effective user interface builder should therefore reduce application development time, as it encourages the design of higher quality user interfaces.

Our Unidraw-based user interface builder, called *UI*, provides a direct-manipulation environment for assembling InterViews toolkit objects into a complete interface. UI defines components that correspond to basic interactors such as scroll bars and push buttons, and it provides components that implement the InterViews composition mechanisms. UI components closely match the composition behavior of their toolkit counterparts, supporting the semantics of interactor attributes such as shape and canvas. Thus the interface designer can experiment with an interface without writing and compiling source code. UI generates C++ code from the graphical specification as its external representation. Once the interface designer is satisfied with the interface's appearance and behavior, he or she can generate the source for incorporation into the application.

User Interface

Figure 10.12 shows a dialog box being built with UI. Along the top edge are state variable views of the internal state, and pull-down menus for issuing commands. In the center is a viewer in which the user composes interfaces. Below the viewer are two rows of controls and a panner for scrolling and zooming the viewer's contents. The upper row's controls engage graphical component tools for instantiating user interface components, while the lower row's controls engage tools that manipulate instantiated components. UI supports multiple views in the same way Drawing does, that is, by copying the editor and editing the original component subject through a new view. UI also incorporates the `Select` and `Move` tools from the Unidraw library, and each UI editor maintains its own selection.

UI provides components for a subset of the predefined interactors in InterViews, including scrollers, buttons, borders, glues, messages, string editors, and file browsers. The graphical component tool controls let the user create these components in the same way that graphical components

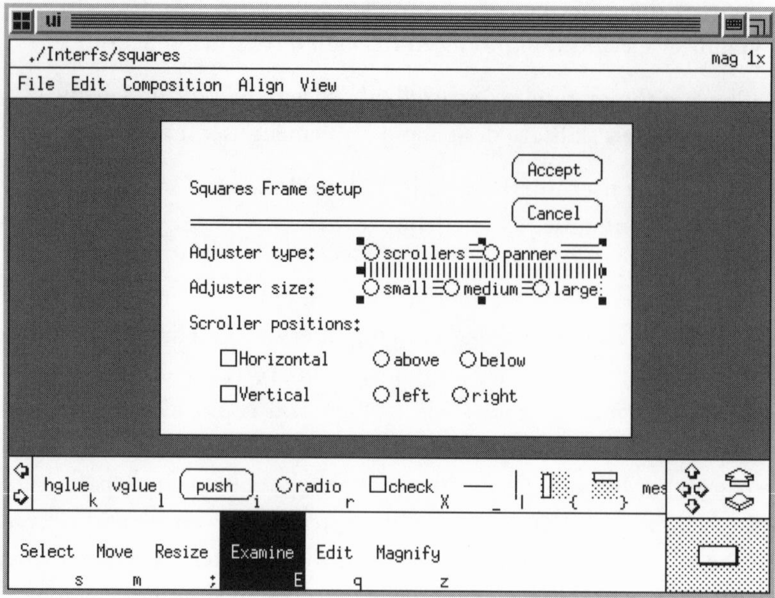

Figure 10.12 User interface builder

are created in Drawing. The user engages the graphical component tool of choice by clicking on the corresponding control; he or she then creates a copy of the prototypical component by clicking in the viewer. Most UI interface components adopt the default behavior of graphical components when they are manipulated by a graphical component tool; that is, a box corresponding to the bounds of the prototypical component appears when the user clicks down in the viewer. The user can drag the bounding box to any position while the button is down, and the prototype is copied and inserted into the interface when the button is released.

UI also defines components that implement InterViews composition mechanisms, including box and tray. These components have no appearance of their own; they compose other interface components in different ways. Composition components are created through commands in the Composition menu. For example, the user can place components into a horizontal box by selecting them first and then choosing the *HBox* entry in the menu. The command inserts components into the box in the same order they are selected. The box then tiles the components horizontally to effect the composition semantics of horizontal boxes. The composition can be treated as a unit and incorporated into larger compositions.

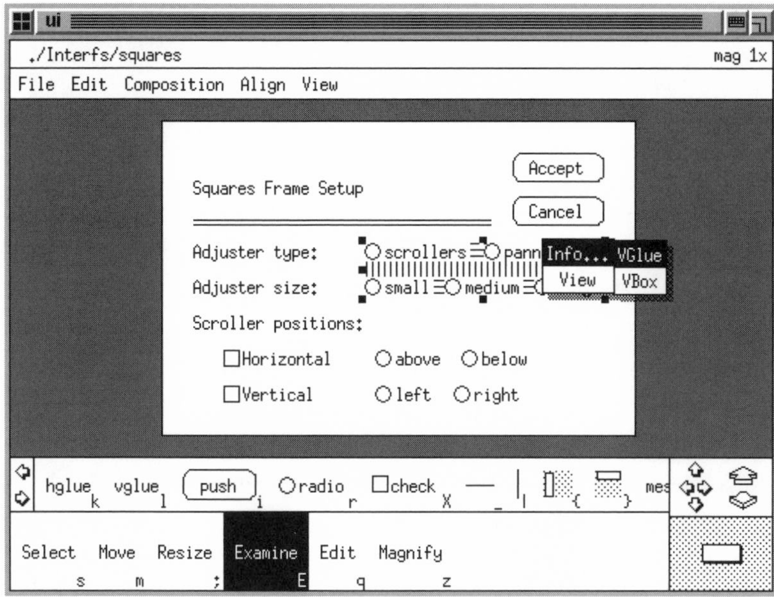

Figure 10.13 Pop-up from a click on a glue component with `Examine`

UI provides `Resize` and `Examine` tools for manipulating interactor components. The controls for engaging these tools lie alongside those for `Select` and `Move`. `Resize` lets the user observe how an interactor (primitive or composite) would be affected by a change in the size of its canvas. This feature can help the user fine-tune the shape (natural size, shrinkability, and stretchability) of glue and other interactors in the interface.

`Examine` lets the user examine and modify a component's internal state, such as its shape, canvas, or button state (if any). Clicking on a component with `Examine` engaged produces a pop-up menu containing two submenus: one for displaying and modifying the component's internal state or that of its parent, and one for creating new views on portions of the composition hierarchy in which the component lives.

In Figure 10.13, the user has clicked on a piece of vertical glue (which renders itself with vertical bars by default for easy identification) and selected the *Info...* submenu, whose body lists the names of interactors in the hierarchy from the glue up to the root interactor. Revealing the hierarchy in this way allows the user to examine internal nodes of the composition without disturbing it. Figure 10.14 shows the result of choosing to examine the glue component: a dialog box containing information about

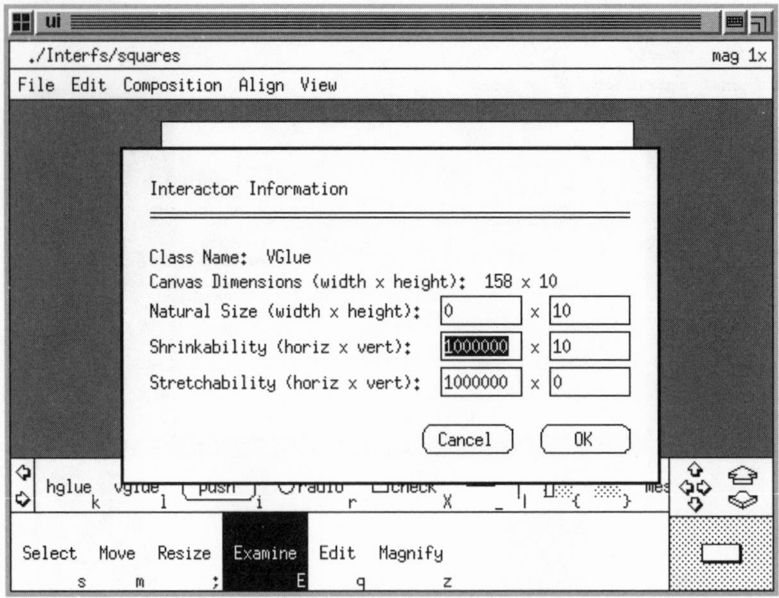

Figure 10.14 Dialog box containing glue component information

the glue's canvas and shape. Since InterViews allows programmers to specify the shape parameters of glue in its constructor, the dialog allows the user to change these parameters. The user cannot alter these parameters for buttons, for example, since one cannot change these values in InterViews without deriving a new button subclass.

The Examine tool also lets the user create views of parts of a composition, which makes it possible to edit otherwise inaccessible parts of the hierarchy. The *View* submenu in the pop-up menu displays a list of the chosen component's parents; Figure 10.15 shows this list for a radio button in the composition. The user clicked on a radio button composed in a horizontal box with two other buttons and some glue. In turn, this horizontal box is composed in a vertical box. By selecting the *HBox* entry in the submenu, the user can see the horizontal box composition in a separate view, as shown in Figure 10.16. The user can then edit the components in the horizontal box without tampering with the rest of the composition. As with all views of the same subject, changes to the composition in either view are reflected immediately in the other.

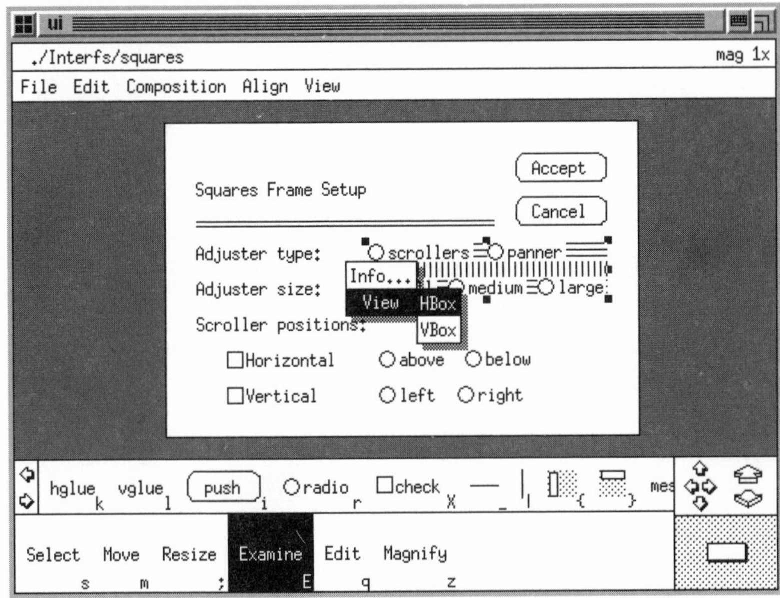

Figure 10.15 Examining a composition hierarchy

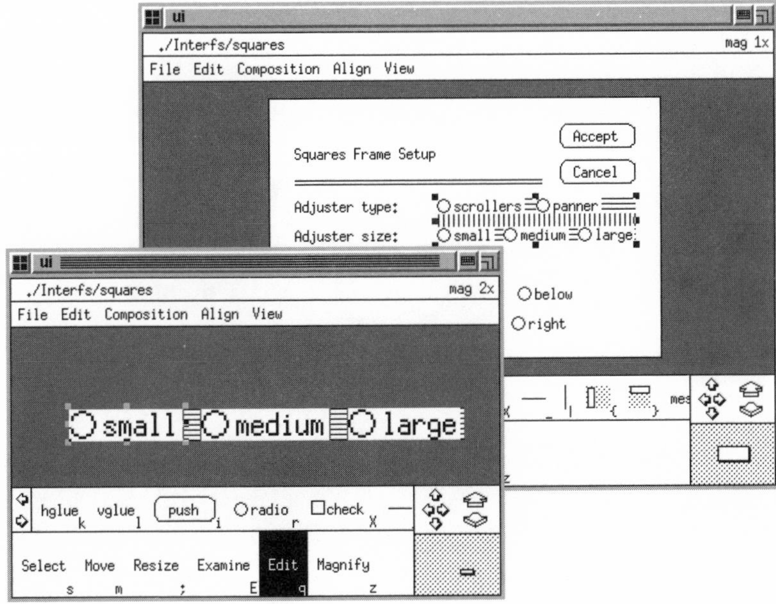

Figure 10.16 Part of the composition hierarchy presented in a separate view

Multiple views are also instrumental in specifying tray compositions. The user specifies a tray's components by selecting the components and invoking the *Tray* entry in the composition menu. Doing so does not, however, define alignments between the tray's components, which is why one would create a tray in the first place. Such alignments are made by creating a view of the tray, in which its components will be individually selectable, and issuing alignment commands from the Align menu. These commands normally align components by simply moving them, but when the commands are applied to components in a tray, the alignments behave as tray alignments—they persist. Once a tray component is aligned to another, therefore, it stays aligned even if the user attempts to move one of them.

The last tool in the palette, `Edit`, lets the user change strings as they appear in the interface. It behaves like `Reshape` in Drawing when reshaping text objects: the user can relabel a button or edit the text in a message by clicking on it and typing the new text.

UI also includes the usual predefined commands for saving and restoring components (which we refer to as *interfaces* in this domain), and editing commands such as `cut`, `copy`, `paste`, `delete`, and `duplicate`. In addition, UI defines a command for dissolving compositions (similar to ungrouping in a drawing editor) and for generating the C++ external representation.

Implementation

UI defines many new classes, as shown in Table 10.10. Class names in boldface type are for objects provided by the Unidraw library, while those in italics are defined by InterViews. Table 10.11 presents a breakdown of the UI implementation in classes and lines of source code.

Like Drawing, UI defines a single editor subclass, `UIEditor`. A new instance of `UIEditor` is created for each view of an interface. Interfaces are compositions of `InteractorComp`, a subclass of `GraphicComps`. There is an `InteractorComp` subclass for each interactor a user can instantiate, each with a corresponding `InteractorView`.

Interactor components. `InteractorComp` adds several operations to the `GraphicComps` interface to access state that characterizes the interactor. This state includes state variables for the interactor's class name, canvas, shape, and button state (if any). An `InteractorComp` also uses a specialized graphic, `UIGraphic`, to define its graphical characteristics, and it provides a `GetUIGraphic` operation to retrieve this graphic without

Table 10.10 UI class hierarchy

Editor	UIEditor			
GraphicComps	InteractorComp	HVComp	BorderComp GlueComp SCrollerComp	
		MessageComp	ButtonComp	FBrowser StrComp
		SceneComp	TrayComp	
			BoxComp	HBoxComp VBoxComp
GraphicViews	InteractorView	HVView	BorderView GlueView ScrollerView	
		MessageView	ButtonView	FBrowserView StrView
		SceneView		
Picture	UIGraphic	HVGraphic	BorderGraphic GlueGraphic ScrollerGraphic	
		MessageGraphic	PushButtonGraphic RadioButtonGraphic CheckBoxGraphic StrEditGraphic	
StateVar	**NameVar**	ButtonStateVar		
	CanvasVar ShapeVar			
StateVarView	ButtonStateVarView CanvasVarView ShapeVarView ClassNameVarView			
PreorderView	CodeView	BorderCode ButtonCode GlueCode MessageCode SCrollerCode StrEditCode FBrowserCode BoxCode TrayCode		
Command	CodeCmd InfoCmd NewViewCmd PlaceCmd			
	BrushCmd	GlueVisibilityCmd		
	GroupCmd	SceneCmd		
BasicDialog	InfoDialog			
Tool	ExamineTool			
Manipulator	PopupManip			
Creator	UICreator			

Table 10.11 UI code breakdown

	Classes	Code (lines)	
		Interface	Implementation
Components	24	500	1870
Commands	7	140	360
Tools/manipulators	2	60	180
External representation	10	170	460
State variables/transfer functions	7	160	520
Editors	1	70	670
Creator	1	20	90
Toolkit-derived classes	12	120	740
Globals	0	100	70
Totals	64	1450	4960

casting. The `UIGraphic` defines its appearance based on information in a canvas state variable, which the interactor component supplies. Most interactor components use a specialized `UIGraphic` that reflects the interactor's appearance based on the dimensions stored in the canvas variable. By deriving a `UIGraphic` and redefining its drawing operation, we can specify the interactor's appearance using immediate-mode graphics.* This approach has two benefits:

- It is generally easier to render the interactor using immediate-mode graphics. Interactors are simple to draw procedurally, their structure does not change, and the drawing procedure can be parameterized to conform to the canvas.
- Since most interactors use immediate-mode graphics, derived `UIGraphic` drawing operations can use the corresponding interactor drawing code virtually unchanged.

* *Immediate-mode* refers to a graphics programming interface comprising operations that draw shapes on the screen without storing information about what was drawn. In contrast, structured graphics involves building a data structure representing the graphics to be drawn. Drawing the graphics requires traversing the structure. Structured graphics provides a higher level abstraction to programmers, supporting facilities like incremental screen update and hit detection. Immediate-mode graphics is simpler and potentially more efficient.

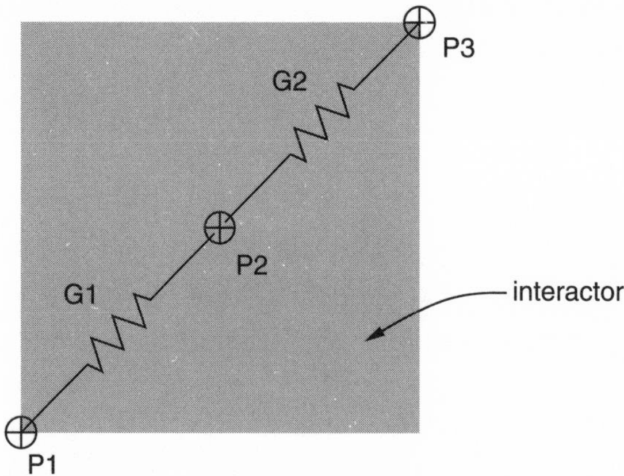

Figure 10.17 Connector construction for tray children

The interactor component class also defines `Reconfig` and `Resize` operations analogous to the corresponding InterViews interactor operations. Conceptually, `Reconfig` notifies the interactor that the library has computed its final graphics state, upon which its shape may depend. `Resize` notifies the interactor that its canvas is defined; the interactor may in turn initialize internal state based on the size of the canvas.

Scene components. The `SceneComp` subclass of `InteractorComp` provides an abstract base class for scene components. SceneComp subclasses include `BoxComp` and `TrayComp`. Subclasses of `BoxComp` implement the tiling semantics of horizontal and vertical boxes using the same algorithms that InterViews boxes use, while `TrayComp` uses connectors to determine the placement of its children. While there is a `SceneView` class for `SceneComp`, box and tray components have no corresponding `SceneView` subclass. No view subclasses are necessary, because the boxes and trays have no appearance or special direct manipulation semantics of their own. Hence the base class `SceneView` can assemble child views for both of them.

Figure 10.17 shows the connector construction that a tray component creates for each of its children. The tray builds these constructions in its `Reconfig` operation after it calls `Reconfig` on its children. The connectors are pins, initially floating, and the glue parameters are based on the child's shape variable, which defines its natural size, stretchability, and shrinkability (in the interactor sense). InterViews makes no distinction between elasticity and deformation limits; they are effectively collapsed into a single parameter per dimension per mode (tension or compression). Therefore, for either `G1` or `G2`,

$$\varepsilon = \lambda = \sigma/2$$

where σ denotes the interactor's horizontal/vertical stretchability/shrinkability, depending on the subscript and superscript we apply to each term.

The tray maintains alignments between its children by establishing connections between the pins in the respective connector constructions. For example, to left-align two children, the tray connects their `P1` connectors together with a piece of connector glue having the following parameters:

$$h = v = \varepsilon_h = \lambda_h$$

$$\varepsilon_v = \lambda_v = \infty$$

(The elasticity and deformation limits are the same in both modes.) These parameters ensure that the children remain left-aligned while still being able to move freely in the vertical direction.

Two-dimensional alignments require two connections. For example, a bottom right-to-bottom left alignment between interactors `I1` and `I2` in Figure 10.18 requires a connection between their `P1` pins and a connection between `P3` of `I1` and `P1` of `I2`. The `P1–P1` connection fixes the components' relative positions vertically, interposing glue `GV`, which is rigid vertically but infinitely flexible horizontally. The `P3–P1` connection fixes the components' relative positions horizontally with glue `GH`, which is rigid horizontally but infinitely flexible vertically.

Once the tray establishes these connections, it must determine its shape. The tray computes its natural size by calling `Update` on the `unidraw` object to solve the network and then determining the pins' bounding box. Calculating its stretchability and shrinkability is more difficult, because there is no way to query the Unidraw library for the network equivalent. The tray must ascertain this information from the dynamics of the network.

First, the tray fixes the bottom leftmost pin in the network. To find the shrinkability, the tray connects a fixed pin (call it `P`$^-$) to the top-rightmost pin. `P`$^-$ is centered at $(-\infty, -\infty)$, that is, a large distance below and to the left of the bottom leftmost pin. Then the tray calls `Update` again to

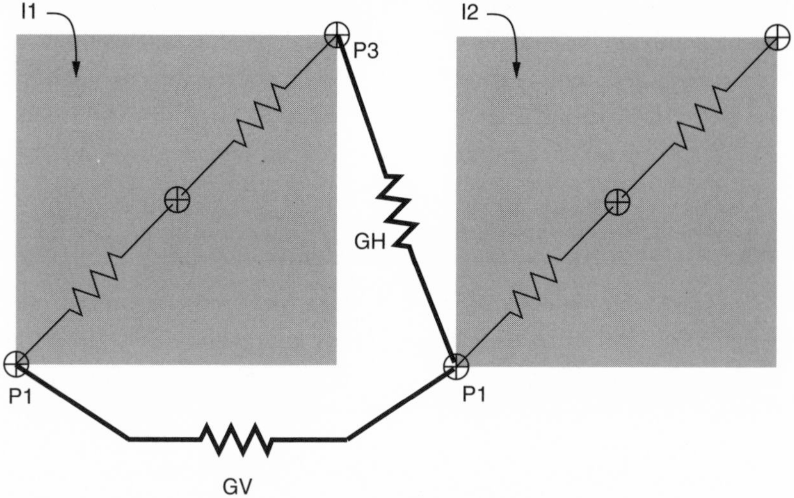

Figure 10.18 Connections for a two-dimensional tray alignment

solve the network. The tray's shrinkability is reflected in the distance the top rightmost pin moved to maintain its connection with `P`$^-$. Similarly, the tray computes its stretchability by connecting the top rightmost pin to a fixed pin `P`$^+$, centered at $(+\infty, +\infty)$, and resolving the network; the stretchability is the amount the top rightmost pin must move to remain connected to `P`$^+$.

With all shape information calculated, the tray can set its shape state variable and return from `Reconfig`. When the tray is later resized, it translates the top rightmost pin so that the bounding box of the tray's pins matches the size of the canvas. The tray then solves the network, and translates and resizes its children to reflect the positions of the pins in its constructions.

State variables. UI defines state variables for interactor attributes that a user can examine, specify, or modify. These include its canvas, shape, class name, and possibly a button state. The views of these state variables are assembled into a dialog box when the user examines the interactor.

`CanvasVar` stores the width and height of an interactor component's canvas. `CanvasVarView` displays this information in an InterViews `Message` object (an interactor that displays a noneditable string of text).

`ShapeVar` defines an interactor component's shape. The shape information can be editable or read-only, depending on whether the interactor's programming interface allows the programmer to specify or change the interactor's shape. `ShapeVarView` presents this information in a tabular format incorporating string editors (interactors that display an editable string of text) if the subject is editable; otherwise it incorporates messages exclusively.

`ButtonStateVar` stores a name, an initial value, and a setting value. All button state variables with a given name share the same initial value. The external representation for an interface will contain an instantiation of a button state object for each unique name among the button state variables. `ButtonStateVarView` provides an interface for changing the subject's name and values.

Finally, interactor components store their class name in a `NameVar`, a Unidraw-defined state variable that stores a string. UI defines a `ClassNameVarView` state variable view that simply presents this name in a message, since it is an unchanging attribute of an interactor.

The `CodeView` subclass of `PreorderView` is the base class for objects that generate UI's external representation. Each interactor component has a corresponding `CodeView` subclass. Figure 10.19 lists a sample UI external representation.

`CodeView`'s `Emit` operation first generates forward declarations for all button states in the interface. `ButtonStateVar` defines a class operation that allows `CodeView` to iterate through all the `ButtonStateVar` instances in the interface and produce the `ButtonState` declarations at the top of Figure 10.19. `CodeView` subclasses for leaf interactor components redefine the `Definition` operation to generate code of the form

new *className (parameters)*

where the parameters reflect the component's internal state. `BoxCode`, the `CodeView` subclass for box components, generates these parameters by calling its children's `Definition` operations. The tray external representation must be handled specially, since its alignments cannot be specified inline (see [Vlissides90 and 91] for details).

A programmer uses the `Interior` function to produce an instance of the interactor composition. `CodeView`'s `Emit` operation generates the `Interior` declaration. The button state initialization code is created by iterating through the `ButtonStateVar` instances as `CodeView` did to

```
static Tray* Tray0 () {
    Tray* tray = new Tray;

    Interactor* i1 = new CheckBox("check", bs0, 1, 0);
    tray->Insert(i1);
    Interactor* i2 = new HGlue(0, 0, hfil);
    tray->Insert(i2);
    Interactor* i3 = new PushButton("push", bs1, 1);
    tray->Insert(i3);

    tray->HBox(tray, i1, i2, i3, tray);
    tray->Align(VertCenter, i1, i2, i3);

    return tray;
}
static Interactor* Interior0 () {
    bs0 = new ButtonState(0);
    bs1 = new ButtonState(0);


    return new Frame(
        new VBox( new VGlue(20, 20, vfil),
            new StringEditor(bs0, "sample"),
            new VGlue(20, 20, vfil),
            Tray0(),
            new VGlue(20, 20, vfil)
        )
    );
}
```

Figure 10.19 Sample UI external representation

generate the corresponding declarations. `CodeView` produces the `Interior` function's return value by calling its own `Definition` operation.

Commands and tools. UI defines several commands. `InfoCmd` creates an instance of `InfoDialog`, which composes state variable views of an interactor component's state variables. A user invokes this command through the examine tool's pop-up menu. Once the user has changed the state variable values and dismissed the dialog, `InfoCmd` applies the changes to the selected interactor component. UI's `NewViewCmd` is analogous to Drawing's: it creates a new UIEditor instance for editing the same component as the current editor. The user directs UI to produce an external representation with the `CodeCmd`. This command lets the user specify a file name in which to store the external representation and then creates a `CodeView` of the editor's interactor component.

The InterViews `Scene` class defines a `Place` operation that makes an interactor hierarchy visible on the screen. This operation initiates two traversals of the interactor hierarchy: one to determine its shape, and another to allocate screen space. InterViews calls `Place` when an interactor is inserted into the top-level window; in UI this occurs when an interactor component is created with a graphical component tool. The interactor view base class creates a `PlaceCmd` in response to manipulation by a graphical component tool. The interactor subject initiates the placement traversals when it interprets this command.

`GlueVisibilityCmd` directs a glue component to make itself visible (by rendering itself with horizontal or vertical bars) or invisible (by erasing the bars). Visible glue is easier to manipulate, while invisible glue is less distracting.

Finally, `SceneCmd` is a subclass of Unidraw's `GroupCmd`, which removes selected components from their parent and inserts them into another graphical component (the *destination*), which in UI will be a scene component. `SceneCmd` extends the behavior of `GroupCmd` to make the destination interpret a `PlaceCmd` after reparenting the components, allowing the destination to determine their shapes and allocate their screen space.

UI defines only one new tool, `ExamineTool`. Other tools in the interface are taken from the framework. In particular, the `Edit` tool is actually an instance of the framework's `ReshapeTool`, which delegates manipulator creation and interpretation to the components being manipulated. Views of interactor components that can be edited with this tool simply redefine their `CreateManipulator` and `InterpretManipulator` operations to respond to it appropriately—a new tool subclass is therefore unnecessary. Similarly, UI's `ResizeTool` is actually an instance of the framework's `StretchTool`.

`ExamineTool` produces an InterViews pop-up menu with two submenus containing controls that execute `InfoCmd` and `NewViewCmd`, respectively. Each of these commands operates on a different level of the chosen interactor hierarchy. `ExamineTool` does not delegate manipulator creation to the selected interactor view; instead, it creates a `PopupManip` with the pop-up menu as an argument, and it relies on the pop-up menu's submenus to execute the desired command. `PopupManip` does little more than forward events to the pop-up menu, to allow it to work within the viewer.

Experience

The user interface building domain is the least mature of the domains for which we have developed Unidraw-based applications. Editors for this domain did not arrive until the mid 1980s, and little has been published relating experience with them in production environments. There is a consensus, however, that they do not eliminate the need for conventional programming, and UI is no exception in this regard. UI is best used to describe the layout of an interface and for experimenting with the dynamics of interactor compositions. UI does not help the user specify an interface's input semantics, nor does it let him or her define new interactors; however, current hand-crafted interface builders do not offer such capabilities either.

On the other hand, UI does support layout semantics as sophisticated as any user interface builder. The composition abstractions that underlie existing builders are not as general or powerful as those that InterViews provides, which include nonlinear deformation (independent stretchability and shrinkability) with two-way layout constraints (via boxes and tray). UI can offer a better direct manipulation model because it is founded upon more powerful InterViews abstractions.

In performance terms, interfaces as they appear and behave in UI actually outperform real InterViews interfaces. Interactor components consume less memory than real interactors, partly because interactor components do not handle input, and partly because each InterViews interactor contains its own X window. The smallest possible InterViews interactor (not including information potentially shared with other interactors) uses about 100 bytes. This figure does not include the X window, which takes up space in both the application and in the window server. In X11 Release 4 the library space is at least 75 bytes, while the server keeps at least an additional 150 bytes. Each InterViews interactor thus consumes at least 325 bytes. The smallest possible interactor component, including a subject and a view, is 188 bytes.

Interactor components also compare favorably at runtime. Interactor views draw themselves as quickly as real interactors do, and scene components compose and place their children substantially faster than real scenes, since placement does not involve communication with the X server. Tray components are even more efficient in comparison. Tray subjects use connectors to determine the proper placement of their components. Unidraw uses a recursive substitution technique to solve connector constraints in time proportional to $O(n^2)$ at worst, where n is the number of alignments [Vlissides90]. InterViews trays use a similar technique to compute placement, but they do not incorporate optimizations developed later for Unidraw that make the search for possible substitutions run in linear time. As a result, InterViews trays take $O(n^3)$ time at worst.

We can conclude, then, that interfaces in UI perform at least as well as the InterViews-based interfaces they implement. However, the code that UI generates could be better. Usually, some modification is required to integrate the code into a larger implementation. The generated interactor instance names are not mnemonic; the user should be able to specify these names at runtime through a state variable view. The programmer will often want the `Interior` function to be a member of a class rather than a static global. This is true for the button states as well. Still, the external representation does encapsulate the trickiest part of the implementation: specifying the composition hierarchy and interactor attributes correctly.

10.5 Summary

Drawing and UI demonstrate how Unidraw facilitates the design and implementation of domain-specific editors. These applications reflect a significant reduction in development effort by almost any measure, and both approach or exceed the functionality and performance of their custom-built counterparts.

Drawing and UI offer different perspectives of Unidraw's capabilities. Drawing is an example of a simple Unidraw-based graphical object editor, demonstrating the power of the predefined library components. Drawing also shows how a Unidraw-based application can give the user considerable control over the application's user interface. UI's components have much more complex semantics; its tray component in particular shows how Unidraw's connector model can support sophisticated connectivity. UI also takes greater advantage of multiple views.

Unidraw greatly simplified the implementation of the drawing editor and user interface builder. Though these editors are not polished systems, they demonstrate that Unidraw is a viable way to build practical applications. Unidraw narrowed the design space for each editor significantly, obviating basic design decisions that are independent of the domain. The framework provides reusable functionality in the form of predefined components, commands, and tools. Debugging time was reduced because much less code was written. Our experience is that developing domain-specific editors with Unidraw is mainly a matter of choosing, designing, and implementing the required domain-specific components. Significantly less effort is spent defining new commands, while specialized tools are rarely needed.

One feature that could be developed further is Unidraw's support for external representations. We would like to go beyond the current predefined external view traversals to develop a more powerful model that supports the *internalization* of one or more different external representations. While Unidraw currently does not preclude this capability, neither does it aid its implementation. Internalization would let a domain-specific editor read representations produced by other applications. For example, a schematic editor could read in a netlist, allow the user to edit it graphically, and generate a new netlist. A logic simulator could then give the user feedback about the modified circuit's behavior, which might prompt him to edit the circuit again. The ability to read as well as write external representations permits iterative design by closing the loop between specification and analysis.

Another useful extension would support automatic component layout. Often in applications such as tree or graph editors the user is not interested in arranging components by hand; instead he or she would rather specify rules for their placement and let the system enforce them. Later the user might tidy up the system's layout via direct manipulation, but the bulk of the work will have already been done. The framework could include an object that positions components according to a specification. Such an object could use established layout algorithms and heuristics to produce pleasing component layouts.

Finally, Unidraw provides a foundation for research into *graphical object editor-building* applications. Just as the concept of assembling user interface components by direct manipulation came into its own when toolkits furnished the underlying abstractions for user interface builders, so too does Unidraw provide the foundation for a direct manipulation approach to building graphical object editors. A graphical object editor builder would offer direct manipulation analogs of classes in the framework, and would generate Unidraw code that uses them. We have implemented the beginnings of such capabilities in a schematic capture system, where new components can be defined at runtime [Vlissides90]. A graphical object editor builder (itself a graphical object editor) would take the metaphor a step further, to let a user specify commands, tools, and external representations dynamically and assemble them into domain-specific editors.

References

[Helm92] R. Helm, T. Huynh, K. Marriott, and J. Vlissides, An object-oriented architecture for constraint-based graphical editing, In *Proceedings of the Third Eurographics Workshop on Object-Oriented Graphics,* pages 1–22, Champéry, Switzerland, October 1992. Also available as IBM Research Division Technical Report RC 18524 (79392).

[Hudson88] S. E. Hudson and R. King. Semantic feedback in the Higgens UIMS. *IEEE Transactions on Software Engineering,* **14**(8), 1188–1206, 1988.

[Linton89] M. A. Linton, J. M. Vlissides, and P. R. Calder, Composing user interfaces with InterViews, *Computer,* **22**(2), 8–22, 1989.

[Stanford92] Stanford University Computer Systems Laboratory. *InterViews Reference Manual, Version 3.1,* 1992.

[Vlissides90] J. M. Vlissides, Generalized Graphical Object Editing, PhD thesis, Stanford University, 1990.

[Vlissides91] J. M. Vlissides and S. Tang, A Unidraw-based user interface builder. In *Proceedings of the ACM SIGGRAPH Fourth Annual Symposium on User Interface Software and Technology,* Hilton Head, SC, November 1991.

CHAPTER 11

Prograph CPX

KURT SCHMUCKER

Preview

Prograph CPX is a commercially supported, self-contained, object-oriented programming language and development environment running on the Macintosh that can produce small-footprint, stand-alone Macintosh applications. It is packaged with an application framework called the *Prograph ABCs* (Application Builder Classes). The ABCs are roughly comparable in the breadth and depth of their functionality to other Macintosh frameworks, like MacApp [Schmucker88] and TCL [Parker93]. While this chapter will touch on all three aspects of Prograph—the language, the environment, and the application framework—the major emphasis will be on the framework, its structure, and its use.

The Prograph 2.5 manual notes that [TGS89], "Prograph integrates four key trends emerging in computer science:

- Prograph is a visual programming language.
- Prograph is object-oriented.
- Prograph supports dataflow specification of program execution.
- Prograph provides an object-oriented application building toolkit."

What is unique about Prograph is:

- Its language: an object-oriented, visual, dataflow language
- The tight integration of the language with the editor, interpreter, and debugger into a single unified development tool

- Several aspects of the ABCs, including the ability to package classes with custom graphical editors for their instances

Prograph CPX is the principal product of Prograph International, and has been shipping on the Macintosh since 1988. It is positioned by Prograph International as a development tool that has the interactive "feel" of the Macintosh Finder, yet with all the power to access any Macintosh internal that can be accessed from any C, C++, or Pascal programming tool. In fact, it would be reasonable to state that Prograph is the first industrial-strength visual programming system.

Prograph users run the full gamut of Macintosh application developers: from former HyperCard scripters or 4D developers, to those who are quite comfortable using MacApp or TCL in C++, and from developers who are primarily concerned with the functionality of their product (application developers), to those who are more concerned with the data content of their work (title developers). They have used Prograph to implement shrink-wrapped products, in-house applications, prototypes, and database front ends, among other uses.

As of this writing (December 1994), the current version of Prograph is limited to producing applications. Nonstand-alone code fragments like XCMDs, WDEFs, PhotoShop plug-ins, etc., cannot be implemented with Prograph, although plans are underway by Prograph International to remove this restriction. In addition, today only 68K-based Macintosh applications can be built, although here too, plans are underway to produce PowerPC-native applications, Windows applications, and UNIX applications.

This chapter will describe the Prograph language and environment, and then discuss the Prograph application framework, the ABCs, in some detail. Where appropriate, comparisons will be made with other Macintosh application frameworks, most notably MacApp. (See Chapter 5 for a detailed description of MacApp.) Prograph demonstrates the power of frameworks when combined with a programming language.

11.1 What Is Prograph?

Prograph is a language and a programming environment. Its language is an iconic visual programming language. The programmer codes by constructing drawings, and the Prograph interpreter and compiler execute those drawings. Figure 11.1 shows a simple piece of Prograph code which sorts, possibly in parallel, three database indices and updates the database.

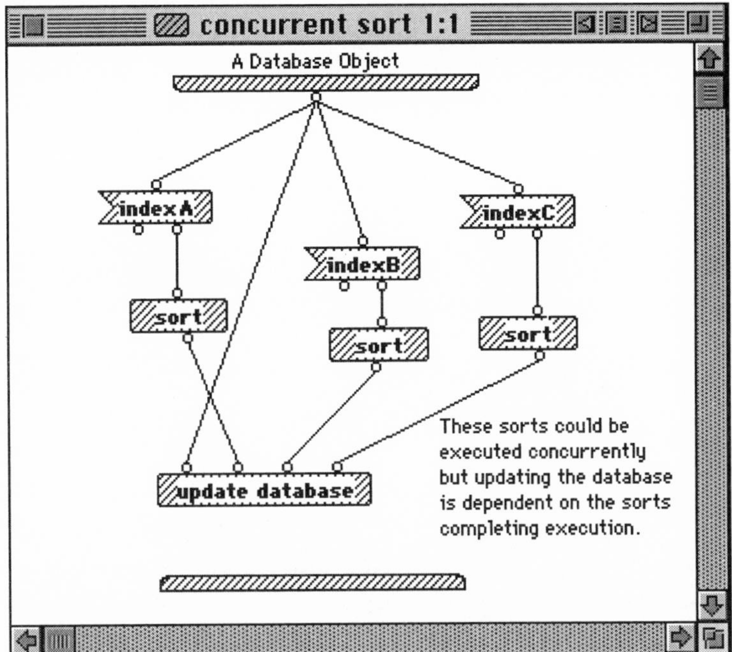

Figure 11.1 A simple piece of Prograph code which sorts—possibly in parallel—three database indices and updates the database. In Prograph code, data basically flows from top to bottom, and operations—represented by icons—can execute whenever all their inputs are satisfied. Note that this graphical code representation is the only representation available for the Prograph language: there is no textual alternative

To many programmers, drawing a program seems very strange at first, but the power and clarity of code expressed in Prograph is undeniable. The power of the language has to do with its primitives and the ways in which they can be used to express a computation. The clarity of code expressed in Prograph is due, in part, to the fact that algorithms, by their very nature, have an inherent internal structure. Often, implementing an algorithm in a textual, and thus necessarily linear fashion, hides this structure. In contrast, the Prograph language brings this structure to the surface, and enables the Prograph-literate programmer to grasp this structure in a single *gestalt.*

The Prograph language has a graphical design and consistency which can be expressed in a small number of basic representations. For instance,

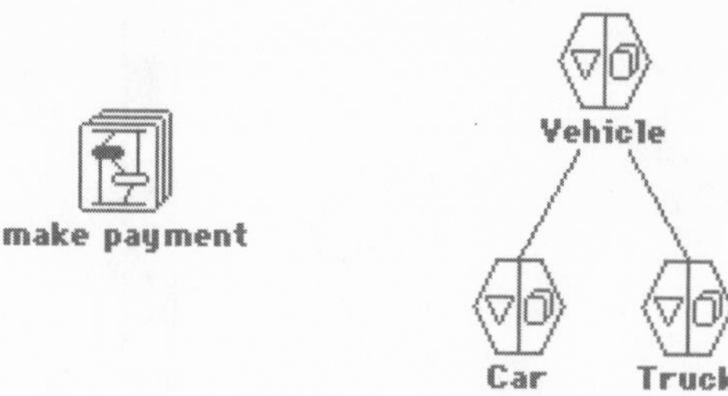

Figure 11.2 Some of the basic elements of the graphical design "language" representations of Prograph. Classes are represented by hexagons, data elements by triangles, pieces of code by rectangles with data flow code inside, and inheritance by lines or downward pointing arrows

classes are represented by hexagons, data elements by triangles, pieces of code by rectangles with a small picture of data flow code inside, and inheritance by lines or downward pointing arrows. In Figure 11.2 some of these representations are used in their simplest forms. The representations can then be combined and used in a variety of language elements. For example, initialization methods—which are associated with an individual class—are depicted as hexagonally-shaped icons with a small picture of data flow code inside; instance variables, being data, are represented by triangles in the data window of a class; class variables, being associated with the class as a whole, are depicted as hexagons, but are drawn with edges and interiors similar to the instance variable triangles. Figure 11.3 shows some of these more complex representations.

11.1.1 Object-Orientation

The Prograph language is object-oriented. In particular, it is a class-based, single inheritance, object-oriented language with dynamic typing and a garbage collection mechanism based on reference counting. The programmer can design and implement new classes, specifying visually the new class's inheritance, additional instance or class variables, modified

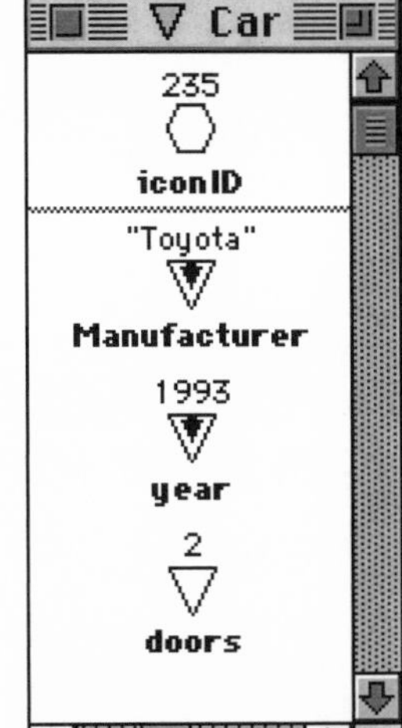

Figure 11.3 The elements of the graphical design "language" representations of Prograph can be combined in ways that are surprisingly self-consistent and easy to learn. In this figure we see three examples of this: initialization methods—which are associated with an individual class—are depicted as hexagonally shaped icons with data flow code inside; instance variables, being data, are represented by triangles in the Data Window of a class; and class variables, being associated with the class as a whole, are depicted as hexagons, but are drawn with edges and interiors similar to the instance variable triangles

default values for inherited instance or class variables, and new or overridden methods. Binding of a polymorphic operation to a method in a particular class happens at runtime and is dependent upon the class of the object to which this operation is employed; however, the syntax for this "message send" is one of the more unusual aspects of Prograph's syntax. The concept of *message sending per se* is not used in Prograph. Rather, the idea of an annotation on the name of an operation is used. There are four cases: The absence of an annotation means that the operation is not polymorphic. The / annotation means that the operation is polymorphic and is to be resolved by method lookup starting in the class of the object flowing into the operation on its first input. The // annotation means that the operation is polymorphic and is to be resolved by method lookup starting in the class in which this method is defined. The // plus super annotation means that the operation is polymorphic and is to be resolved by method

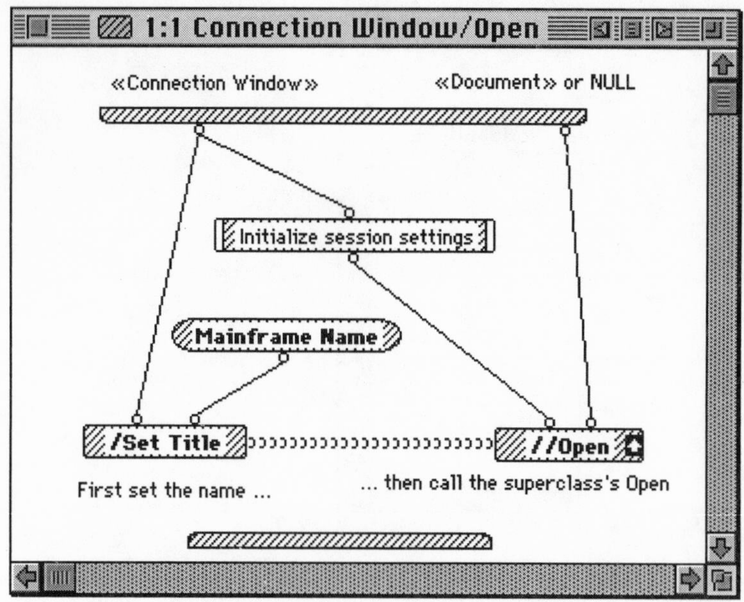

Figure 11.4 A typical piece of Prograph code showing comments, use of different types of operations (with their respective iconic representations), data flow (straight lines) and synchronization primitives (the wavy line)

lookup starting in the superclass of the class in which this method is defined. In addition, Prograph is one of the few object-oriented languages in which there is no `SELF` construct (or a `this` construct, to use the C++ terminology).

Prograph has an almost completely iconic syntax, and this iconic syntax is the only representation of Prograph code (Figure 11.4 shows a small code fragment typical of the Prograph language.). There is no textual equivalent of a piece of a Prograph program—the Prograph interpreter and compiler translate directly from this graphical syntax into 68K code. The icons of the Prograph language represent some twenty types of operations, and Figure 11.5 shows most of the lexicon of the language. The inputs and outputs to an operation are specified by small circles at the top and bottom, respectively, of the icons. The number of inputs and outputs— the operation's arity—is enforced only at runtime. In addition, there are a variety of annotations that can be applied to the inputs and outputs, or to the operation as a whole to implement looping or control flow. The visual syntax of Prograph has been formally specified [Cox88].

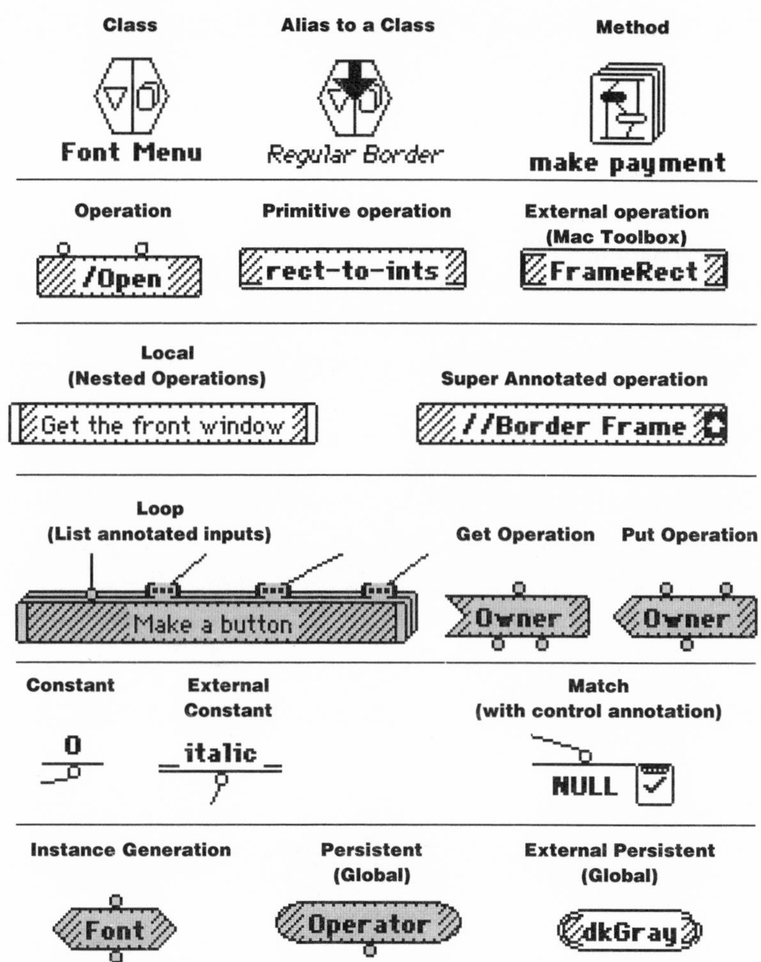

Figure 11.5 Examples of most of the iconic syntax of the Prograph language

Visual languages like Prograph sometimes suffer from the spaghetti code problem: there are so many lines running all over that the code for any meaningful piece of work actually ends up looking like spaghetti. Prograph deals with this issue by enabling the programmer to *iconify* any portion of any piece of code at any time during the development process. This iconified code is called a *local.* Effectively, locals are nested pieces of code. There is no limit to the level of nesting possible with locals, and there is no execution penalty to their use. In addition, locals can be named and this naming, if done well, can provide a useful documentation for the code. Figure 11.6 shows the same piece of Prograph code with and without the use of locals. Note also that long names, often containing punctuation or other special characters, can be used for the names of locals. The proper use of locals can dramatically improve the comprehensibility of a piece of code. The one negative aspect of their use is the so-called *rat hole* phenomena—every piece of code in its own rat hole. This can sometimes make finding code difficult.

Three of the most interesting aspects of the Prograph syntax are *list annotation*, *inject*, and *control annotation*. Any elementary operation can be made to loop by list annotating any of its inputs. When this is done, the operation is invoked multiple times—once for each element of the list that is passed on this input. Thus, list annotation on an input causes the compiler to construct a loop for the programmer. Since this annotation can be made on a local as well as a primitive operation, the looping construct is quite powerful. In addition, list annotation can be done on a output. On an output terminal, list annotation causes the system to gather together all the outputs at the terminal for every iteration of the

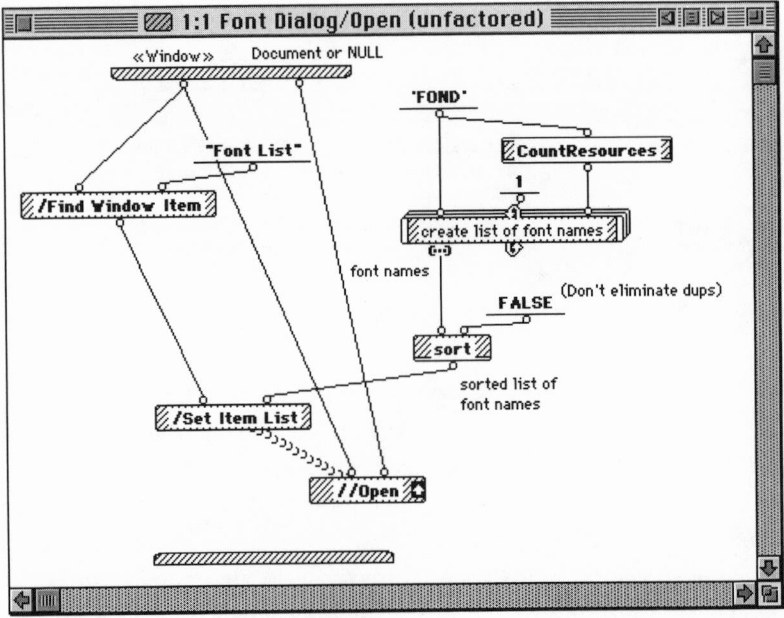

Figure 11.6a The code to build a dialog box containing a scrolling list of the installed fonts without the use of Prograph locals to factor the code

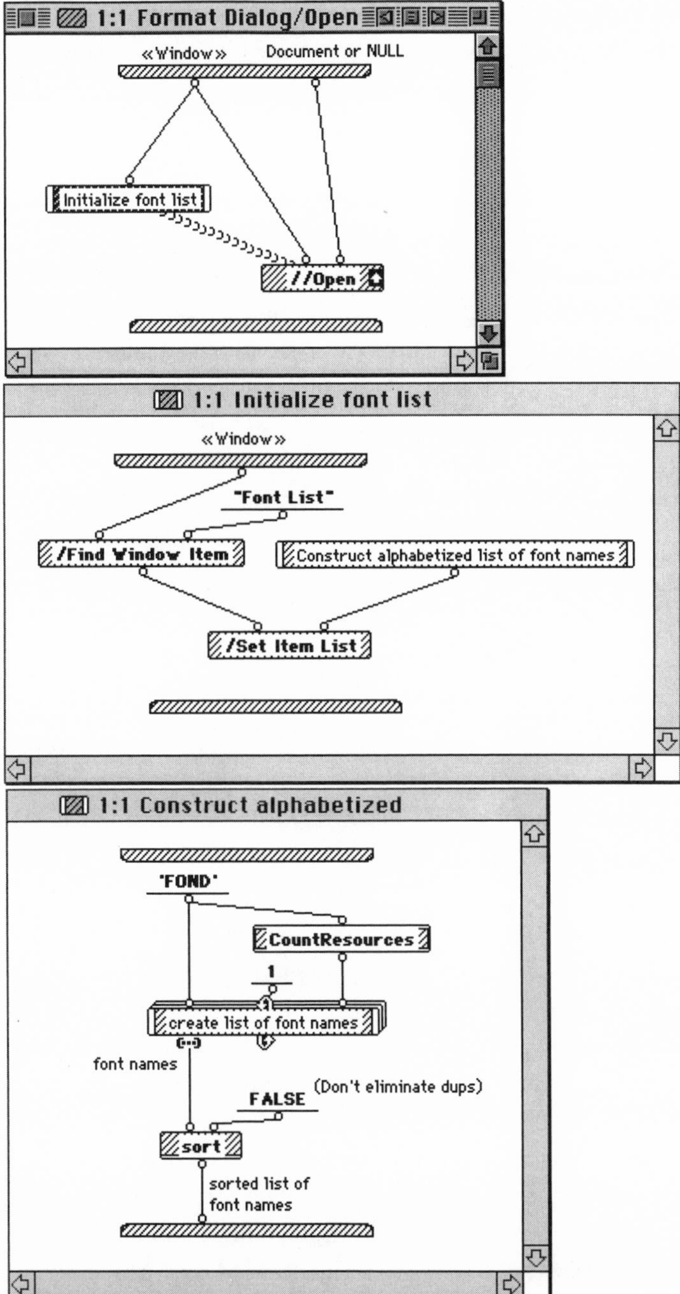

Figure 11.6b The code to build a dialog box containing a scrolling list of the installed fonts with the use of Prograph locals to factor the code

operation and to pass, as the *final* output of the terminal, this collection of results in the form of an output list. List annotation, then, enables the programmer to easily make a operation into a loop that either breaks down a list into its component elements and runs that operation on the elements, or that builds up a list from the multiple executions of an operation. An individual operation can have any number of its inputs or outputs list annotated. Figure 11.7 shows several examples of list annotation.

Inject is a means of determining the operation's name at runtime. (For those familiar with Smalltalk, Prograph's inject is similar to Smalltalk's *perform.* It is also not too dissimilar to procedure variables in Pascal or function pointers in C.) Suppose, for example, that you want to implement a function, `FooMe`, that takes two arguments: a list of objects, and a reference to a method to be applied to each of those objects. In Object Pascal pseudo code, this function might look something like this:

```
Function FooMe(theList: TList; Procedure DoThis(object: TObject));
{ Iterates through the list of objects applying the DoThis procedure }

    BEGIN
        theList.Each(DoThis);
    END;
```

The Prograph implementation of `FooMe` would look something like Figure 11.8. Note that just the name—as a string—of the method to be applied to each object is passed to `FooMe`. This string is turned into a method invocation by the inject.

The Prograph representation of inject—a nameless operation with one terminal descending into the operation's icon—is a particularly well-designed graphic representation for this programming concept. When properly used, inject can result in extremely powerful and compact Prograph implementations of complex functions. However, when used improperly, it can result in code that is very difficult to read or debug, not unlike the computed `GOTO` of FORTRAN.

Control flow is the most unusual aspect of the Prograph language, and is perhaps the most difficult aspect of Prograph for the inexperienced user. It is a combination of annotations on operations and a case structure. A Prograph method can consist of a number of mutually exclusive *cases.* These cases are somewhat similar to the cases in a Pascal `CASE` statement or a C `switch` expression. The main difference is that, unlike Pascal or C, the code to determine which case will be executed is inside the case,

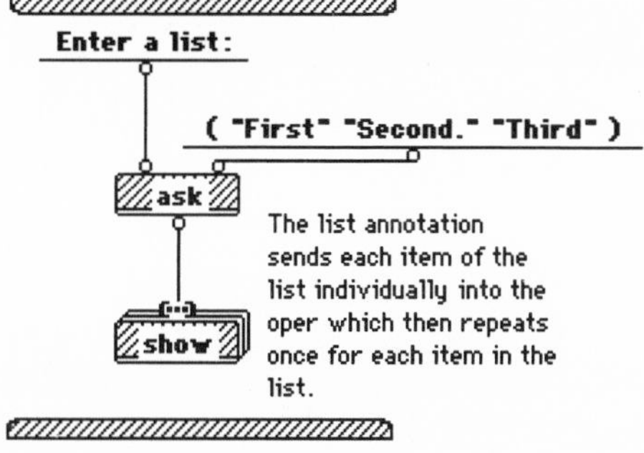

Example 1

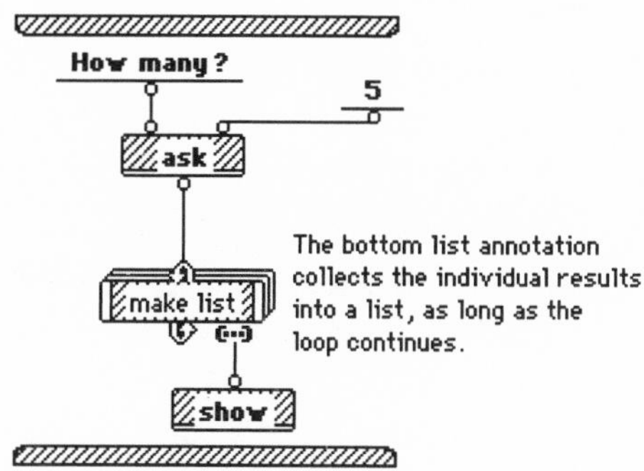

Example 2

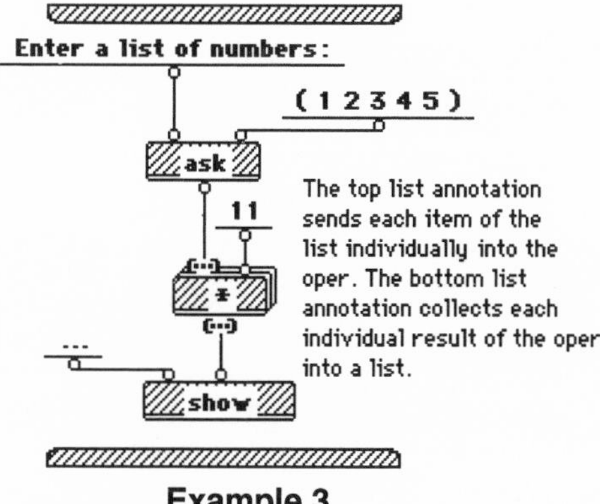

Example 3

Figure 11.7 Examples of list annotation in Prograph. List annotation is an extremely easy-to-use and efficient mechanism for iterating over a list. All the programmer has to do is to change a single input or output on an operation, and that operation will automatically be called repeatedly for each element of a list, or its outputs will be packaged together into a list

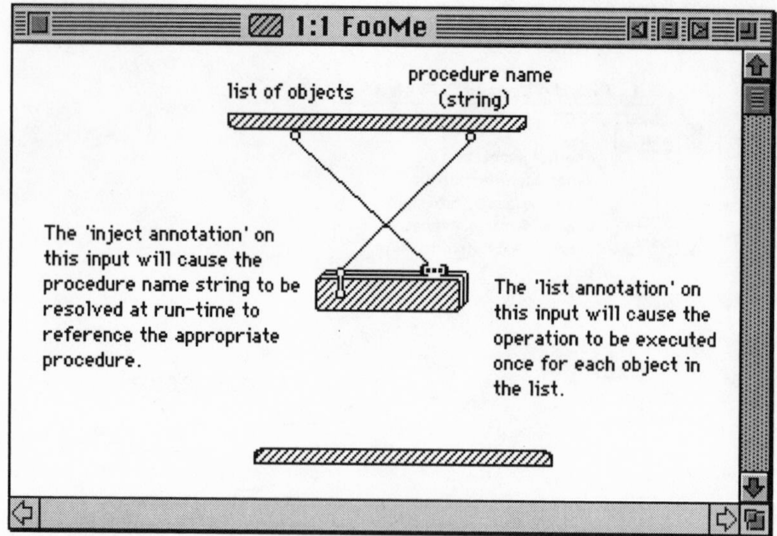

Figure 11.8 A simple use of inject to determine a procedure at runtime. Note that Prograph's inject is similar in its semantics to Smalltalk's perform

not outside it. A small example may make this clear. Suppose that we want to implement a small function that has one integer input, and if that input is between 1 and 10, the value of the function is computed one way; if it is between 11 and 100, another way, and if it is anything else, yet a third way. In Pascal-like pseudo code, this function would look something like this:

```
Function Foo( i: Integer): Integer;
Begin
    Case i of
        1..10:          Foo := Calculation_A(i);
        11..100:        Foo := Calculation_B(i);
        Otherwise       Foo := Calculation_C(i);
    End; {Case}
End; {Foo}
```

The implementation of `Foo` in Prograph would also involve three cases, and it would look like Figure 11.9. The control annotations are the small boxes on the right of the match primitives at the top of the first two cases. (Note that the window titles show the total number of cases in a method, and which case this window is, as in *2:3*, the second of three cases.) In this simple example, the same annotation—a check mark in an otherwise empty rectangle—is used. The semantics of this annotation

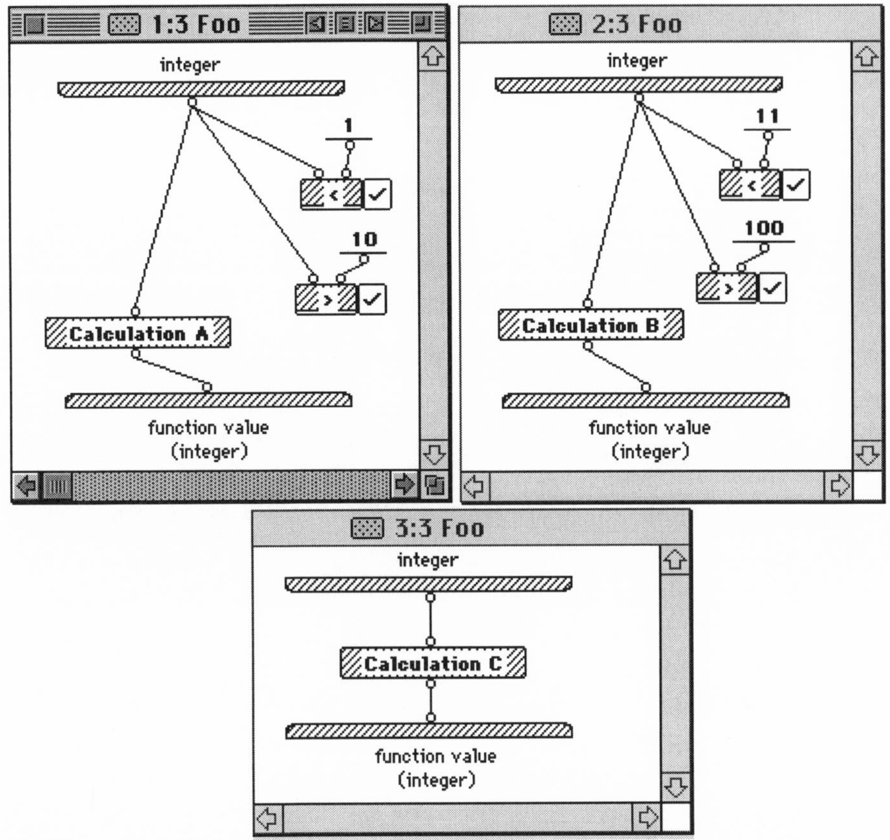

Figure 11.9 The Prograph equivalent of a small Pascal Case statement

are: "If this operation succeeds, then go to the next case." The check mark is the iconic representation of success, and the empty rectangle represents the *go to the next case* notion. If the check mark were replaced by an *x*, then the semantics would have been: "If this operation fails, then go to the next case." In addition to the otherwise empty rectangle, there are four other possibilities, and the five different semantics of control annotations are shown together in Figure 11.10. It is a runtime error and a compile-time warning to have a next-case control annotation in a location where it cannot execute, for example, in the last case of a method.

11.1.2 Dataflow

The Prograph language is also a *data flow language*. Typed data elements flow along the data wires from the outputs of one operation to the

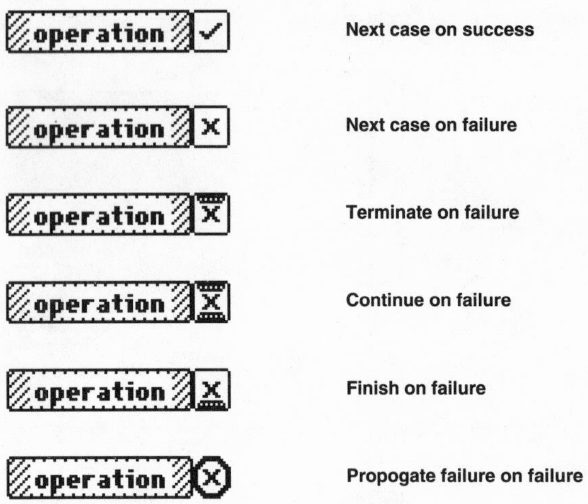

Figure 11.10 The different types of actions possible with a control annotation

inputs of another. Execution of an operation can take place any time that data is available on all of its inputs, but otherwise the order of execution is nondeterministic. This is often a conceptual stumbling block for the new Prograph programmer, probably because of prior training in linear, textual languages with their implicit execution order. In reality, however, order of execution is often an unnecessary detail in the implementation of an algorithm, and Prograph frees the programmer from having to specify this unneeded detail—once, of course, the programmer learns to differentiate the unnecessary specification of ordering from that which is necessary. Should an algorithm require that a particular operation, *A*, be executed prior to another operation, *B*, the programmer can enforce this by connecting a *synchro* from *A* to *B*, and Prograph will guarantee that A is executed before, although not necessarily immediately before, *B*. (An example of a synchro in use can be seen in Figure 11.4. This synchro ensures that the window's title is set before the superclass's Open method is invoked.) As you would probably expect, the use of unnecessary synchro connections is the mark of a beginning Prograph programmer.

11.1.3 Data Types and Primitives

There are ten data types in the Prograph language: boolean, integer, real, string, list, external structure, NULL, NONE, undefined, and object. Type checking is performed at runtime at the execution of each operation.

A type error will cause the application to halt. If the application is being run under the interpreter when a type error occurs, then control will be transferred to the interpreter and the programmer will be given the opportunity to correct the error—either by modifying the code or by modifying the data value—and continuing execution. If the error occurs in a compiled application, the application will quit and return to Finder.

In addition, there are 307 primitives that are effectively part of the language. These primitives include functions in the following areas, among others: math, list processing, I/O, string processing, and interpreter control. Figure 11.11 presents the entire set of primitives.

New external primitives can easily be added. In fact, this is how the Mac Toolbox traps are supported: as *external* primitives defined in files that are supplied with CPX. It is relatively easy to add new external primitives, and this is the means by which existing libraries of C or Pascal functionality can be brought into Prograph. Once this is done from some library, these external primitives are supported at exactly the same level as Mac Toolbox traps. Thus, it is not the case that C or Pascal libraries that you bring into Prograph are somehow "second-class citizens" in the Prograph language. This is the means by which new Mac system calls (e.g., QuickTime or Drag Manager) are added to Prograph. Prograph International tries to keep up with the steady stream of additional Mac APIs coming out of Apple, but if for some reason they have not yet gotten to the nifty new API that you want to use, you can just do the work yourself to bring this functionality into Prograph as a new external primitive. There is no easy way today, however, to bring in C++ libraries, especially in a way that would retain the inheritance structure of the C++ library.

Method and procedure names can include spaces, punctuation, and other special characters, and they can be of any length. This may seem like a very minor point, but it is really nice to be able to name a local *Bring to Front, if necessary* or ??. In fact, a Prograph naming convention has been informally adopted in which, among other conventions, a name ending in a ? returns a boolean.

11.2 Prograph Environment

In this section a quick (and necessarily incomplete) overview of the Prograph programming environment will be presented. Normally, the programming environment, although of great importance to the actual

ABC Support
- draw-style-text
- popup-menu

AppleTalk
- ATP-Close
- ATP-Get-Request
- ATP-Get-Response
- ATP-Open
- ATP-Send-Request
- ATP-Send-Response
- NBP-Close
- NBP-Confirm
- NBP-Lookup
- NBP-Open
- NBP-Register

Bit Manipulation
- bit-and
- bit-not
- bit-or
- bit-shift-l
- bit-shift-r
- bit-xor
- test-all?
- test-bit?
- test-one?

Callbacks
- callback
- dispose-callback

Data
- copy
- inst-to-list
- list-to-inst
- shallow-copy

DataFile Manager
- cluster-delete
- cluster-lock
- cluster-read
- cluster-replace
- cluster-unlock
- cluster-write
- db-backup
- db-close
- db-compact
- db-delete
- db-flush
- db-info
- db-list
- db-new
- db-open
- db-rename
- db-shutdown
- db-wait
- key-close
- key-delete
- key-find
- key-first
- key-info
- key-last
- key-list
- key-new
- key-next
- key-open
- key-previous
- key-read
- key-rename
- key-value
- table-close
- table-delete
- table-export
- table-import
- table-info
- table-list
- table-new
- table-open
- table-rename

Environment
- gestalt
- gestalt-attribute?
- trap?

File
- close
- create
- delete
- file-size
- get-file
- get-position
- open
- put-file
- read
- read-line
- rename
- resource-file
- set-position
- write
- write-line

Graphics
- find-bounds
- ints-to-point
- ints-to-rect
- ints-to-rgb
- point-to-ints
- point-to-rect
- rect-to-ints
- rect-to-points
- rgb-to-ints

Input/Output
- accept
- answer
- answer-v
- ask
- display
- print-text
- select
- set-dialog-font
- show

Interpreter Control
- abort
- abort-callback
- call
- compiled?
- debug
- execute
- find-method
- halt
- open-info-window
- open-method-window
- switch-to-prograph
- trace
- yield-cpu

Lists
- (in)
- (join)
- (length)
- attach-l
- attach-r
- detach-l
- detach-nth
- detach-r
- find-instance
- find-sorted
- get-nth
- insert-nth
- make-list
- pack
- reverse
- set-nth
- set-nth!
- sort
- split-nth
- unpack

Figure 11.11 Prograph primitives, organized by category

Load and Save/Data Clustering

clear-bytes-map
from-bytes
load
save
to-bytes

Logical/Relational

<
<=
=
>
>=
and
choose
not
or
switch
xor
~=
≠
≤
≥

Math

*
**
+
++
+1
-
--
-1
abs
acos
annuity
asin
atan
atan2
compound
cos
div
exp
idiv
ln
log10
max
min
pi
power
rand
round
round-down
round-up
set-seed
sign
sign-extend
sin
sqrt
tan
trunc
÷
÷÷

Memory

address-to-object
block-address
block-size
compact-memory
from-handle
from-pointer
get-integer
get-point
get-real
get-rect
get-string
get-text
heap-size
lock-block
lock-string
make-direct
make-handle
make-pointer
memory-callback
new-block
object-to-address
put-integer
put-point
put-real
put-rect
put-string
put-text
string-address
to-handle
to-pointer
unlock-block
unlock-string
valid-heap?

Serial Port

break-serial-port
clear-serial-port
configure-sport
count-sport-input
get-sport-buffer
get-sport-refs
kill-serial-port
open-serial-port
receive-serial-port
send-serial-port
send-sport-done
set-sport-buffer
sport-configuration

String

"in"
"join"
"length"
format
from-ascii
from-string
integer-to-string
middle
prefix
string-to-integer
suffix
to-ascii
to-string
tokenize

System

ancestors
attribute-com
attributes
called-from-get
called-from-meth
called-from-set
calls-to-get
calls-to-meth
calls-to-set
children
class-com
class-section
classes
create-class
create-method
descendants
editor-methods
meth-com

Figure 11.11 *(Continued)* Prograph primitives, organized by category

meth-com-g	persistents	**Type**
meth-com-s	section-com	boolean?
meth-io-com	section-content	external-type
meth-io-com-g	sections	instance?
meth-io-com-s	set-attribute-com	integer?
method-arity	set-class-com	list?
method-classes	set-meth-com	number?
method-section	set-meth-com-g	real?
methods	set-meth-com-s	string?
pers-com	set-pers-com	type
persistents-section	set-section-com	

Figure 11.11 *(Continued)* Prograph primitives, organized by category

use of the language and framework, is tangential to a discussion of the syntax of the language and the design of the framework. For Prograph this is not true, due to the highly integrated nature of all three of these. However, to keep this chapter of manageable length, and because the main subject of this book is frameworks, this subsection on the Prograph environment will be brief.

The Prograph environment consists of two tools: a compiler and a combined editor/interpreter/debugger, usually called the interpreter or the just simply the *environment* (Calling this second tool the i*nterpreter* is an historical artifact that is now technically inaccurate, since the current version of the *interpreter* is an incremental compiler.). Typically, an application is designed, implemented, and debugged in the environment, and then as a final step, compiled by the compiler. In this section, each of the three aspects of the environment will be described separately. This separation is a convenience for the purposes of exposition.

11.2.1 Editor/Interpreter/Debugger

The editor is a structured graphics editor that understands the syntax of the Prograph language. This editor simultaneously assists the user in entering Prograph code with a minimum of hassle and enforces Prograph syntax, so that it is not possible enter a syntactically incorrect Prograph expression. The editor also enters the correct arity for any primitive, universal, or method after the programmer enters the name. (There is also a mechanism such that the name does not have to be typed in.) Figure 11.12 shows the sequence of editor actions for entering a simple Prograph method.

The environment includes an incremental compiler, and the programmer can run the application being developed under the control of

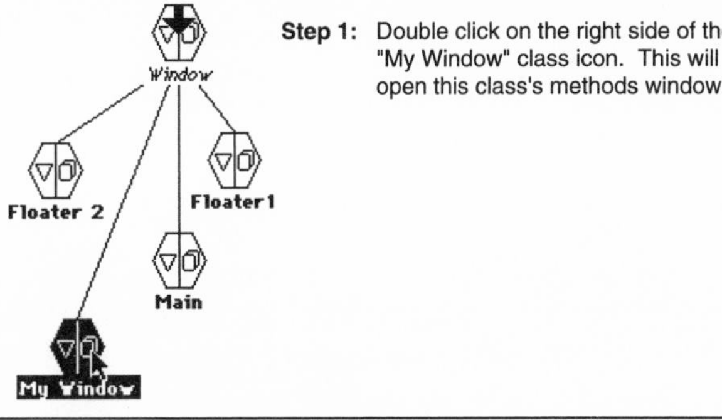
Window
Floater 2
Floater1
Main
My Window
Step 1: Double click on the right side of the "My Window" class icon. This will open this class's methods window.

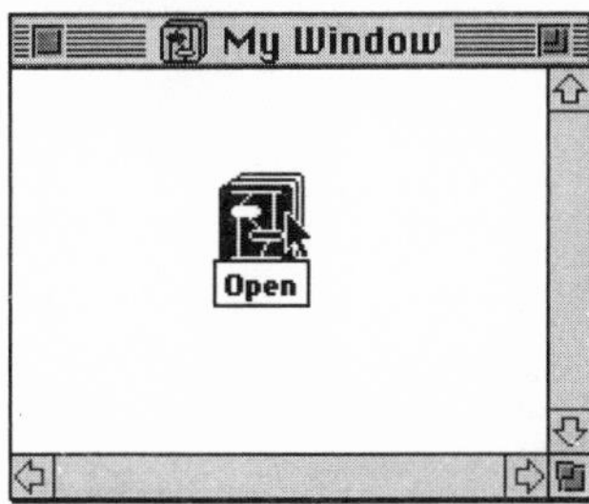
My Window
Open

Step 2: Click in the methods window to create a method. Type "Open" for its name.

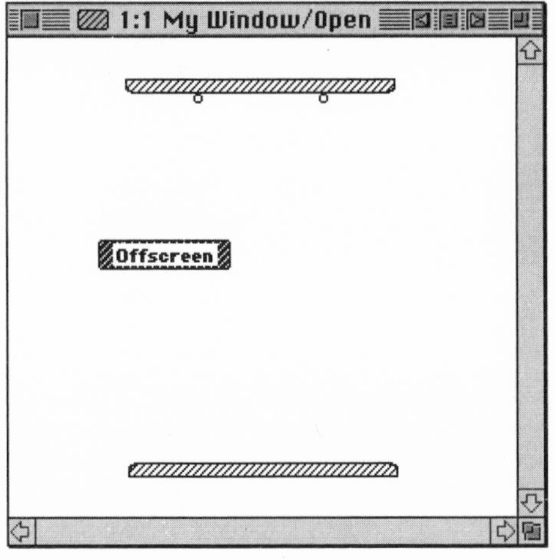
1:1 My Window/Open
Offscreen

Step 3: Click twice just beneath the input bar in order to create two inputs, since the arity of Window/Open is two inputs and no outputs.

Click to create a new operation, and name it “Offscreen”.

Figure 11.12 The Prograph editor provides an ideal environment for entering, testing, and debugging Prograph code. This long figure documents the series of actions that a programmer would take to enter a small method. Note that because of the support of the Prograph editor, it is not possible to enter a syntactically incorrect Prograph expression. In effect, the Prograph editor is to the graphical Prograph language what a syntax-directed editor can be to a textual language

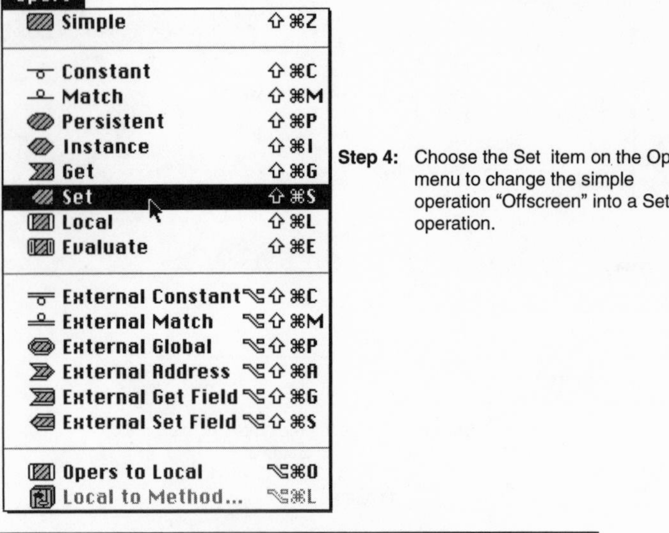

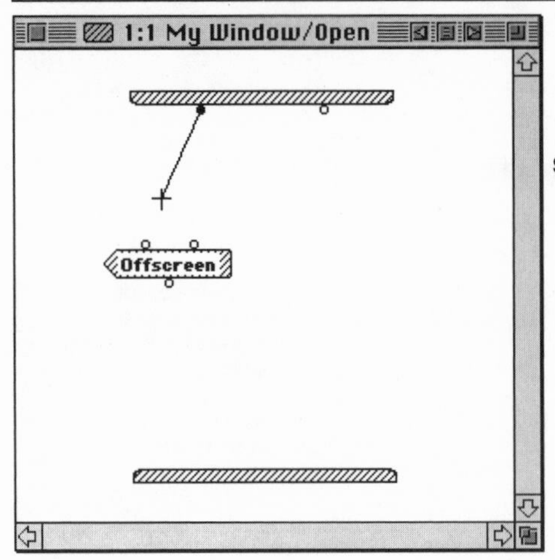

Step 5: Select the left input, and then hold down the Option key. Move the mouse to the left input of the Get operation to draw a flow line.

Figure 11.12 (*Continued*) The Prograph editor

the environment. While doing so, the application can be interrupted, data values can be examined (Figure 11.13), data values and code can be changed, and the execution of the application can be continued.

In effect, the environment includes a graphical interface builder; however, the manner in which this capability is implemented is somewhat unusual. Specific editor classes—themselves written in Prograph—provide individualized graphical editors for each one of the main ABC classes.

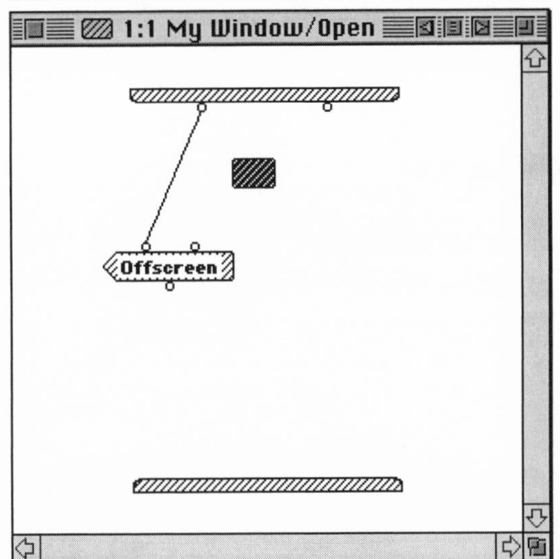

Step 6: Click to create a new operation.

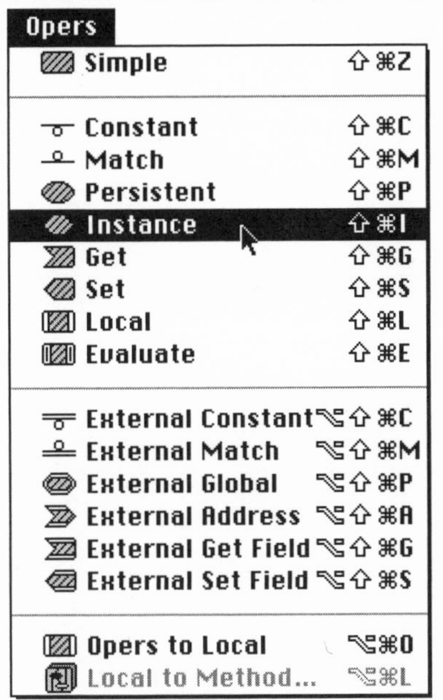

Step 7: Choose the Instance item on the Opers menu to change the simple operation into an Instance Generator.

Figure 11.12 (*Continued*) The Prograph editor

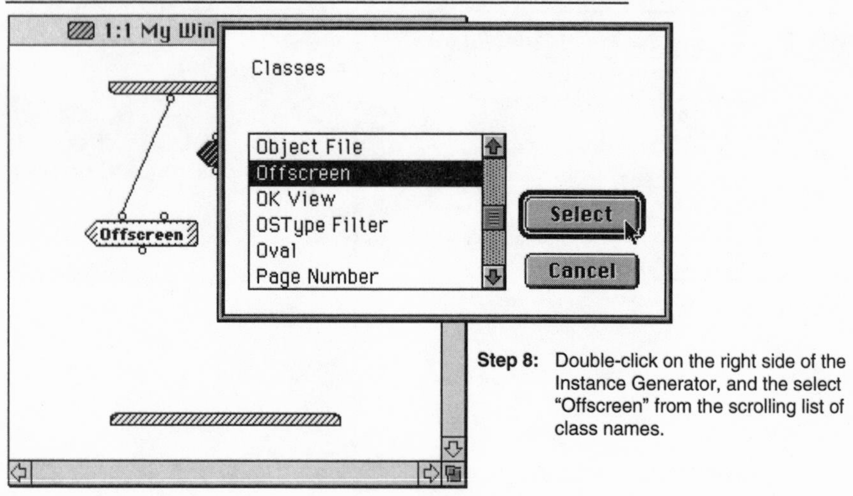
1:1 My Win
Classes
Object File
Offscreen
OK View
OSType Filter
Oval
Page Number
Select
Cancel
Offscreen
Step 8: Double-click on the right side of the Instance Generator, and the select "Offscreen" from the scrolling list of class names.

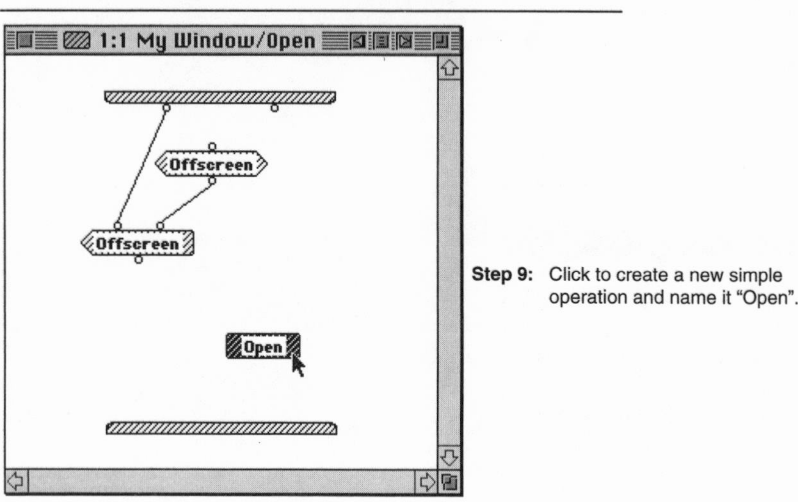
1:1 My Window/Open
Offscreen
Offscreen
Open
Step 9: Click to create a new simple operation and name it "Open".

Figure 11.12 (*Continued*) The Prograph editor

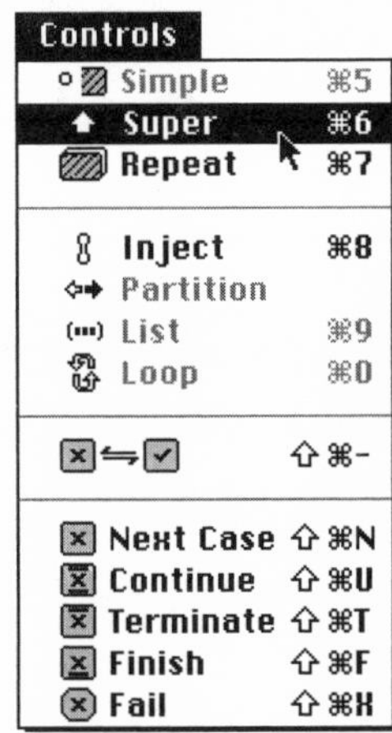

Step 10: Choose the Super item from the Controls menu to add the Super annotation to the simple "Open" operation.

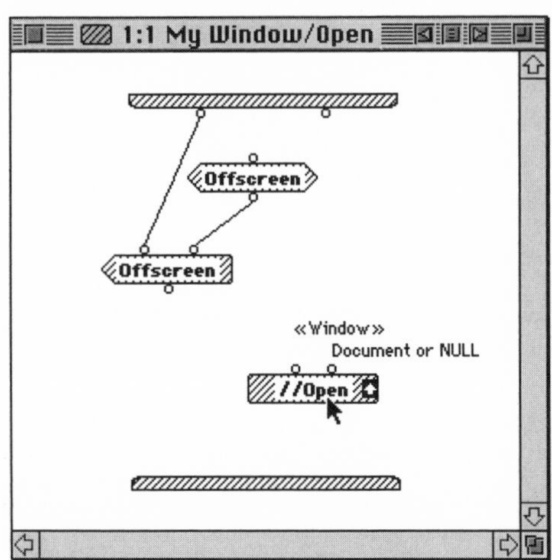

Step 11: The super annotation, plus the "//", plus the comments from the overridden method are added to the operation.

Figure 11.12 (*Continued*) The Prograph editor

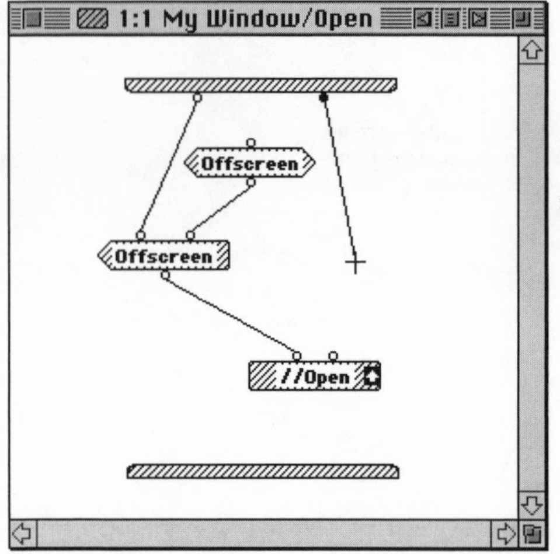

Step 12: Command-click on the inputs to the super annotated Open, in order to hide the comments. Then connect the inputs to this operation by clicking, holding down the option key, and moving the mouse. Do this for each of the two inputs.

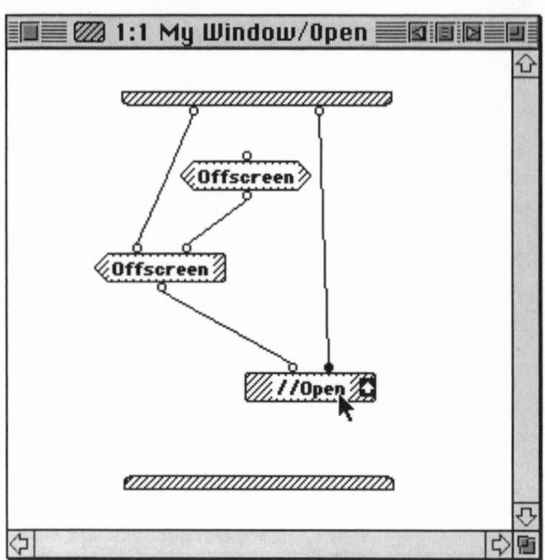

Step 13: The method is now complete, but in order to 'straighten' things up a bit, click on the second input to the super annotated Open, and press this space bar. This will make the flow line vertical.

Figure 11.12 (*Continued*) The Prograph editor

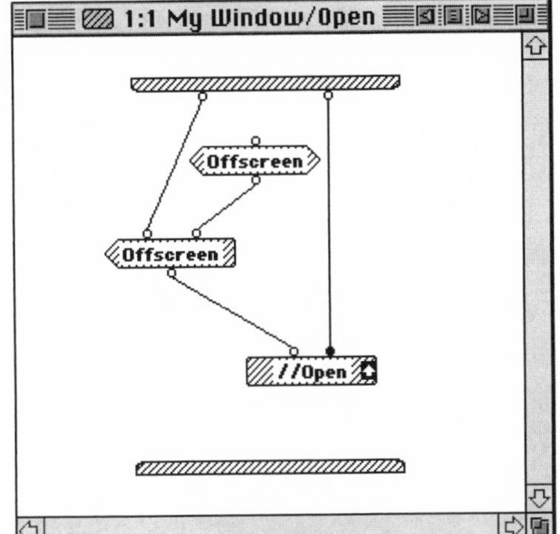

Step 14: The method is now finished.

Figure 11.12 (*Continued*) The Prograph editor

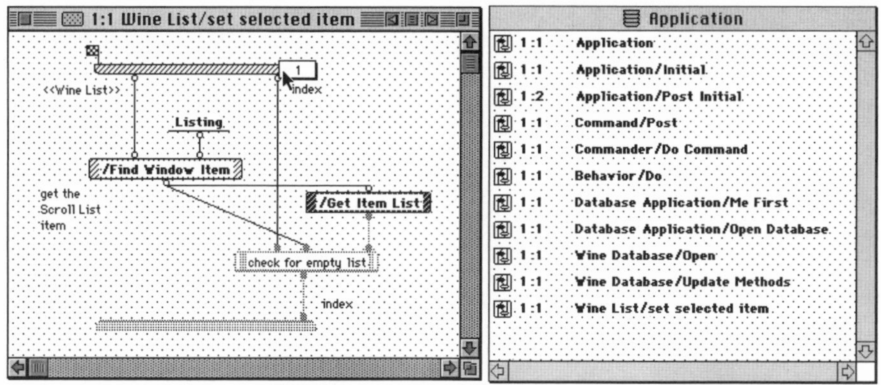

Figure 11.13 Inspecting data values in code when execution is interrupted at a breakpoint. Note that execution can be resumed, or can be carried out operation by operation (analogous to line-by-line execution in debuggers of textual languages)

Figure 11.14 shows a collection of these editors. These editor classes—called the ABEs—are executed in separate lightweight processes when the programmer is graphically editing one of the ABC instances. The ABEs are present only in the environment, and are not included when an application is compiled. For this reasons, they are also called *interpreter only* classes or sections.

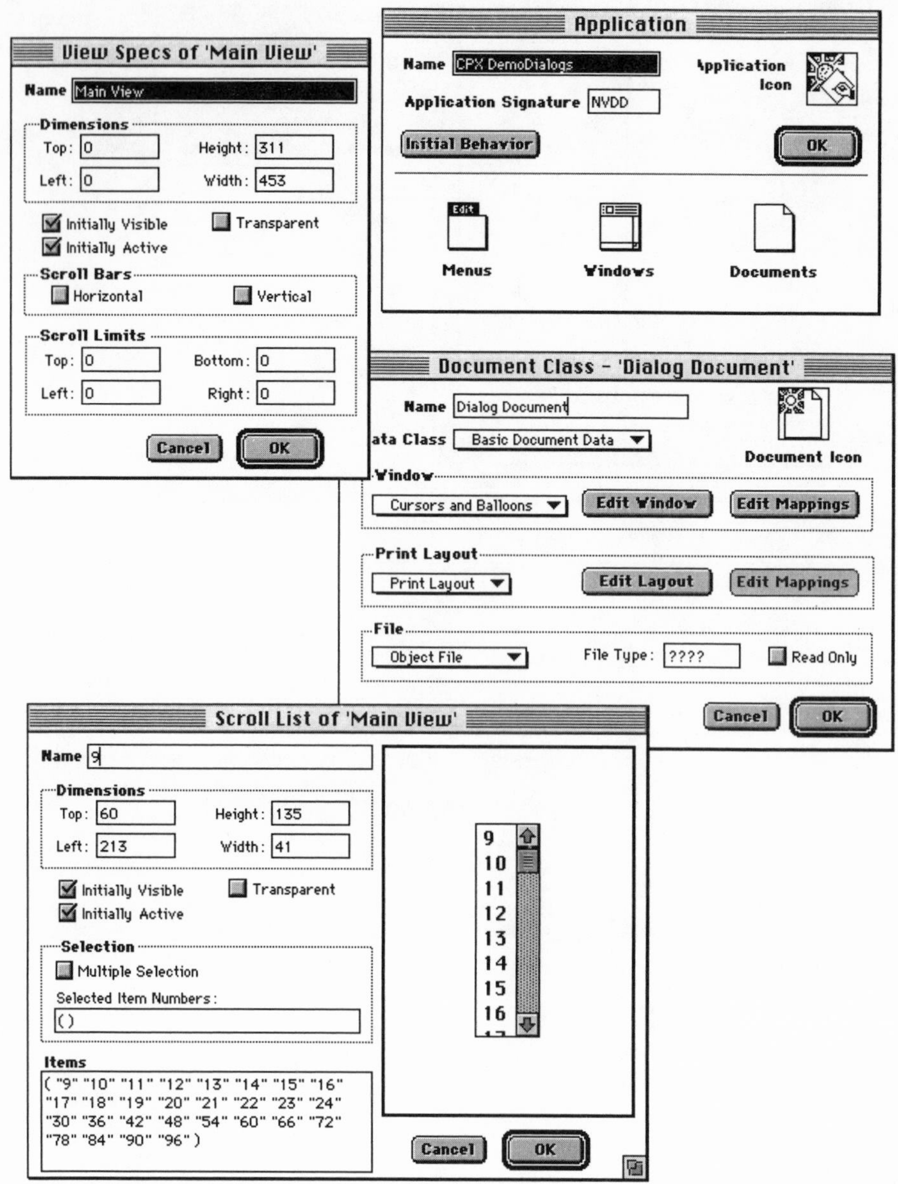

Figure 11.14 A collection of the Application Builder Editors—graphical editors for many of the classes in the Prograph application framework

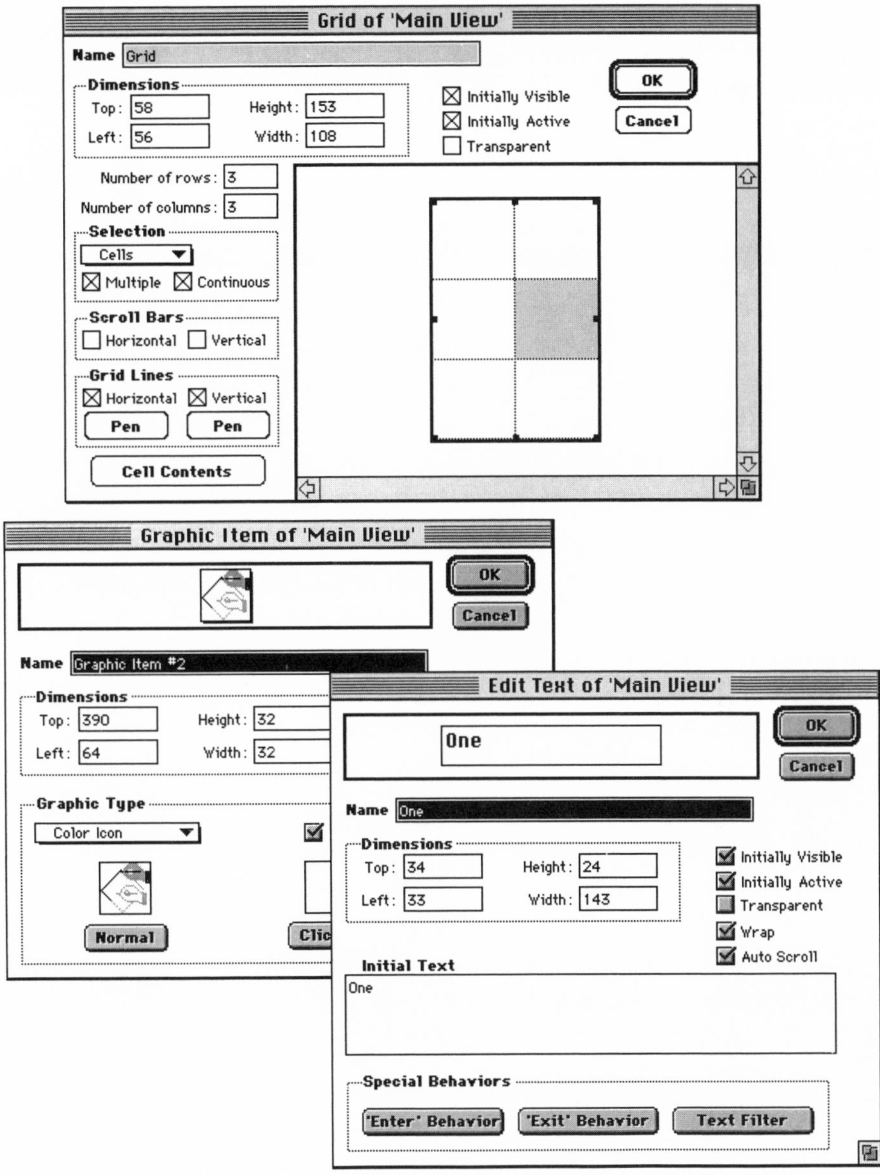

Figure 11.14 (*Continued*) A collection of the Application Builder

11.2.2 Compiler

After an application has been developed and debugged, it can be compiled in what is essentially a batch process. The resulting application is a standard, double-clickable Macintosh application. In Section 11.4, comparisons of the RAM footprint and execution speeds for compiled applications will be made.

11.2.3 Other Features of the Environment

There are many more aspects of the Prograph CPX environment than can be covered in this short chapter, including a help system for all the Prograph primitives and ABC classes and methods, as well as all the Mac Toolbox calls, a variety of accelerators for *power* users, the manner in which comments and other documentation are supported by the environment, and the way in which the environment is actually used in practice to support an *outside-in* development style.

11.3 Prograph Framework

In this section, the basic statistics and runtime architecture of the Prograph ABCs are explained. Particular attention is paid to the runtime interconnections between the objects that make up a running application, as opposed to the static inheritance structure of the class library. Since the ABCs and the Prograph language itself are tightly integrated with the development environment, a lengthy explanation of how the programmer uses the ABCs in the Prograph environment is given. This section concludes with some measurements of RAM and disk footprints of several applications written with the ABCs, and compares these to the equivalent MacApp applications.

11.3.1 Basic Statistics and Static Structure

The 161 classes of the Prograph ABCs are structured as 46 sections—independent units of compilation which can each have classes as well as global functions and global data. References to the sections that comprise a complete application are stored as a project (The project stores little else besides references to sections and Macintosh resources—icons, sounds, cursors, and other Macintosh Toolbox structures.). Names of classes, global functions, and global data must be unique in a project. The programmer can add any number of new sections to a project.

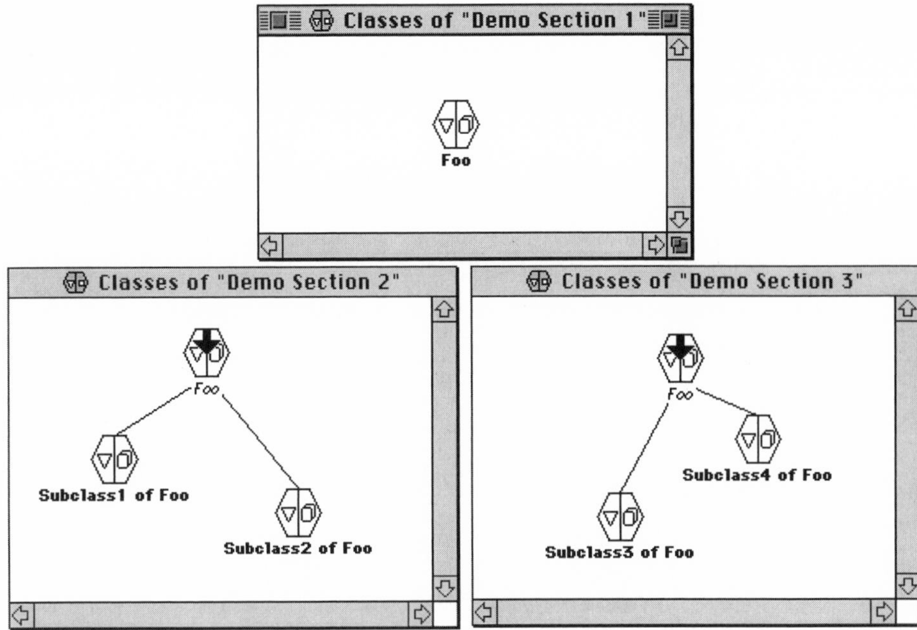

Figure 11.15 The use of aliases to classes in different sections. Note that the iconic representation for the alias—a class icon with a superimposed downward-pointing arrow and an italic name—is a nice mix of the graphical language of the Macintosh Finder and that of the Prograph language

Inheritance links can span any number of sections. The programmer's interface for this is a particularly elegant extension of the notion of an alias from the Macintosh Finder [Apple93]. While there can be only one class named `Foo` in a project, there can be any number of aliases to this class in other sections. In all respects except adding new instance variables and changing the superclass, aliases act just like the original class. Thus, if there was a need to implement subclasses of `Foo` in two different sections, the programmer would only have to add an alias to `Foo` in each section, and then to implement subclasses of each alias. Figure 11.15 shows how this would look to the programmer. The representation of the alias follows both the graphical design of the Finder (names in italic) and that of the Prograph language (hexagons, downward-pointing arrows).

The inheritance structure of the ABCs is that of a forest of a large number of short trees. There is no single *object* class that is the superclass of all or most of the ABC classes. In fact, a large number of classes (approximately 60) inherit from no other class. Normally, this would be an unusual and perhaps suboptimal structure for an application framework. This is not the case for the ABCs because *object* is a basic data type of the Prograph language and because of the large number of language primitives (approximately 300), many of which provide much of the functionality found in the `Object` class in other systems. For example, cloning, both shallow and deep, is accomplished via the copy primitive rather than via a `Copy` method in class `Object`. This seems to work quite well, especially since even the built-in primitives like `copy` can be overridden using the data-determined reference mechanism. Figure 11.16 shows the inheritance structure of the ABCs.

There are 2327 methods in the 335 classes in the ABCs and ABEs, and all methods are provided in source code with the CPX product. Method sizes range from 0 operations (null methods) to more than 10 cases and 60 operations. Figure 11.17 shows one of the more complex methods.

11.3.2 Framework Architecture

The Prograph ABCs structures a running application in a way similar to other Macintosh application frameworks. This is not too surprising, since all Macintosh frameworks are basically extensible object-oriented applications that implement the same Macintosh user interface specification. The look and feel of that user interface specification dramatically influences the functionality of the objects that make up any framework that supports it. Thus, most of the major objects of the Prograph framework will be familiar to users of these other frameworks:

- Application. The root object that governs the application's behavior and visual appearance. The application object allocates and initializes most of the other objects that comprise the application's runtime structure
- Window. Object wrapper for a Macintosh window
- View. Rendering object
- Document. Defines a relationship between a window, a data file, and a print layout. This object also provides the file and disk I/O behavior for the application. The actual data controlled by a document is stored in an auxiliary Document Data object

Prograph CPX Class Forest

- Application
- Background
- Balloon Help
  - Window Item Help
    - Toggle Item Help
    - Target Item Help
- Bandor
- Behavior Specifier
  - Attribute Specifier
  - Class Specifier
  - IAC Attribute Specifier
  - IAC Parameter Specifier
  - Menu Item Specifier
  - Menu Specifier
  - Method Specifier
  - Persistent Specifier
  - Window Item Specifier
    - Value Specifier
  - Window Specifier
- Clipboard
- Column
- Command
  - Behavior
    - IAC Event Behavior
    - Menu Behavior
    - Window Item Behavior
      - Control Behavior
  - Task
    - Deferred Task
      - Periodic Task
    - Text Task
      - Clear Task
      - Copy Task
      - Cut Task
      - Paste Task
      - Typing Task
- Commander
- Control Color
- Cursors
- Desktop
- Document
- Document Data
  - Basic Document Data
- Draggor
  - Autoscroll Draggor
  - Scroll List Draggor
- Environment
- Event
- Event Handler
  - Finder Handler
  - Multifinder Handler
  - Modal Handler
- File
  - Data File
    - Object File
    - Picture File
    - Text File
      - Style Text File
  - Resource File
- File Alias
- Font
- Graphic
  - Line
  - Rectangle
    - Round Rectangle
    - Oval
  - Text
- Help Message
  - Pict Res Help
  - STR Res Help
  - String Res Help
  - TERes Help
- IAC Data Type
- IAC Descriptor
- IAC Event
- IAC Object
- IAC Suite
  - IAC Required Suite
- Marquee
- Menu
  - Basic Edit Menu
  - Basic File Menu
  - Document File Menu
  - Help Menu
  - Standard Apple Menu
    - Apple Menu
  - Text Edit Menu
  - Text Font Menu
    - Font Menu
    - Font Size Menu
    - Font Style Menu
- Menubar
- Offscreen
- Pen
- Print Layout
- Printer
- Rainy Day Fund
- Regular Border
  - Drop Shadow
  - Select Border
    - Default Border
- Resize
- Resizor
- Resource
  - B&W Pattern
  - Color Pattern
  - Graphic Resource
    - Color Icon
    - Icon
      - Finder Icon
    - Pict
    - Small Icon
      - Finder Small Icon
- Row
- Screen
- Selector
- Special Keys
- Text Editor
- Text Filter
  - Integer Filter
  - Integer List Filter
  - List Filter
  - Natural Filter
  - OSType Filter
  - Range Filter
  - Real Filter
- Utility
- Window
- Window Item
  - Control
    - Check Box
    - Push Button
    - Radio Button
    - Scroll Bar
  - Edit Text
    - Scroll Text
  - Graphic Item
    - Target Graphic Item
  - Popup Menu
  - Print View Item
    - Date
    - Page Number
    - Time
  - Scroll List
    - Drag & Scroll List
  - View
    - Grid
    - Multiple View
    - OK View
    - Print View
    - Radio Set
    - Selection View
      - Autoscroll Selection View
- Window Item Mapping

Figure 11.16 Inheritance structure of the Prograph class library

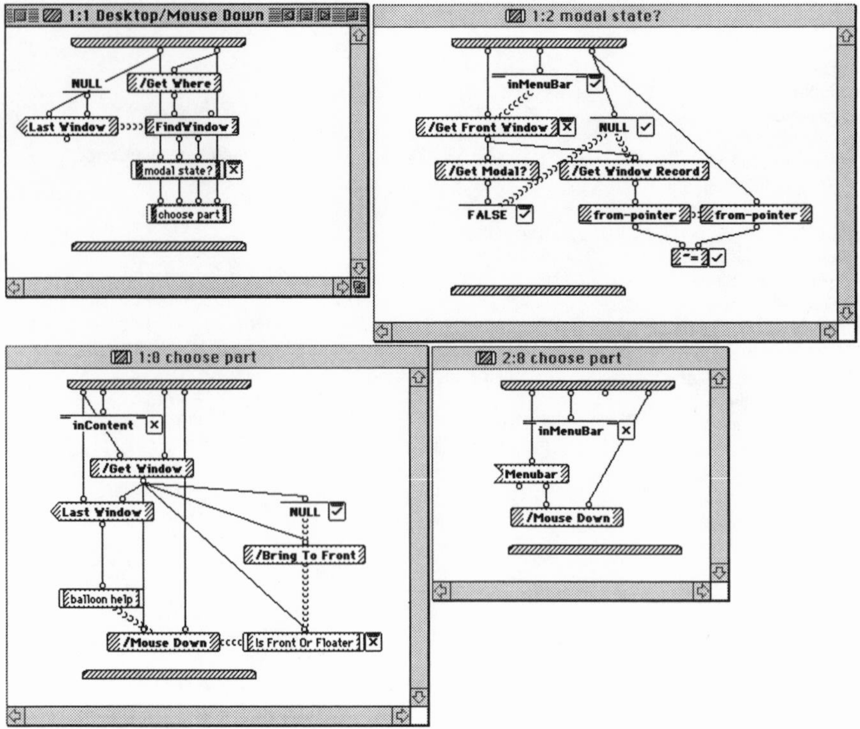

Figure 11.17 Event handling for a mouse click—one of the larger methods in the ABCs. Note the use of locals to make the code more understandable

- Task. An object wrapper for request for an action, initiated by the user, or internally (not unlike the MacApp command object)
- Desktop. The root object that controls all the visual aspects of the application: windows, menubar, menus, palettes, etc. The single instance of the Desktop class manages the Mac desktop for the application, including its menubar and windows. It is the root of the application's visual hierarchy
- Commander. The event and command handler for the application
- Menubar and MenuObject wrappers for the Macintosh menubar and menus.

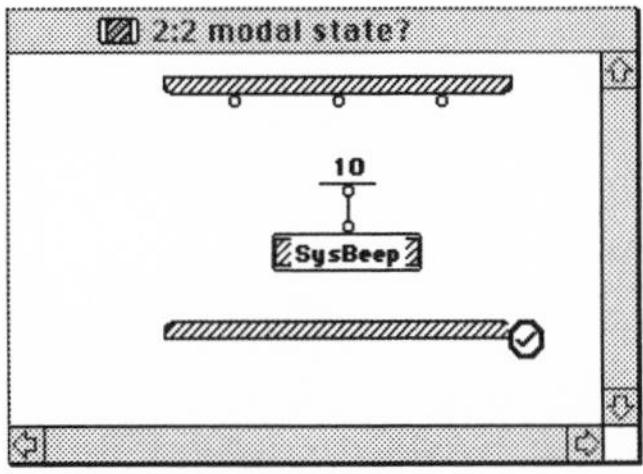

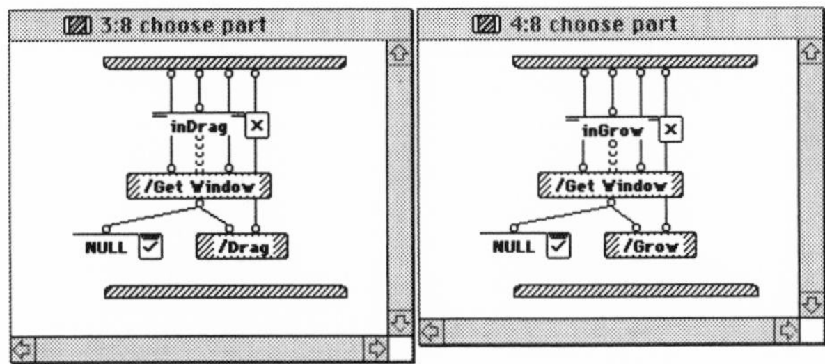

Figure 11.17 (*Continued*) Event handling for a mouse click

Figure 11.18 shows the runtime interconnections between these objects, as they occur in a small database application that is shipped with CPX as a sample program.

In particular, like most of the other application frameworks for the Macintosh, the CPX ABCs do not use a strict Smalltalk-80 MVC architecture, but rather use an architecture heavily influenced by MacApp. In the MacApp approach, the data that is to be rendered is managed by a `Document` object (the model) and the rendering and user interaction management is handling by the `View` (combining the view and controller classes of Smalltalk). The `Document` class, in addition, handles most of the details of files, disk I/O, and in the case of CPX in particular, much of the mapping from the document to the components of the window (which particular field of the document fills this text view, and which field controls the state of a checkbox widget, for example) is done by the Document, in conjunction with a specialized `Window Item Mapping` object owned by the `Document` (See Chapter 5.).

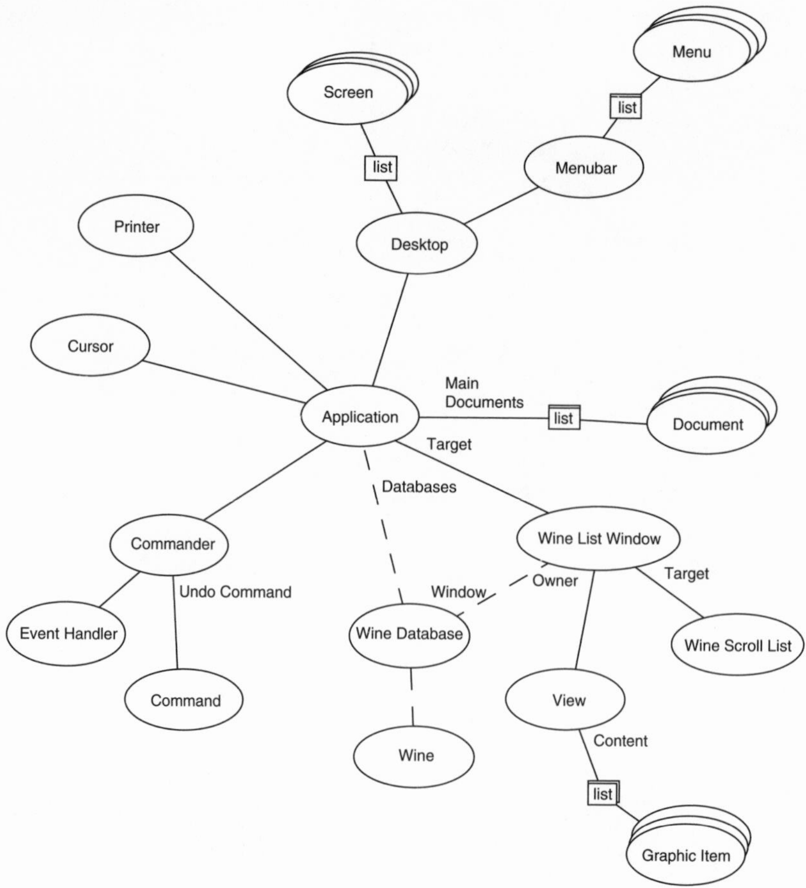

Figure 11.18 Runtime interconnections between the instance of an application written with the Prograph ABCs

11.3.3 Use of the Framework in the Environment

In order to build an application, the user of the Prograph ABCs, as with any application framework, designs and implements subclasses to the ABC classes, adding new instance variables and adding and overriding methods as needed, extending the functionality of the ABCs to reach the feature set of the desired application. This often involves the overriding of null methods in the framework which are placeholders through which the framework accesses the programmer's code (For example, `View/Draw` is overridden so that the framework can access the user's rendering code, and `Command/Undo` is overridden so that the framework is able to handle undo processing automatically.). These null methods are sometimes called *hook* methods. [Schmucker88]

For the ABCs, this includes the following tasks:

- Subclass `Application`, override `Application/Update Menus` to handle any application-wide menus
- Subclass `Window` for each type of window desired
- Subclass `Menu` for each menu that will be inserted in the menu bar. Add a method or universal to handle the menu event associated with each menu item
- Subclass `Task` (or `Command`, or `Behavior`) for each undoable action that the user can perform
- Subclass `Document` and `Document Data` for each type of file that the application deals with. Override, at a minimum, `Document Data/Get Data` and `Document/Put Data` so that these files can be read and written

(Notice that designing a custom `View` subclass for each rendering is not part of this list. More on this later.)

The environment relieves the programmer of the tedium of constructing the many `Window` and `Menu` subclasses that are needed for any significant application, as well as providing a great deal of flexibility in the design and implementation of hook methods.

The `Window` and `Menu` subclasses are typically implemented indirectly via the graphical interfaces of the ABEs. Using the `Window` editor, for example, the programmer not only can design the graphical layout of the window instances, but also can specify the window's resize properties (whether its views grow or shrink as the window's size changes, for example), the draw behavior and the key handling for its views, and the click behavior for its buttons. This is all done in a Behavior Editor. (Figure 11.19 shows the Window Editor and the associated Behavior Editor for one of its buttons.)

Behaviors provide an elegant solution to a problem that many frameworks share: the rigidity of hook methods. Because most object-oriented languages, including Prograph, require that the interface of an overridden method be identical to that of the method it is overriding, the programmer is forced into using whatever the framework designer

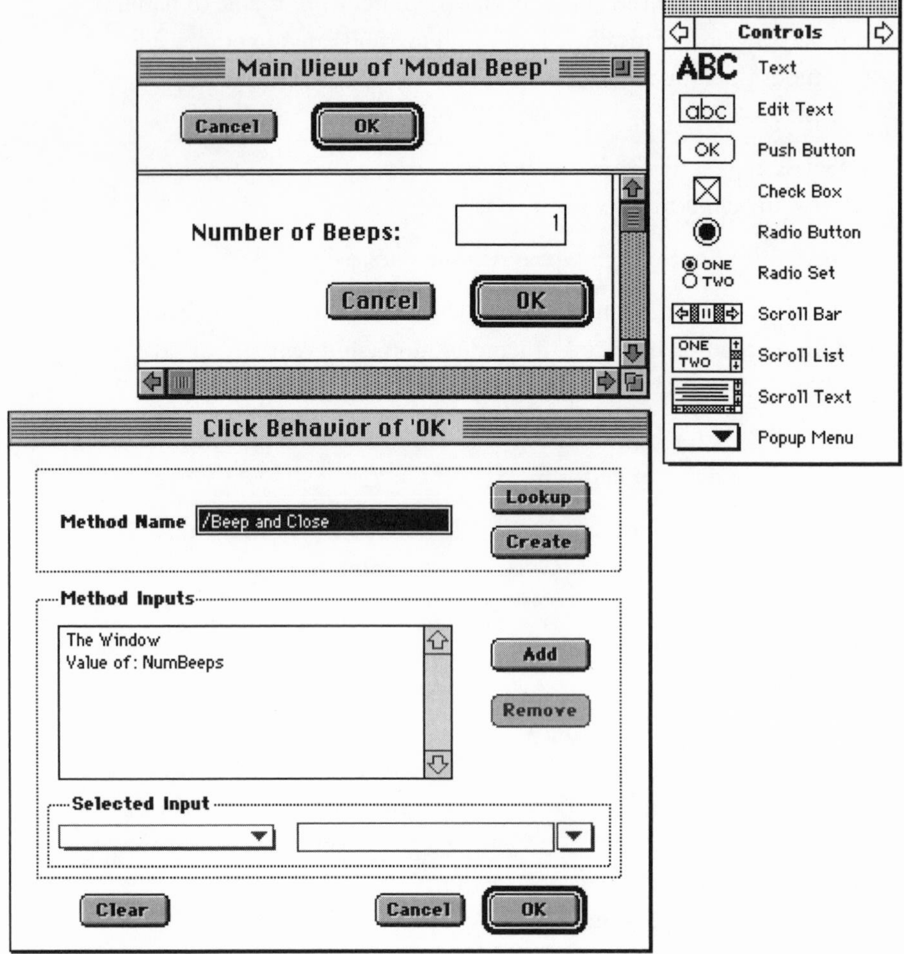

Figure 11.19 The `Window` and `Button Click Behavior Editors` for a simple window. (Note that the widget palette—one of three—is also shown)

has specified. (Conversely, the framework designer is required to anticipate the needs of all the users of the framework when designing the interfaces to hook methods.) This can result in either an interface that does not pass all the necessary information, or one that is overly complex for simple or average cases. The ABCs avoid all of these problems by providing what is in essence a layer of indirection between the framework and the code that will be called. This layer of indirection is the `Behavior Specifier` object.

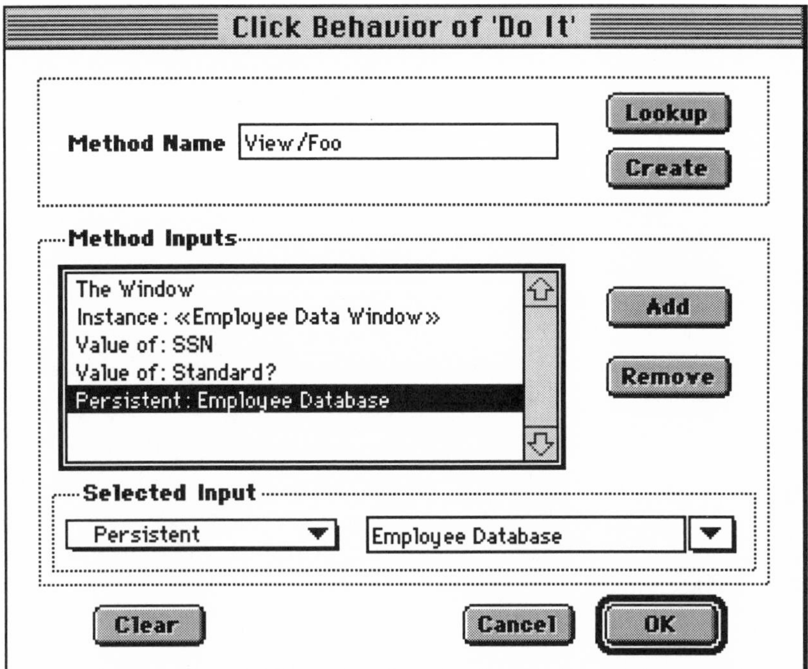

Figure 11.20 A `Click Behavior Editor` specifying a button that will allocate an instance of the class `Employee Data Window`, retrieves the current value from the editable text item named *SSN*, and the boolean value of the checkbox named *Standard?*, retrieves the value of the global (persistent) named *Employee Database*, and then includes these as arguments, together with the window that owns the button, in a call to the method `View/Foo Button`. Note that all the behavior for this button is obtained without writing any Prograph code

A `Behavior Specifier` enables the programmer, in effect, to custom-design the hook method for each object. Figure 11.20 specifies a click method for a button that will do the following:

- Allocate an instance of the class `Employee Data Window`.
- Retrieve the current value from the editable text item named *SSN*, and the boolean value of the checkbox named *Standard?*.
- Retrieve the value of the global (persistent) named `Employee Database`.

- Include these as arguments, together with the window that owns the button, in a call to the method `View/Foo Button`.

11.3.4 Achieving Certain Common Tasks in the ABCs

In order to give you a feeling for the use of the ABCs, the manner in which they are used to perform several common tasks in application development will be sketched.

Activating a menu item

To activate a menu item you have to write some code—typically in an override of the `Update Menu` method present in many of the CPX classes—deciding programmatically what object controls the activation of this particular menu item, and under what circumstances it should be activated.

Menu items, for the purpose of enabling, are identified by the name of their associated menu behavior, an object that encapsulates the action that a menu item represents. Your code enables the menu behavior named `Foo` and the framework determines that this is, for example, the fourth item on the third menu.

While the MacApp menu enabling is handled by a background process executing periodically, the menu enabling in CPX is done on demand when the user clicks in the menubar (or types a command key equivalent to a menu item). The `Event Handler/Mouse Down` method passes responsibility for handling mouse downs to the Desktop object. When the `Desktop/Mouse Down` method determines that the mouse down occurred in the menubar, it calls the `Menubar/Mouse Down` method. One of the first things this method does it to update the enabling on all the menus.

Consider, for example, two menus named App Menu and Win Menu. The App Menu has three items, and Win Menu has two items. Let's consider Win Menu first. Its two items, Win1 and Win2, are enabled by the windows Win1 and Win2. The code to do this, which is executed whenever one of these windows is the frontmost window, is shown in Figure 11.21. This code merely calls the inherited `Update Menus` method as well as executing a small local that uses the `Set Item Enabled?` method to enable the menu item whose behavior is named "Win1." (In this case the behavior, the menu item, and the enabling object all happen to have the same name.)

All the items in App Menu are enabled by the application object. This menu also shows that the menu item text can be different from an item's

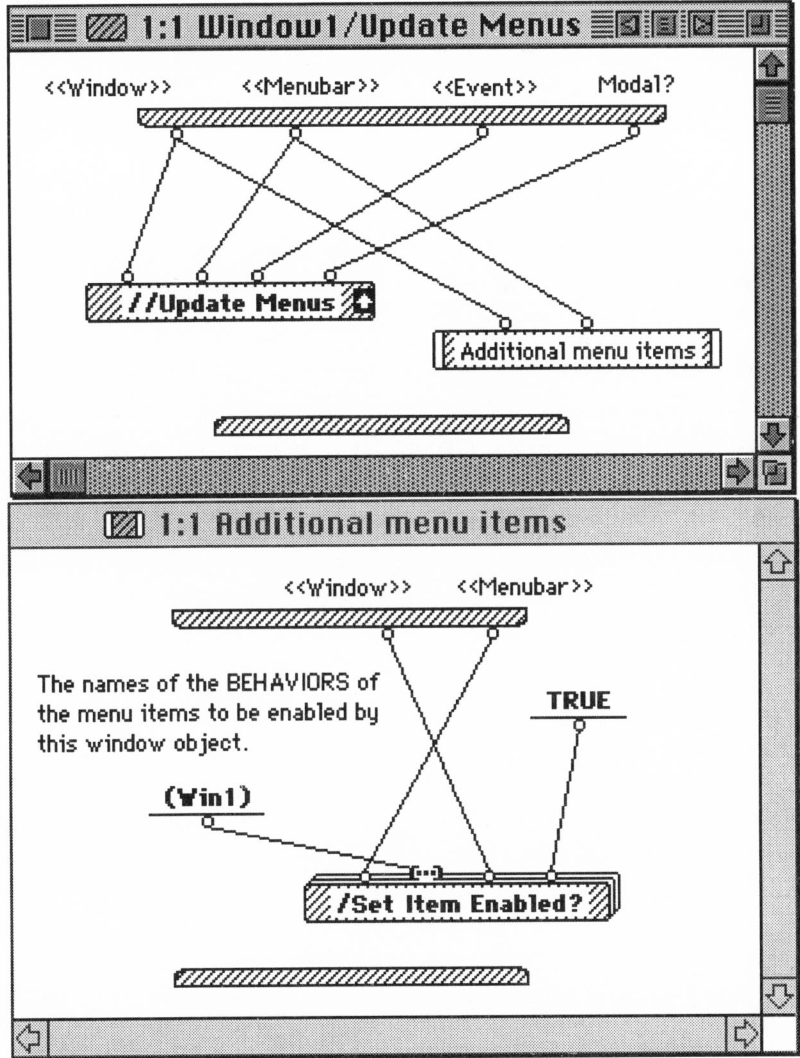

Figure 11.21 The menu enabling code for two menu items controlled by a window subclass. This is the simplest example of menu enabling

associated behaviors. The behaviors are named App1, App2, and App3 and these are listed in the application object's Update Menu code. However, the menu item text strings are App1, El App2, and Lé App3. The menu item strings can be localized to different natural languages, or just changed in any way you require, without affecting your code.

Handling a menu event

In most cases you don't even have to write code to handle a menu event, but need only specify a `Menu Item Behavior`—using a graphical editor which is part of the `Menu` class's ABE. This behavior can be constructed so that it calls the method or primitive of your choice, with whatever arguments are needed by that code.

Of course, whatever actions you want to take place as a result of the menu item being chosen will have to be coded, but the connection between the menu item and that code is done with a behavior.

Drawing the Interior of a Window

Surprisingly, you often don't need to write any additional code to connect your drawing code to a particular view—this connection is done with a behavior. One advantage of this approach is that you do not typically need as many View subclasses in a CPX application as you would in a MacApp application. In effect, the connection between a particular view and its drawing (and also interaction behavior) is stored in its `Drawing Behavior` (and `Click Behavior`) instance variables rather than being done by subclassing `View` and overriding its `Draw` (and `DoMouseClick`) methods.

11.3.5 Measurements

Prograph, used in conjunction with the ABCs, produces small footprint, stand-alone applications. The minimal Macintosh-style "Hello, World" application—with multiple windows, the standard Apple, File, and Edit menus, and printing—has a RAM footprint of about 700K.

Figure 11.22 presents the results of a test to compare the RAM footprints of MacApp and Prograph CPX by reimplementing several of the MacApp sample programs in Prograph. These sample programs ranged in size from about 50 to about 3000 lines of C++. The RAM footprint of the Prograph version is generally about 300-400K larger than that of MacApp. About half of this difference is attributable to the overhead of the additional symbolic data necessary to support the inject feature of the Prograph language, and a portion of the remainder can be attributed to the Prograph garbage collector.

The Prograph application framework is comparable in its breadth and depth to other commercially supported frameworks, but when the power of the Prograph language and the speed of its development environment are taken into account, Prograph CPX stands out as a superb application development tool.

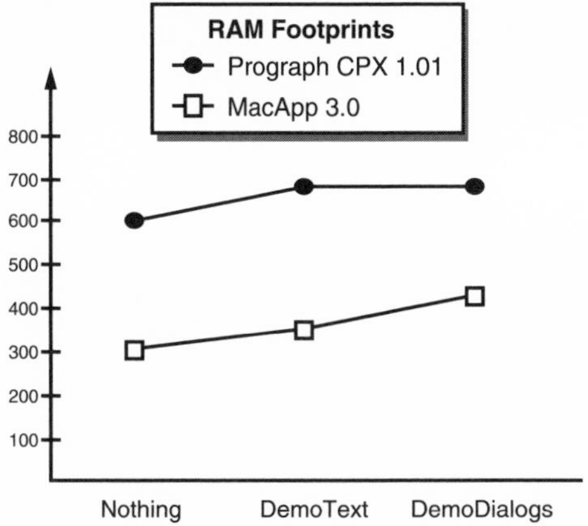

Figure 11.22 RAM footprint comparisons (in K) for the re-implementation of three of the MacApp sample programs in Prograph CPX. The size of the source code for these three applications (in C++ using MacApp 3.0) ranges from about 50 lines to over 3000

References

[Apple92] Apple Computer, *Macintosh Human Interface Guidelines*, Addison-Wesley, 1992.

[Cox88] P.T. Cox and T. Pietrzykowski, Using a Pictorial Representation to combine Dataflow and Object-orientation in a language-independent programming mechanism, *Proceedings of the International Computer Science Conference,* 1988, pp. 695–704.

[Parker93] R.O. Parker, *Easy Object Programming for the Macintosh using AppMaker and THINK Pascal,* Prentice-Hall, 1993.

[Schmucker88] Kurt Schmucker, *Object-Oriented Programming for the Macintosh*, Hayden, 1988.

[Schmucker94] Kurt Schmucker, DemoDialogs in Prograph CPX, *FrameWorks,* **8** (2), 8–13, 1994.

[TGS89] TGS Systems, "Prograph Syntax and Semantics," in the Prograph 2.5 manuals, Appendix IV, Sept. 1989 (first printing), July 1990 (second printing).

CHAPTER 12

Epilog

12.1 The Long and Winding Road

Designers of computer software have been searching for a rigorous, building-block approach to the design and construction of programs for many decades. In the early days of programming, the fundamental building block was the *subroutine.* Advocates of COBOL, FORTRAN, and most other first-generation languages held subroutines in high regard and proclaimed, "This is the way to build complex software from simple parts."

The world of software was still young when this notion faded, as a crack in the foundation appeared in the form of failed projects, cost overruns, and low quality. *Structured programming,* based on procedural languages like ALGOL, Pascal, and C, was touted as the fix to unbridled complexity even in modular code. If the control paths in a procedure (subroutine) form a tree structure, then a complex program can be simplified, indeed reduced, to its basic building blocks. This time, the basic building blocks came in three flavors: *concatenation, looping,* and `if-then-else` *branching* statements. Thus, gluing together statements, or blocks of statement was called concatenation; iteration of a block of one or more statements was called looping; and structured branching through an `if-then-else` construct was called branching. These were the permissible flow constructs, which gave rise to the *goto-less* programming dance craze of the 1970s. The structured programming fanatics claimed structuralism as the one true path to knowledge.

Structured programming raised everyone's consciousness. What were the "good practices" of "good programmers?" We learned that isolation of variables and procedures is good; too much flow of information across boundaries (interfaces) is bad. *Coupling* (the flow of values from one procedure to another) should be minimized. *Cohesion* (the clustering of functionality within a procedure or module) should be maximized. The fundamentals of structured programming are still valid today, but they do not take us far enough toward the finish line.

The next step in the evolution toward perfection is object-oriented programming (OOP) and its supporting technologies, such as OOD, OODBMS, etc. The object-oriented technologies (OOTs) are better than structured programming, and better than procedural programming because OOP incorporates many of the lessons learned from the structured programming generation. Plus it adds reuse, inheritance, and polymorphism, which you have heard a lot about already in this book. OOP resets the software developer baseline, because it keeps the good practices found in structured programming, but discards nearly everything else associated with procedural programming. It is a departure from earlier practices.

12.2 The Dark Side of Objects

OT is being touted, just like its predecessors, as the one true path to knowledge. It is not. Even though this book has been heavy-handed in its advocacy of object-oriented programming, all is not milk and honey in the world of OT. Procedural programming does not go far enough, and neither does OOP. We should recognize that OT is simply another step toward Nirvana.

In fact, there is a dark side to OT. The first crack in OOP's foundation is the so-called *fragile base class problem.* When designing a class hierarchy for a framework, we are actually designing a house of cards. Each interface between a class and its subclasses is a form of coupling. In fact, inheritance is an extreme form of coupling that would make a structured programming whiz shudder with fright. Inheritance leads to a high degree of coupling within a framework. This is bad because coupling is the root cause of the *ripple effect* in software. If coupling is high, a small change in one place can propagate changes throughout a large part of the entire system.

In a framework, everything is connected to a few top-level base classes. What happens when the top level interface changes? Everything depends on these fragile base classes, hence the name of the problem. Changes ripple throughout the class hierarchy, leaving one's design in a shambles. Framework designers must be absolutely sure that the hierarchy will stand the test of time, and who can tell the future?

The second major weakness of framework design stems from the static structure of the class hierarchy and the monolithic nature of inheritance. Even though objects are easily created and destroyed during a program's execution, we need more flexibility in modern systems. In reality, class hierarchies cannot be static. They must be dynamic, which means that their interfaces must be created and destroyed during execution of the system; the interfaces (in addition to the objects themselves) must be *dynamic.* This means that the class hierarchy of a framework can be created as the system runs.

Consider the case of a real-time system constructed as a framework. This might be a small operating system or a distributed client/server application. Here is the limitation imposed by a static class hierarchy: when a new device is plugged into the running system its interface must be made known to the application framework. For example, the system may be a desktop computer and the device may be a network interface card. How does the running system recognize the new interface? Polymorphism will not work in this case, if the device interface has nothing to override.

In current framework technology, the new device overrides an abstract class which is statically defined by the framework programmer. The new interface must conform to the hooks or protocols of the static design. When the framework conforms in every detail, everything works; otherwise, the framework breaks.

In *distributed client/server systems,* this problem is being addressed by OMG (Object Management Group), which is a group of vendors who want to set standards for frameworks interoperability. OMG is working on CORBA (Common Object Request Broker Architecture), which defines how objects and their interfaces are dynamically created and destroyed within a distributed inhomogeneous network of object-oriented software systems.

An ORB (Object Request Broker) is a control program which sorts out and manages interfaces as they come and go in a network of systems. For example, a network of three computers requires the services of an ORB before they can interoperate. Whenever one machine creates an object, it broadcasts the object's interface specification to the other machines via the ORB. If the other machines want to use the services of the new object, no problem. The ORB makes the connection, and the distributed system carries on much like a monolithic system inside of a single computer. The ORB manages a pool of dynamically created interfaces, and also keeps track of where all objects are within the system of distributed objects.

Traditional framework technology cannot handle the dynamic interface fluctuations demanded by CORBA. In fact, CORBA interoperability goes against the grain of pure OOP because it violates some of the strict encapsulation rules of OOP. CORBA is so controversial that even the members of the OMG disagree on the definition of OOP. In other words, the OMG has found some cracks in the foundation of OT, and the word on the street is that OT is not the one and only true path to knowledge.

12.3 The True Path to Knowledge

Throughout the late 1990s the definition of OOP will be revised, thus shaking up the very foundation of what started out to be the true path to knowledge. Framework technology is attempting to unify the lessons learned over the past 30 years at exactly the same time that it is under siege to change. Fads will come and go before the framework approach evolves into the next stage of development. Frameworks are long-term players in this evolution.

Patterns, or collaborations among classes in frameworks (or subframeworks) is one of the most recent fads to hit the framework camp. These advocates claim that patterns are the one and only true path to knowledge. Expect more buzzwords to appear on the horizon.

The truth is that we have a long way to go before we discover the one true path to knowledge. Software design in 1995 is about where medicine was in 1895, where physics was at the time of Newton, and where mathematics was when Roman numerals were hi-tech.

12.4 What Have We Learned?

We are approaching the 50-year mark in the evolution of software design, programming, and software engineering in general; what have we learned? The framework movement is an attempt to condense all that we know about programming into a unified approach to the construction of large, complex, and reusable software systems. It attempts to solve the age-old problem of how to build large systems from many small simple parts. Yet, frameworks possess their own forms of complexity. The fragile base class problem, the lack of dynamic interfaces, and the confusion brought on by buzzwords are but a few of the intrinsic complexities of frameworks. Still, progress has been made:

- Building blocks: objects are in fact self-contained building blocks; hence they are ideal for a unified theory of composition. If we can discover a solution to the fragile base class problem and dynamic interfaces, we may be on to something powerful.
- Reuse: frameworks are in fact reusable. And if we have a sufficient supply of application-specific frameworks such as the Taligent set, then we can build 80% of the world's applications with only 20% of the effort required when starting from scratch. Yet, a framework is an extremely complex structure. Therefore, reusable frameworks in themselves are not sufficient to solve the software crisis. We need higher level tools. Are visual languages language like Prograph the answer? Are visual tools the true path to knowledge?
- Testing: components of a framework are assumed to be highly reliable because of exhaustive testing. After all, they have been reused many times. Yet these tried-and-true components interact with one another in subtle and complex ways. In addition, they also interact with newly created objects from programmers unfamiliar with the inner workings of the framework. How do we test the specialization that is created whenever a framework is reused? Further complicating the testing problem, we want the framework itself to be created and destroyed as the program executes! This is a very nasty testing problem in the making.

12.5 Frameworks 2000

The following speculations are pure fantasy, based on the arguments given above. If framework technology is only a step toward the light at the end of the tunnel, then what lies ahead? These are guesses for the year 2000 AD:

- The rise of end-user programming: The number of application programmers will not continue to grow until the point is reached where every adult in the country is a programmer. Instead, tasks which are now considered programming tasks will be largely done by the same people who need the program. For example, an accountant requires a programmer to modify the accounting code to add or change the payroll system. A retail sales clerk is not expected to change the screen forms on his or her point-of-sale terminal. These end-users are not expected to know how to program computers. Yet the reality is that they will have to perform some "programming" tasks in the future, because it will become too costly and time-consuming to rely totally on professional programmers to do all of these tasks. Thus the rise of the end-user programmer. How will end-users be able to do this? Framework technology will play a major role in making end-user programming possible. In this respect, framework technology is an invisible enabling technology.

- The rise of automation: Programmers have dreamed of automation since the days of John von Neumann. Very high-level languages have failed. Program generators have failed. Artificial intelligence technology has failed. OOP is merely the latest in a number of attempts to challenge this age-old problem. Still, by the year 2000 AD, a significant fraction of all new applications will be created by end-users who use high-level tools (beyond Prograph) to construct sophisticated applications on top of distributed computers. Once again, the technology will be packaged as a collection of application-specific frameworks.
- The rise of components: By the year 2000, the component industry will be thriving. It will be populated by an entirely new breed of computer company that is much like a parts supplier to a major automobile manufacturer. These companies will provide plug-in objects to existing frameworks. For example, a basic word processing application, based on a framework for doing word processing, will be enhanced by many components: one for spell-checking, others for graphics, and still others to do e-mail and handle the telephone, etc. Components based on Microsoft OLE/COM and OpenDoc/DSOM will number in the thousands, creating yet another opportunity for programming tools that assist end-users to plug together components with little knowledge of programming. None of this kind of programming is possible without frameworks.
- The rise of global computers: The frameworks of the late 20th century will run over CORBA-compliant networks containing thousands of computers located in homes and offices. For example, a single computer game might be played by 100,000 people

over the Internet using a distributed framework. The game may run for months, and involve extremely large terrain databases (simulations of actual places around the world), multiple natural language translation capabilities to handle human interactions from any nationality, and complex economic or political rules that simulate the real world. None of this will be possible without software that can handle complexity. Framework technology is not in itself powerful enough to handle such complexity, but it is a step in the right direction. (Further speculation: most of the lower level complexity of current frameworks will be absorbed into the hardware of future processors, thus making it possible to focus framework design on the higher-order issues).

- The rise of software appliances: The result of frameworks, components, end-user programming, and globalism is the *appliance.* An appliance is a useful, flexible, and yet specialized collection of frameworks embedded within a special-purpose device such as a video tape recorder, automobile, refrigerator, or automated home. A *Software appliance* is a megacomponent which can be downloaded into a device, modified by its user to customize its features, and set loose to do its thing. For example, a literary appliance might be downloaded from an on-line library, modified by a child at home to search for information on Diophantine Equations, and then set loose to search the libraries of the world for 24 hours, while the child plays a global game. In 24 hours the appliance might have found 10,000 references to Diophantine Equations, applied the child's customizations to these references to reduce them to 500 cases, and constructed a 20 page report, 3 examples, and 4 unanswered questions. Appliances may be used for many different kinds of applications. However, all appliances are derivatives of frameworks.

The future of frameworks is bright but incomplete. Over the next 5–10 years, we will witness rapid change in the definition and application of what we now call a framework. In 1954, a *compiler* was a program that collected subroutines together to construct another program. Today, a compiler is a program that translates a high-level language into machine language. The term has taken on an entirely different meaning than that intended by its author. The same fate awaits the term *framework.*

Index

N

O

P

Q

R

S

T

U

V

W

X

Z